PURCHASING AND SUPPLY
CHAIN MANAGEMENT

PURCHASING AND SUPPLY CHAIN MANAGEMENT

ANALYSIS, PLANNING AND PRACTICE

THIRD EDITION

Arjan J. van Weele

Professor of Purchasing and Supply Management
Eindhoven University of Technology
Eindhoven, The Netherlands
Nyenrode, The Netherlands School of Business

THOMSON
LEARNING™

Australia • Canada • Mexico • Singapore • Spain • United Kingdom • United States

THOMSON

LEARNING

Purchasing and Supply Chain Management: Analysis, Planning and Practice

Copyright © 2002 Arjan J. van Weele

Business Press is a division of Thomson Learning. The Thomson Learning logo is a registered trademark used herein under license.

For more information, contact Business Press, Berkshire House, 168–173 High Holborn, London, WC1V 7AA or visit us on the World Wide Web at: http://www.itbp.com

British Library Cataloguing-in-Publication Data
A catalogue record for this book is available from the British Library

First edition published by Chapman & Hall 1996

Second edition published 2000 by Thomson Learning

Third edition published 2002 by Thomson Learning

ISBN 1–86152–978–3

Typeset by LaserScript, Mitcham, Surrey
Printed in the UK by TJ International, Padstow, Cornwall

CONTENTS

PREFACE

It is almost impossible to monitor the developments which are going on in most management disciplines nowadays. This is certainly true for the area of purchasing and supply management. This was the main reason to review the text of this book.

Over the past few years there has been an ever-increasing interest in purchasing and supply management, not only from professional purchasing managers; the interest from general managers, functional managers and business consultants is stronger than ever before. Many professionals have become aware that purchasing in general, and supplier relationships in particular, represent a fantastic area for improvement. The number of articles on purchasing management issues has increased, as has the acceptance of purchasing and supply management as a key area for improving competitive strength.

The business chain is as strong as its weakest link. One of the important links in the business chain is the purchasing and supply function. Many top managers are becoming increasingly aware of how much money is involved in purchasing decisions. In general, only the money related to the purchase of production materials is considered. However, in practice, large sums are also spent on investment goods, and let us not forget the purchase of all kinds of services. In many industrial companies the purchasing share takes up more than half of the cost of goods sold. In most trading companies this figure is even higher! This implies that purchasing decision making has a large influence on the company results: one dollar saved in purchasing costs contributes directly to the company's bottom line. However, the reverse is also true. A non-professional, amateur approach to purchasing decisions can readily lead to overlooking cost-savings opportunities, which in the end may lead to a significant financial loss.

In their efforts to arrive at a sustainable competitive advantage managers increasingly differentiate between core and non-core activities. Companies try to focus on those core activities which provide them with a competitive edge in their end-use markets. Activities which have been defined as non-core, then, are subcontracted to suppliers. As a consequence of this development the effect of purchasing decisions on the company's financial results is growing in many sectors.

When dealing with suppliers, suboptimization must be prevented because it is very tempting to make price the central issue in negotiations. Strategic purchasing and supply management is more than just negotiating a deal with suppliers. It is about managing supplier relationships in such a way that suppliers actively support the company's overall business strategy. It is about fostering a climate where suppliers are challenged to continuously improve their performance and value added. It is about integrating suppliers in the company's overall business processes to boost productivity. It is about developing the physical and information infrastructure to enable these new ways of working . . .

This book aims to introduce the reader to some important principles underlying purchasing and supply management. The ideas are derived from my experience as a management consultant, trainer and academic, obtained from working with a large number of companies in Europe. Regarding its structure and presentation, the underlying idea is that this book should be both balanced and easy to teach.

The idea of writing this book dates back a number of years. The success of the original version which appeared in Dutch in 1988, together with the many positive reactions which I received, convinced me that a translation would be worthwhile. This version, in English, based on the many reactions I have received since the book was published, appeals to a large audience. It is used as a leading textbook in many universities and business schools, in many countries. Hence, I decided to make the investment and to review it carefully. I hope you will find even more value in using it.

Those who are familiar with its contents will soon find out that the second and third edition cannot be used alongside the first edition. Too many topics needed to be rewritten and updated. This is particularly true for the first chapter where more is written now on the changes going on in the business context of organizations and how these impact the role and position of purchasing and supply management. It is also true for Chapter 5, where I have added a section on how purchasing and supply develops over time as a management discipline. Chapter 6 includes new material on the value of the Internet for purchasing market research, whereas new material on developing leveraged purchasing strategies and portfolio management has been included in Chapter 7. Chapter 8, in fact, is completely new text which deals with how to get better results from suppliers. Chapter 10 holds all the material on supply chain management, part of which was in other chapters in the first edition. Chapter 11 has been significantly updated and brought in line with how large companies organize for purchasing nowadays. The same is true for Chapter 13, where new material on developing cost models has been added. Finally, Chapter 15 on buying for retail companies has been changed and updated significantly whereas Chapter 17 is a whole new chapter on public procurement and the EC Directives.

Throughout the text, introductory cases have been replaced and updated, as have memos and other illustrations.

Writing a book is like choosing from a restaurant menu, in that it is often more difficult to decide what **not** to include. In this sense the book displays several personal choices and some subjects may not have received (sufficient) attention. In due course I would appreciate hearing from you, the reader, as to whether you agree with the selection made. Realization of this book has been made possible thanks to the enthusiastic support of several people, and its contents have been enriched as a result of their critical and constructive comments. Thanks to the diligence of the staff of Thomson Learning, this book can be presented to you in its present form. I am grateful to them for the meticulous examination of the text, for the many improvements made, and for the valuable suggestions concerning the layout and design.

I am grateful to the many practitioners I have met over the years with whom I was happy to work as a consultant. Without exception, this work gave me the feeling that purchasing and supply management is a challenging area to work in and that it represents a business area of still-unknown potential for companies. Next, I also would like to thank my colleagues at both the Institute for Purchasing and Supply Development at Eindhoven University of Technology and the Supply Chain Management Center at Nyenrode University for their support, endeavour and superb working climate. It is both rewarding and fun to work at those places. Especially, I would like to thank the Dutch Association of Purchasing Management (NEVI) in The Netherlands, which for so many years has supported me consistently in my academic teaching activities and research projects.

Finally, my wife Ineke encouraged me to (re)write this book. She knew, as no other, the sacrifices which this personal project, again, would entail for my beloved family. Ineke, Vivianne and Marijn accepted these and gave me constant moral support. It is thanks to them that I found the time and the inspiration necessary to complete this task. It is undoubtedly their book too.

Prof dr Arjan van Weele
NEVI Chair Purchasing and Supply Management
Eindhoven University of Technology/Nyenrode University
Maarssen, The Netherlands

Preface to the 3rd Edition

The rapid changes going on in the Internet nowadays and the solutions which these changes provide for general managers, purchasing managers, buyers and suppliers, have made an update of this book inevitable. Compared to the second edition, a new chapter (Chapter 9) has been included providing an overview of the most important terms and definitions and the developments that are going on in the Internet, which we feel are relevant to purchasing managers. Moreover, this chapter provides a comprehensive overview of the most important electronic solutions that are available in the area of purchasing and supply chain management and the conditions that should be met in order to implement them effectively. Next some minor alterations have been made to Chapter 18, Public Procurement and EC Directives, in order to keep this up to date with some recent changes in legislation and regulations. I am grateful to Mr J. von Berkel, at Compendium Public Procurement, for his useful comments on this chapter. Given the positive reactions we have received on the book, the remainder of the text has not been changed.

INTRODUCTION

Purchasing and supply management on the move

During the past few years purchasing and supply management as a discipline has changed considerably in many companies. This is reflected in the increased attention this discipline is receiving from business managers and practitioners. Considering the amount of money generally involved in the preparation and execution of purchasing and supply decisions, this is not so strange. An effectively and efficiently operating purchasing and supply function can make an important contribution to company results. However, there is more. As a result of the implementation of improvement programmes in engineering, manufacturing and logistics management, many companies feel the need for improved relationships with suppliers. These relationships necessarily should result in lead time reduction in new product development, and just-in-time delivery and zero defects on components. Traditionally, the purchasing department acts as the intermediary which records the agreements with suppliers on these issues and supervises their fulfilment. This traditional role, however, is changing rapidly as can be seen from the purchasing practices in some major, leading-edge companies. Moving away from their traditional, operational roles, purchasing and supply managers are assuming more strategic roles in their organizations, focusing on getting better performance from suppliers and the active management of supplier relationships.

These are a few important reasons why management is becoming increasingly interested in purchasing and supply management as a business discipline.

Why this book?

Compared to other management, relatively little academic research has been undertaken in the area of purchasing and supply management. This explains why there is quite a gap in the development of a solid body of knowledge compared to other disciplines in business administration. As a result, it is far from simple to disseminate knowledge across organizations concerning this discipline. Most handbooks on purchasing are of American origin and date back to the 1950s. The well-known texts do not cover the developments which are at present taking place in the purchasing and supply practices of leading-edge companies. Practical descriptions of purchasing situations, which can serve as a learning vehicle and study material for students, are few. This contrasts with disciplines such as marketing, financing, organizational behaviour and other management disciplines, where many major textbooks exist.

It is gratifying that several business schools, polytechnics and academic institutions have decided to include purchasing and supply management in their curriculum. This initiative has no chance of success, however, if there is no effective and up-to-date supportive material. This book aims to fill that gap.

Intended audience

This book is intended for those who are interested in purchasing and supply management in the broadest sense. Its contents aim to provide an in-depth discussion of purchasing and supply issues, both from a strategic and managerial perspective. Reading this book will not make you a buyer or a purchasing manager. In this the text differs from the more pragmatic-oriented literature.

In particular this book is intended for:

- Polytechnic and academic students in business administration and industrial engineering who want to specialize in business strategy, manufacturing strategy and/or supply chain management.
- Professional managers in trade and industry, active in purchasing and/or supply chain management, who are interested in opportunities for improving the effectiveness and efficiency of the purchasing and supply function in their companies.
- Participants in management development programmes in the area of strategic management, manufacturing and supply chain management.
- Account managers and industrial sales representatives who in their professional capacity regularly meet with professional buyers, and who are interested in the way these buyers execute their tasks.
- Those who supervise purchasing staff directly or indirectly, and who come from a non-purchasing background and are interested in the latest developments in the area of purchasing.

Framework

The book has been developed using the following principles.

- **Strategic management perspective**. In this book the subject of purchasing and supply management is presented as an essential link of the business system. This business system is only as strong as its weakest link. The way purchasing and supply management is executed or should be executed is presented from a strategic management perspective. This implies, for example, that attention is given to subjects such as how company objectives may influence purchasing and supply strategies and policies, how purchasing and supply strategies should support overall business strategy, how to develop these strategies, how to execute them, how to manage the purchasing process, and how to monitor purchasing performance.

- **Practical orientation**. Business administration and industrial engineering are concerned with analysing and solving practical business problems. For this reason, the various subjects are discussed from a practical point of view. This book does not aim to transform the reader into a professional buyer. The intention is to introduce the reader to the discipline and familiarize him/her with the key concepts.
- **Scientific basis**. In discussing the subject matter, repeated reference is given to existing management literature. In this way the individual reader can broaden his/her orientation if he or she so desires. When possible, views on purchasing issues are illustrated with research results from national and international specialist literature.
- **Identical structure of each chapter**. Every chapter is alike in structure and encompasses:
  - the learning objectives;
  - an introductory case to illustrate the practical relevance of the subject;
  - an introduction which provides a survey of the most important subjects which will be discussed in the chapter;
  - practical illustrations and memos to emphasize certain subjects in a chapter;
  - a summary at the end of each chapter;
  - assignments for classroom discussion, if desired.

Structure

The book is divided into three parts; each containing several chapters. The overall structure is presented in the figure overleaf.

Part One: Analysis is aimed at getting acquainted with the discipline. The key concepts and terms are presented here.

Chapter 1 focuses on the role and significance of the purchasing function for industrial companies. This is done by describing the purchasing role in the company's value chain. Further, definitions of some important terms and concepts are provided. In the remainder of the book a clear distinction will be made between the activities of the purchasing department and the purchasing function. The latter term, as we will see, has a broader meaning than the first. An active, market-oriented purchasing policy can make a large contribution to innovation and quality improvement. This chapter also discusses the differences in the purchasing function of industrial companies, trade and retail companies and government institutions. In doing so, this chapter provides a framework for the rest of the book.

Chapter 2 addresses the buying behaviour of organizations. The major differences between buying behaviour of consumers and organizations are discussed. Several stages may be distinguished in the decision-making process

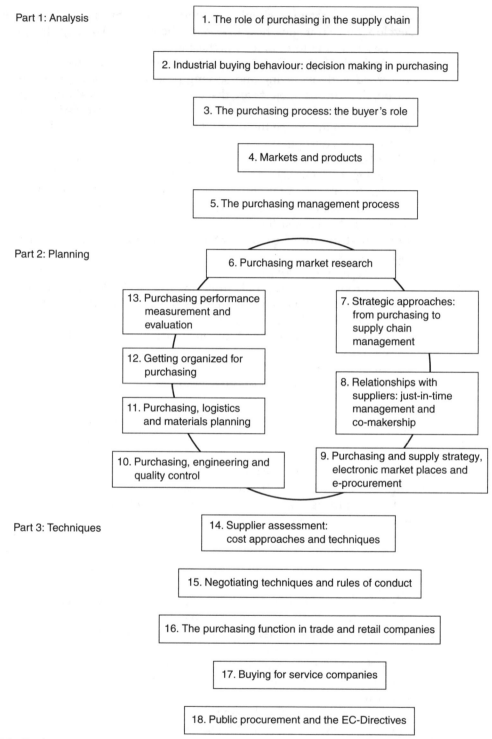

Part 1: Analysis

1. The role of purchasing in the supply chain

2. Industrial buying behaviour: decision making in purchasing

3. The purchasing process: the buyer's role

4. Markets and products

5. The purchasing management process

Part 2: Planning

6. Purchasing market research

13. Purchasing performance measurement and evaluation

7. Strategic approaches: from purchasing to supply chain management

12. Getting organized for purchasing

8. Relationships with suppliers: just-in-time management and co-makership

11. Purchasing, logistics and materials planning

9. Purchasing and supply strategy, electronic market places and e-procurement

10. Purchasing, engineering and quality control

Part 3: Techniques

14. Supplier assessment: cost approaches and techniques

15. Negotiating techniques and rules of conduct

16. The purchasing function in trade and retail companies

17. Buying for service companies

18. Public procurement and the EC-Directives

Figure 0.1 Book structure.

regarding organizational buying behaviour. These are illustrated by presenting a purchasing process model, in which each of the steps is briefly described. Various models of organizational buying behaviour, developed in the (industrial) marketing literature, are also presented. In this way the reader will gain insight into the complexity which characterizes many purchasing decisions in organizations.

The purchasing process model is elaborated in Chapter 3. First, how to arrive at a consistent purchasing order specification is discussed, which serves as a basis for the request for quotation. Next, all activities required in order to arrive at a systematic supplier selection are described. Major aspects of contracting are then discussed. Various subjects which should be considered when making a contractual agreement with suppliers are discussed in depth. Finally how to order and expedite are explored. All these subjects are dealt with from the buyer's point of view.

Chapter 4 deals with the subject of markets and products. First the focus is on the different types of markets that buyers encounter. Second, several specific characteristics are described, related to the purchase of materials, components, supplies for maintenance, repair and operating supplies, investment goods and services.

Chapter 5 deals with the purchasing management process. Purchasing practices vary in different organizations, depending not only on the strategic importance of purchasing, but also on management's view of purchasing. In order to manage purchasing effectively, management must pay attention and give substance to every element in the purchasing management process. This chapter concludes with a discussion on how purchasing and supply management develops within organizations over time.

Part Two: Planning discusses in detail the elements of the purchasing management process described in Chapter 5.

Starting with purchasing market research in Chapter 6, this task consists of continuously tuning the technical developments which occur in purchasing markets and the needs of the company. The supply department is an important observation post for the company on its supply markets. In particular, this chapter looks at the ways in which this task can be realized and the different techniques with which to conduct purchasing market research. Extensive attention is given to how the Internet can be used to generate purchasing market information.

Chapter 7 focuses on purchasing strategy. Attention is given to the issue of how purchasing strategies can be linked to, and can support, the overall business strategy. Following developments in the area of marketing, a portfolio approach is presented on which four basic, differentiated supplier strategies are based.

In Chapter 8 the central issue is how to get better results from suppliers. Major changes, which are occurring in the relationship between industrial companies and their suppliers are described. It will become clear from this chapter that suppliers do not always act in the interest of their customers. Hence, an active approach to the management of supplier relationships is required. This chapter explains how companies may develop such an approach.

Acknowledging the rapid growing influence of information and web-technology, Chapter 9 deals with the role of electronic market places and

E-Procurement. Here, an overview is provided of the most important terms and definitions and the developments that are going on in the Internet, which are of interest to purchasing managers. Moreover, this chapter provides a comprehensive overview of the most important electronic solutions that are available in the area of purchasing and supply management and the conditions that should be met in order to implement them effectively.

The purchasing function has a complex network of relations in the company because it maintains relationships with nearly all departments within a company. Chapter 10 presents the possible problems and opportunities in the relationships between purchasing and engineering, and purchasing and quality management. Special attention is given to how to improve supplier quality. Here, supplier quality assurance and supplier certification are presented as techniques which can be used in this respect.

Chapter 11 describes the role of purchasing within supply chain management. After providing some important definitions the basics of materials planning are presented. This is achieved by providing a logistics reference model, which differentiates between several manufacturing situations (assembly type of operations versus job shop). This model explains why purchasing situations within different companies and industries may be vastly different. Next, it covers a detailed discussion on materials scheduling, just-in-time management and the required information systems technology.

The subject of how to organize for efficient purchasing is covered in Chapter 12. In practice a large variety of organizational structures is observed and the most important of these are discussed. Specific attention is given to the issue of centralized versus decentralized purchasing in a multi-plant environment. Here different co-ordination structures are discussed through which companies try to capture purchasing synergies. Next, the issue of how to organize for efficient purchasing at the business unit level is presented.

Chapter 13 concludes Part Two with a discussion on purchasing performance measurement and evaluation. The central issue here is how to measure and assess the performance of the purchasing department. Several important methods and (benchmarking) techniques are presented.

Part Three: Practice presents a number of operational purchasing methods and techniques. This part also gives specific attention to the purchasing policies of retail and service companies and those of governmental bodies.

All purchasing decisions, and decisions concerning supplier selection, must be based on sound business analyses. In Chapter 14 some methods and techniques which can be used to support the decisions involved are discussed. Among other things, special attention is given to the learning curve and cost modelling.

In industrial and trade practice intensive negotiations often precede signing of the purchasing contract. Chapter 15 describes how to conduct purchasing negotiations. It focuses on the procedures used in purchasing negotiations and the rules of conduct when considering relationships with suppliers.

Chapter 16 examines the purchasing function in trade and retail companies. The most important differences with the industrial purchasing function are discussed. Some modern retail concepts such as efficient consumer response

(ECR), direct product cost (DPC), direct product profitability (DPP) and 'Spaceman' are presented here.

Chapter 17 shows how to deal with the purchasing function in service-oriented companies. Here, the purchasing cost relative to total sales turnover is much lower than for industrial and trade companies. The role of the purchasing function and its perceived importance to management therefore differs widely, and purchasing practices obtained from industrial and trade companies have only limited value.

Finally, Chapter 18 describes the specific characteristics of buying for governmental institutions. From this chapter it will become clear that there are large differences between buying for the government versus buying for private enterprise. Governmental bodies are not free in choosing their purchasing procedures. Therefore, this chapter gives elaborate attention to the most important EC Directives on public procurement and how to work with these.

PART ONE

ANALYSIS

THE ROLE OF PURCHASING IN THE SUPPLY CHAIN

1

Learning objectives

After studying this chapter you should understand the following:

- How changes in the business context affect business strategy and the supply structure of organizations.
- The role and importance of the purchasing and supply function in business.
- The difference between concepts such as supply chain management, procurement, purchasing, buying and ordering and how these are interrelated.
- The most important tasks and responsibilities related to the purchasing and supply function.
- The different products which may be sourced from suppliers.

CASE STUDY
How suppliers add value to Audi's quality compact

With the launch of the new Audi A3, Audi is now a leading player in the compact car market. The A3 is setting new standards through its design, high quality, safety and extensive standard equipment levels. The A3 was specially developed for the compact class premium segment in only 24 months. Without the enthusiasm and commitment of Audi's suppliers this would have been an impossible task.

Audi had already broken new ground in the integration of the automotive supply industry during the development of the A4 saloon and Avant. The buzzwords here are 'simultaneous engineering'. Simultaneous engineering means that development steps take place in parallel. This saves time but demands an extremely disciplined and responsible procedure. As a result of this process, the requirements profile for employees in all company divisions and at Audi suppliers had to be changed drastically. This was particularly true in purchasing, which acts as the direct interface to the supplier industry.

Continued on page 4

In the 1980s purchasing merely represented a parts procurement process primarily oriented towards purchasing at low cost. However, today, purchasing bears co-responsibility for the overall product development process. A result of this is the holistic approach to the selection of Audi suppliers. As a part of forward sourcing, the suppliers are integrated by Audi at a very early stage and sometimes even participate in the design phase in some cases. Suppliers have the opportunity to bring their knowledge and experience to bear, and of designing the product in order to facilitate production.

At a very early stage of the product planning, logistics, R&D, controlling and purchasing jointly define the development and production depth, taking into account core competencies. This is a decisive factor governing the entry of the Audi brand in the premium segment. The objective is to create process chain responsibility for modules and systems with the greatest possible continuity . . . Audi expects its (supplier) partners to gradually develop into systems suppliers offering an all-round service . . .

(Source: 'Suppliers add value to Audi's quality compact', *European Purchasing & Materials Management*, 1998, Issue 10, p. 18)

Introduction

The description of Audi's A3 illustrates some major developments in purchasing and supply strategy which also are occurring within other manufacturing companies. As with other companies, Audi increasingly focuses on what it considers to be its core activities. For Audi these activities relate in the first instance to the development of a superior brand image in the car market and the design and assembly of top quality cars. For this reason suppliers are involved in major design decisions in order to arrive at the best technical and economically feasible solutions. Cars, systems and components should be manufactured at low cost, without waste, at high and consistent quality levels and at short and reliable cycletimes. Audi does not just merely buy components from their suppliers. Through their forward sourcing programme they want to mobilize and benefit from their suppliers' expertise as much as possible. This is why Audi invests so heavily in improving relationships with suppliers. In doing so the suppliers' role gradually evolves from just supplying products to the role of a systems supplier, designing and delivering technologically advanced modules or sub-systems (such as axles, dashboards, climate control systems, chairs).

Elements of Audi's purchasing and supply strategy can also be traced in those of other international manufacturing companies. Because of fierce international competition European manufacturing companies need to investigate and pursue all the possibilities for cost reduction, quality improvement and efficiency improvement. Managers are becoming increasingly aware that the largest part of their end products' costs are related to the materials and services purchased from suppliers. Therefore, suppliers are increasingly involved, directly or indirectly, in their marketing, development and manufacturing programmes. As the case study of Audi illustrates, there is much more to purchasing than just negotiating materials prices.

In this chapter we discuss the role and importance of the purchasing function. We will limit our discussion mainly to manufacturing companies, taking Porter's value chain as the leading concept. Some time is spent in defining important terms and concepts and we elaborate on the role which buyers may play in cost reduction, and product and process innovation. The chapter concludes by describing some important trends and developments, which may be perceived in the purchasing strategies of a few progressive manufacturing companies. In this way Chapter 1 sets the stage for the remaining chapters in Part One.

Changes in the business context

The business context of many companies is nowadays radically changing. Most changes are not mere trends but the result of large, unruly forces which have a lasting effect on the world economy. Examples are the increasing globalization of customer markets, the rapid development of information technology and computer networks, the increasing importance of services in our economies, and the ongoing changes in customer demands and preferences. All these changes happen to businesses at the same time – and they are happening fast. Some leading authors have predicted that these changes will cause a revolution in business, and will change the nature of competition dramatically (Hammer and Champy, 1993; Peters, 1992).

The message is clear: business is changing, but to what extent? In what way? What are the consequences? What are the challenges large companies are confronted with? And how will they impact purchasing and supply strategies? Let's have a closer look at some of the most important changes.

Globalization of trade

Competition in many industries has intensified all over the world in just a few years. The reasons why this has happened are many. They relate to:

- deregulation in many industries (such as energy supply and airlines);
- intercultural homogenization and the resulting homogenization of consumer preferences;
- the forming of trade regions (GATT, NAFTA, EEC) in some areas in the world;
- improved transportation facilities;
- the more sophisticated information and communications technology which has become available.

The latter especially enables people and organizations to overcome the barriers of physical distance. It is assumed that modern information technology will challenge and redefine commonly accepted notions of geographic nations, companies, industries, and communities. Ohmae (1994) stated that modern information technology will make traditional borders obsolete. Not only between nations but especially between organizations. He forecasts that the world increasingly will become one 'global village'.

Thanks to the new information technologies, companies in some industries are reallocating and reconfiguring their activities into global value chains (see Memo 1.1). Adopting these value chain concepts seems most appropriate for products with a high value-to-weight ratio, like semiconductors and memories. However, also in some service industries (like transportation and logistics) we see a rapid development of global supply networks (for example: DHL, Federal Express, UPS) which are enabled through advanced computer and Internet technologies.

Also some important changes in the international trade-blocs have affected global trade flows. Post-war tariffs under GATT have gone down to an historically all-time low level. Some developed countries have established free-trade zones. Examples here are the EEC (Europe), NAFTA (US, Canada, Mexico) and the 'Yen bloc', that includes the Asian nations. It is expected that these three trade zones will greatly affect the world economy in the early years of the twenty-first century. It will be clear that as a consequence of these developments opportunities for global sourcing have increased.

By the early twenty-first century it is expected that there will be five Asian countries among the top ten economies of the world. Today, Japan is the only Asian country in the G-7. It is expected that it soon will be joined in a new G-10 by India, Indonesia, China, and Korea (Ohmae, 1994).

The Information Society

In the aforementioned it has been argued that knowledge and application of modern information technologies will be crucial to competitive advantage of companies. Given its importance we will elaborate here on this subject.

Information technologies are the core of today's economy. The economic value from generating, using, and selling information is growing fast. Examples can be found in modern retail, where retail companies apply database marketing to monitor changes in consumer buying behaviour and preferences. Detailed information about buying patterns and consumer profiles is readily available, enabling retail-buyers (or category managers (see Chapter 16)) to quickly adapt their product assortments and services. Moreover, advanced retail information systems enable an efficient tracing and tracking of good flows and a detailed monitoring of supplier performance. Through EDI interlinkages manufacturers of fast moving consumer goods are requested to schedule their deliveries based

---

MEMO 1.1: Towards the global value chain

Some Japanese companies have already become 'global' in that their R&D is networked, involving American and Asian scientists. Their design concepts are detailed by low-cost Indian engineers in Bangalore or Bombay and then switched over to Singapore. Their components are produced in Taiwan and shipped to Tianjin for final assembly and inspection. And then final products are sold in Europe and North America (Ohmae, 1994).

on continuous replenishment and to take care of logistics activities which traditionally used to be done by the retailer.

This is not only becoming common practice in modern retail. Similar trends can also be perceived in some leading-edge industrial manufacturing companies. The Xerox Corporation has adopted in many of its manufacturing plants the concept of 'pay for production'. In this concept suppliers of major (and costly) components are paid by Xerox only for the products that actually have been consumed in the production of a specific day. Suppliers have been made totally responsible for materials planning, managing pipeline inventory and efficient replenishment. Advanced electronic linkages lie at the heart of these modern manufacturing and logistics concepts.

Electronic networks will be in many industries one of the key success factors for the years to come. As the Audi case has shown at the beginning of this chapter this is nowhere more evident than in the automotive industry. The electronic capabilities of suppliers increasingly will determine whether they will be able to survive in a specific customer relationship. It is expected that manufacturers will increasingly shun suppliers for future business who do not offer electronic linkages, or who have incompatible information systems.

Changing consumer patterns

Of course we cannot underestimate the importance of changes in consumer patterns nowadays. In the past consumers would value a product or service on the basis of some combination of quality and price. Tomorrow's consumers, by contrast, will use an expanded concept of value that includes convenience of purchase, after-sales service, dependability, uniqueness and so on (Treacy and Wiersma, 1993). This idea is also reflected by some leading authors on business marketing where value is defined as: 'the worth in monetary terms of the economic, technical, service and social benefits a customer firm receives in exchange for the price it pays for a marketing offering' (Anderson and Narus, 1998, p. 5).

Increasingly, customers are demanding quality products which are tailored to individual needs and tastes. During the 1990s, the well-informed and highly educated consumers are more aware of their purchasing power, and exhibit more critical buying behaviour. We see the empowerment of the consumers against remote and irresponsible organizations (as can be illustrated by the reaction of some action groups against the dismantling of the Brent Spar by Shell in 1997). In essence, people will no longer settle for whatever companies are offering. Instead, they will seek out and command their first choices in products and services. Consumers take charge: they now tell manufacturers *what* they want, *when* they want it, *how* they want it and *what* they are willing *to pay*. They demand products and services designed for their unique and particular needs.

As a result many manufacturers of consumer products (ranging from fast moving consumer goods to cars and furniture) need constantly to look for opportunities to reduce costs and improve efficiency. At the same time however, they need to constantly innovate and renew their product and service offerings. In more and more industries services are becoming an integrated part of the market proposition. In many cases companies simply do not have the knowledge and resources to develop all the solutions in-house. This is one reason (as we will see in Chapter 7 in more detail) why outsourcing has become so widespread a phenomenon. In order to be able to confront these challenges companies need to work together with suppliers more closely in the area of manufacturing, logistics, services and product development.

This poses new demands on the purchasing and supply function of those companies. Let's identify how these changes affect purchasing and supply strategies.

Impact on business strategies and structures

This section discusses the impact of changes in the business environment on the strategy and structure of large companies. As a result of the new unruly forces coming on to them, companies need to rethink their position in the value chain. Doing so effectively requires a clear idea of their core versus non-core activities. In order to improve their competitive position companies need to focus their core activities on the needs and requirements of their customers. Non-core activities are increasingly outsourced to specialist suppliers, which explains why supplier management is becoming a core issue in corporate strategies. These issues are addressed now in more detail.

Value Chain Management

The term value chain is used to describe the various steps a good or service goes through from raw material to final consumption. Michael Porter considers every firm basically as a collection of primary and supporting value activities that are performed to design, produce, market, deliver and support products that are valuable for customers. As he argues, a firm's value chain and the way in which it performs individual value-activities are a reflection of its history, its strategy, its approach to implementing its strategy, and the underlying economics of the activities themselves (Porter, 1985). This explains why there can be explicit differences between organizations with regard to structure, operations management, ways of planning, style of management, and sometimes notable differences in strength of competition between organizations operating within the same sector.

Seen from this perspective competitive advantage depends primarily on the art of positioning a company in the right place on the value chain. According to Quinn (1992) each company should focus on a just a few core activities, where it thinks it can achieve and maintain a long-term competitive advantage. All other activities in which it cannot achieve world-class status should be outsourced. Contracting out non-core activities to specialized suppliers can contribute to cost reduction, quality improvement, lead time reduction and innovation at the same time. This explains the high and rising purchasing to sales ratio which can be perceived in many companies.

Quinn (1992) has suggested the following ideas for developing a sustainable competitive advantage through core competencies:

- Companies need to focus their internal resources on those core sources of intellectual or service capabilities, which presently create a meaningful distinctiveness in their customers' minds.
- The next step to competitive advantage is to consider the company's remaining capabilities as a group of service activities that could be either 'made' internally or 'bought' externally from a wide variety of suppliers specializing or functionally competing in that activity.
- For continued success companies need to actively command, dominate, and build barriers to entry around those selected activities critical to their particular strategic concept. Concentrating more power than anyone else in the world on these core competencies as they affect customers is crucial to strategic success.
- Managers need to plan and control their outsourced activities so that their company never becomes overly dependent on, or later is dominated by, their partners. This means consciously developing and monitoring multiple competitive sources and strategically controlling certain critical steps in the process.

Using this approach to core competencies, companies, according to Quinn, can develop a much higher level of focus, and hence a higher leverage, for their business strategies than through traditional product-focused strategies. Quinn's ideas, which have been refined by Hamel and Prahalad (1994), have been adopted by a score of companies worldwide. It is fair to say that these ideas have set the stage for the emergence and widespread acceptance of advanced purchasing and supply strategies.

Process orientation

Given the pressure that consumers and some industrial manufacturers exert on their suppliers, companies increasingly are organizing their activities around processes, which are relevant for their customers, rather than functions. The functional organization gradually is being replaced by the process organization. By process we mean a set of activities that, taken together, produce a value to a customer. Hammer and Champy (1993) suggests that by adopting a process orientation we need to look at the entire process beyond organizational boundaries. In these companies staff actually may work for several managers, making the traditional one-line-of-command obsolete. More and more work is being done in cross-functional teams or cross-departmental project teams or even joint customer–supplier teams. Staff are encouraged to take initiative and to collaborate with their peers to solve problems rather than to await instructions from their departmental managers. Later in this book we will see that the process orientation and cross functional teams are very powerful concepts in the area of purchasing and supply management.

Outsourcing and managing best-in-class supplier networks

Outsourcing is, as has already been argued, becoming more and more a strategic issue in many industries, with great importance for the survival of the company. Often specialist suppliers can perform the outsourced activities at lower cost and with higher value-added than the buying company.

To be able to outsource, excellent suppliers are needed, referred to by some companies as world-class suppliers, or best-in-class suppliers. More and more suppliers are professional enough to deliver complete functional units or subsystems with the required quality, flexibility and innovativeness. The key to strategic success for many firms in the future will be their coalition with the world's best suppliers, product designers, advertising agencies, distribution channels, financial houses, or other outside sources. Nike has served for some time as a nice example, since this highly successful company concentrates on design, marketing, and distribution, while virtually all production of its sporting goods lines is made through co-manufacturing arrangements with suppliers (Quinn, 1992). However, over the past years other companies, like Dell and Gateway, have followed Nike's example.

The role of purchasing in the value chain

In many business strategies the concept of value chain management plays a central role. Therefore this subject is elaborated on in this section. There will be an explanation of what value chain management is. When describing the role and position of the purchasing and supply function in industrial companies, the value chain of Porter (1985) is taken as a term of reference (see Figure 1.1).

The value chain in Figure 1.1 is composed of value activities and a margin which is achieved by these activities. Value activities can be divided into physically and technically different groups of activities. Porter differentiates between primary activities and support activities.

Primary activities are those which are directed at the physical transformation and handling of the final products, which the company delivers to its customers. As can be seen from Figure 1.1 distribution to the customer(s) and providing (product) services are part of these primary activities.

Support activities enable and support the primary activities. They can be directed at supporting one of the primary activities as well as supporting the whole primary process.

Porter differentiates between five generic categories of primary activities (1985, pp. 39–40).

- *Inbound logistics*. These activities are related to receiving, storing and disseminating inputs to the product, such as materials handling, warehousing, inventory control, vehicle scheduling and returns to suppliers.

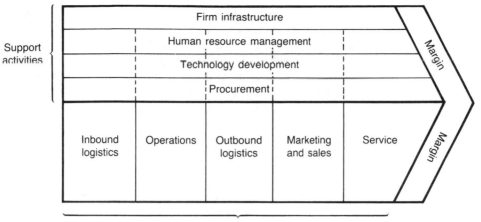

Figure 1.1   Purchasing and the value chain. (Redrawn from Porter, 1985.)

- *Operations*. Activities associated with transforming inputs into the final product form, such as machining, packaging, assembly, equipment maintenance, testing, printing and facility operations.
- *Outbound logistics*. These are activities associated with collecting, storing, and physically distributing the product to buyers, such as finished goods warehousing, materials handling, delivery vehicle operations, order processing and scheduling.
- *Marketing and sales*. These activities relate to advertising, promotion, sales, distribution channel selection, the management of channel relations and pricing.
- *Services*. Activities associated with providing services to enhance or maintain the value of the product, such as installation, repair, training, parts supply and product adjustment.

Support activities are grouped into four categories.

- *Procurement*. Procurement relates to the function of purchasing inputs used in the firm's value chain. These may include raw materials, supplies, and other consumable items as well as assets such as machinery, laboratory equipment, office equipment and buildings. These examples illustrate that purchased inputs may be related to primary activities as well as support activities. This is one reason why Porter classifies procurement as a support activity and not as a primary activity.
- *Technology development*. 'Technology' has a very broad meaning in this context, since in Porter's view every activity embodies technology, be it know-how, procedures or technology embodied in process or product design. Most value activities use a technology that combines a number of different subtechnologies involving different scientific disciplines.

- *Human resources management.* These are all the activities directed at recruiting, hiring, training, developing and compensation of all types of personnel, active in both primary and support activities.
- *Firm infrastructure.* The whole company is customer of these activities. They don't support one or more primary activities – rather, they support whole company processes. Examples of these activities are management, planning, finance, accounting, legal, government affairs, and quality management. In larger companies, which often consist of different operating units, one sees these activities divided among headquarters and the operating companies. This division is often the subject of discussion which is why it changes so frequently.

All activities need to be performed in such a way that the total value generated by the company is more than the sum of its costs. In Porter's terms, the total value of the company is determined by the whole of its sales value. The margin reflects the reward for the risks run by the company. Porter regards procurement as a support activity. He uses the term procurement rather than purchasing since, as he argues, the usual connotation of purchasing is too narrow among managers (1985, p. 41). 'The dispersion of the procurement function often obscures the magnitude of total purchases and means that many purchases receive little scrutiny.'

Based on these observations the conclusion is that procurement may provide support to the following:

- *Primary activities.* The procurement function should be able to meet the material requirements related to inbound and outbound logistics, and, often more importantly, related to operations. Operations may have a different structure among manufacturing companies. Usually manufacturing processes can be characterized according to the following categories.
  - *Make (and distribute) to stock (MTS).* Standard products are manufactured and stocked, customers are serviced from an end product inventory. Production is on dedicated machinery, often in large batches. Materials requirements planning (and therefore also planning of purchased products) is based on sales forecasts. Examples are steelplate, most maintenance, repair and operating supplies.
  - *Make to order (MTO).* Products are manufactured from raw material or the purchased components inventory after a customer order has been received and accepted. This is common in situations with very large or customer-specific product ranges (e.g. packaging materials) or bulk products that are very expensive to stock (e.g. insulation materials).
  - *Engineer to order (ETO).* All manufacturing activities from design to assembly and even purchasing of the required materials are related to a specific customer order. Production is usually on multipurpose machinery, requiring highly skilled operators, for example large customer-specific installations.

These constrasting manufacturing situations explain why procurement activities may be radically different between companies and industries.

Procurement operations for a manufacturer producing cars in large batches, controlled by a materials requirements planning system, may differ largely from those in a job-shop environment, where every project may be new to the organization and where materials are obtained from a vast, frequently changing supplier base! Buying for primary activities will be referred to throughout this book as 'production buying' or 'buying of production items'. Usually this area gets most of the attention from management.

- *Support activities.* Procurement activities may be also related to supplying products and services for the other support functions. Some examples are the buying of
  - laboratory equipment for research and development;
  - computer hardware and software for the central computer department;
  - lease-cars for the sales force and senior management;
  - office equipment for accounting;
  - food and beverages for the catering department;
  - cleaning materials for housekeeping, etc.

Again we see that the procurement function aimed at the support activities may be very different in character. Some of the purchases to be made are routine purchases (maintenance, repair and operating supplies (MRO-supplies)) and may be repetitive and low in value. Other purchases may have a 'project character' and may be unique and high valued (investment goods, capital equipment, buildings). In general this type of purchases will be referred to as 'non production buying' or 'general expenses'. They may be classified into: MRO-supplies, investment goods and services. The high variety of this type of purchases makes it extremely difficult to support these by one uniform computer information system and/or buying procedure. The character of this type of purchases also explains why professionalism in purchasing usually is low. This is one reason why some international companies, which have set up special programmes in this area (such as Lucent, Philips Electronics and SAir Group) have reported high savings. Table 1.1 summarizes the most important differences between buying for primary and for support activities.

Table 1.1 Main differences between buying for primary activities and buying for support activities

Aspects	Buying for primary activities	Buying for support activities
Product assortment	Limited to large	Very large
Number of suppliers	Limited, transparent	Very large
Purchasing turnover	Very large, considerable	Limited
Number of purchase orders	Considerable	Very large
Average order size	High	Small
Control	Depends on type of production planning	Limited, forecast-related or project-related planning
Decision-making unit	Engineering, manufacturing specialists dominant	Fragmented, varies with product or service.

Definition of concepts

The purchasing function traditionally encompasses the process of buying. It involves determining the need, selecting the supplier, arriving at a proper price, specifying terms and conditions, issuing the contract or order, and following up to ensure proper delivery. In short, the purchasing function should obtain the proper equipment, material, supplies and services of the right quality, in the right quantity, at the right price and from the right source (Aljian, 1984, p. 3). In this description, the purchasing function is regarded primarily as an operational activity.

In practice, as well as in the literature, many terms and concepts are used in the area of purchasing. However, no agreement exists about the definition of these terms. Terms like procurement, purchasing, supply and logistics management are used interchangeably. Throughout this book the definition of purchasing is:

> 'obtaining from external sources all goods, services, capabilities and knowledge which are necessary for running, maintaining and managing the company's primary and support activities at the most favourable conditions.'

The purchasing function in this definition covers specifically activities aimed at

- determining the specification (in terms of required quality and quantities) of the goods and services that need to be bought;
- selecting the most suitable supplier;
- preparing and conducting negotiations with the supplier in order to establish an agreement;
- placing the order with the selected supplier;
- monitoring and control of the order (expediting);
- follow up and evaluation (settling claims, keeping product and supplier files up-to-date, supplier rating and supplier ranking).

Figure 1.2 schematically illustrates the main activities within the purchasing function. It shows that these activities are closely interrelated. This picture is referred to as the purchasing process model.

The purchasing function does not include the responsibility for materials requirements planning, materials scheduling, inventory management, incoming inspection and quality control. However, in order to be effective, purchasing operations should be closely linked and interrelated to these materials activities. In the author's opinion a purchasing manager should support each of the six activities mentioned above. However, this does not necessarily imply that all these activities should be conducted by the manager's department, as illustrated in the following example.

A buyer who is responsible for maintenance, repair and operating supplies, is often confronted with the 'small-order problem'. Many requisitions which he receives from internal departments concern simple products of low expense. Handling these requisitions, however, is often a laborious task if that buyer is to issue a purchase order for every requisition. An alternative may be to arrange for a so-called 'umbrella' agreement with a specific supplier for the delivery of hand-tooling. In this arrangement he may establish the product range, which will be

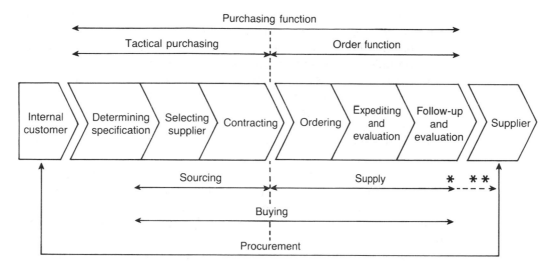

Figure 1.2   Purchasing process model and some related concepts: * = USA; ** = UK.

bought from that supplier including the prices per product. Furthermore he may negotiate a bonus from that supplier tied to the total purchasing turnover over 12 months. Next he may communicate terms and conditions of this contract to the staff of Technical Services. Through an agreed (computer-supported) order-routine, employees of this department can order directly from the supplier, without involving the purchasing department. In this example it is the task of the buyer to develop an overall commercial agreement with the supplier and to establish an (electronic) order routine with that supplier on the one hand and the internal customer on the other hand. In fact, what happens is that the ordering function is delegated, in a rather controlled way, to the internal customer. In this manner it is possible to combine the purchasing power of the organization with optimal flexibility and efficiency for Technical Services.

From the definition of **purchasing** it may be derived that this covers all activities for which the company receives an invoice from outside parties. Hence the playing ground of purchasing includes intercompany business, countertrade arrangements, hiring of temporary personnel from outside agencies, contracting for advertising. However, many of the activities for which the company may receive invoices from suppliers may be arranged for without interference from the purchasing department (this will be discussed later). Therefore the scope of the purchasing function is usually much broader than that of the purchasing department.

The term **ordering** refers to the placing of purchase orders at a supplier against previously arranged conditions. Furthermore, this term will be used when purchase orders are placed directly, without questioning the supplier's conditions. Call-off orders fall into this category as telephone orders for products bought from a supplier catalogue. Ordering is considered to be a part of the purchasing process. In fact it relates to the last three steps of the purchasing process. The use of the term 'tactical purchasing' refers to the first three steps.

As seen from Figure 1.2 **procurement** is a somewhat broader term. It includes all activities required in order to get the product from the supplier to its final destination. It encompasses the purchasing function, stores, traffic and transportation, incoming inspection, and quality control and assurance. Some firms also consider salvage and environmental issues (as they are related to materials) as a part of procurement (see also Memo 1.2). This task is expected to become more important in future years, with the increasing impact of environmental issues.

It is difficult to find a description of **buying** in management literature. It differs from purchasing in the sense that it does not encompass the first step of the purchasing process. This is in line with the practice of trading and retail companies (e.g. department stores), where this term is most often referred to. Here, discussions about the specifications of products to be purchased are more limited compared to industrial companies, since in many cases these are decided by the supplier.

Another term often used in the materials area is **supply**. This is somewhat more difficult to grasp, because it appears that there are differences in connotation between North America and Europe (Leenders *et al.* 1989, p. 3). In America 'supply' covers the stores function of internally consumed items such as

---

MEMO 1.2: The vision of Shell International Oil Company on procurement

In October 1991, in the introduction to the Procurement Business Strategy, I wrote: "It is simply no longer acceptable to treat the supply of goods and services as an administrative issue – it can and should be a potent force to make competitive gains and generate significant financial benefit".

In 1994 the Shell Group's spend on goods and services was $30 billion and a target to reduce this by 7% was set for the Group. Although good results have been achieved, in some areas we have fallen short of our targets.

The Shell Group urgently needs to improve its performance and do so more quickly. In December 1998 I set a target for reducing our overall costs by $2.5 billion a year in 2001. We cannot afford to fail; we must deliver more than we promise, not less. It is vital that all staff working in positions where they influence the costs we incur with our third parties acquire the portfolio of skills they need to manage these costs in a professional manner.

New terms such as Supply Chain Management and Value Chain Management have become commonplace in the procurement world. In those areas where these ideas have been applied they have been consistently successful. Yet, while this experience exists within the Group, it is clear that so far we have not succeeded in achieving the transformation we need in people's commercial behaviour across all of our organisations.

To achieve this change, we need to improve our commercial skills to a level that is commensurate with our best technical skills and we must work together to obtain the combined benefits that excellence in these two areas will bring . . .

(Mark Moody Stuart, Chairman of the Committee of Managing Directors, Shell Group)

(*Source*: Quoted with permission from the Introduction to Shell's Commercial Learning Guide (1998))

office supplies, cleaning materials, etc. However, in the United Kingdom and Europe, the term supply seems to have a broader meaning which includes at least purchasing, stores and receiving. The governmental sector also uses this broader interpretation.

A term which has become increasingly popular in the materials area is **sourcing**. Vollman *et al.* (1984) include the following activities under this term: finding sources of supply, guaranteeing continuity in supply, ensuring alternative sources of supply, gathering knowledge of procurable resources (p. 148). Most of these activities relate, as the author sees it, to the second step of the purchasing process, i.e. finding and selecting adequate suppliers.

Purchasing management refers to all activities required to manage supplier relationships. It is focused on structuring and continuously improving purchasing processes within the organization and between the organization and its suppliers. Purchasing management, hence, has an internal aspect and an external aspect. The idea behind purchasing management is that if suppliers are not managed by their customers, customer relationships will be managed by the suppliers. Given the widespread acceptance of marketing management and customer and account management in business, suppliers usually are in a favourable position. Given the cross-functional nature of purchasing management and its wider playing ground it is also referred to in this text as **business resource management**.

Purchasing management is part of **supply chain management**. The latter concept can be described as the management of all activities, information, knowledge and financial resources associated with the flow and transformation of goods and services up from the raw materials suppliers, component suppliers and other suppliers in such a way that the expectations of the end users of the company are being met or surpassed. Supply chain management differs from purchasing in that it encompasses also all logistics activities. Moreover it entails the management of relationships not only with first tier suppliers but also with lower tier suppliers (supply chain management is covered in more detail in Chapter 11 of this book).

Importance of purchasing to business

An analysis of the cost structure of manufacturing companies immediately shows the importance of purchasing to organizations. In general the largest part of the cost of goods sold (COGS) appears to be taken up by purchased materials and services. Figure 1.3 shows that the purchasing value in relation to cost of goods sold is approximately 50%. If the **other business costs**, which have an important purchasing component, are added to the purchasing value, the total amounts to approximately 68%.*

---

*Purchasing value** is defined by the Central Statistical Office (CSO) as 'the invoice value of the purchased goods, raw materials and catalysts, packaging goods and work done by third parties, excluding sales tax and returned import duties and levies'. **Other business costs** are defined by CSO as 'the rent of buildings, sites, machines, installations and transport, the costs of maintenance and insurance, banking costs, auxiliary materials not included in the use of raw materials and catalysts, car costs, communication costs, office supplies, subscriptions, advertisements and costs of professional services.'

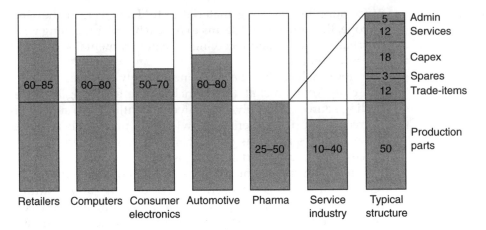

Figure 1.3 Purchased goods and services as a percentage of Cost of Goods Sold (adapted from Kluge (1996)).

Through the DuPont chart (Figure 1.4), the effects of purchasing savings on the company's (Du Pont) return on investment can be illustrated. Figure 1.4 shows how a 2% saving on purchasing related expenditure for a company (in this case Philips Electronics) may lead to an improvement of the return on net assets (RONA) of 15%. Of course, the reverse is valid also: due to a lack of a well defined purchasing policy and a lack of structure in the purchasing (decision making) process, the resulting lack of control on purchasing costs may lead to an unforeseen financial loss.

Figure 1.5 shows how purchasing costs savings may affect the financial performance of some major international companies. .

The Du Pont analysis shows that purchasing contributes to improving the company's RONA in two ways:

- Through reduction of all direct materials costs – this will immediately lead to an improvement of the company's sales margin, which in turn will affect RONA in a positive manner. A number of measures may lead to lower direct materials costs such as introducing new suppliers, competitive tendering, looking for substitute materials, etc.
- Through a reduction of the net capital employed by the company – this will work out positively on the company's capital turnover ratio. Measures which will lead to a lower capital employed are many. Examples are longer payment terms, reduction of (pipeline) inventories of base materials through just-in-time (JIT) agreements with suppliers, supplier quality improvement (which will lead to less buffer stock required) and leasing instead of buying equipment.

In many manufacturing companies managers have for a long time pursued a policy of reducing direct materials costs. Volkswagen AG may serve as an example here, where Lopez (Volkswagen's purchasing director at the time) in the early nineties shook up the European supplier industry with his unorthodox and

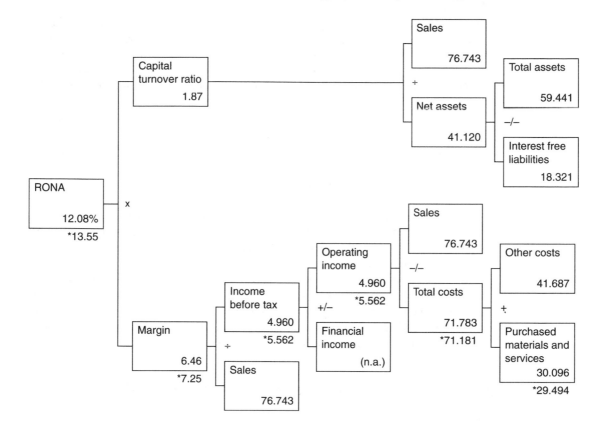

Amounts: EC million

Figure 1.4 DuPont analysis Philips (1997): a 2% savings on purchased materials and services leads to a 12,1% RONA improvement.

Company	Purchasing's share in turnover (1997)	Rona 1997	Rona 1997 as a result of 2% purchase savings	Rona 1997 as a result of 5% purchase savings
Ahold	80%	12.8%	18.2%	26.4%
Oce	48%	9.1%	10.0%	11.5%
Philips	42%	12.1%	15.7%	15.7%
Stork	50%	14.5%	17.9%	23.1%
DSM	75%	13.1%	15.0%	17.8%
Shell	76%	16.6%	18.7%	21.8%
Heineken	60%	13.9%	15.6%	18.2%

Figure 1.5 Effect of a 2% purchasing cost saving on Rona of some major international companies (Van Weele and van der Vossen, 1998).

straightforward purchasing tactics. He certainly set an example for other companies, who in turn introduced aggressive and strict targets in their purchasing strategies aimed at materials cost reduction. Nowadays these companies increasingly turn their attention to measures aimed at improving logistics, improving quality of incoming materials and cycle time or lead time reduction in their relationships with suppliers.

It can be concluded that purchasing policies fundamentally contribute to business success in several ways. First, purchasing policies can significantly improve sales margins through realizing substantial cost savings. A dollar saved in purchasing is a dollar added to the bottom line. Second, through better quality and logistics arrangements with suppliers, purchasing can contribute to a higher capital turnover ratio. Third, suppliers may contribute, when addressed properly, significantly to the company's innovation processes. As has been demonstrated even small improvements in the relationship with suppliers may have a significant impact on the company's return on net assets.

The conclusion we can draw from this discussion is that as the purchasing to sales ratio increases for a specific company, purchasing decisions will have a more profound impact on the company's net results. The same goes for the capital turnover ratio. A higher ratio will lead to a greater leverage of savings on direct materials costs. Let us now turn to a more detailed discussion on how the purchasing function may contribute to a reduction of the company's basic costs.

Purchasing, cost reduction and technological innovation

Apart from immediate savings on purchasing prices, the purchasing function can also contribute to the improvement of the company's competitive position in a more indirect manner. This indirect contribution can take the shape of standardization of the product assortment, reduction of stocks, product and process innovation, reduction of quality costs (costs related to inspection, rejection, repairs), and cutting down on production lead times. In practice, these indirect contributions often turn out to be more substantial than the amounts of money which are saved directly (i.e. exclusively by purchasing).

To give an idea of the way in which purchasing can contribute indirectly to corporate performance, consider the following examples.

● *Reduction of quality costs.* It was mentioned earlier that purchasing can contribute to a reduction of quality costs. When products are delivered by suppliers, many companies conduct both an incoming and a quality inspection. Part of purchasing's task is to minimize quality costs in the enterprise, as far as they are related to purchased materials. The costs of incoming and quality inspection of purchased goods can be reduced by selecting suppliers who have their production well under control, and who possess a sound quality organization. However, this often is not enough, since many companies experience is that most of the causes of bad quality are related to a lack of internal procedures and organization. Therefore quality improvement should be given first priority.

- *Product standardization.* Purchasing can contribute to cost-price reduction by striving for a reduction in product variety. This can be arrived at through standardization of specific standard products (instead of supplier-specific brands) and/or suppliers. This may lead to less dependence on certain suppliers, better use of competitive bidding and a lower number of items to be kept in stock.

- *Contribution to product design and innovation.* Von Hippel (1978) showed that successful industrial innovations often follow from an intensive interaction between suppliers and buyers. To actively pursue this kind of interaction is a task for purchasing. In this way, purchasing can actively contribute to a continuous innovation and improvement of products, which may result in a stronger competitive position of the company in its end-user markets. Other publications also show that the purchasing function and suppliers can play an initiating role regarding innovation processes (Wijnstra (1998)).

- *Stock reduction.* In the Western interpretation of management, stocks are seen as insurance against scheduling. These problems can result from the difficulty in predicting the outgoing materials flow (sales forecasts are hard to give, or are not made). On the other hand, they may be due to irregularities in the delivery of purchased materials. This kind of scheduling problem used to be absorbed by safety stocks (van Weele, 1984). Through imposing a solid discipline on suppliers and enforcing it, through careful scheduling of deliveries and/or through special stock arrangements with suppliers (e.g. consigned stock agreements), purchasing can significantly contribute to a reduction of stock and hence the capital employed.

- *Increasing flexibility.* Forced by international competition, more and more companies attempt implementation of flexible manufacturing systems. These systems are geared towards improving the company's market responsiveness. Some ways in which attempts are made to accomplish this are striving for improved quality, minimizing stocks, and higher turnover rates in production.

  Implementation of this kind of system (also known as manufacturing resources planning, KANBAN[1] and just-in-time scheduling) demands a high performance level from suppliers. Purchasing will have to impose these demands on carefully selected suppliers. A purchasing policy which also aims at improving supplier performance will definitely benefit the company's competitiveness in its end-use markets.

- *Fostering purchasing synergy.* Over the years many companies have adopted a business unit structure, where operating companies have a fairly large autonomy. In such a structure every business unit manager needs to report on the profit and loss account for which he/she is fully responsible. Hence, business unit managers are responsible both for revenues and for costs, including materials costs. In such cases the company as a group can benefit significantly from co-ordinated contracting of common materials requirements from a smaller supplier base.

The list of examples cannot be complete within the scope of this chapter. It is obvious that companies can benefit significantly from effective purchasing and supply strategies and that opportunities for improvement are many. In general, however, these improvement measures require a better collaboration and harmonization between the different functional domains with the company. This explains why there is often such a large potential for improvement.

Classification of purchasing goods

The purchasing process may concern a large variety of goods and, of course, services. In general, purchased materials and services can be grouped into the following categories.

- *Raw materials.* Raw materials are materials which have undergone no transformation or a minimal transformation, and they serve as the basis materials for a production process. We may differentiate between **physical raw materials**, such as iron ore, copper ore, coal, and **natural raw materials**, such as grains, soya and coffee.
- *Supplementary materials.* These are materials which are not absorbed physically in the end product; they are used or consumed during the production process. Examples of this type of product are lubricating oil, cooling water, polishing materials, welding electrodes and industrial gases.
- *Semi-manufactured products.* These products have already been processed once or more, and they will be processed further at a later stage. They are physically present in the end product. Examples are steelplate, rolled wire and plastic foils.
- *Components.* Components are manufactured goods which will not undergo additional physical changes, but which will be incorporated in a system with which there is a functional relationship by joining it with other components. They are built into an end product. Examples are headlight units, lamps, batteries, engine parts, electronic parts and transmissions. A distinction can be made between **specific components** and **standard components**. Specific components are produced according to design or specification of the customer, whereas standard components are produced according to specification of the supplier.
- *Finished products.* These encompass all products which are purchased to be sold, after negligible added value, either together with other finished products and/or manufactured products. Examples of this product category are accessories which are supplied by car manufacturers, such as stripings, car radios and ornamental wheel rims. The manufacturer does not produce these products, but obtains them from specialized suppliers. Commercial products and articles sold by department stores are also in this category.
- *Investment goods or capital equipment.* These are the products which are not consumed immediately, but whose purchasing value is depreciated over a period of time. In general the book value is stated on the balance-sheet annually. Investment goods can be machines used in production, but they also include computers and buildings. These examples illustrate the varied character of this category of goods.
- *Maintenance, repair and operating materials (MRO items).* These products, sometimes referred to as indirect materials or consumable items, represent

materials, which are necessary for keeping the organization running in general, and for the support activities in particular. These products are often supplied from stock; examples are office supplies, cleaning materials and copy paper, but also maintenance materials and spare parts.

- *Services*. Services are activities which are executed by third parties (suppliers, contractors, engineering firms) on a contract basis. Services can range from providing cleaning services and hiring temporary labour to having a new production facility for a chemical company designed by a specialized engineering firm (a **contractor**).

Having defined the most important categories of purchased goods and services we now turn to a short description of major new developments going on in the area of purchasing and supply management.

New developments in purchasing

Many companies are now confronted with diminishing growth opportunities, which results in a situation where an increase in turnover can only be realized at the expense of the competition and only with a great deal of effort. This leads to increased pressure on sales prices and consequently on cost prices and margins, which causes two developments.

On the one hand it has resulted in shifts of power between purchasing and selling parties in many markets. Due to the fact that in many cases the market has changed from a seller's-market to a buyer's-market, the role of the buyer is now more dominant than a number of years ago.

On the other hand the increasing pressure on sales prices and margins has resulted in an increased pressure on direct materials-related costs. Because the purchasing prices determine the sales prices in the industrial sector to a large extent, the company will be constantly on the look-out for opportunities to keep these prices as low as possible.

As a result of both developments, the purchasing and supply strategies of industrial companies have undergone major changes. Several examples of these changes are presented below.

- *Co-ordination of purchasing requirements*. In companies with several manufacturing plants, important purchasing advantages can be realized by combining joint purchasing requirements. A trend towards a co-ordinated purchasing policy is seen to emerge in many European companies of this type, even across national borders. Traditionally this was already common for raw materials; at present however, a similar approach is used for the purchase of computer hardware and software, capital goods and components. Good examples of companies with an active policy concerning purchasing co-ordination are, apart from the automotive and computer industry, Shell, Philips Electronics Ltd and Alcatel.
- *Integration of purchasing in logistics*. Automation enables companies to improve materials planning and supply systems. It furthermore may

significantly improve productivity within the materials area. An integrated approach of materials management requires close co-operation between production planning, inventory control, quality inspection and purchasing. To achieve successful automation, system standardization is a prerequisite. Purchasing cannot be allowed to follow its own course. To ensure effective integration of the different materials-related areas, purchasing increasingly is integrated into supply-chain management.

- *Integration of purchasing in engineering and production planning.* In practice, supplier selection is determined to a large degree by the technical specifications. Once established, this specification is often very difficult to change (and only at high cost). From a commercial point of view it is undesirable that specifications are defined towards a particular supplier; in that case purchasing often ends up with a monopolist, which seriously hampers negotiating. To prevent this, it is desirable to include purchasing in the development process at an early stage. The goal is to make optimal use of purchasing's knowledge of products and markets for the benefit of the product design. To this end some progressive companies have brought in specialists (referred to as purchasing engineers), who form the link between purchasing and the engineering department.
- *Make or buy.* Practice shows that several production activities can be done cheaper and faster by specialized suppliers. Moreover, companies may make greater demands in terms of quality on external suppliers than on their own production departments. This is why in some industrial branches the purchasing to sales ratio has been steadily rising. For some companies this conclusion has resulted in detailed make-or-buy studies. Purchasing should always be closely involved in this type of study, because they are the logical source of market information (in the form of prices, alternative suppliers, etc.).
- *Reciprocity agreements and compensation obligations.* Companies operating on the international markets are often obliged to compensate (part of) their sales turnover by counter-purchase obligations. The recent opening up of the Eastern European bloc has made countertrade an actual issue. Buying from these countries may even open up interesting sales opportunities. Purchasing becomes involved in fulfilling such obligations.
- *Total quality control and just-in-time production.* In several companies (especially those companies whose manufacturing operations are characterized by assembly) a growing interest in quality improvement and increased productivity can be observed. The activities of the European Foundation for Quality Management, initiated by the Presidents of 14 European industries on 5 September 1988, illustrate the first; several EEC programmes (such as Cargonaut), aimed at logistics, the second. There is a growing awareness in the international business scene that, if Europe wishes to remain competitive on a world scale in several sectors, improvements must be made in both the level of costs and the level of quality of the end products.
- *Purchasing and the Internet.* One of the most important challenges that have affected traditional purchasing strategies and organisation are the solutions

that are provided by modern information technology and the Internet. In just a few years manufacturing companies have invested millions of Euro's in setting up electronic market places (such as Covisint in the car manufacturing industry, WorldWideRetailExchange in the retail sector, and PaperXchange by the paper industry). Equal amounts are invested in electronic procurement systems, which are now implemented to speed up business to business transactions, whilst reducing the cost of these. More information about the opportunities which the Internet represents for buyers and purchasing managers is to be found in Chapter 9.

- *Environmental issues*. Environmental problems in many European countries become more and more prevalent. National governments have become more strict in their regulations on this point. In Germany, for instance, strict regulations on (industrial) packaging recently came into force. In due course all superfluous packaging needs to be avoided (e.g. blister packaging and the box-packaging of toothpaste). Manufacturers of packaging will increasingly be held responsible for its disposal after use. This is one reason why Volkswagen constructed its latest Golf (America: Rabbit) in such a way that the different parts and components can be easily disassembled and reprocessed at the end of the car's lifespan. Volkswagen has even founded its own rework facilities for this purpose. Environmental issues pose a whole new challenge to purchasing. They will increasingly pose problems to manufacturing companies. It is purchasing's task to work out ideas and measures with suppliers, which may solve or mitigate them!

It can be appreciated from this discussion that purchasing and supply represents a business area which is being confronted with many changes and challenges. Most of the problems, however, require intensive interaction, communication and co-operation with other disciplines in the organization. Purchasing and supply is developing increasingly as a business function which cuts across other disciplines. Managing the purchasing and supply function requires a thorough understanding of the purchasing processes that take place within the organization. Only then can these challenges be dealt with effectively.

Summary

One of the conclusions that can be drawn from this chapter is that purchasing is more than supply. The field of the purchasing function extends from the purchasing market to inside the company gate.

Buyers apparently have an important role to play in development and engineering projects. They should be able to translate technical developments at the supplier's end in terms of the company's needs.

The purchasing function should ensure an optimal supply system, which must be geared towards the needs of production and materials planning. In other words, the purchasing function is a very important link in the production and supply chain of organizations.

The purchasing function is concerned with obtaining all goods necessary for running, maintaining and managing the company; in principle this also includes contracting services. The fact that there is such a rich variety of purchasing requirements in many companies makes it difficult to delineate the field of purchasing in practice.

Purchasing management is the activity aimed at systematizing the purchasing process and achieving specific improvement of this process following changes in purchasing requirements.

The importance of the purchasing function for an organization can be deduced from the effect of (potential) purchasing savings on the company profits. However, there is more: through a market-oriented purchasing policy, interesting contributions can be made to product and process innovation and a reduction of product cost price achieved.

Finally, it has been established that the purchasing function is subject to many changes. Higher demands on the quality of the goods to be purchased, reduction of stocks and cutting down on the lead times in logistics and production cause higher demands on suppliers. The purchasing department is the logical party to communicate these demands to the suppliers and to see to it that they are met.

Assignments

1.1   Take the annual report of an industrial company. Calculate the purchasing value in relation to the turnover. Calculate the effect of a 2% saving on the purchasing value.

Do the same for a 2% increase in the purchasing value *ceteris paribus*.

Describe the elements in the Du Pont chart (Figure 1.4) that are affected by purchasing policy directly or indirectly.

1.2   What would you consider to be purchasing's added value to a company? What would you consider to be purchasing's core and non-core activities?

1.3   What are the major differences between purchasing, supply, sourcing and supply management? Would you consider the purchasing function to be part of supply chain management or would you favour the reverse? Discuss!

1.4   What are the major differences between the activities of the purchasing function and the activities conducted by the purchasing department? Do you think it is important to differentiate between these two concepts? Why?

1.5   The chapter describes a number of new developments in purchasing and also addresses the aim for total quality control in companies. Describe the major consequences of total quality control on the purchasing policy in general and on the relationships with suppliers in particular.

Note

1   A KABAN is a pull system in which production orders for components are generated on small cards (KABANS) indicating the volume of products that need to be produced based on actual consumption.

INDUSTRIAL BUYING BEHAVIOUR: DECISION MAKING IN PURCHASING

2

Learning objectives

After studying this chapter you should understand the following:

- The major differences between organizational and consumer buying behaviour.
- The key elements of the purchasing process.
- The various roles in a decision-making unit.
- The involvement of the purchasing department in the acquisition of various goods.
- How to model organizational buying behaviour and network-theory.

CASE STUDY
Buying computer systems in a car leasing company

The management of a car leasing company has requested its business systems manager to prepare a proposal for further automation of all activities related to customer order handling. This management decision is in line with the intention to increase the efficiency of the sales back office: in the future, more administrative work must be done with fewer people. The management already has its eye on a particular system: contact has been made with a software supplier, who has references from the automobile branch. Documentation has been requested and the systems manager is asked to give his opinion.

The systems manager thinks that the management's ideas on further computerization of administrative sales tasks is best elaborated in close co-operation with the future users of the system. A project group is installed, consisting of employees from the internal sales department, the field sales organization, the internal control department and an external consultant. The

Continued on page 28

working group's course is plotted. It immediately becomes clear during the first meetings that the compatibility between the intended software system and the organization's present ways of working is not optimal. When asked, the supplier states that this is usually the case: the current operating procedures will have to be adjusted here and there. However, before going ahead, the systems manager decides to get information from other suppliers. It appears that adjustments in the sales organizations are necessary no matter what software system management decides to implement. There is no system readily available on the market that corresponds exactly with the organization's present needs. The working group decides to invite another software company to help determine whether the organization will have to develop its own system. The question is what form of software will qualify.

The systems department at headquarters is asked about their experience with software companies. Several names are provided, and it is decided to approach four companies. After talking to these four suppliers, the group decides to go ahead with one selected supplier for the time being.

The supplier in question proposes to start with a thorough analysis of the information needs of the company. Only then can the system requirements be defined. Supervision of these first steps will cost money, of course! A $150,000 quote is submitted and accepted. All this has taken three months.

The activities turn out to be more complex than expected. They also turn out to take much more time than anticipated: it has taken four months to describe the system requirements. Analysis of available software systems is then commenced. This reveals that one system will do, but that a considerable amount of 'application engineering' will be necessary. The software company can be of help in this too. A quotation is solicited: it amounts to $650,000. The systems manager has the strong impression that this price is far too high and again wants to invite competitive quotations from other software companies. However, the management is opposed: the current supplier is well-informed about the organization's problems. A new supplier would have to start all over, and that would cost too much money and time . . .

Introduction

The situation described above outlines one part of a complex decision-making process related to an important purchase. Decision-making processes concerning the purchase of products that are still to be developed, are generally characterized by a high degree of complexity and uncertainty. For this reason the decision making in such situations usually involves many disciplines and departments in the organization. In this car-lease company it involved the management, the systems manager, the marketing department, the sales department, and the internal controlling department. In addition, the external consultant and the suppliers involved exerted considerable influence on the decisions that were made. So, various disciplines and stakeholders are involved, with varying interests and different views and opinions about what should be done! Circumstances such as these often make the purchasing decision-making process complex and obscure. When ill structured, these processes can easily end up in frustration, considerable loss of time and budget overruns. Hence, a major question is how decision-making processes in purchasing can be structured in such a way that all parties involved arrive at solutions which are satisfactory to them.

In this chapter different models that are available to answer this question will be explained, starting with the main differences between organizational and consumer buying behaviour. Next, the purchasing process will be described in more detail. Thereafter are some sources from business marketing theory on how organizational buying behaviour can be modelled and analysed.

Organizational buying behaviour: basic characteristics

It is tempting to take the literature on consumer buying behaviour as a frame of reference for studying buying processes in organizations. However, it soon becomes clear that these theories have only limited value in this regard. There appear to be major differences between **consumer marketing** on the one hand and **industrial** or **business-to-business marketing** on the other. The industrial marketer has to deal with companies, governmental organizations or institutions, who need the purchased product to feed, support and maintain their primary and supporting processes. In consumer marketing, however, the marketer faces individuals who strive for an immediate satisfaction of their needs. Table 2.1 summarizes the major differences between both types of marketing.

The following are a few important characteristics of industrial markets.

- *Professional purchasing.* Usually, professional buyers are involved in purchasing decision-making and purchase operations. Because of their education, experience and responsibilities, they usually are experienced discussion partners for industrial salesmen and account managers.

Table 2.1 Main differences between industrial and consumer markets (adapted from Matthijssens and Rijcke (1982))

Aspect	Industrial market	Consumer market
Buying objective	Enable production	Personal need satisfaction
Buying motive	Mainly rational	Also emotional
Purchasing function	Professional buying, predominantly men	Consumers, mainly women
Decision making	Many persons involved, much discussion	Often impulsive, without consulting others
Characteristics	Negotiations, intense interaction	Often without negotiation, little interaction
Product and market knowledge	Large	Limited
Order size	Often large	Mostly small
Demand	Derived demand, may fluctuate strongly	Autonomous demand, relatively stable
Price elasticity	Rather inelastic	Rather elastic
Number of customers	Mostly limited	Very large
Spread of customers	Sometimes large geographic concentration	Large geographical spread

- *Derived demand*. Most companies sell to other companies. Few manufacturing companies deliver directly to the end user. For this reason developments in industrial markets are often related to changes which occur in the end-user markets.
- *Inelastic, fluctuating demand*. Due to the complex decision making, the price-elasticity in industrial markets is frequently lower than for consumer products.
- *Geographical concentration*. Many industrial markets are geographically concentrated (unlike consumer markets, which are geographically dispersed). The European chemical industry, for example, is concentrated in the Ruhr area in Germany, the automobile industry in southern Germany, France and northern Italy (as the microchip industry is concentrated in Silicon Valley in the United States).
- *Large order quantities and large amounts of money involved*. Business-to-business transactions often involve large quantities of goods and services and, therefore, large sums of money.
- *Limited number of customers*. The customer market of industrial suppliers often consists of only a few companies. In Europe, the automotive industry – if limited to the producers – is made up of approximately 10 major independent manufacturers! Manufacturers of fast moving consumer products are confronted with only a handful of supermarket chains in most European countries. Therefore, only a limited number of buyers in fact determine the success of a new product!

A major difference between the consumer sector and the industrial sector is related to the **interaction** and **(mutual) interdependency** between buyer and seller. Unlike the consumer sector, business-to-business markets are often characterized by long-lasting relationships between the buying and the selling parties. As a consequence, business-to-business marketers must regard their markets as a **network of relationships.** Their marketing strategies are aimed at extending, investing in and continuously maintaining these networks. In other words, business-to-business marketing, and professional purchasing, require active management of relationships within complex organizational networks (see Figure 2.1).

The purchasing process

In Chapter 1 some purchasing terms and definitions were given. In this chapter the purchasing process model described there will be elaborated on, based on Figure 2.2. The purchasing process model shows how the different purchasing activities are interrelated. Some of the important aspects of this model are now emphasized and explained.

- *Process approach*. Throughout this book purchasing and supply issues will be considered from a process approach. The various steps in this model are closely connected. The quality of the output of the preceding steps

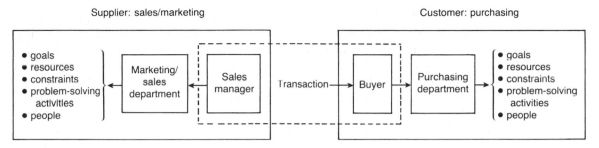

Figure 2.1 Purchasing management requires management of supplier relationships within organizational networks.

	Define specification	Select supplier	Contract agreement	Ordering	Expediting	Evaluation
P & S Role	• Get specification	• Assure adequate supplier selection	• Prepare contract	• Establish order routine	• Establish expediting routine	• Assess supplier
Elements	• Functional specification • Technical changes • Bring supplier-knowledge to engineering	• Prequalification of suppliers • Request for quotation	• Contracting expertise • Negotiating expertise	• Develop order routines • Order handling	• Expediting • 'Trouble-shooting'	• Supplier evaluation • Supplier rating
Documents	• Functional specification • Norm/spec control	• Supplier selection proposal	• Contract	• Order	• Exception report • Due date listings • Invoices	• Preferred supplier list • Supplier ranking scheme

Figure 2.2 Purchasing process approach: managing interfaces. (Redrawn from Van Weele (1994)).

determines to a large extent the quality of the output of the subsequent steps. Deficiencies in one step will lead to problems in the next steps. As an example, quality problems related to purchased materials often become visible at the end of the purchasing process in terms of rejected deliveries (step 5). In practice, however, bad quality of incoming materials can frequently be traced to incorrect or incomplete specifications (step 1), or to an incorrect sourcing decision in that a supplier has been selected who cannot deliver against required specifications (step 2). Also the contract that has been drawn up may have been incomplete in that it did not provide for any penalty clauses when delivering bad quality (step 3).

- *Defining the interfaces.* The purchasing process model implies that in order to get a full grip on buying operations, the output of each phase is clearly defined. Preferably it should be possible to trace and track every activity that has been done in the purchasing process. Every consecutive step should only be started when the previous step has been concluded by a decision.

Therefore, it is recommended that the result of each step is documented in the form of a 'go-no-go' document. This will help to structure the purchasing process and to formalize it. The way this is done usually is explained in the company's purchasing procedures, which are laid down in a purchasing manual. When such procedures are absent, this usually results in highly unstructured purchasing decision-making processes and operational problems.

- *Determining responsibilities.* The author considers purchasing to be a *cross-functional* responsibility. As indicated before, the purchasing process is not limited to the purchasing department only. Many echelons in the organization are usually involved. This demands adequate communication and co-operation among the disciplines involved. The tasks, responsibilities and authority of each department should be indicated in each phase, to prevent misunderstandings and role conflicts. For example: when deciding on specifications of technical components, engineering departments often have the sole authority to do this. Engineering departments, however, are in most cases not responsible for the supply of base materials in the manufacturing stage. What often happens is that engineers, after careful selection, decide to integrate supplier and brand-specific components in their final designs leaving the buyer with a monopolist supplier. The author suggests that deciding on specifications of purchased materials and supplier selection are considered as a joint activity between engineers and buyers. (See also Wijnstra (1998). This author has presented an interesting framework which may serve as a terms of reference to structure collaboration on product development between engineering, purchasing and suppliers.)
- *Combining different skills, different types of knowledge and expertise.* The first three steps, called the initial or tactical purchasing function, are primarily of a technical–commercial nature. The remaining three steps, referred to as the ordering function, are of a more logistics–administrative nature. A key problem in many companies is how to combine the different types of knowledge, skills and expertise in such a way that all parties involved arrive at an optimal solution for the company. It would be almost impossible to combine all these elements in one person, which is why we see an increasing tendency towards specialization in purchasing jobs, while at the same time cross-functional co-operation between different disciplines is growing.

The added value of the professional buyer primarily lies in his ability to act as a facilitator for the entire purchasing and supply cycle. This includes, among other things:

- Being involved in new product development projects and investment projects at an early stage, based on proven expertise.
- Preparing a list of approved suppliers in co-operation with the internal customer, and after that drawing up requests for quotations and preparing their evaluation together with the user, as well as selecting a supplier by mutual agreement.

- Preparing and carrying out the contract negotiations as well as drawing up and reviewing the terms and conditions of the contract.
- Setting up requisitioning and ordering routines in such a way that the users (if possible and so desired) can place orders themselves, within the terms and conditions established with the suppliers.
- In case orders cannot be placed by users themselves, take care of orderhandling i.e. handling internal requisitions; place orders at suppliers and maintain and monitor order and supplier files.
- Expediting (arranging) or follow-up of outstanding orders and monitoring outstanding financial obligations.
- Follow up and evaluation in terms of settling claims, evaluating supplier performance and maintaining and keeping up to date the relevant supplier documentation.

The cause of delivery problems of purchased materials is often related to late requisitioning by other departments (often due to time pressure). In practice this leads not only to a higher price being paid (as a result of extra work, speed delivery, buying from stock-keeping wholesaler), but also in many cases to higher organizational costs and operational problems (the delivered materials do not comply with the specifications, many partial deliveries, postponed delivery of critical parts, etc.). The presented purchasing model may help managers to structure their purchasing decision-making processes and the operational processes involved. The results will not only pay off in terms of lower prices paid for materials and services, but certainly also in lower organizational costs and a higher productivity.

There are relatively few situations in which all of the steps in the purchasing process are passed through. This only happens in the case of a first-time purchase of a product and/or service. In practice, most purchasing transactions involve more or less straight rebuys. In general, three types of purchasing situations are distinguished (Robinson, Faris and Wind, 1967; see for the first studies on this subject Brand (1968)).

- *The new-task situation*. This situation occurs when the organization decides to buy a completely new product, supplied by an unknown supplier. This type of transaction is characterized by a high degree of uncertainty and high risk in that the specifications of the product still have to be mapped. The decision-making process is characterized by extensive problem solving and becomes protracted because various disciplines, distributed across various hierarchical levels in the organization, will probably assert their influence. The new-task situation occurs, for example, in the acquisition of capital goods and the purchase of new components which must be produced to the organization's specifications (see Figure 2.3). The case example of the car-lease company at the beginning of this chapter also falls into this category.
- *The modified rebuy*. This is when the organization wants to purchase a new product from a known supplier, or an existing product from a new supplier, and usually occurs when there is some dissatisfaction about the current supplier, or when better alternatives for existing products have become

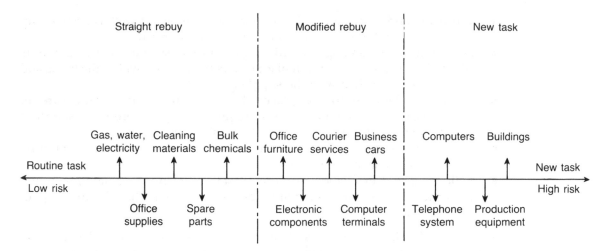

Figure 2.3   New task-situation, modified rebuy and straight rebuy illustrated by some examples.

available. This situation is less uncertain than the new-task situation because the relevant criteria on how to value the functionality of the product or service or how to select the supplier are more or less known. The purchasing process focuses in particular on the last four steps of the model and decision making is characterized by **limited problem solving**.

- *The straight rebuy.* This is the most common situation and it entails the acquisition of a known product from a known supplier. Uncertainty regarding the outcome of the transaction is low because the terms and conditions of the contract are known and are periodically re-established in negotiations with the supplier. In the case of regularly recurring (repetitive) deliveries of identical goods, blanket orders or annual agreements are used that cover the main terms and conditions. Ordering takes place **through call-off orders**, often placed directly by the user department. This benefits both the speed and efficiency of the transaction (for buyer as well as supplier). In this situation the purchasing process only covers the final three steps of the model. Straight rebuy situations relate to all kind of consumable items (such as office supplies, fixing materials, cleaning materials, catering products). After negotiations with distributors about the contract, orders should be placed directly by the users without interference from the purchasing department. As will be explained later, Internet technology and especially E-Commerce provide interesting solutions for efficient orderhandling in this area.

This typology of buying situations explains that the degree of uncertainty and risk that buyers may deal with, strongly depends on the type of purchasing situation. This is reflected in the way the decision-making process evolves. The higher the sums of money involved and the higher the technical complexity, the higher the perceived risk will be, and more functions and persons will become involved in the decision making. The involvement of these persons as well as their role, will vary in each step of the purchasing process model. They are sometimes referred to as the Decision-Making Unit (DMU) (Webster and Wind, 1972). In light of the interdisciplinary nature of many purchasing decisions, it is essential that the decision-making process is well organized. Many problems with supply and suppliers are caused by a lack of organization within the DMU.

Major bottlenecks and problems

The purchasing process model is a construct, an abstraction from reality, and in the real world organizational purchasing processes deviate from this model. Observation of numerous companies and institutions over many years has demonstrated that the purchasing process can be obstructed by the following situations.

- *Supplier or brand specifications*. With the exception of some leading-edge companies in the automotive, computer and consumer electronics industry, most buyers are involved only to a minor extent in the specification phase. Product specifications are usually determined unilaterally by the user, which means that they are often defined 'towards' a particular (approved) supplier. The use of a particular brand or supplier specification seriously limits the buyer's commercial latitude (in terms of negotiations) with the supplier – who in most cases is well aware of the selection of his product. Moreover, it may lead to situations where the supplier selected cannot meet the capacity and logistics requirements of the company.
- *Inadequate supplier selection*. Selecting a supplier is one of the most important decisions in the purchasing process, particularly if the products delivered require many years of maintenance and service (as in the case of many investment goods). Failure to check the supplier's (bank) references, can produce very unpleasant surprises in the shape of unexpected bankruptcy, inability to meet quality requirements, unwillingness to keep up to warranty obligations, etc. It may become clear that the supplier, in order to land the contract, has made promises about delivery times he cannot keep.
- *Insufficient contracting expertise*. If there are problems during or after delivery, the contract's fine print comes into play. It can turn out that things thought to be handled by the supplier, have to be paid for separately by the customer. Misunderstandings about the handling of problems can be prevented by means of a solid contract. Prevention is better than cure and editing of the contract is better left to the buyer.
- *Too much emphasis on price*. Especially when buying capital equipment buying decisions need to be based upon total-cost-of-ownership (TCO) rather than price only. Many equipment manufacturers have adopted a sales strategy where they charge a fairly low price for their equipment. However, their warranties and service contracts require the customer to source spare parts and all maintenance services from the original equipment manufacturer. If not done so by the customer, the supplier will not guarantee the functioning

of the equipment. Examples of this type of sales 'tactics' are many: copying machine manufacturers, manufacturers of computer mainframes, manufacturers of earth-moving equipment and trucks, systems packaging suppliers exert this kind of practices. In order to handle this type of purchase effectively, buyers need to base their decisions on TCO models where the initial purchase of the equipment is balanced against the life-of-type costs of the equipment.

● *Administrative organization.* Placing orders can also cause big problems. Sometimes there are no clear procedures with regard to procurement or authorization of orders, which can lead to random ordering by everybody in the organization. The result is lots of extra work in the inspection of deliveries (who is this product for?) and in making invoices payable (to what order or delivery does this invoice refer?). Inadequate administrative procedures could result in payment of invoices without any kind of check (see Memo 2.1).

The role of the purchasing department in the purchasing process

In general the scope of the purchasing function is far wider than the activities of the purchasing department. In many companies, various goods and services are bought without intervention of the purchasing department (see Table 2.2). Apart from buyers, therefore, many other disciplines within the company are actively

---

MEMO 2.1: How inefficient administrative purchasing procedures can pay off handsomely . . .

The Profit Recovery Group is a successful US-based consultancy firm which has reported considerable growth and profit. Founded in the early seventies, the company went through a fast growth stage from 1991 on. In 1999 the company reported a sales turnover of 40 million US-dollars; at that time 1800 people were employed. From 1996 on this firm also set foot in Europe. What is the basis of its success?

Profit Recovery Group works on the basis of no cure-no pay. It targets its activities on large retailers and manufacturing firms. Based on the annual report of its prospective clients the company presents a proposal to investigate the invoices that have been paid for goods and services (including transport) by that client during a certain period. This investigation consists of checking whether the quantities invoiced and the price paid match the company's purchase orders and whether these data comply with the contract that has been negotiated with that supplier. If any variances are found (unfair prices being charged or delivered quantities lower than those invoiced) these are reported. Savings will be shared on a 50:50 basis with the client.

The activities of Profit Recovery Group are successful also in Europe. This illustrates how a consulting firm, operating in a niche market, may benefit from apparent deficiencies in the information and financial flows between buyers and suppliers.

Table 2.2 Examples of items purchased outside the purchasing department

Type of purchasing item	Purchased by
Key raw materials	Management
Computers and software	Accounting, computer department
Lease contracts	Accounting
Insurance	Management, accounting
Accounting services, legal and management consulting services	Management
Advertising, sales brochures, business gifts	Sales, marketing, sales promotions
Catering	Catering manager, facilities manager
Travel	Administration (or separate department)
Licences and development contracts	Research and development manager
Books and magazines	Library
Sales promotion items	Sales, marketing
Temporary labour and training	Personnel department, Human resources
Cleaning materials	Facilities manager
Maintenance, repair and operating supplies	Technical maintenance

engaged in buying products and services. This is one reason why such large savings usually can be realized. This is especially true for the facilities area, where a growing number of management consultants have found interesting prospects.

Limiting this discussion to the role of the purchasing department in the purchasing process, it can be seen that this role varies from company to company and from situation to situation. Table 2.3 shows the involvement of purchasing departments in the acquisition of

- production-related items such as raw materials, catalysts and semi-manufactured products;
- indirect materials, such as spare parts, office supplies, cleaning materials and workclothes;
- investment goods, such as buildings, manufacturing equipment and computers, trucks, cars, etc.

Although this survey was conducted some time ago, the picture with regard to the role of purchasing within many manufacturing companies, apart from some leading-edge companies, is still valid. However, due to the interest that can be observed in purchasing and supply issues from some large multinational companies and leading management consultancies, this picture will rapidly change in the years to come.

Table 2.3 shows that in general the purchasing department's involvement is highest in the purchase of indirect materials (referred to in many companies as consumable items, or maintenance, repair and operating (MRO) supplies).

Considering the various purchasing activities, it can be seen that the involvement of the purchasing department is limited during the first stages of the purchasing process. Purchasing's role becomes more important when quotations must be solicited; however, when these quotations are evaluated, involvement decreases. Involvement is at its highest in the last stage of the

Table 2.3 Involvement of the purchasing department in the acquisition of production-related items, indirect goods and investment goods. Numbers represent average scores. (Source: van Weele and van Hespen, 1987)

	Purchasing fully responsible		Shared responsibility		Purchasing not responsible	
	100% (5)		75% (4) 50% (3) 25% (2)		0% (1)	
	Production-related goods		Indirect materials		Investment goods	
	PM	GM	PM	GM	PM	GM
Determining purchasing requirements (quality)	1.6	1.5	1.8	2.0	1.3	1.1
Determining purchasing requirements (quantity)	2.4	2.2	2.0	1.8	1.1	1.0
Market research and supplier selection	4.3	4.0	4.1	4.0	2.8	2.7
Requests for quotation	4.6	4.5	4.5	4.8	3.7	4.0
Evaluating requests for quotation	4.1	4.2	4.2	4.3	3.0	3.1
Negotiations with suppliers	4.4	4.5	4.4	4.5	3.3	3.6
Final supplier selection	3.9	4.0	4.1	4.2	2.7	2.8
Preparing contract	4.6	4.9	4.8	4.9	4.1	4.4
Order handling and expediting	4.4	4.4	4.4	4.4	3.9	3.9
Invoice handling	2.7	3.0	2.5	2.8	2.4	2.5

PM = Purchasing manager
GM = General manager

purchasing process, i.e. when the purchase contract is drawn up and when orders need to be placed. This seems to be true for all three types of purchasing goods. Apparently checking invoices is usually a responsibility that purchasing shares with the accounting discipline.

It can be concluded from this survey that the involvement of the purchasing department in the initial stage is rather low. Purchasing appears to be most involved in the operational activities of the purchasing process, which explains the administrative orientation of most purchasing departments. There is a certain risk involved when this situation applies to a certain company. In the first place the administrative work may prevent buyers from spending sufficient time on their tactical and more strategic purchasing tasks. Second, the administrative orientation may prevent a more strategic vision on purchasing and supply management to develop. Both are underlying reasons why purchasing and supply management in many organizations represent a business area with such great improvement potential!

Figure 2.4 shows that purchasing and supply activities in general have four different **dimensions**:

- a **technical dimension**, which concerns the functionality, specifications and quality of the purchased products;

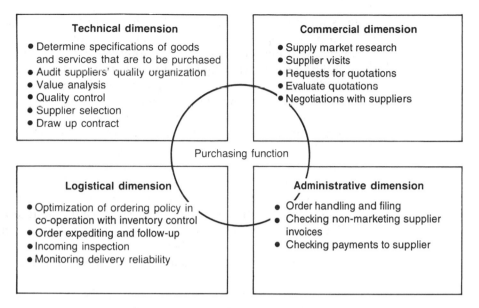

Figure 2.4 Four main dimensions of the purchasing function.

- a **commercial dimension**, related to managing the relationship with the suppliers and the contractual conditions which must be negotiated and arranged;
- a **logistics dimension**, which concerns all activities related to optimizing the incoming materials flow from the supplier up to the point where the materials are needed and actually consumed;
- an **administrative dimension**, relating to the efficient orderhandling, expediting and follow up and handling of invoices.

Models of industrial buying behaviour

In the previous section the stages of the purchasing process were identified. The variables that affect the course and/or the outcomes of this process will now be addressed, distinguishing between

- variables that affect the buying **process**;
- variables that affect buying **behaviour**.

Variables that affect the buying process

- *Characteristics of the product*. Decisions about the purchase of raw materials differ from, for example, those for the purchase of spare parts. The differences stem from the financial importance (and therefore the influence on the cost price of the end product) of both types of goods, their technical complexity and the supply risk involved. In practice, many differences in the way the buying process develops can be traced to specific product characteristics. Decisions about the purchase of technically complex products are usually made by technical specialists (designers, engineers, technical/maintenance department, etc.). Decisions concerning the purchase of standard-grade, high-volume products (such as raw materials and commodities) are made primarily by financial managers and/or top management. Purchase decisions about routine products in general are left to the lower echelons of the organization.

- *Strategic importance of the purchase*. The higher the importance of the purchase to the company, the more involved management will be in the purchase decision. The strategic importance is not merely determined by the amounts of money or the investment involved in the purchase. For example, low-cost bottleneck items can sometimes show significant risk in terms of availability and supply, and often turn out to be a direct threat to the continuity of production. For this reason they are of prime interest to top management. Other examples of key purchase decisions are contracting for licenses or development contracts.

- *Sums of money involved in the purchases*. As the amounts of money involved increase, management's role in the purchase decision will grow. This is why the management is often directly involved in negotiations about important raw materials and investment goods.

- *Characteristics of the purchasing market*. The approach towards suppliers varies depending on the organization's freedom of choice in terms of purchasing. In a monopolist or oligopolist market, negotiations with suppliers will be far more complex and difficult than in markets characterized by free competition. The management of the company will therefore be more interested in the former.

- *Degree of risk related to the purchase*. As the risk related to the purchase decision is higher, more disciplines will be involved in the process. The case study at the beginning of this chapter illustrates this situation. The risk attached to the purchase decision decreases and the lead time of the process diminishes as the organization has more experience with the purchase of a particular product or a particular supplier.

- *Role of the purchasing department in the organization*. The tasks, responsibilities and competence of the purchasing department vary between organizations. Purchasing departments in large companies usually operate more professionally than those in smaller ones, and very small companies usually dispense with having a specialist explicitly in charge of the purchasing task. The internal structure of the organization generally governs the way in which the purchasing decisions are made.

- *Degree to which the purchase product affects existing routines in the organization*. The decision making will be more complex, take more time and require the involvement of more disciplines as the products that are to be purchased require adjustments in the internal organization or necessitate education and training. This situation occurs, for example, when implementing new computer and new manufacturing technology.

Lehman and O'Shaughnessy (1974) provide an interesting elaboration of the second last aspect. These authors distinguish four categories of products, based on the potential post-purchase problems: (1) routine products; (2) products that require instruction; (3) products whose adequate technical functioning in the organization is uncertain; (4) products that can result in problems in the internal organization. As more adaptation within the organization is required, more disciplines will be involved in the buying decision, and the decision-making process will be more complex.

According to Fisher (1970) the purchasing decision-making process is primarily determined by two aspects, **product complexity** and **commercial uncertainty**. If these two aspects are combined, statements can be made about what disciplines will be involved in the decision-making process (see Figure 2.5).

Variables that affect the buying decision

Here the ideas developed by Webster and Wind (1972) are adopted. These authors distinguish between 'task' variables and 'non-task' variables. They define task variables as those variables that are related to the tasks, responsibilities and

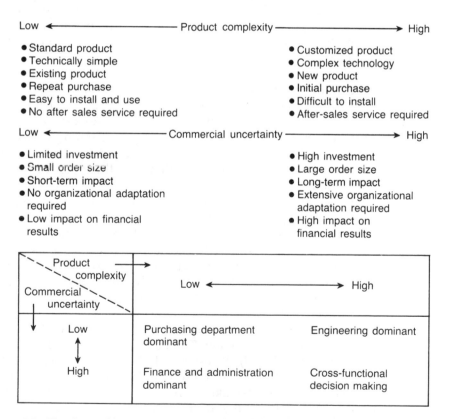

Figure 2.5 Typology of buying situations. (Adapted from Fisher, 1970.)

competences assigned by the organization to the person involved in the purchase decision. The engineer's main focus will be on the design, construction and quality aspects of the purchase product. A materials planner will focus mainly on logistic aspects, such as minimum order quantities, packing requirements, delivery times, etc. Every specialist will want a say in the discussion from his/her own perspective and interests.

The non-task variables are related to the professional's personality. People differ in terms of personality, for example the degree to which the person involved either accepts or avoids risks, his/her ambitions, the degree to which he/she avoids or confronts personal conflicts with suppliers, etc.

According to Webster and Wind (1972), task and non-task variables can be identified not only on the level of the individual, but also on a departmental level, at the level of the organization, and the level of the company and its environment. For example, the group culture in a purchasing department may focus on strengthening its own position within the organization, which may lead to boundary problems with other disciplines and suboptimal decisions. Another example: when the culture in an organization is highly informal, this will prevent as successful introduction of formal purchasing procedures. As an illustration of how the relationships between a company and its environment may affect relationships with suppliers, the organization's implicit objective might be to avoid introducing environmentally sensitive products to the market. As a result this company may impose requirements on its suppliers to formally comply with environmental legislation. Figure 2.6. depicts Webster and Wind's model.

This description clearly shows that the authors attach a great significance to the influence of psychological, social, organizational and environmental factors on the buying process. They place purchasing decision processes in a larger context, suggesting that purchasing processes can only be understood if the researcher takes these factors into consideration. This perspective is also shared by Sheth (1973) and provides an understanding of the large differences which exist between organizations in the field of organizational buying behaviour.

Based upon observations from a number of purchasing practices the author feels that the importance of social, psychological and emotional factors on purchasing decision making can hardly be overstated. There have been many examples where rational purchasing decision making was blurred and obstructed by the fact that deeply felt emotions and personal preferences were insufficiently recognized. Remarkably, these aspects of purchasing decision making have gained only little interest from researchers up to now.

Collectively, the relevant literature makes it clear that organizational purchasing processes are very complex, always involving more than one person, i.e. group decision making. The literature refers to this group as the 'decision-making unit' (DMU). Webster and Wind (1972) speak of the 'buying center', which they define as 'all those individuals and groups who participate in the purchasing decision-making process, who share some common goals and the risks arising from the decisions'. Within the DMU various roles can be distinguished.

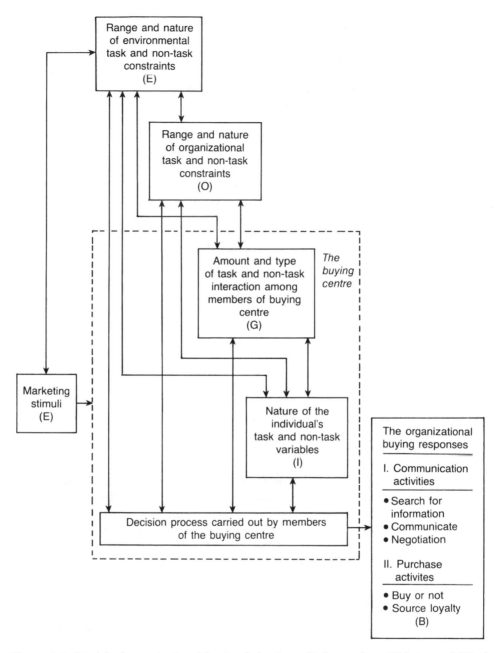

Figure 2.6 Model of organizational buying behaviour. (Redrawn from Webster and Wind, 1972, p. 30.)

- *Users.* These are the people who will work with the product, either on an individual basis or in a group context. It is obvious that the user has an important say when it concerns the specification and selection of the product.

- *Influencers*. The influencers are able to affect the outcome of the purchasing process by means of solicited or unsolicited advice. In the construction business, for example, architects have an important say in the choice of materials. Software specialists can exert influence on the selection of the hardware supplier (and vice versa).
- *Buyers*. Buyers are not necessarily the same individuals as the users. In large organizations, it is often the buyer who negotiates with the supplier about the terms and conditions of the contract and who places the order.
- *Decision makers*. These are the professionals who actually determine the selection of the supplier. Sometimes the decision maker is a designer who writes his specifications 'towards' a specific supplier because of positive experiences with this supplier's products in the past. In other cases the decision maker is the person who controls the budget.
- *Gatekeepers*. Gatekeepers are the people who control the flow of information from the supplier towards the other members of the DMU (and vice versa). In some cases the gatekeeper may be the technical director's secretary who screens contacts with (particular) suppliers. In other cases the buyer is the gatekeeper, when he has the power to decide whether or not to circulate specific supplier documentation within the organization.

Table 2.4 relates these roles to the various phases of the purchasing process. It can be seen that the importance of individual roles can differ, depending on which phase the purchasing process is in.

Buying behaviour considered as an interactive process

One salient feature of the models that have been discussed so far, is that they are typically based on consumer research. In line with the consumer marketing models, these models attempt to describe organizational buying behaviour as occurring primarily within the boundaries of the organization itself. Influences which may be exerted from stakeholders outside the organization are not reflected in these models. A major drawback of these models is that they ignore the fact that industrial buying behaviour actually should be studied as an interactive process in which two (or even more) organizations participate

Table 2.4 Decision stages and roles in the decision-making unit. (Webster and Wind, 1972, p. 80)

	User	Influencer	Buyer	Decider	Gatekeeper
Identification of need	x	x			
Establishing specifications and scheduling the purchase	x	x	x	x	
Identifying buying alternatives	x	x	x		x
Evaluating alternative buying actions	x	x	x		
Selecting the suppliers	x	x	x	x	

simultaneously. Although these early models on organizational buying behaviour provide a systematic account of all the variables that may play a role in the purchase decision, it is unlikely that the effect of customer behaviour on the industrial market will be totally independent from the supplier. Industrial markets have a far higher degree of mutual interdependency, and it is therefore essential that buying behaviour is analysed as an interactive process. This proposition is supported by literature in the field of industrial buying behaviour, e.g. Hakansson and others (1977, 1979, 1982) and Ford (1980).

The approach of Hakansson, Johansson and Wootz

These authors describe the interaction process between buyers and sellers in terms of the following physical characteristics:

- the number of times the parties make contact;
- the properties of the object of exchange: the product;
- the degree in which the process is formalized (written record, rules and regulations);
- characteristics of the parties involved.

Based on these elements, the transaction process in terms of the **physical exchange** can be described.

The interaction process can, however, also be studied from a '**social exchange**' perspective: in what way does the process take place, how do organizations achieve a particular interaction, under what conditions can this social process evolve? In terms of time, the interaction process will proceed faster as the parties get to know each other better and develop more trust in their mutual relationship.

A third aspect of this model is the mutual **adaptation** of the parties involved. During the interaction, the understanding of the mutual positions grows and the parties get closer. This is expressed in, among other things, the adjustment of the supplier's commercial and manufacturing organization to the client organization. It is of major importance for any organization to maximize the chances of a successful interaction process. Seen from the other side, the supplier will try to increase its chances for a successful interaction process by limiting its activities as much as possible to those transactions where the fit between the supplier's marketing policy and production system on the one hand and the customer's requirements on the other hand, is optimal. The supplier can furthermore attempt to change the customer's preferences and perceptions, by influencing three different types of uncertainties:

- *Uncertainty with regard to the definition of the requirements ('requirements uncertainty')*. The supplier responds to the question: 'Are we buying the right product for our problem/our needs?'
- *Uncertainty with regard to the outcome of the transaction ('transaction uncertainty')*. The question anticipated here is: 'Will the supplier actually perform in accordance with the agreement (i.e. regarding delivery times and quality)?'

> • *Uncertainty with regard to the right choice of supplier ('market uncertainty').* This type of insecurity is reflected in the question: 'Are we selecting the right supplier from the group of potential suppliers?'

These three types of uncertainty will ultimately determine the characteristics of the buyer–seller relationship and how it will develop over time.

Buying situations can now be characterized with the aid of these three types of uncertainty. Figure 2.7 provides an illustration.

The supplier is therefore well-advised to limit himself as much as possible to interactions in which the fit between his and the customer's organizations is optimal. As will be clear from this approach, the supplier can influence the intensity of the interaction by reducing, maintaining or increasing the uncertainty about requirements, transaction uncertainty and market uncertainty.

The approach of Ford

Ford (1980) emphasizes that the crucial element of industrial marketing is viewing the market as a network of relationships between organizations. Marketing policy should not employ a strategy of broad market segmentation only, it should strive to maintain and expand a particular portfolio of concrete relationships with organizations. This underlines the long-lasting nature of the relations between supplier and customer on industrial markets. This view

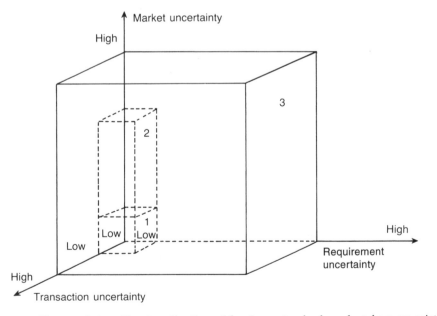

Figure 2.7 Characteristics of buying situations: 1 buying a standard product from an existing supplier; 2 buying a standard commodity from a new supplier; 3 buying a reactor for a new nuclear power plant. (According to Hakansson, Johansson and Wootz, 1797.)

implies that the mutual dependency between the two parties increases as the permanence of the relationship increases. These lasting relationships also form a barrier against competitors of the supplier getting into contact with the customer. One will have to 'break into' the existing relationships. Ford describes the development of relationships between organizations as a process in three stages. It starts with the first contact between the organizations, develops into an ever closer relationship, and gradually becomes more and more institutionalized (Chapter 8 of this book describes how companies may be able to foster partnership-relationships with their suppliers).

Management of the portfolio of relationships is not only a matter of operational importance (short term), it is primarily a strategic policy issue (long term). Based on this reasoning Ford suggests that relationship managers be appointed, who co-ordinate all aspects per relationship in time. (Ford proved to have a good foresight: account management in business-to-business marketing has since then been widely adopted.) This applies of course to the most important relations or groups of relations. This account manager is more than an industrial sales representative, since apart from direct sales he is responsible for developing the relationships with his key accounts in the long term.

Ford's ideas are interesting and although initially intended for business-to-business marketing and sales organizations, his ideas are also very valuable for purchasing and supply management.

The network approach

The network approach goes beyond the interaction approach. Supporters of this approach (for example Hakansson (1982) and Wijnstra (1998)) are convinced that the dyadic relationship between supplier and manufacturer is not only influenced by the characteristics of the product and the involved organizations, but also by the relationship between these organizations and other organizations which are part of the supplier network (see Memo 2.2). Effective purchasing and effective management of supplier relationships requires a thorough understanding of the cost structures and the balance of power in the entire buyer–supplier network. The value of this approach is confirmed by the experiences of some leading manufacturers such as Honda and Chrysler in the United States. These automotive manufacturers have focused their supplier strategies upon developing intensive relationships with relatively few selected suppliers of parts and subassemblies. Business is done based on detailed cost breakdowns, showing the high level of knowledge of the producer concerning the supplier's cost position. Components are divided into the individual sub-parts. The cost-price of these individual parts is analysed in detail in terms of direct and indirect costs of labour, overhead, depreciation and materials. Also the operational costs as incurred by the manufacturer are analysed relative to incoming inspection, materials handling, storage, etc. Based upon this information both buyer and seller develop a common understanding of the cost drivers and the opportunities for cost reduction and improving business processes. As a rule ideas are developed on how to take advantage of these

MEMO 2.2: Case example of how buyer–seller networks interact

In recent years many industries in Europe, like the Japanese industries, have developed a tiered supplier structure. Often, this structure resembles a pyramid. The original equipment manufacturers (OEMs) (producers of end-products, such as truck manufacturers, manufacturers of PCs) are at the top of this pyramid. They often buy their products (mostly subassemblies) from first-tier suppliers (main suppliers). The main suppliers purchase their subassemblies and components from second-tier suppliers (jobbers). Jobbers are companies which specialize in electro-mechanical activities (such as drilling, cutting, milling, grinding, etc.) on base materials (steel, steelplate, plastics). The base materials, however, are supplied by big international (process) manufacturers like DuPont, Dow Chemical Hoechst and Akzo Nobel. Examples of other manufacturers of base materials are steelmills and manufacturers of basic foodstuffs.

Usually these process-manufacturers target their marketing and sales strategies towards two different market segments. First, through their account managers and technical specialists they focus on getting a favoured status in the relationship with the OEMs. For it is important to have their brands and/or materials described in the specifications of new products. Therefore, sales efforts are primarily targeted at the OEM's research and development departments and engineering people. Once the OEM has decided to integrate the base supplier's materials in its components (for example to use DSM-plastics for a new bumper), the supplier of this component is limited to this sole source of supply.

Of course, these suppliers often do not have any other choice but to accept the terms of conditions of these base materials suppliers.

Nowadays some leading-edge OEMs, through value chain analysis, have identified this problem and now try to integrate the first-tier suppliers into their development and operations processes. Often this leads to a situation where the OEM actually will support its first-tier suppliers in their negotiations with their second-tier suppliers and base materials suppliers. Contracts for base materials may be negotiated by the much more powerful OEM; the first-tier supplier, however, is entitled to use this contract to call off deliveries.

opportunities leading to detailed improvement plans to be implemented on both sides.

As both organizations go through this process over time, relationships will become more intensive and co-operative and supply chain integration will be the result.

In practice, many organizations take the developments within the market of the supplier into account when defining their own purchasing policy. For example, a take-over of a supplier by a direct competitor can result in the end of the relationship with this supplier. This happened when a major supplier of bottles to the Heineken organization was taken over in the early nineties by Saint Gobain. Saint Gobain owns Kronenbourg, which is one of the main competitors of Heineken in France. When Saint Gobain became the owner of this bottle supplier, Heineken decided to look for another supplier. This example illustrates that changes in the supplier network actually influence individual relationships between buyers and sellers. The network approach, therefore, provides a useful and valuable concept to study the dynamics in relationships between manufacturers and their suppliers.

The network perspective is complementary to the other models and approaches which have been described in this chapter. What model to be used in a specific situation will depend, of course, on the object of study.

Summary

This chapter describes how organizational buying behaviour can be studied and analysed. The conclusion is that the buying behaviour of organizations differs significantly from consumer buying behaviour. Industrial companies, governmental organizations and institutions buy their goods and services to feed, support and maintain their primary and supportive processes, while consumers purchase products to immediately satisfy their needs. The value of the models which have been developed for explaining consumer buying behaviour is therefore, in the author's opinion, limited when studying industrial buying processes.

Although organizational purchasing processes may vary to a great extent, clear stages are still recognized. In this chapter the purchasing process model has been elaborated. The essence of this outlook is that effective purchasing decision making requires a cross-functional approach. The key issue is to direct and guide the efforts of the various organizational parties involved in such a way, that an optimal result is achieved for the organization. The professional buyer can make a major contribution here. Not all phases of the purchasing process are passed through in all cases. Three types of buying situations can, roughly, be distinguished, i.e. the new-task situation, the modified rebuy and the straight rebuy. The composition of the decision-making unit (DMU) will be different for each of these situations.

In this chapter the position of the purchasing department was discussed. In general, the purchasing department's involvement is highest when it concerns the purchase of indirect goods or consumable items. Its role is more limited when it concerns investment goods. It has furthermore been demonstrated that purchasing's involvement is highest during the operational stages of the purchasing process; purchasing's involvement is relatively low in the early stages of product development (when specifications are determined and materials selected). Theory runs ahead of practice here.

Finally, this chapter discussed several theoretical models in the field of industrial buying behaviour. A distinction can be made between the models that view the purchasing process exclusively from an organizational perspective, and the models that regard the buying process as an interaction between two or more parties. Both types of models have their value: they explain why it is often so difficult for an outsider to fathom organizational purchasing processes and why they are often so hard to organize.

Assignments

2.1   In paragraph two of this chapter it is stated that industrial markets, unlike consumer markets, are often inelastic. Do you agree with this statement? Please explain why and provide some examples.

2.2   As the strategic importance of a product increases, management's involvement in the purchase decision will also grow. Which criteria determine the strategic importance of a particular good that is to be purchased for the organization? Give examples of products that, in your opinion, can be earmarked as strategic (a) for an automobile manufacturer and (b) for an academic hospital.

2.3a   The management of a medium-sized metal working company is considering buying a CNC-milling machine. This is a completely new type of machine for the company in question. Describe:
       (a) the purchasing process phases that this company will go through;
       (b) which disciplines will probably be involved in each phase of the buying process.

2.3b   One production plant, where numerical milling machines have been in use for a number of years, is considering the purchase of an additional one. Describe how the purchasing process in this production company differs from the purchasing process described above.

2.4   What are the differences between buying standard-grade raw materials and buying customized electrical components? Discuss the differences in market structure, required expertise, product characteristics, etc. in your analysis, using Fisher's typology as a framework.

2.5   According to the interaction approach of Johansson, Hakansson and Wootz, the industrial seller can influence the course of the purchasing process by anticipating three kinds of uncertainty. First, describe these three types of uncertainty. Then indicate what arguments a seller of copying equipment can use to either (a) enlarge or (b) reduce each of these uncertainties in his relationship with a potential customer.

THE PURCHASING PROCESS: THE BUYER'S ROLE

3

Learning objectives

After studying this chapter you should understand the following:

- The most important elements of a purchase order specification.
- The various methods of contracting out, their advantages and disadvantages.
- The most important activities that precede the supplier selection decision.
- The main elements of a purchase contract.
- The way in which order follow-up and expediting can take place.

CASE STUDY
Purchase of new carriages by a national railway company

In 1992 in one European country the following story was published in various newspapers. It revealed the problems related to the purchase of new carriages by the national railway company which suffered a major financial setback because the new two-deck carriages turned out to be 30 cm wider than the railway could accommodate. The new carriages could not pass each other in at least 16 places in the country and on these (mainly curved) sections the distance between the tracks needed to be widened by at least 16 cm. The railway company was also compelled to replace or shift overhead wires, signals, signs, platform covering and tiling in many additional places throughout the country. The unforeseen costs involved were estimated to be at least $57 million.

These problems were caused by the design of the new trains which had five seats across the width of the carriages instead of the usual four. More passengers on a train means greater revenue; however, due to the new design the carriages had become 30 cm wider.

Introduction

This case study demonstrates that a lot can go wrong in the process of buying capital equipment. Several aspects in connection with the use of the carriages were obviously overlooked and, as a result, expensive adjustments in the railway infrastructure had to be made. This type of problem is not uncommon in the purchase of capital goods because the decision-making process usually focuses on the purchase of the equipment itself. Aspects such as training and education, after-sales service, aspects of maintenance and the supply of spare parts often receive attention only after the machine has been put into operation. It then becomes clear that the supplier, who was so keen to deliver the machinery, is not very service oriented and that spare parts are extremely costly.

This chapter further elaborates the purchasing process model presented in Chapter 2; each of the stages distinguished there will be addressed in detail. The description will be based on the purchasing procedure for capital equipment, starting with the question of how to achieve a sound purchase specification, to be followed by a description of the main activities preceding the supplier selection. The purchasing contract is then discussed, including several special terms and conditions. Finally, several expediting methods are described.

The different stages will be illustrated by a project concerning the purchase of body carriers by an automotive manufacturer, used to transport car bodies inside the plant.

First step in the buying process: determining on purchase order specifications

During this initial stage of the purchasing process, the purchasing requirements are determined and the company is also faced with the 'make-or-buy' question. It has to determine which products or activities will be produced/performed by the company itself, and which products or activities will be contracted out. In what follows only the contracting-out issue will be discussed. This process starts by drawing up the specifications of those items that will be purchased, which may have a different level of detail. In general it is possible to differentiate between:

- A **functional specification** – this describes the functionality which the product must have for the user (in this chapter, the term 'user' is employed in a broader sense. It can refer to the person who actually uses the product that is to be bought, but it can also refer to the person who has to make the financial decision about the purchase, who allocates the budget). An example. When outsourcing greenkeeping a buyer may state in its contract with the gardener that he is expected to mow a lawn once every week, using personnel with a specific educational background and using a Qualcast low-noise, high-performance mower. However, he also may state in his contract that the gardener will keep the grass at a maximum of one inch, whilst keeping noise below a certain number of decibels during execution. The difference will be clear: in the first situation the gardener will probably mow the lawn every week (also during wintertime), since that is what has been agreed with the customer. In the second situation the gardener will only mow the grass when needed. (This example may seem trivial to the reader; however, it is based on a real situation!)

The advantages of working with functional specifications will be clear:
- potential suppliers are given the best possible opportunity to contribute their expertise;
- new technologies can be used, technologies that the buyer is not familiar with;
- it creates one standard, against which all concepts can be evaluated.
- A **detailed technical specification** – this describes the technical properties and characteristics of the product as well as the activities to be performed by the supplier. Usually these technical specifications are laid down in detailed technical drawings and activity schedules which can be used to monitor the supplier's activities in detail. This way of working by the contractor can easily lead to overspecification, where the user imposes requirements on both product and supplier which easily lead to higher cost but no better functionality.

Both functional and technical specification are part of a wider concept, which is referred to as the **purchase order specification**. This document (usually a set of documents) comprises the following:

- **quality specifications**, describing how the product should be delivered (with or without a quality certificate) and what technical norms and standards the product should meet;
- the **logistics specifications,** indicating the quantities needed and the delivery time to be respected;
- a **maintenance specification**, describing how the product will be maintained and serviced by the supplier (and whether or not spare parts need to be supplied in the future);
- **legal and environmental requirements,** determining that both product and production process should be in compliance with health, safety and environmental legislation;
- a **target budget**, which indicates within what financial constraints the solution to be provided by the prospective supplier should be found.

In the purchase of construction work and civil projects, the purchase order specifications are usually recorded in a **scope-of-work** description.

The user or budget holder is responsible for specifying the purchasing order requirements and the buyer's task is to ensure that the specification is drawn up in objective, supplier-neutral terms. Several manufacturing companies (including Xerox) have regulated this responsibility in so-called **sign-off procedures**. Before a specification is released to a supplier, it must have the formal approval of purchasing and/or the (potential) supplier(s). The purpose of this procedure is to prevent misunderstandings in the consecutive stages of the purchasing process. In this way the costs of so-called 'problem-solving changes' are reduced. Experience has shown that this type of preparation will result in a considerable reduction of the project's total engineering lead time.

Technical changes that occur during the project must be dealt with in accordance with the **change order procedures**. The buyer's job is to ensure that the supplier's work is conducted according to the last specifications sent to him.

Suppliers should ideally confirm each approved change, preferably in writing – sound **configuration management** can prevent many problems!

In summary, the added value of the buyer during the specification stage is:

- ensuring unambiguous functional, technical, logistics and maintenance specifications;
- preventing the use of supplier or product brand specifications – to keep the possibility of alternative sources of supply open;
- recording clear procedures regarding approval of specification changes;
- ensuring a clear sample inspection procedure;
- ensuring clear descriptions of the methods to be used by both buyer and supplier for testing of the quality of the product;
- (if possible) ensuring a general cost breakdown and/or calculation to help assessment of quotations at a later stage.

Memo 3.1 illustrates this first stage of the purchasing process, for the purchase of car-body carriers by a large automotive manufacturer.

Second step in the buying process: supplier selection

After the purchasing requirements have been defined and described in the specifications, the buyer can start his market exploration. In practice these steps are interwoven. When drawing up the technical specifications, the practical feasibility and the costs are estimated. The selection of basic technologies – through which the product design will have to be realized – is frequently made

---

MEMO 3.1: Deciding on the specification of the body carriers

The department of 'Advanced Engineering' has been requested by the technical director of the assembly plant to investigate the way in which car bodies can be transported more efficiently through the plant. For this project an Advanced Engineering team is created, consisting of experts from both the Engineering and the Assembly organization. Some preliminary investigations led to the conclusion that transportation basically can take place in three fundamentally different ways: through carriers, conveyors or chains. The carrier concept is chosen for reasons of flexibility. The assignment is then passed on to the Technical Operations department. Headed by a project engineer, a project team is formed, consisting of representatives from various technical disciplines (manufacturing engineering, process-control and automation and human engineering) and purchasing. Disciplines such as cost engineering and finance and controlling are involved on an *ad hoc* basis. The project group first focuses on defining the scope of the project – what is it we want? These discussions result in a technical specification, which does not express any preference for a particular supplier. The major guiding principles are that the project should, whenever possible, use 'proven technologies' and suppliers with 'proven abilities', since the car-manufacturer has no wish to serve as a 'guinea pig' for suppliers in this type of project. It is decided to choose potential suppliers, who may be contacted for the next step.

with the names of a few suppliers in mind. In practice, the step of 'selection' contains a number of separate steps:

- determining on the method of subcontracting;
- preliminary qualification of suppliers and drawing up the 'bidders list';
- preparation of the request for quotation and analysis of the bids received;
- selection of the supplier.

The first issue to be dealt with in supplier selection is whether to opt for turnkey or partial subcontracting.[1] In the case of **turnkey subcontracting** the responsibility for the execution of the entire assignment (often including design activities) is placed with the supplier. In the case of **partial subcontracting** the assignment is divided into parts which are contracted out separately, often to various suppliers. Co-ordination rests with the principal. Partial subcontracting usually results in savings, but obviously has some important drawbacks. Table 3.1 lists the advantages and disadvantages of both types of subcontracting.

A major point against partial subcontracting is that the principal must be sure that the separate contracts are attuned to one another. In this case, full responsibility for the continuity of the whole of the project activities rests with the principal. If he fails, it is clear that the expected cost advantage will not materialize, and considerable additional costs will result.

A second decision to be made at this stage is whether the work will be awarded on a **fixed-price, lump-sum** or a **cost-reimbursable** basis.

When work is executed based on a fixed-price contract, the principal orders the supplier to perform the required activities at a fixed price, and to have the work completed by a predetermined date. The advantages of this method are:

Table 3.1 Advantages and disadvantages of turnkey and partial subcontracting

	Advantages	*Disadvantages*
Turnkey subcontracting	Limited interference by principal during project execution	No insight in cost/price structure of project
	No experience in similar projects required from principal	Limited influence only on materials used (quality and quantities)
	Limited efforts from principal required	
Partial subcontracting	Better insight in cost/price structure of project by principal	In-depth knowledge and experience from principal required
	Better grip on suppliers and materials used	Much time and effort required for project co-ordination and monitoring
	Lower overall project costs in general	Risk that communications problems may delay project activities

[1] The term subcontracting is used here. Alternative terms used in literature for the same activity are 'outsourcing' and 'contracting out'.

- The principal knows exactly where he stands financially.
- After completion of the work there is no need for **settlements** because all risks are carried by the supplier.
- A firm completion date.

As the price is fixed, it is in the supplier's interest to execute the work as efficiently as possible. The fixed price is an incentive to complete the work, or deliver the goods, as quickly as possible within the agreed term. Disadvantages of this method are:

- It is difficult to get insight into the supplier's cost breakdown if the principal lacks expertise; this problem can be avoided by requesting quotations from more than one supplier.
- Preparation requires time – the question is whether there is enough time to prepare a detailed specification and have a formal bidding procedure.
- One does not know in advance which supplier will turn out to be the best.

In the case of a cost-reimbursable contract the nature and scope of the activities to be performed are not established in advance. The principal orders the supplier to perform the required activities at a predetermined hourly rate, sometimes in combination with a prearranged percentage to cover the overhead costs. Settlement follows after completion of the activities based on the supplier's day reports (stating the man hours worked) and (if relevant) the materials which have been consumed. The advantages of this method are:

- The principal obtains an exact picture of the cost structure of the work.
- The principal is free in his choice of suppliers; it is known in advance what supplier he will be dealing with.

Naturally, there are also some disadvantages:

- There is no predetermined fixed price, so the buyer is not quite sure about the financial consequences.
- There is no incentive to work faster, as the supplier is reimbursed for every hour he works; every setback is charged to the principal.
- There is no certainty about completion date.

An additional disadvantage of this method is that the principal is not forced to specify exactly what it is he wants. Frequently this specification is left to the supplier for the sake of convenience. Due to the uncertainty of the final cost, many buyers avoid working with cost-reimbursable contracts. Some only use them in the case of specific, minor maintenance/repair activities, for which the financial risks are relatively clear. Cost-reimbursable contracts are not without problems and several points have to be discussed with the supplier in advance (see Figure 3.1). The decision in favour of either fixed-price or cost-reimbursable contracts is determined by a number of factors, such as:

- *Comprehensiveness of the specification.* The availability of extensive specifications is a crucial prerequisite of lump-sum contracting. Absence of specifications makes a fair comparison of the various quotations impossible.

- Wages and salaries
- Percentage for general expense
- Profit percentage/mark-up
- Reporting procedures for hours worked and consumption of materials
- Costs of tooling and special equipment
- Costs related to co-ordinating the work of third parties
- Agreement on cost estimates for extra work
- Agreement on what to be supplied by principal
- Agreement on what facilities (telephone, electricity, housing) to be provided by principal/contractor
- Key personnel to be assigned on the job by contractor
- Arrangement of required licenses and permits from local authorities
- Selection of sub-suppliers of contractors

Figure 3.1   Aspects to be considered when contracting on a cost-reimbursable basis.

- *Available time.* Does the principal have enough time for a tender procedure and price negotiations or should the work be started immediately?
- *Technical expertise.* If the work requires specialized knowledge and skills, a cost-reimbursable contract is often preferred.
- *Knowledge of the industry.* The degree to which the principal knows the methods and price arrangements operating in that particular industry.

In summary, the first step in the stage of supplier selection consists of determining whether to opt for partial or turnkey contracting out. Second, it should be decided whether execution will take place by means of fixed-price or a cost-reimbursable agreement.

A third type of contract which is often used in the subcontracting world and which should be mentioned here is the **unit-rate contract**. These contracts determine the cost per activity for standardized and routine work. Petrochemical companies, for example, annually negotiate unit-rates for simple installation and maintenance activities which are subcontracted to suppliers (for instance unit-rate per metre of piping that is installed, or unit rate per square metre of groundfloor, which is cleaned). Unit-rate contracts are used for activities which are standardized but which are difficult to estimate in terms of volume and time.

The selected contracting method determines to a great extent how the next steps of the buying process will evolve. For that reason, these decisions must be made together with the user and/or budget holder. However, the buyer presents the different contracting methods which he thinks are possible and outlines the considerations that may influence the decision.

The selection of a supplier is one of the most important steps in the purchasing process and several activities precede this decision.

- Summarizing the **prequalification requirements**, based on the purchase order specification, that the suppliers who are going to be approached for a quotation will have to meet.
- Assembling the initial bidders list (so-called **bidders' long list**) that indicates which suppliers may probably do the job. Next, these suppliers are contacted to provide references and information about their qualifications. At this stage it may be necessary to conduct a supplier visit or audit in order to get a precise idea on their capabilities. Large companies generally work with 'approved vendors lists' in order to select the suppliers for the long list.

  Sometimes there is not a sufficient number of approved suppliers available. Then, new suppliers need to be found. For important assignments these are first scrutinized and screened before any bids will be solicited from them.

It is common practice to identify three to five prospective suppliers, from whom quotations will be solicited. These suppliers make up the **bidders' short list**. If circumstances give cause to revise the invitation to bid, then all of the competing suppliers should be given the opportunity to respond to this revision.

After receipt of the quotations, the purchasing department will make a preliminary technical and commercial evaluation, during which all relevant aspects are acknowledged. The technical, logistic, quality, financial and legal aspects need to be weighed. Ranking schemes may be used with a different degree of sophistication in order to facilitate the process of evaluating the supplier bids. These schemes are used jointly between users and buyers involved. Usually this step ends with a supplier selection proposal, which consists of (a) a decision to select a certain supplier, (b) the underlying ranking schemes and (c) the underlying quotations which have been considered.

The next step is to carry out a risk analysis for critical suppliers and purchase parts. During this step potential risks related to a particular choice of supplier are investigated. An example is presented in Memo 3.2.

Ultimately one supplier will be selected with whom the delivery of the product (or service) will have to be negotiated. (In some cases, however, the assignment may be given to two or more suppliers (when dual or multiple sourcing is the preferred sourcing strategy).) The suppliers who are not selected are informed about the reasons for rejecting their proposals.

Summarizing this section, the added value of the buyer's role in the selection phase is in:

- Determining (or having others determine) the most adequate way of subcontracting (turnkey versus partial subcontracting and deciding on fixed-cost , cost-reimbursable or unit rate contract).
- Identifying reliable supplier–partners by means of an adequate procedure of prequalification; preliminary selection of the most suitable suppliers by means of a tender and ranking procedure.
- Drawing up the request for quotation in such a way that comparison of the quotations, which are received at a later stage, is possible.

> ## MEMO 3.2: Risk analysis by the Ministry of Defence
>
> If a supplier does not fulfil his obligations in the realization of complex and extensive projects, this can lead to considerable damages or loss for a military organization. To limit the risk of problems as much as possible, the Ministries of Defence of several European countries sometimes carry out an analysis of the risks related to doing business with suppliers for strategic projects. In general three categories of risks are distinguished.
>
> 1 **Technical risk** regarding the suitability/professionalism of the management, the means of production, the skills, tools and testing equipment of the company in question, for the manufacture of the required goods and services, which must meet the agreed requirements and must be delivered within the agreed term.
> 2 **Quality risk** with regard to the quality management of the company in general and the quality control system of the project in question in particular.
> 3 **Financial risk** related to the degree in which the company is considered to function soundly and effectively for the duration of the project. Of importance in this respect are: financial condition, investment elasticity and a solid financial condition in the near future.
>
> In large and technologically complex projects the risks can be so large that additional measures and arrangements are required. These measures should consist of at least periodical preventive audits aimed at assessing the technical capacity and quality control (the so-called 'pre-award survey'), to be conducted by the military; and the financial status of the company in question, to be conducted by the accounting department. This latter analysis concerns the actual and the anticipated results of the company activities (such as turnover and company results) and ratio analysis of several financial parameters (such as liquidity and solvency).

- Handling requests for information from suppliers in a similar manner; channelling the information between project team and supplier.
- Conducting a balanced analysis of quotations in close co-operation with the user, making a clear distinction between the technical evaluation and the commercial evaluation.

Memo 3.3 illustrates the course of this phase in the case example.

The objective of this stage of the buying process is to arrive at a balanced selection of the most suitable supplier–partner based upon total cost of ownership. Statements that would result in premature obligations towards particular suppliers must be avoided at this stage.

Third step in the buying process: the purchasing contract

After the supplier has been selected, a contract will have to be drawn up. Depending on the industry, the contract may refer to specific additional terms and conditions.

The technical contents of the purchase agreement naturally depend on the product or project that is to be purchased. Specific commercial and legal terms and conditions will vary per contract, differences being caused by purchasing policy, company culture, market situation, product characteristics, etc. This limits the use of standard purchase contracts. The next section proceeds to discuss several important aspects of the purchase agreement.

Prices and terms of delivery

In general the buyer should insist on a **fixed price**, arrived at through competitive bidding or negotiation, which is acceptable to both principal and supplier. Financial obligations should be defined unequivocally. Ideally the supplier should be willing to accept all risks, in so far as these are not excluded contractually. A fixed price is definitely preferred from the perspective of cost control or budget management.

In practice, different price arrangements are used in purchase agreements.

- *Fixed price plus incentive fee.* This type of contract is designed to motivate suppliers by means of rewards to execute the work above the agreed standard. The incentives do not have to relate to immediately visible cost reductions, which are realized by the supplier. They can also relate to earlier delivery, a better delivery reliability and/or a better quality performance than agreed.
- *Cost-plus contract.* This type of contract may have different forms: cost-plus with a percentage fee, cost-reimbursable plus a fixed fee, and cost-plus with a guaranteed maximum. In practice this type of contract often turns out to be more expensive for the buyer than other types of contracts. Cost-plus contracts are used in situations where the work cannot be specified adequately, or when a fixed price constitutes too big a risk for both the supplier and the buyer.
- *Cost-reimbursable contracts.* This type of contract is usually based on fixed hourly rates for labour and equipment. However, without a bonus or penalty clause these contracts provide little incentive to minimize labour hours or costs. The buyer should therefore always make sure that
  - the supplier keeps a sound cost administration, so that inspection is possible;
  - a maximum price is recorded in the contract;
  - this amount may only be exceeded after written agreement has been obtained from the buyer;
  - the costs which are to be reimbursed are made payable to the supplier on a well-specified invoice.
- *Agreement with price-adjustment* (**escalation clauses**). This type of contract is used mainly for agreements with a long-term delivery, or when very specific, market-sensitive materials are processed. The price is linked to a price adjustment formula, which is based on external factors such as material costs or changes in labour costs.

It is recommended to record **optional prices** for future deliveries of spare parts, and, when appropriate, service rates. Finally, when buying from foreign

> ## MEMO 3.3: Preparation of supplier selection
>
> Based on the technical specifications, the project team of the car manufacturer submitted an 'internal request for quotation' to the section of Investment Buying of the Purchasing Department. This request included a pre-selection of suppliers, the desired delivery time and an estimate of the required budget. With the aid of this information the purchasing department designed a request for quotation accompanied by purchasing conditions, etc., which was then sent to six suppliers. After a number of consultation rounds with these suppliers, the project team eventually received three quotations. These were evaluated by the team through a detailed, multi-page quotation analysis form. The three suppliers presented their proposals to the board of directors, after which one supplier finally was selected.

suppliers, currency risks need to be dealt with. Although working with currency exchange clauses is an acceptable approach, it is recommended that such clauses are excluded from the purchase agreement because the supplier can cover this type of risk fairly simply by applying financial hedging techniques.

Terms of payment

When capital goods or installations are purchased, it is common practice that payment takes place in several **terms**, partly because the supplier will have to make large investments to be able to produce the desired product. If this method of payment is used, account should be taken of the influence of the payment terms on the final price. Attention should also be paid to covering the currency risk related to paying for goods that have not yet been delivered.

In general, the preferred method of payment is based on the supplier's performance **(performance bond)**. For instance: payment of 20% of the total sum when 25% of the work is completed. The last 5 or 10% of the payment is held back until the client is absolutely sure that the equipment operates exactly as it should or in the case of a service, that the supplier's work has been up to the customer's satisfaction.

Advance payments should preferably be covered by a **bank guarantee** in which the supplier agrees to fulfil his obligations. Such a bank guarantee completely covers the prepaid sum and is valid for the period of delivery of the part that the bank guarantee relates to. If appropriate, a **concern guarantee** from the holding company (which is often less expensive) will suffice.

Subsequently, attention should be paid to drawing up an agreement providing specifically for the transfer of ownership.

Penalty clauses and warranty conditions

According to the general purchase conditions of several large companies, suppliers must guarantee with respect to the delivered goods that

- They are of good quality and completely in accordance with the agreed requirements, specifications, conditions, drawings, samples, etc. and that they are suitable for their intended purpose.
- The goods will be completely new and free of defects, that new materials of good and suitable quality will be used for the manufacture of these goods and that first-rate technical and expert personnel will be used.
- The legal and government regulations of the country where the supplier is domiciled have been met and that the goods, or the use of them, do not contain any risk regarding the health or security of persons, property and environment.

Agreements will also have to be made with the supplier about the performance of the goods to be delivered. In the case of acquisition of investment goods a **performance guarantee** can be agreed upon, for example by agreeing that a particular production unit will produce 10 tons of end product of a certain quality per day. If the agreed performance is not met, one should first discuss corrective measures. If these also turn out to be inadequate then the resulting costs are to be recovered from the supplier. This procedure must be agreed upon in the terms and conditions of the contract. **Penalty clauses** do not, therefore, provide a solution for problems occurring at the stage of execution or delivery; at most they can limit the resulting damages afterwards.

In some circumstances, a penalty clause is unacceptable. If, for example, performance is found to be more than 5% under the agreed standard, or if the legal environmental regulations are not complied with, the client must have the right to refuse the product or installation in question.

It is also important that the period during which the supplier is liable for the reliability and adequate functioning of the delivered goods in the specified circumstances, is recorded in the contract. In general a period of 12 months is included as the **warranty period** in the terms and conditions of the agreement. The agreement should also state when the warranty comes into effect; this can be the date that the goods are put into service, or it can be the delivery date.

One special aspect in the case of investment goods is the **systems responsibility**; it is common to demand from the supplier that he takes measures to maintain the delivered product during the **life-of-type**. Maintenance and spare parts must be available during this life-of-type. In this context manufacturers of trucks are required to be able to maintain their products, sometimes for a period of more than 20 years!

Other arrangements

In many companies the issues described above will be recorded in the **general purchase conditions**. Other subjects that can be addressed in these regulations include

- insurance and safety regulations;
- transfer of rights and obligations;

- contracting out to third parties;
- terms of delivery.

In general, buyers should strive for a situation in which they can prescribe the company's terms of purchase. In practice, however, a supplier will frequently accept an order only on his own terms of sale. If the supplier does not explicitly reject the terms of purchase in his order confirmation, the terms of purchase are still valid (from a legal point of view). If he does reject them, however, then there is basically no consensus and therefore no purchase agreement. In this type of situation, additional negotiations will be necessary. This tug-of-war about terms of sale and purchase is sometimes referred to as the 'battle of forms'.

Naturally, attempts have been made in international trade to standardize much-used trade terms. The Incoterms are an example. The main standard terms and conditions are discussed in Memo 3.4, whereas Memo 3.5 describes the course of the contractual stage for the carriers.

In summary, the main tasks of the buyer in the contracting stage are considered to be the following:

- Supplying the required contracting expertise in the form of modular purchase contracts and general terms of purchase, in which all aspects are taken into account.
- Determining what price and other commercial conditions will be negotiated.
- Preparing specific contractual arrangements to minimize risks and liabilities which are related to the purchase.
- Preparing and conducting the negotiations about all terms and conditions of the contract with the supplier.
- Editing the purchase agreement.

Steps four and five: ordering and expediting

After the terms and conditions of the contract have been agreed and recorded, the order can be placed. In some cases the contract in fact **is** the purchase order. In other cases, for example in case of a routine buying situation, buyers will negotiate a call-off agreement, covering the materials needed for a longer period (one year or even longer). Next, purchase orders are placed against this agreement. In those cases contracting and ordering are separate activities.

A purchase order usually is initiated (electronically) through a purchase order requisition or a materials requisition. For production and inventory items this requisition is generated through the materials requirements planning systems through the matching of the materials volume needed for production for a given period and the available (pipeline) inventories. When inventories seem to get lower than their minimum acceptable levels, the MRP-system generates a signal to the purchasing department by means of a detailed materials or purchase order requisition. Most advanced (integrated) materials planning software

MEMO 3.4: The Incoterms 1990

'Incoterms' is short for international commerce terms (see van Weele and Gelderman, 1998). These terms relate to several important standard conditions in connection with the delivery and transportation of, and risk attached to, goods. The Incoterms have been carefully defined: it has been established how each condition must be interpreted. Using the Incoterms may prevent misunderstandings between supplier and buyer.

The Incoterms were first published in 1936 and they have been adapted regularly since. The newest version, Incoterms 1990, distinguishes the following standard conditions:

EXW	Ex Works
FCA	Free Carrier
FAS	Free Alongside Ship
FOB	Free On Board
CPT	Carriage Paid To
CIP	Carriage and Insurance Paid to
CFR	Cost and Freight
CIF	Cost, Insurance, Freight
DAF	Delivered at Frontier
DES	Delivered Ex Ship
DEQ	Delivered Ex Quay
DDU	Delivered Duty Unpaid
DDP	Delivered Duty Paid

Each Incoterm arranges the distribution of the costs (transportation, insurance) and the risk (in case of loss and damage) of the physical delivery. In addition the Incoterms regulate which documents should be provided by the supplier, or that the supplier must help the buyer in this, and who is to pay the costs of these documents. Incoterms do not regulate the legal delivery, the legal transfer of title. This is arranged in the legal system that applies to the purchase agreement.

An Incoterm only applies if both parties have reached an agreement about it and the contract will then refer to the Incoterm in question. Incoterms are not part of permissive or imperative law and parties are free to agree to deviations from an Incoterm. This is risky, however, because adding a word or even a single letter to an Incoterm may lead a judge (especially a foreign judge) to a different interpretation than was intended by the buyer.

The 13 Incoterms 1990 can be organized according to:

- type of transportation;
- type of agreement.

Table 3.2 reflects the resulting classification of Incoterms. This classification, as well as their meaning will be briefly explained, but for a complete explanation see the *Guide to Incoterms*, 1990 edition, published by the International Chamber of Commerce.

The first classification is a very rough one: sea carriage versus 'other' methods of transportation; traditionally, the Incoterms have played an important role in sea carriage. The classification into

Memo 3.4: continued

Table 3.2 Incoterms 1990 classification

Transportation method	Type of contract			
	Departure	Main carriage unpaid	Main carriage paid	Arrival
Sea carriage	EXW	FOB	CIF	DES
		FAS	CFR	DEQ
Other transportation	EXW	FCA	CPT	DAF
			CIP	DDU
				DDP

types of contract determine to a high degree where the physical delivery from supplier to buyer takes place. Four types of contracts can be distinguished:

- departure;
- main carriage unpaid;
- main carriage paid;
- arrival.

The first group consists exclusively of the Incoterm EXW (Ex Works). In the case of EXW the buyer is responsible for arranging and settling everything. The supplier only makes the goods available for the buyer, who has to collect these from the factory or warehouse.

In the second group of Incoterms the buyer arranges most of the physical delivery. In the case of sea carriage, the supplier delivers the goods to the quay (FAS) or on board (FOB). Then the ship can leave at the expense and risk of the buyer. The Incoterm FCA rests on the same principle: the supplier has met his obligations as soon as the goods have been transferred to a transporter at the agreed location. In this situation also, the supplier carries the costs and responsibility up until the moment that the goods are delivered.

Characteristic of the third group is that the supplier takes responsibility for most of the transport. In the case of sea carriage the supplier will bring the goods into a harbour in the buyer's country. In the case of CIF the supplier pays the costs of loading, transportation and the transport insurance. The risk is transferred to the buyer (as it is in the case of FOB) when the goods have passed the ship's rail. Incoterm CFR is a variation on CIF in which the buyer carries the risk of transportation. It is of course wise to cover this risk by means of transport insurance. The same difference (who carries the risk?) applies to CIP and CPT. In the case of CIP the supplier carries the risk and pays for transportation to the agreed location of transfer; in the case of CPT the buyer carries the transportation risk. Within the fourth group of Incoterms, arrival, the most extreme Incoterms are DDU and DDP. DDP is the exact opposite of EXW in that the supplier brings the goods to the buyer's 'front door'. The same goes for DDU, except that the buyer pays the import duties. Less extreme is delivery to a ship (DES), to the quay (DEQ) or to the border (DAF). There are now two versions of the Incoterm DEQ: duty paid and duty unpaid. This difference is important in view of import duties. Figure 3.2 shows where the supplier is supposed to deliver under the various Incoterms.

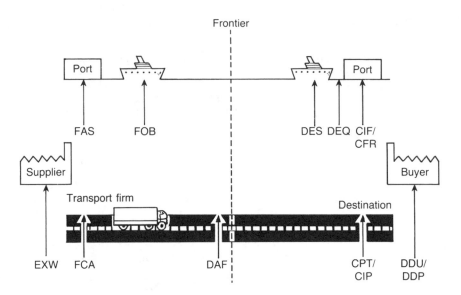

Figure 3.2   Delivery under Incoterms.

MEMO 3.5: Preparation of the purchasing agreement

The project team started negotiations with the selected supplier. Eventually these negotiations resulted in a contract acceptable to both parties. Based on the invitation to bid, the engineers in the project team evaluated the technical aspects of the contract while purchasing negotiated the commercial terms. As the company initially needed only 100 carriers, and more would definitely be required at a later stage, a price adjustment formula was included in the contract. This formula read:

$$V_1 = \frac{V_0}{100} \left(A + B_1 \times \frac{M_1}{M_{10}} + B_2 \times \frac{M_2}{M_{20}} + C \times \frac{S_1}{S_{10}} \right)$$

in which:

V_1	= Final order value
V_0	= Total order value (in a base month)
A	= Constant (0,10)
B_1	= 0.30 × the price increase of mechanical components
B_2	= 0.25 × the price increase of electronic components
C	= 0.30 × the average wage increase
M_1, M_{10}	= CBS indices (in supplier's country)
M_2, M_{20}	= CBS indices (in supplier's country)
S_1, S_{10}	= CBS indices (in supplier's country)

The value of such a formula would be that in the future no negotiations on price would be required when ordering extra car body carriers from the supplier.

packages enable the transfer of this requisition to a purchase order electronically.

When ordering from a supplier, it is very important to be specific about the information and instructions to the supplier. Generally, a purchase order will include the following entities: an order number, a concise description of the product, unit price, number of units required, expected delivery time or date, delivery address and invoicing address. All of these data need to be reflected on the delivery documents and invoice, sent by the supplier in order to facilitate (electronic) matching.

Usually the supplier is requested to send in an order for each purchase order received. Together, the purchase order, the supplier's delivery documents and invoices form the basis for the buyer's vendor rating system (see Chapter 14 for a more detailed discussion of this subject).

If all of these preparatory activities have been executed adequately, there will be less work in the ordering and order handling stages. In practice, however, things often work out differently, and considerable efforts are required from the buyer during the phase of ordering and expediting. Expediting demands a lot of attention and is often conducted based on an **overdue list**, which records all deliveries that are late. There are several types of expediting (Kudrna, 1975, p. 45).

- *Exception expediting*. This method in many organizations is referred to as the 'beep system' which means that the buyer only undertakes action when the organization sends out signals of (impending) material shortages. Late deliveries from suppliers usually disrupt production. It is therefore important that deliveries are monitored closely by the buyer or materials planner in order to prevent materials shortages. Therefore this method is not recommended.
- *Routine status check*. This method of expediting aims at preventing materials supply and quality problems. A particular number of days before the promised delivery date, the buyer will contact the supplier with the request to confirm the delivery date again in order to secure delivery.

MEMO 3.6: Order handling

Now that the actual negotiations with the supplier have been concluded, the car manufacturer can proceed to order the desired equipment. During these phases of the purchasing process, the purchasing department will carry co-responsibility for

- follow-up of the order at the supplier's plant;
- negotiations about the consequences of requested engineering changes;
- expediting the orders up to the agreed delivery times;
- settlement of all financial matters;
- all commercial correspondence with the supplier;
- handling possible warranty claims.

- *Advanced status check*. This method is used for critical purchase parts and suppliers. Critical may refer here to supplies which are on the critical path of a materials planning. Critical may, however, also refer to materials with tight quality tolerances and unreliable suppliers. In those case it is recommended to negotiate in the contracting stage with the supplier that a detailed production plan, which lists the various steps of the production ('milestones'), will be handed over to the buyer before production starts. Monitoring production progress is done by means of periodical checks against the established production programme. At critical moments during the production process, the buyer will carry out inspections. In the case of very large purchase contracts (e.g. orders for heavy equipment from the petrochemical industry) the buyer may want to have a specialist permanently based at the supplier's premises **(field expediting)**.

When the products or equipment are delivered they will have to be checked to ensure that they meet the specified requirements. Acceptance of equipment often consists of a number of steps:

- acceptance test at the supplier's site before shipment;
- acceptance test at the user's site after delivery;
- acceptance test when the equipment is put into operation for the first time.

Depending on the size and technical complexity there may be more than one acceptance test at the supplier's site during installation of the equipment.

The business world is far from ideal. Notwithstanding good contracts and purchase orders, things may go wrong at delivery. Delivery times may not be respected by the supplier, quality problems may occur with purchased materials, suppliers may charge more for their products than allowed, etc. Therefore it is very important that the company has a reporting system for all the problems which may occur. Quality and delivery problems should be daily reported to the buyer (electronically) through a supplier complaint reporting procedure. These problems should be immediately communicated to the supplier in order to prevent a recurrence in the future. In other chapters in this book this matter will be discussed in more detail (see Chapters 10 and 11).

In summary, the added value of the buyer during the ordering and expediting phase lies predominantly in:

- developing efficient ordering routines between the buying company and supplier;
- checking that all purchase orders are confirmed by the supplier;
- developing and executing a computer-supported, differentiated method of expediting and inspection;
- maintaining a computer-supported database with regard to critical purchasing and supplier information (preferably arranged according to key technologies);
- developing a sound procedure for order handling;
- applying effective 'trouble shooting' when necessary.

Follow up and evaluation of the buying process

The buyer's role continues even after the new product has been taken into production, or the new installation has been put into operation. Things which can go wrong in the relationship with the supplier and which have to be taken care of at this stage are

- settling warranty claims and penalty clauses;
- settling the results of work in excess of, or work less than, that stated in the specification;
- organizing the purchase and supplier documentation;
- recording project evaluations, etc.

With regard to excess work, it is important to establish that this must be reported to the principal in advance, and that the principal must give permission first. Extra work must always be reported to the purchasing manager so that the purchase costs remain clear. Furthermore, it stimulates an adequate administrative processing of the invoices that are submitted later on.

In the case of investment goods, maintenance activities will become necessary after a while. At that time it becomes clear whether the supplier can substantiate his promises about service, maintenance and the supply of spare parts.

Experiences with individual suppliers should be documented carefully. It is recommended that buyers keep track of the supplier's quality and delivery record, his competitiveness and innovativeness since these data can lead to an adjustment of the so-called vendor rating (Chapter 12). It is important to have a thorough and up-to-date record of the actual capabilities of each supplier. Reporting this kind of information, both to management and the supplier's management, is one major source of added value contributed by the buyer. That concludes the cycle, because this information can be used in a subsequent purchasing cycle to assemble the 'bidders short list' for future projects and contracts. In this way the company learns to work with suppliers with proven capabilities. When companies learn to work this way, this usually results in a reduction of the supplier base. Companies, then, will gradually concentrate their business among fewer but more capable suppliers.

During the after-sales phase, the buyer's added value is primarily related to

- settling claims, with regard to work not covered in the specification;
- recording the user's experience with specific products and suppliers by means of a detailed vendor rating system;
- recording maintenance experience;
- supervising compliance with agreements concerning the supply of spare parts and maintenance.

Summary

This chapter has described the purchasing process in detail. The starting point was to discuss a new-task buying situation, i.e. a situation where every step of the buying process model needed to be prepared and conducted. Each step was illustrated through a practical example relating to the purchase of a new piece of equipment (car body carriers). For many other products the purchasing process is, fortunately, much simpler.

The starting point of the purchasing process is the purchase order specification which describes the whole of the user requirements in detail. In addition to technical requirements, the purchase specifications also reflect maintenance requirements and the logistic requirements the contract or order must meet. The purchase specification becomes in turn the basis for the supplier selection process. During this step choices need to be made about the method of contracting out (partial or integral) and the type of contract (fixed-price or cost-reimbursable). Only after this has been done can the bidder's list be assembled and the request for quotation be designed. For the evaluation and appraisal of quotations a distinction should preferably be made between the technical evaluation and the commercial evaluation. These evaluations will result in a clear and unambiguous selection of a supplier, and the selection phase concludes with the preparation of the contract negotiations.

Contracting is an art in itself. The terms and conditions which have to be included in the contract are numerous and varied. In this chapter were discussed prices and terms of delivery, terms of payment, penalty regulations and warranty regulations and other, more general, terms and conditions including the much-used Incoterms.

After the agreement has been signed, the order must be placed. The order indicates quantities, product description and unit price, as well as the desired delivery date and other information necessary for effective logistic and administrative processing. The purchasing process is concluded with the follow up and evaluation phase.

This description of the purchasing process clarifies once again that a buyer must be an all-rounder with sufficient technical knowledge, a feeling for the commercial side of the process, and be familiar with the basics of logistics and administration. Every step in the buying process must be executed carefully and systematically in order to provide the internal customer with what he needs: a product which is fit for its use, on time, in the required quantity and at a reasonable cost.

Assignments

3.1   In this chapter fixed-price contracting and cost-reimbursable contracting were distinguished. What are the most important advantages and disadvantages of both types of contract? Describe situations in which you would prefer one or the other type of contract.

3.2   General terms and conditions sometimes include a penalty clause for late delivery, delivery of products that do not comply with the specification, etc. What advantages and disadvantages do you see in the application of penalty clauses?

3.3   This chapter describes three different methods of expediting. In which circumstances do you think each of these methods is useful? Explain your answer.

3.4 The case study at the beginning of the chapter describes the problems that arose when a railway company purchased new carriages. In your opinion, how could these problems have been avoided? List at least five measures.

3.5 Large companies want to carry out a preliminary qualification of suppliers before they place an order. What does prequalification mean? Name at least five criteria you would use in the prequalification of a supplier of packaging materials.

MARKETS AND PRODUCTS

4

Learning objectives

After studying this chapter you should understand:

- The various types of supply market structures.
- The influence of market structures on purchasing policy.
- The specific characteristics related to the buying of raw materials, components, maintenance, repair and operating supplies, investment goods and services.

CASE STUDY
The effect of frost on Brasilian coffee bean production

Thursday, July 16th, 1975. The market is slow this morning. The assistant buyer of a medium-sized coffee roasting factory somewhere in North-West Europe is slightly ticked off. Of all the times when he could have taken a vacation, his boss decided to leave during the frosty season in Brasil, the world's largest producer of coffee. He left a telephone number and a somewhat odd instruction: in case of frost, call immediately! And that is exactly what makes the assistant buyer so nervous. Yes, he knows the stories, but how do you judge such a situation?

It is four in the morning of that same day when Joao gets out of bed again. The weather forecast said there could be early morning frost in the area around Campinas in Parana, which is where his coffee plantation is located. Nothing serious, but it has been cold for a couple of days, and frost has already been reported in Rio Grande to the south. As he goes outside an icy wind sweeps the land. The thermometer indicates minus 2°C. He calls his broker in Rio who was still asleep, but who is instantly wide awake when Joao tells him it is freezing. 'Buy London futures'. It is midday over there, so he can make the transaction before lunch-close. 'Buy at the market, i.e. the price is irrelevant. Buy at market price'.

In Londeina the special weather correspondent of one of the major traders in the market also checks the thermometer and sees to his alarm that it reads minus 4°C. And at this early hour! This is going to be a major frost! So his boss is called out of bed at a quarter past four, and he succeeds in getting through to his London branch office ten minutes later, just before the noon close of the London futures exchange. £375 per ton, little trade, a single order from an unknown source. The comment from London is: no real excitement. Rumours about frost? Haven't heard a thing. The message from New York is: 'O.K. we buy. Buy anything you can get your hands on'. First the

Continued on page 74

futures, then the effective trade. In a few minutes £390 is reached, at which price the market closes for lunch. What is going on? Frost? Nobody knows exactly. Now the assistant buyer really starts to worry, and with good cause. These signals from a futures market must not be missed. If there is any purpose to the futures exchange at all, it is to pick up this type of signal. At two o'clock in the afternoon the senior buyer's siesta is rudely interrupted by a puzzled waiter who states, while it is 30°C outside: 'Il gèle au Bresil'. The senior buyer's reaction to this message is even more incomprehensible to the waiter: he races to the nearest telephone and won't move from there. Not until half past five, after the London close, when he rejoins his wife and states that he is going to take the eight o'clock plane home. It is only frost, but his wife knows this is the end of her vacation. 'Why don't you stay on?', her husband tries, but one hour later the suitcases are packed and the taxi is waiting. The next morning, July 17th, eleven o'clock. Reuter reports that although there has been some frost, the damage to the crops is minimal. The market has been open for half an hour and immediately opened $100 (25%) higher because of the news. This market climbed up to £4200 in March 1977. The futures market gave the industrial buyer the opportunity to cover part of his purchasing needs at an early stage.

(Source: Vanhorick (1986) pp. 17–18)

Introduction

The number of sales transactions equals the number of purchasing transactions, for in each buy/sell transaction there is a buyer and a seller. Both operate in a market. The seller has various market segments or target groups and, based on a number of criteria, he will attempt to segment his market in such a way that the market opportunities are optimally aligned with his company's technical and commercial possibilities.

The buyer also has a choice. Based on his experience or on a deliberate purchasing strategy, he can decide to place his purchasing orders with a particular group of suppliers. In this decision he will be guided on the one hand by the assortment carried by the suppliers. On the other hand his choice will depend on the quality of the service these suppliers provide. And, like the seller, the buyer will also strive for an optimal fit between the product and quality of service offered by suppliers and the needs of his internal customers.

Depending on the commercial choices that sellers and buyers make in their commercial policy, different types of markets emerge. Every type of market leads to a specific type of purchasing and selling behaviour. The objective of this chapter is to describe a few of the most common types of supply market structures. The introductory case indicates that purchasing raw materials is often a complex undertaking: knowledge of the market and experience, in combination with a sound analytical attitude, are indispensable properties for the raw materials buyer. Apart from supply market structures, this chapter examines the following issues: the specific problems in connection with the purchase of raw materials, the purchase of specific and standard components, the purchase of MRO goods and investment (capital) goods. The chapter concludes with a discussion of the purchase of services.

Markets and market structures

The patterns of relationships between supplier and buyer are primarily determined by the underlying pattern of the goods and services deliveries, the **external structure** (Figure 4.1). The external structure consists of a number of links (companies, institutions) that are connected via markets. Within the external structure, industrial branches and industry columns can be distinguished.

An **industrial branch** is defined as the horizontal relationship of organizations that experience each other as effective competitors (for example: the leather and footwear industry, the electronics industry).

An **industry column** is defined as a series of companies (links) in which the consecutive stages of production of an economic product take place – from primary producer to consumer.

Depending on the number of stages one can speak of a short or a long industry column. Depending on the location of the link in the industry column, the materials-flow between successive links can take the following forms (see Figure 4.2).

- *Diverging materials flow.* The finished product of one link is the main or sole input for the next production stages of various **industry columns**. This applies to industries which process raw materials.
- *Linear materials flow.* The finished product of one link is the main or sole input for the subsequent link.
- *Converging materials flow.* Various finished products of links of various industry columns are the input for the next link. This situation is found in companies with assembly-oriented production.

Diverging materials flows are usually found at the beginning of an industry column. Converging materials flows are found at the end of an industry column.

External factors are those which determine the degree of availability of a certain product and which cannot be influenced by individual companies. Examples are

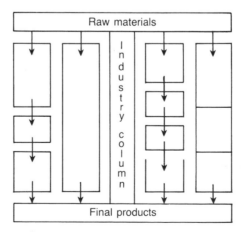

Figure 4.1 The external structure on a macro level.

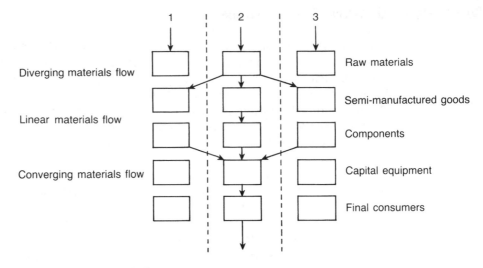

Figure 4.2 The materials flow structure.

- the number of customers or buyers in a market;
- the number of suppliers;
- the market structure (transparency, pricing method);
- the stock situation of the product in question;
- speed of technological innovation.

External factors are relevant because they determine the **market structure**. Market structure is defined in this book as the total set of conditions in which a company sells its products, with special attention to the number of parties in the market and the nature of the product being traded. Central to this definition are, therefore:

- the number of suppliers;
- the number of buyers;
- the degree of product differentiation.

The **market** is the total of supply and demand. Sometimes this refers to a physical market, where buyers and sellers actually meet, but in general abstract markets are dealt with. Economic theory uses a number of constructs to explain the relationship between the variables mentioned and market price. It distinguishes various market structures both on the supply side and the demand side, which in reality do not exist in their pure form.

Supply side

Four types of market structures are usually distinguished on the supply side.

- *Pure competition.* Characteristic of this market structure is that neither the supplier nor the buyer can influence the price of the product. Thus, the price is a given one for all parties involved. Furthermore it is assumed that in this market structure complete information is available. In other words, there is a high degree of market transparency. In addition, the product is homogeneous and fully replaceable by substitutes. Examples of this market type are commodities markets for natural products such as wheat, cocoa, coffee, and for metals such as iron, copper and aluminium. Most auctions (flowers, vegetables) resemble this situation.

- *Monopolistic competition.* This market structure is similar to many actual markets and is characterized by a high degree of product differentiation. Each supplier tries to make his product stand out in order to create a monopoly situation for himself. This situation is favourable for the supplier because it provides him with some room to manipulate his prices, within a given bandwidth. There is no direct pressure on his prices from competitors' offers. Examples are the markets for cigarettes, detergents, hi-fi equipment and other durable consumer goods.

- *Oligopoly.* An oligopoly is a market type characterized by a limited number of suppliers and a limited product differentiation. Moreover, it is very difficult to get a foothold in the market, due to some important entry barriers. The suppliers are familiar with each other's market behaviour. An oligopoly can have various forms (see Figure 4.3). Depending on the situation the market price can be set by a market- or price-leader, or arranged through some form of price arrangements (cartels). Also, it may happen that the players in the market cannot combine to pursue cut-throat competition.

  When there are few suppliers, but a differentiated or heterogeneous product, it is referred to as a **heterogeneous oligopoly**. As soon as there are more suppliers in such a situation, the preferred term is **monopolistic competition**. Examples are found primarily in the industrial sector: the markets for forklift trucks, chemical semi-manufactured goods, flavourings, etc.

- *Monopoly.* A monopoly is characterized by the presence of only one supplier of the product in question. Substitutes are (virtually) absent. This enables the monopolist to pursue his own pricing policy. **Natural monopolies** exist when

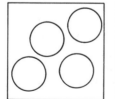  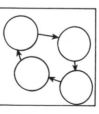 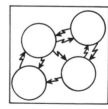

At price P1 and quantity Q1, all capacity is used: *price stability*

There is a *price leader* and this is accepted

Price agreements are reached

At price P1 and quantity Q1 one party operates below cost price and starts a *price offensive*

Figure 4.3   Examples of the oligopolistic market type.

the entire supply of raw materials or a particular manufacturing process is owned by just one producer or manufacturer, excluding others by means of contracts or patents (e.g. oil concessions, diamonds). **Government monopolies** exist when based on special licences which are required from the government or when based on state law. Examples are postal services, railways and some public utilities (gas, etc.).

The big advantage of a monopoly for the supplier is that it enables him to dictate the price and other contractual conditions to the market. Naturally this dictate has its limits in so far as the buyer is not obliged to purchase the product. Purchasing practice shows many situations which resemble monopolies:

- An original equipment manufacturer's (OEM) rule in the service contract that only original spare parts are to be used under penalty of lapse of the warranty conditions.
- Purchase requisitions on which the applicant merely indicates brand name and a specific supplier's name.
- Strict guidelines from an engineering department to use only one particular technology for some component that needs to be purchased.

Through his marketing and communications policy the supplier's account manager tries to influence the customer's preferences. The buyer needs to be attentive to these matters and should continuously reflect whether the perceived differences in value of the product that is offered by the supplier outweighs his price variance and the risk of a larger dependency.

Demand side

In general three types of market structure on the demand side can be distinguished.

- *Pure competition*. The description given above also applies here.
- *Oligopsony*. This is the oligopoly situation in reverse: there are only a few buyers and a large number of suppliers. The (frequently large) buyers are aware of one another's behaviour and in this way collectively occupy a position of power *vis-à-vis* the usually smaller suppliers. One example of this market structure is the automobile industry in its capacity of buyer of semi-manufactured products and components. Other examples are agricultural **co-operatives** or **buying consortia** which can be found in numerous branches. These organizations in fact co-ordinate the buying volumes of their members *vis-à-vis* usually much larger suppliers.
- *Monopsony*. In this situation there is only one buyer of the product versus a large number of suppliers. In reality this is a very rare situation. Examples are the sugar industry, dairy industry, the railways (as buyer of locomotives and trains) and public utilities in some countries (gas, electricity, water supply).

The supply and demand situations described above can be placed in a matrix and the result is shown in Figure 4.4. Depending on the number of suppliers in

Number of suppliers \ Number of buyers	One	Few	Many
One	Bilateral monopoly, 'captive market' (spare parts)	Limited supply-side monopoly (fuel pumps)	Supply-side monopoly (gas, water, electricity)
Few	Limited demand-side monopoly (telephone exchanges, trains)	Bilateral oligopoly (chemical semi-manufacturers)	Supply-side oligopoly (copiers, computers)
Many	Demand-side monopoly (weapons systems, ammunition)	Demand-side oligopoly suppliers (components automobile industry)	Polypolistic competition (office supplies)

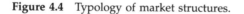

▨ = Demand-side stronger than supply-side

☐ = Demand and supply more or less in balance

▤ = Supply-side stronger than demand-side

Figure 4.4 Typology of market structures.

the market and their positions relative to those of immediate competitors, the buyer's position can be dominant, equal or subordinate in comparison to the opposition. To assess one's position of power it is important to take into account one's position relative to the opposition. SAS may be one of the few buyers of turbo-jet engines but, compared to a company the size of General Electric, SAS's negotiating position is minor. To take another example, DAF Trucks only has a minor power position compared to ZF, the largest German supplier of gearboxes. DAF Trucks order's add up to tens of millions of UK pounds annually but, compared to Daimler Chrysler, DAF Trucks is only a small player for ZF.

When developing a purchasing policy, the purchasing manager should reflect on the following questions

- Which types of markets are we dealing with in relation to article X; how many (potential) suppliers are in the market, from whom we could, in principle, obtain this article?

- What reactions will placing an order of volume Y and price Z with one supplier generate from the other suppliers?
- What is the degree of differentiation for a particular product in the supplier market; which alternatives or substitutes are available?
- What is our company's market share for product X in the supply market and who are our competitors with regard to this product? Who else is buying this product?
- What is likely to happen in the short and the long term with regard to the supply of product Q and what effect will the expected developments have on price setting and availability?

Knowledge of market structures is important to the buyer because these determine to a large extent the desired strategy on the one hand, and the negotiating strategies that will be used on the other hand. Chapter 7 discusses these strategic consequences in more detail.

Purchase of goods

Raw materials and Commodity Exchanges

Raw materials are a substantial component of many companies' purchasing portfolios. In this context one can think of oil as the raw material for oil refineries and the chemical industry, vegetable oils and fats for the margarine industry and iron ore for the steel industry. These examples clearly show that a distinction can be made between natural raw materials (which include natural products such as cattle, corn, wheat, coffee, cocoa, sugar, cotton and soya), and minerals (for example coal, iron ore, copper and bauxite). The purchase of raw materials often involves large sums of money. In addition they partly determine the cost price of the finished product. For these reasons they will often be earmarked as strategic products.

The **commodity exchange** plays a significant role in the purchase of raw materials. The major commodity exchanges are in the United States, for example Comex in New York where precious metals are traded, and the Chicago Board of Trade where grain, rice and soya are traded. One major commodity exchange outside the United States is the London Metal Exchange (LME). This futures market deals primarily with non-precious metals such as copper, zinc, tin and aluminium.

The origins of these commodity exchanges are often historically determined. Past attempts to establish exchanges in Amsterdam, Paris, Singapore and Hong Kong were all in vain. The reasons why these efforts failed are to be found in the absence of one or several crucial conditions that must be fulfilled. The most important criteria for the effective functioning of a futures market are (Vanhorick, 1986, p. 5):

- A logical geographical location – this is important, bearing in mind the transportation of raw materials, coupled with a highly developed banking network, because it must be possible to conclude large numbers of financial transactions.

- Liquidity of the article – the raw material must be available in sufficient quantity, but also in manageable units. The manageability of crude oil has always presented a problem, because the quantities involved are usually too large to be able to achieve a standard quantity through the futures market. Furthermore, it must be possible to standardize the quality of the article.
- Liquidity of the market – there must be sufficient parties willing to participate in the futures market.
- Political stability – there must be a certain degree of political stability in the country where the exchange is established, because of the huge financial interests connected with the futures trade. For this reason a futures market in a politically unstable country is doomed to fail.

Futures trade is forward trade, which means that goods are purchased to be delivered at a future time, not with the intention to receive or deliver these goods at that agreed time, but to fulfil the contract by settling the price difference between the original and a new transaction. There is, therefore, no physical trading of goods on the futures market, but a trade in contracts concerning goods.

A futures market is used to hedge the price risk of a particular transaction (purchase or sale of a commodity), which will be concluded at some future date (for example a future receipt or delivery). Future trading is a complex, and for outsiders, not very accessible process. Not much has been published about it. The author's description is based on Vanhorick (1986).

Participants in a futures market always take 'an open position' which can be either long or short. A **long position** refers to the situation in which on balance a party buys more of the product or the futures (including stocks and options) than he has sold. The balance of purchases and sales is therefore positive. A **short position** is taken when there have been more sales than purchases so that the balance of purchases and sales is negative.

The futures market functions by means of the **clearing house**. This body guarantees the contracts and takes care of the financial settlement. Normally, trading is possible six to eight months ahead, based on delivery per calendar month, spread across the entire year, for example January–March–May–July–September–November, or any other combination of months. Each month, or rather, each position, has its own quotation, bid price, asking price, last traded price, daily high–low prices and closing value (see Table 4.1).

The quotations for all the major futures markets are published daily in the financial newspapers. Many trading houses and brokers have direct access to the

Table 4.1 Example of a futures quotation

Month	Last traded	Bid	Ask	Open	High	Low	Close
November	2350	2349	2352	2330	2360	2325	2345
January	2392	2385	2388	2361	2398	2358	2370
March	2428	2426	etc.				

rates by means of Reuters screens or the Internet, so they can monitor them by the minute.

Registration as a party is a precondition for buying or selling a standard quantity of the standard quality commodity/raw material in a previously determined month of delivery (delivery position) at any given moment during the opening hours of the market. After the month of delivery has been concluded, the participant should be back to a zero-position on that futures. He can achieve this by means of a counter transaction at a certain point in time: buying when he is short or selling if he is long. This is the principle of the futures market in a nutshell.

As a rule, four groups participate in the futures market: the producer, the trader, the buyer and the speculator. Each group has its own primary goals and so introduces a different element to the market process.

The **producer** will use the futures market to secure the yield of his crop. Farmers, for example, who have sold their grain crop to the co-operative for a fixed price in the spring, are confronted with the risk of a rise in prices. Had they waited until August, they might have negotiated a better price. This risk can be hedged by means of a forward transaction.

The **trader** is the main user of the futures market. He is both buyer and seller and is satisfied with small profits over large positions.

The main goal of the **buyer** is to limit the market or price risk. Breweries often purchase the barley harvest from the farmer when the seeds have only just been planted. This means that they run a price risk for several months, until the moment of delivery. By delivery time the prices can be substantially lower. The brewery can hedge this risk by means of a forward transaction.

The only goal of the **speculator** is profit. He operates on both sides of the market, buying and selling. Speculators provide the market with dynamics: the larger the number of speculators, the higher the liquidity of the market becomes.

How does a forward transaction work? Memo 4.1 shows an example of a hedge. To hedge means that price risks, which are related to a physical transaction, are covered by taking up a counter transaction on the futures market. The example indicates in what way buyer and seller can limit their risks of either a rise or a fall in prices.

Purchasing will make use of futures markets especially in the following situations:

- The raw material that is purchased is an essential constituent of the cost price of the finished product.
- It is almost impossible to pass on a price increase on the purchasing side to the sales price. If this is the case, using the futures market is to be recommended.
- The raw material which is used in the finished product cannot be substituted by other products (for example: natural rubber as a substitute for synthetics). If there are many possible substitutes it is less necessary to use a futures market. However, if one is dependent on one particular raw material, a futures market can be very useful.

MEMO 4.1: The purchase of coffee

On 1 January a trader buys 50 tons of coffee from a producer at £1800 per ton. The consignment will be delivered on 1 April. The trader therefore runs the risk of a fall in prices from January through March. If the market falls to £1600 he would sustain a loss of £10 000. Therefore, the trader is 50 tons long. He can limit his price risk by entering into a forward transaction, doing this by taking a short position on the futures market for the same amount of money. In other words he can obtain 10 futures contracts of sale of 5 tons each on a three-month term; at that time the price of a three-month contract is £1800.

If by 1 April the market price for coffee has gone down from £1800 to £1600, he loses the £10 000; however, at that moment he sells his forward futures contract for 50 tons at £1800 while the current rate is £1600. In other words, he makes a profit of £10 000:

Effective purchase		Sale forward contract March	
50 tons at £1800	= £90 000	50 tons at £1800	= £90 000
Decreased market value:		Forward price:	
50 tons at £1600	= £80 000	50 tons at £1600	= £80 000
Market loss	£10 000	Profit futures market	£10 000

The balance of both transactions is zero. In this way the trader can limit his price risks by means of a forward transaction. Of course there are costs in connection with forward transactions, but compared to the total financial interest they are extremely low.

Buying components

Components are parts which are to be built in the final product, to be sold by the manufacturer. They can be either **standard** or **specific**. Standard components are manufactured based on specifications provided by the supplier, e.g. tyres, light bulbs, fuses, small electric motors and condensers. Specific components are manufactured according to designs, specified by the buyer. Examples of specific components are forgings and castings, gears, gearboxes and axles.

Components are often purchased for serial production. This enables buyers to negotiate annual agreements with suppliers, or to negotiate even longer-term price and delivery agreements. This simplifies the administrative process significantly, because as the conditions have been agreed, orders can be placed directly at the supplier (through **call-off orders** or **blanket orders**).

Quality aspects play an extremely important role in buying components, for every defect in the production line can result in delays and production losses. Furthermore, the quality of the constituent parts determines the quality of the finished product.

It is for this reason that quality requires special attention in the purchase of components. In their pursuit of quality improvements, buyers increasingly take a preventive approach: before suppliers qualify for an order, they are first audited with regard to their prevailing quality system and production process (see also Chapter 10). A supplier is only included in the 'approved suppliers' file after it has been determined that he is capable of delivering a product of the required quality. The relationship with suppliers who repeatedly fail to meet the quality standards is terminated. After the evaluation there will be joint efforts to reach a quality agreement, which, among other things, establishes targets for quality improvement. If these targets are met, incoming inspection and quality inspection of the deliveries can be abolished, or the frequency of inspections can be lowered considerably.

When a quality agreement has been entered into, it will be checked periodically as to whether all conditions are still being met. In case of doubt or in the case of proven quality problems, extra quality inspections will be carried out until the agreed quality level has been reached. Information on the quality behaviour of suppliers is systematically recorded in a quality control system (part of the vendor rating-system). Based on this information action can be taken in the case of negative trends in the supplier's performance. Vendor rating can also be used to compare quality levels of suppliers. Chapter 14 will further address methods to assess suppliers.

Finally, the directive concerning liability for defective products is of importance. This directive was established in July 1985 by the Council of the European Communities, to protect the consumer from damage which results from defective products. In addition this directive serves to harmonize the legislation regarding this subject between the various member states. When a purchased component is defective, both the supplier and the manufacturer of the finished product are liable for the entire damage. If one of the liable parties has compensated for the damage, then the aggrieved party cannot address the others.

Buying maintenance, repair and operating supplies

The buying of **maintenance, repair and operating supplies** has its own specific problems. The major purchasing-related characteristics of these goods are:

- Very extensive article assortment – in a medium-sized company an assortment containing 10 000 to 15 000 articles is no exception. This also results in an extensive supplier file. The turnover per article and per supplier is low.
- High degree of specificity – many articles are company-specific (for example spare parts for production or processing equipment).
- Many of these articles have a low, but irregular consumption rate – this implies that these articles usually have a very low inventory turnover rate.
- The user has substantial influence on the choice of the product.

In practice, MRO items take up 80% of the product codes. At the same time they rarely make up more than 20% of the purchasing turnover and, as a result of the characteristics mentioned earlier, quite often 80% of the buyer's work concerns these articles.

Measures aimed at increasing purchasing efficiency should primarily focus on reducing the administrative work involved. Several measures may be used for this, including drastic reduction of product variety through standardization, outsourcing materials planning and purchasing to specialized distributors, electronic ordering and invoicing, working with electronic catalogues through E-commerce and Internet technology (see also Chapter 6). Arrangements with suppliers can be negotiated through so-called call-off agreements, which specify price, delivery terms and conditions and the contract period covered. Usually bonus arrangements are part of the contract specifying what bonus will be paid depending on the volume ordered by the company. Orders actually are placed by the users themselves, who refer to the overall contract terms that have been agreed. This frees the buyer from an important administrative workload.

A greater level of co-operation is afforded by the **systems contract**. A systems contract usually covers a plant or department's requirements for MRO supplies. It generally provides for the supplier to carry inventory and to make regular, timely deliveries. How to arrive at such a contract? Let's use office supplies as an example. First a particular product group or assortment (e.g. office supplies) is analysed. Based on a thorough inventory it is decided to reduce the product variety and standardize. This usually requires ample discussions between the users and the buyer involved, who for this reason work together by means of a **buying committee**. Also the number of suppliers is analysed. The idea is to bring the whole product group to only one specialized supplier, usually a distributor who will take stock and take care of all deliveries. Ordering routines are then established which, as a rule, mean that the internal users can order directly from the supplier (often through a detailed electronic product catalogue), without intervention of the purchasing department. Also, a specific customer service level is agreed upon with the supplier, such as delivery of the assortment within three days at a 98% delivery reliability, directly to the user. Finally, the supplier invoices the administration once a month and provides the manager of every department or the person responsible for the budget with an overview of the orders from that department on a monthly basis. It is clear that this solution prevents a lot of work and solves the so-called 'small-order problem' of many purchasing departments. Larger companies use this method for the purchase of office supplies, hand tools, electro-technical articles, fasteners and so forth. Although systems contracting seems to resemble other forms of contracts, it is characterized by the high degree of integration between the supplier and the customer organization. The recent upswing of **E-Commerce** and the availability of Internet technology has improved the practical application of this type of thinking considerably. E-Commerce provides not only electronic ordering right from the users desk, but also electronic tracing and tracking of deliveries and, more importantly, electronic payment. One way of solving payment issues is to integrate the purchasing card within E-Commerce.

In recent years **corporate credit cards** have widened in scope from travel and entertainment purposes to those of non-production buying, facilitating the incidental purchases that offices and plants make at last moment's notice. Such transactions are too small for national contracts, yet accounting for them costs a fortune in paperwork. Many companies in the US distribute the purchasing cards to foremen, clerks, and secretaries. Companies can specify the use and billing so that they can be available, say, for only hardware items up to 500 dollars. The cards incorporate codes that set credit limits and restrict where they can be used and for what commodities (see Memo 4.2).

At the time of transaction the electronic checking process validates that the type of commodity is allowed, and the person buying is requesting a job code for the items being purchased. The credit card company pays the suppliers,

---

MEMO 4.2: Gillette and the Purchasing Card

Bob Edwards, Manager Corporate Purchasing at The Gillette Company sees a bright future for the Purchasing Card. Purchasing in his view adds little or no value to the buying of non-production, Maintenance, Repair and Operations (MRO) items. 'We just take a purchase requisition and convert it to a purchase order and pass it on to a supplier. We have become high-priced clerks'. The cost of processing an order is often more then the cost of goods/services Gillette is buying. 'My goal is to eliminate 50 to 80% of non-value added work from the Purchasing and Accounts Payable Departments', says Edwards. 'First, I have to draw the people, i.e. requisitioners, in to using the Purchasing Card. I want a few restrictions at first on the card, i.e. Dollar-limit per transaction, because otherwise they are not going to use it. I will let them buy almost anything that they have bought previously using a purchase requisition. I want them to get so used to using that Purchasing Card that they cannot live without it. Second, in a year's time I will do an analysis of what goods/services have been purchased, and from whom these were bought. After that analysis is done, purchasing will go out and negotiate national or international company-wide contracts and then restrict the use of the Purchasing Card only to those preferred suppliers under contract'.

Accounts payable will not pay an invoice without the issuing of a purchase order. Purchasing is not going to issue a purchase order, as long as they don't have a purchasing requisition, and if purchasing gets a purchasing requisition they will say: Hey, why a requisition? You have a Purchasing Card, buy it yourself! It's a closed loop. This eliminates the issuing of purchase orders, receiving reports, invoices and checks. Our credit card company pays the supplier within 72 hours and bills Gillette once a month for all transactions.

In the near future Gillette is going to set up electronic catalogues in their personal computers. When a requester wants, let's say, toothpicks, he or she types in 'toothpicks': the name of the supplier, contact person, telephone number and price will come up on their screen. The requester then calls the supplier and orders their toothpicks and gives them his Purchasing Card number. They buy it themselves. It doesn't come through purchasing anymore, it is automated. The purchase order processing costs can be reduced from approximately 125 dollars to less than 3 dollars per transaction. The credit card company has developed the software so they can send Gillette an electronic invoice once a month and Gillette can run it directly into their general ledger. Gillette pays this company once a month by doing Electronic Funds Transfer. 'We have completely automated the process'.

Says Edwards: 'Now Purchasing is going to add real value in the non production (MRO) area, because we will have the time to negotiate better/more contracts, find better suppliers, and we have the leverage of the total dollars.'

(Source: Van Weele and Rozemeijer, (1996), p. 89–91)

eliminating thousands of purchase orders and cheques. At the end of the month the company receives one bill, hard copy and/or on tape, with all transactions sorted by purchaser, store, and/or job code. These systems greatly reduce cash use and provide cost control over the many small purchases often needed in the field or on the spot. Credit card companies generally provide quickly redigitized hard copies of any purchase slip for verification. In this way the purchasing card cuts processing costs to a few cents (Tully, 1995).

Buying investment goods

The process of purchasing investment goods takes place as described in Chapter 3. This section is therefore limited to a general outline. In general, the purchase of investment goods entails

- the purchase of machinery, installations and services;
- monitoring the progress (expediting);
- ensuring the required quality and verifying that the requirements as specified in the order are met.

The purchase of investment goods usually takes place on a project basis, within an approved budget and established planning, in accordance with the agreed procedures. Often, a specific project team is installed. Such a team for larger investment projects is frequently composed of

- A project leader, ultimately responsible for the optimal realization of the project in terms of technology, budget and planning.
- A project engineer, responsible for the coordination of the various technical disciplines.
- A planning engineer, responsible for setting up and maintaining up-to-date planning and documentation.
- A project administrator, responsible for budget management.
- A process engineer or environmental expert.
- Engineers as representatives of disciplines appropriate to the project, such as civil engineering, mechanical engineering, electrical equipment, instrumentation, accessories, pipeline systems and power supply.
- A project buyer, as representative of the purchasing department and responsible for all purchasing aspects, including order handling, inspection and quality inspection at the supplier's site, and monitoring progress/expediting.

The criteria used for selecting suppliers include:

- *Production.* What experience does the supplier or contractor have in projects like those in question?
- *Organization.* What is the state of the quality and experience of the staff that will be employed? To what extent is the supplier able to supply all required disciplines?
- *Financial status.* What about the supplier's financial reliability? What is the state of his liquidity and profitability? How pressing is his need for work?

- *Design and manufacturing capacity.* Which assembly instructions will the supplier use? How does he plan to monitor his costs? Does he have any experience with the materials that will be used?
- *Quality assurance.* What guarantees is the supplier willing to provide regarding design specification and technical specifications? What quality standards will he adhere to?
- *Experience and references.* What are the experiences of other client organizations with regard to the work done by the supplier? What references can the supplier provide?

After the supplier has been selected, a purchase contract will be drawn up, in which a large number of issues are set down. Quite frequently such an order consists of several hundreds of pages, including the **project specifications**. Many issues must be regulated, including

- What is to be delivered, to be set down with extensive technical specifications.
- Where the goods are to be delivered or where the service is to be performed.
- The conditions under which the delivery is to be made; these concern price, delivery, payment and warranty.

Apart from these general issues there are several specific aspects involved in purchasing for investment projects, such as

- *Bank guarantees.* Demanded of the supplier by the buyer to ensure that the supplier will fulfil the obligations which follow from the contract.
- *Transfer of title.* By means of which ownership of the material is transferred to the buyer when the supplier has received payment for these materials.
- *Performance guarantees.* In which the supplier guarantees that the performances specified in the order will be met in the circumstances described (frequently the supplier will have to demonstrate this in an acceptance test).

Buying services

Buying services takes place according to more or less the same principles as for the purchase of goods. Specific attention will also have to be given to matters such as the law concerning ultimate responsibility for the payment of taxes and social security, flexwork, insurances, safety regulations, and ownership. Several types of services can be distinguished:

- Services in the fields of architecture and civil engineering.
- Services in the fields of machine construction, production equipment, transportation and generation of energy.
- Services regarding electrical engineering, instrumentation, production automation, etc.
- Facilities services regarding offices, laboratories, business computers and peripheral equipment, cafeterias, safety and health care.

A frequent question with regard to services is whether to 'do it yourself' or to buy these from suppliers. Buying of services may be necessary because of insufficient internal capacity to perform the work planned; this is called **capacity buying**. A lack of expertise to perform the planned work internally at an acceptable quality level or at a justified cost level gives rise to the need for **specialist buying**. Table 4.2 shows the advantages and disadvantages of subcontracting from suppliers.

In case of subcontracting the principal can choose between a fixed-price contract or a cost-reimbursable contract (see also Chapter 3). Popular methods for arriving at a fair selection of the best supplier are **the open tender with pre-selection** and the **open tender without pre-selection**. In the first case, the principal explicitly indicates which companies qualify for the activities and only invited companies can submit proposals. With an open tender, every supplier can submit a proposal, because the principal makes no pre-selection.

One feature that regularly leads to misunderstandings in this type of contracting is the surplus work – the unforeseen activities for which often no price has been agreed. This work is frequently an unwelcome surprise for the buyer.

When work is contracted out, the principal must take into account that the laws have been tightened up. Important regulations in some European countries are those related to payment of social securities and taxes in the case of subcontracting. Put simply, these are arrangements applied by national government to prevent 'moonlighting' and illegal recruitment or contracting practices. The essence of these regulations is that the principal is liable for payment of social insurance premiums and taxes. This does not only apply to the activities executed by the contractor – the principal is also responsible for payment of the premiums and taxes of the subcontractors that are engaged by the contractor! In some European countries this law may apply to all sectors.

Other laws that require attention in the context of buying services are

Table 4.2 Advantages and disadvantages of contracting out

Advantages	Disadvantages
Investments can be focused on core activities	Increased dependency on suppliers
Optimal use of knowledge, equipment and experience of third parties	Constant monitoring of costs related to contracting out is necessary
Flexibility is increased; fluctuations in workload can be absorbed more easily	Risk of communication and organizational problems during transfer of activities to third parties
Contracting out leads to a more simple primary process in the organization	Risk of information 'leaks' (confidential information)
Input of an independent vision prevents organizational shortsightedness	Risk of social and legal problems in case of execution of activities by third parties
Part of the company risk is transferred to third parties	

- laws concerning flexitime;
- laws concerning foreign labour;
- laws concerning health, safety and the environment;
- laws related to general labour conditions;
- collective labour agreements which may be present within a specific sector;
- laws concerning income tax and social insurances.

Summary

To be able to purchase effectively, the buyer must have a sound knowledge of the supply-markets in which he operates and of the products he buys. Supply market structures determine the buyer's tactics – his attitude towards a monopolist will differ greatly from the attitude he adopts when dealing with an oligopoly situation. When deciding on his tactics the buyer will take into account the demand side and the supply side of a specific market. A sound analysis of the buyers' power position requires understanding of the behaviour of both buyers and suppliers.

This chapter has described the purchasing process related to raw materials, components, MRO items, investment goods and services. The descriptions show that the buying of each of these goods requires its own knowledge and experience – there is a world of difference between buying raw materials, hedging price risks by means of futures contracts, and buying for investment projects. In the purchase of services, it was seen that in addition to the specialist aspects, legal requirements also play an important role. Due to some EC directives, legislation in this area is subject to change and it is essential for the buyer to keep informed of changes which are going on.

Assignments

4.1   In this chapter the function of the project buyer was discussed. In your opinion, what characteristics should a project buyer who purchases for large investment projects possess? Answer the same question for the buyer of raw materials. What knowledge and skills should this person possess?

4.2   Describe the major differences between the execution of work based on fixed-price contracts and on cost-reimbursable contracts. Describe the circumstances in which each of the methods would be preferred by you.

4.3   The board of a trade company is considering expanding the stockroom. This entails adding to the existing stockroom and will cost approximately £2 million. Indicate:

- How you would proceed in a similar situation.
- Who you would involve in the project team.
- What criteria you would use for the selection of potential suppliers or contractors.

4.4 In the purchase of MRO goods there is the small-order problem: the smallest part of the turnover is made up by a very large amount of low-consumption articles.

- Name some examples of MRO articles.
- What measures would you as purchasing manager take to make the purchase and/or ordering of these articles as effective and efficient as possible?

4.5 One of the unsolved problems in many companies is who should be responsible for the purchase of services. Indicate who in your opinion should take care of the purchase of the following services. Describe how you see the involvement of the Purchasing Department for each situation:

- buying consulting expertise;
- hiring temporary labour;
- buying advertising and PR material;
- buying technical design expertise;
- buying automation services

THE PURCHASING MANAGEMENT PROCESS

5

Learning objectives

After studying this chapter you should understand the following:

- The major tasks and responsibilities of purchasing.
- The basic principles on which purchasing policy can be based.
- The major policy areas in purchasing.
- How purchasing may develop over time as a business function.

CASE STUDY
Purchasing's new muscle

The role of purchasing has changed dramatically in the last 25 years. Back in the early days, requisitions were sent 'down' to the purchasing department – it seemed that purchasing always was in the basement. People did not know to whom they were sending their requisitions; they certainly never spoke to anyone down there. They simply sent down a piece of paper that said 'Buy five of these'.

In the 1970s and 1980s, companies like AT&T downsized and reengineered to stay competitive, but they ignored the importance of their purchases. In most companies, purchases consume 40 to 60 percent of total revenue. Fortunately, the last few years have witnessed a revolution that *Fortune Magazine* referred to as 'purchasing's new muscle'.

I would have preferred a different title for a couple of reasons. First, we at AT&T call it 'procurement' rather than purchasing because out process goes far beyond what is traditionally known as purchasing. Second, I do not like referring to this new influence as 'muscle' because it implies the use of force. Rather than raw power, purchasing's new status is based upon respect for what it can contribute to the business. Clearly, businesses are waking up to the real value of purchasing. In other words, purchasing has finally risen from the basement . . .

Nothing is more important than purchasing but few executives understand the size of the opportunity. For example, one result of our restructuring will be the formation of a systems and technology company. This $20 billion business will spend $10 billion, half of its total revenue, on

Continued on page 94

outside suppliers. If there is anything in that business that is more important than purchasing, it is a well kept secret . . .

Interview with William B. Marx jr., Executive Vice President Multimedia Group Products, AT&T, as quoted from 'Purchasing's New Muscle', in Strategic Purchasing: Sourcing for the Bottom Line, The Conference Board, 1996, pp. 9–10.

Introduction

There are major differences between organizations in the area of purchasing and supply management. Observations from business practice have shown that tasks, responsibilities and the degree of authority, assigned to the purchasing departments, differ. These differences can be traced to differences in the purchasing portfolio, the characteristics of supplier markets, the production technology and organizational structures. However, differences also stem from the way in which purchasing actually is being managed.

The objective of this chapter is to systematically answer the question as to how an organization's purchasing policy can be structured, building on the concepts presented in Chapter 1.

Tasks and responsibilities assigned to the purchasing department vary widely among companies. In one organization the purchasing department may simply represent an ordering agency, whose main activity is processing purchasing orders, whereas in another organization purchasing is considered a strategic activity which is integrated into all major business processes. This chapter describes the major tasks and responsibilities of purchasing and supply management, the basic principles on which purchasing and supply strategies can be based and the elements of the purchasing management process. Moreover, the way in which purchasing and supply management may develop as a business discipline over time is discussed.

Primary tasks and responsibilities

Based on the framework of concepts developed earlier, the following responsibilities are considered to be core to the purchasing function in any organization.

1 *Contribution to the continuity of the company's primary activities* (see also Chapter 1). The materials and services which are to be purchased, must become available in line with the requirements of purchasing's internal customers. Purchasing's primary task is, therefore, that of securing supply from reliable suppliers at consistent quality at reasonable (total) cost. Effective and efficient supply is mandatory. If this task is not executed effectively the buyer, or the purchasing department, will lose credibility. The internal customers, such as engineering, manufacturing and technical services, will then bypass the purchasing department and start doing

purchasing on their own. Effective purchasing therefore requires an explicit supply orientation.

2   *Control and reduction of all purchasing-related costs.* Having secured supply, purchasing needs to make sure that goods and services are supplied at the lowest total cost of ownership (TCO). Total cost of ownership consists of two major elements: direct materials cost and all (indirect) costs related to the handling of these materials (costs related to incoming inspection, materials handling, inventory, administration, and scrap, etc.) Of course, a major task is to make sure that materials and services are bought at fair and competitive prices from the best suppliers that can be found.

However, buyers should also attempt to reduce or prevent indirect costs. They can do so by reducing the 'buffers' or 'waste' that may be built into the materials process or supply chain (e.g. safety stocks, incoming inspection, quality inspection, field expediting, etc.).

In view of the fact that on average 60% of the production value of industrial companies consists of purchased products, it is obvious that purchasing's contribution on this aspect is a major one. (See also Chapter 1 on purchasing's impact on the company's return on net assets (DuPont analysis).)

3   *Reduction of the company's risk exposure in relation to its supply markets.* If possible, the company should avoid becoming too dependent on just a few suppliers. Both in terms of supply and technology. 'Captive' sales situations must be prevented or reduced and it is important to have access to reliable suppliers because high quality and punctual delivery are often more important than price. In order to minimize its technological and supply risks in the long term, the company's management preferably should aim to spread its purchasing requirements among different suppliers.

4   *Contribution to product and process innovation.* Suppliers are often a source of new products and production technologies. In many industries technological developments take place at such a rate that even large enterprises, such as General Motors and IBM, are unable to generate all the investments needed to keep up with technology development in every area. In some cases this leads to partnerships with suppliers in the research and development field. The Smart Car, which was developed by Daimler-Chrysler in co-operation with Swatch company is one example; another is the development of high precision wafersteppers (for the manufacture of microchips) by ASM Lithography in The Netherlands with Carl Zeiss, manufacturer of high-tech lenses, from Germany.

The company's image is partly determined by what it communicates to its customer markets and the financial community. It is certainly also influenced by what it communicates to its suppliers. A fair and open attitude towards suppliers can help the company position itself as an attractive business partner. Buyers must make sure that the company actually meets its contractual obligations towards suppliers. It is therefore important that purchasing works according to a minimum set of purchasing procedures which describe how orders are placed, who is authorized to make purchasing decisions and how to structure the purchasing process (see Chapter 3). The ways of working should be described preferably in purchasing procedures, which are simple to use and easy to communicate. Examples of such procedures are the simple rule that no invoice will be paid to suppliers unless it can be matched by a purchase order. Or, another example: that all purchases beyond a certain amount of money (for instance, $10 000) need to be covered by at least three quotations from suppliers. Of increasing importance are some clear rules of conduct on how to deal with supplier relationships, on what is allowed when accepting gifts and other fringe benefits from suppliers. As co-operation with suppliers becomes more intensive the need for this kind of (formal) arrangement grows (see also Chapter 15 on 'rules of conduct' and 'purchasing ethics').

The importance of a clear and professional communication on the company's purchasing policies is increasingly being recognized by (mainly) larger companies (see Memo 5.1). Most of them have developed over time brochures to explain their policies both internally and externally.

Having described the most important tasks and responsibilities of purchasing, the following observations are worth mentioning.

- Acceptance of these ideas implies that in order to be successful, an explicit (internal) customer orientation is adopted. Buyers need to support the business the company is in. Buyers should therefore spend a substantial part of their time in contact with internal users, such as production, product development and engineering. Bureaucracy ('this order must be placed according to our purchasing procedures') and too strong an emphasis on price aspects ('let's see what discount we can get!'), which many buyers are accused of in practice, are incompatible with a true customer orientation. Experience shows that internal users will only consider costs when they are convinced the buyer will ensure timely delivery and/or availability at the quality they want. Those aspects should be of primary concern to them (see Memo 5.2)
- The various purchasing tasks cannot necessarily be applied collectively, and in certain situations they can even be contradictory. Single sourcing is often based on the objective of reducing materials costs – by placing all purchasing requirements with one supplier it is often possible to negotiate substantially better conditions. However, this policy certainly has its price in that it will lead to increased supply risk and/or dependency on one supplier. Balancing the pros and cons of this particular problem exceeds the authority of a buyer. This is one reason why strategic supplier decisions can only be made by (top) management.

MEMO 5.1: 'Selling' The Purchasing Policy

Many large companies now have sometimes very attractively designed brochures which explain their purchasing policy. By means of these brochures both internal staff and suppliers are informed of the methods used by the company's purchasing department, the way in which it is organized and also of the division of the different commodities among the buyers (see Figure 5.1).

Figure 5.1   Brochure which explains company purchasing policy. Reproduced with permission from Alcatel Bell. 'Quality on Time' is a registered trademark of Bell Telephone Manufacturing Company, NV, Francis Wellesplein I, Antwerp, Belgium and forms part of the Alcatel Group.

- The idea that buyers can indeed make significant contributions to product and process innovation, implies high demands on buyers' technical competence and personal qualities. Co-operation between engineering or research and development on the one hand, and the purchasing department on the other hand, can often not be realized in practice. Engineers and developers don't believe that buyers can make a significant contribution to their work because buyers often lack the required technical background and have insufficient affinity with product development and design and engineering problems. In those cases the purchasing department's professional staff should be upgraded to bring it in line with the level of professionalism, which is present in the surrounding business areas.

Policy principles

In this section the major principles on which purchasing policies should be based are described. Preferably, purchasing policies should be based on a sound business orientation, reflect a cross-functional approach and be directed at improving the company's bottom line.

Business orientation

Developing a purchasing and supply strategy requires a thorough understanding of the company's overall business policy. What end-user markets is the company targetting and what are the major developments going on in those markets? What competition is the company suffering from and what leeway does the company have in setting its own pricing policies. To what extent can materials price increases be passed on to the final customer or is this impossible? What changes are happening in the company's product, production and information technologies? What investments will be made by the company in terms of new products and technology and what products will be taken out of the market for the years to come. Understanding these kinds of questions is important since it

---

MEMO 5.2: Value versus price

It is unwise to pay too much, as it is unwise to pay too little. When you pay too much, you lose a little money, that's all. When you pay too little, you sometimes lose everything, because the thing you bought was incapable of doing the thing you bought it to do.

The common law of business balance prohibits paying a little and getting a lot. If you deal with the lowest bidder, it's well to add something for the risk you run. And if you do that, you will have enough to pay for something better.

(Source: anonymous)

will determine how purchasing and supply strategies will need to support the company in meeting its goals and objectives.

Integrated, cross-functional approach

Purchasing decisions cannot be made in isolation, and should not be aimed at optimization of purchasing performance only. Purchasing decisions should be made taking into account the effects of these decisions on the other primary activities (such as production planning, materials management and transportation). Therefore, purchasing decisions need to be based on balancing total cost of ownership. When buying, for instance, a new packaging line it is important to consider not only the initial investment, but also the costs which will be incurred in the future for buying accessories, spare parts and services. Moreover, unplanned downtime needs to be guaranteed by the supplier to be kept to a minimum during the packaging lines' technical and economic lifespan. The selling of equipment by a supplier is one thing; servicing that same equipment satisfactorily over a large number of years by that same supplier is often something different. This example illustrates the complexity of this type of purchases and the different kinds of decisions that need to be made. Careful decision making in those circumstances, therefore, requires a cross-functional and team-based approach among all the business disciplines affected by it. Purchasing and supply strategies can only be developed effectively in close co-operation with all disciplines and (top) managers involved. The purchasing and supply manager will lead the developing of such views and visions.

Bottom-line orientation

The author does not share the view that purchasing should only operate as a service function which should work on behalf of and comply with its customers' requirements without asking too many questions. Rather, that purchasing should provide a healthy commercial opposition *vis-à-vis* its internal customers. Through their activities buyers should make the company more cost aware. They should consistently look for improving the price/value ratio of the goods and services bought by the company. To accomplish this, purchasing should be able to suggest alternatives to existing product designs, materials or components to be used and alternative suppliers. Experience with companies in which purchasing is recognized as a bottom-line-driven activity shows that this function contributes to a permanent reduction of the cost price of the end product, whilst stimulating innovation from suppliers at the same time.

Purchasing management process

It has been argued that purchasing policies and strategies should be based on the company's overall (financial) objectives and product/market strategies. A company that operates in a highly competitive end-user market (e.g. the automotive industry), will beyond doubt have a strong focus on cost reduction and innovation. Hence, its purchasing and supply strategies should reflect those aspects and the purchasing activities will be directed through detailed materials budgets and well-prepared cost reduction projects. Constantly looking for new and more competitive sources of supply on an international basis (global sourcing) will be part of these projects. As an example, Volkswagen AG, since 1993 has pursued an aggressive sourcing strategy for its components. Having sourced traditionally from German suppliers, its flamboyant purchasing director Ignacio Lopez changed its sourcing strategy into one based upon global sourcing. Volkswagen's international purchasing offices nowadays invite quotations from suppliers world-wide, which are compared by an executive board which convenes weekly at Wolfsburg. As a result Volkswagen reported significant materials cost savings. (Important savings (up to 20% of initial materials costs) were reported during 1994–1995; after these years however, severe delivery problems occurred: most suppliers were not capable (or willing) to keep up with Volkswagen's growing materials volumes. Hence, many disruptions in production.)

A high-tech company operating in a niche market where it sells unique products, however, will have other concerns in the area of purchasing and supply strategy. Early supplier involvement, securing proprietary knowledge, reducing development lead time here will be of prime interest to the (technical) management. Apart from that the purchasing and supply function needs to secure flawless delivery of components and materials required. Innovation and supply come first; next price and cost aspects are considered. Philips Medical Systems, manufacturer of advanced medical equipment, may serve as an example here. This company has gone to great lengths to involve purchasing and suppliers at an early stage of development. Suppliers are primarily selected on their technological capabilities and invited to take an active role during the development stage. After development, suppliers are requested to submit quotations which, in most cases, are very competitive due to the fact that the supplier has gone through its learning curve earlier than its competitors. Also ASM-Lithography, a manufacturer of high-tech wafersteppers in The Netherlands, is practising this approach in its purchasing policies.

In order to describe the elements of the purchasing management process, much can be learned from the literature available on marketing management (e.g. Kotler, 1997). There are some striking similarities between marketing and purchasing:

- The primary focus of both company activities is on the exchange of values between two or more parties, resulting in the sell/buy transaction.
- Both activities are externally oriented, i.e. aimed at outside parties.
- Neither activity can be done adequately without sound knowledge of markets, competition, prices, technology and products.
- As a result of the amounts of money involved, both activities have great impact on the company's bottom line.

Analogous to marketing management, the following successive elements are identified in managing purchasing and supply:

- purchasing and supply (market) research;
- determining purchasing and supply objectives;
- determining strategy;
- action planning;
- implementation;
- control and evaluation.

The purchasing management process is schematically illustrated in Figure 5.2. Each of these elements is discussed briefly now.

Purchasing and supply (market) research

Purchasing and supply (market) research refers to the systematic study of all relevant factors which may affect supply and demand of goods and services, for the purpose of securing the company's current and future requirements.

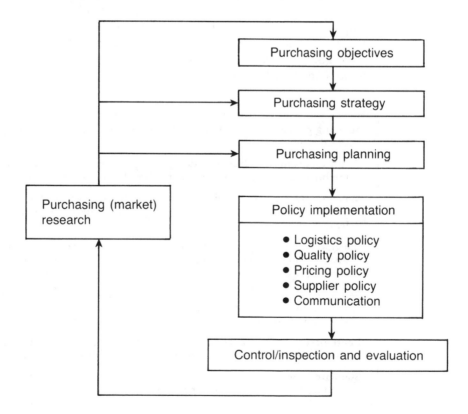

Figure 5.2 The purchasing management process.

Purchasing (market) research is used first of all to support purchasing policies and decision making; it must generate data and alternatives on which the buyer and or management can base better purchasing decisions. Purchasing research can have both an external and an internal focus. Examples of the former are supplier studies, supply market studies and materials cost and price analyses. Examples of the latter are analysis of the company's purchasing portfolio and analysis of the costs that may be related to holding inventory and the quality costs of incoming materials.

A detailed description of the role and significance of purchasing market research is included in Chapter 6.

Purchasing and supply objectives, strategy and planning

Based upon the company's overall objectives, purchasing objectives will relate to cost-reduction, reduction of the supplier base, improving product quality, lead time reduction and so on. Through these objectives the company directs, manages and controls its purchasing activities and relationships with suppliers. In line with these purchasing and supply objectives purchasing management can focus on different areas for action (see Figure 5.3).

Important decisions need to be made in terms of supplier strategies. How many suppliers are needed per product category? For what product categories are we going to reduce or increase the number of suppliers? Are we going to pursue a relationship based upon partnership or one based upon competitive

---

Sourcing policy – determining dependency on suppliers and designing plans to reduce this dependency.

Direct versus indirect buying – determining the (possible) cost benefits of buying from importers and distributors, or buying directly from the manufacturer.

Make-or-buy analysis – analysis of savings opportunities by eliminating particular production activities and buying the required products from third parties; buy-or-lease may be considered as an alternative.

Integration between purchasing and other functional areas – plans aimed at removing interface problems between purchasing and materials management, purchasing and engineering, and between purchasing and financial administration or treasury.

Setting up a purchasing information and control system – analysis of purchasing's information needs and design of an automation plan; possibilities of linking this system with existing information systems in other functional areas.

Centralized or decentralized purchasing – balancing cost benefits and strategic considerations related to a centralized or decentralized organization of purchasing.

Standardization – determining possibilities to achieve standardization in order to reduce product and supplier variety; balancing savings and risks.

Figure 5.3 Examples of areas for action in purchasing.

bidding? For what products do we need to source globally and for what products do we need to find local suppliers? These and other aspects are covered in the commodity sourcing strategy document.

Implementation of purchasing policy

Important areas to consider when implementing purchasing and supply policy are supply, product and supplier quality, materials costs and prices, supplier policy and communication policy (see Table 5.1).

- *Supply.* Supply is aimed at the optimization of both the ordering process and the incoming materials flow. Purchasing order processing entails handling of purchasing requisitions, orderprocessing and expediting, and development of efficient, computer-supported order routines. Materials and supply planning relates to issuing materials delivery schedules to suppliers, reducing supplier lead times, troubleshooting in case of delivery problems, reducing (pipeline) inventories, and monitoring supplier delivery performance.
- *Product and supplier quality.* Central to this aspect are the materials specifications. Two important subjects of concern here are purchasing's early involvement in design and product development and improving product and supplier quality performance. Activities which may contribute to both areas are:

  - standardization of materials – by striving for simplification or standardization of product-specifications, the buyer may reduce product variety resulting in both cost reduction and a lesser supplier dependence at the same time;
  - a purchasing policy focused on the life cycle of the end products – there is not much point in investigating material quality improvements used in products which will be eliminated shortly;
  - specific quality improvements – negotiating targets on improving reject rates, reducing incoming inspection, and negotiating quality agreements;

Table 5.1   Aspects of purchasing policy

Tools	Aspects
Supply policy	Purchasing order processing
	Materials and supply planning
Product and supplier quality policy	Early involvement in development
	Improving suppliers' quality performance
Materials cost policy	Control of materials costs and prices
	Reduction of materials costs and prices
Supplier policy	Sourcing policy
	Improvement of supplier performance
Communication policy	Internal contacts
	External contacts

- agreeing on and gradually extending permanent warranty conditions that are to be provided by the supplier;
- initiating special programmes in the field of value analysis to simplify product design and/or reduce product costs.

- *Materials cost policy.* The objective of materials cost policy is twofold: first, to obtain control of materials cost and prices in such a way that suppliers are unable to pass on unjustified price increases to the company. Second, to systematically reduce the supplier's materials cost through joint, well-prepared action plans. In order to be successful on both aspects a thorough knowledge of the supplier's pricing policies and cost structure is required. In this context, understanding and knowledge of market structures and of the susceptibility of the price paid to market and cost factors is necessary. It should be decided for what products to build detailed cost-models, for what products to monitor underlying cost factors, and for what products to develop detailed materials budget estimates.
- *Supplier policy.* The supplier policy is focused on the systematic management of the company's supplier base. First, decisions need to be made for what commodities to pursue a multiple sourcing strategy or to go for single sourcing or a partnership relationship. Suppliers who actually perform best should be rewarded with more business in the future. Targets and possible projects for future co-operation should be determined carefully. Relationships with suppliers who consistently fail to meet the company's expectations should be terminated. However, such decisions need to be made based on detailed data on how the supplier performed in the past and be implemented carefully.
- *Communication policy.* The company's purchasing policies need to be communicated both internally and to suppliers. Increasingly, companies use their Intranet for the former. At this time many companies employ their own Purchasing Website (see Memo 5.3) in order to communicate their future materials requirements and ways of working to their suppliers. The next step is that preferred suppliers have access to the customer's Intranet through which internal users can order directly from them through their electronic catalogues. The facilities to communicate both internally and externally for buyers have considerably improved over the past years. Most companies at this time are only at the beginning of discovering the vast opportunities in purchasing and supply that the new electronic media offer.

Control/inspection and evaluation

Purchasing management must see to it that both results and activities, that have been planned, are realized within the available financial resources. To this end the actual performance, obtained through purchasing activities, must be periodically checked against the purchasing plans. In most cases reports are required about the savings and costs reductions realized through (cross-functional) purchasing activities. Furthermore, the performance of suppliers

MEMO 5.3: Reverse marketing: Sony

The Internet site of Sony (see Figure 5.4) provides an interesting example of how large manufacturers communicate with their suppliers nowadays. New suppliers are explicitly invited to study Sony's purchasing policy and pre-qualification procedure and to react to vacant orders for components. In fact, Sony uses the WWW as a marketing instrument in order to attract new suppliers.

Also other progressive manufacturers have a purchasing website on the World Wide Web – interesting sites are those of NASA and Siemens (Website addresses of these and other companies can be found at the website of the Institute for Purchasing and Supply Development of Eindhoven University of Technology (www.tue.nl/tm/ipsd). On their Internet sites the following information can be found:

- description of the organization and product/market;
- description of the purchasing and supplier;
- questionnaire for suppliers for prequalification;
- structure of the purchasing department;
- list of persons to contact;
- invitation to submit quotations for certain products or services;
- description of the quality system used for supplies;
- general purchasing conditions;
- recent information from the press which may be relevant for suppliers.

This is just one example of how manufacturers are using the Internet to communicate with their (future) suppliers. See Chapter 6 for a more detailed discussion on how the Internet can be used for supplier market survey and actual buying transactions.

should be checked periodically through vendor performance reports. These subjects need to be reported to management through a consistent procedure so that management is able to assess overall purchasing performance.

As Figure 5.2. shows, the purchasing management process in fact is a closed loop. If one of the elements gets unsufficient attention, the effect will be that activities will get out of control. When objectives and concrete targets are absent, this will lead to a situation in which purchasing activities will lack clear guidance. When objectives and targets have not been translated into detailed action plans, this will lead to a lack of understanding of who is responsible for doing what. The absence of a management reporting structure often is a prime reason why managers do not understand what purchasing has contributed to the company's bottom line. In many companies, elements of this purchasing management process are ill structured. This is one of the reasons why purchasing in those companies has little professionalism. Most problems related to purchasing and supply management, therefore, are problems of management rather than that they are related to the purchasing area itself.

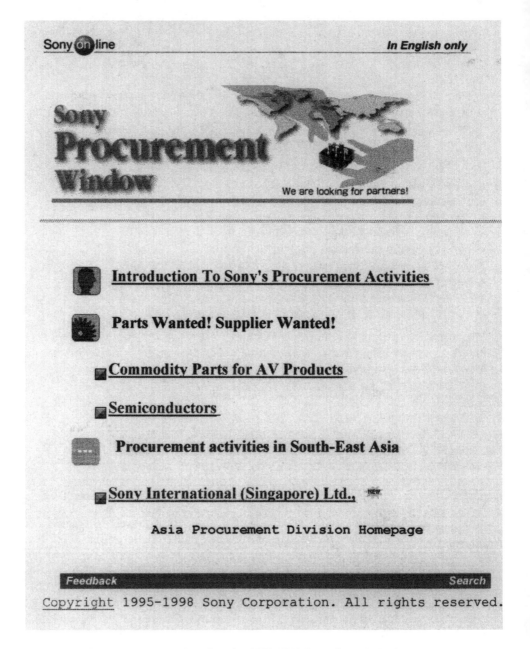

Figure 5.4 Sony Procurement Window (© 1995–1998 Sony Corporation)

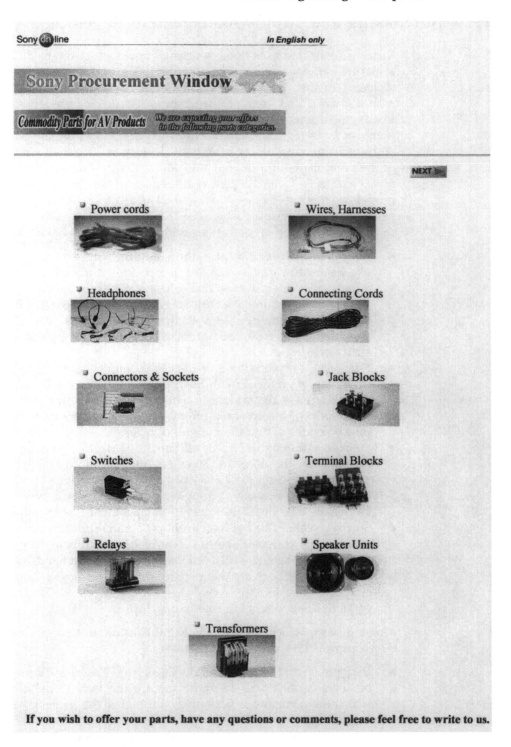

Figure 5.4   *(continued)*

How purchasing and supply management develops over time

Purchasing structures in large companies nowadays are very different from those structures in place during the 1970s or 1980s, and they will, beyond doubt, be different in the future. Two decades ago concepts like purchasing portfolio management, total cost of ownership, supplier-partnerships, early supplier involvement and cross-functional buying teams were not known. Since then many new strategic and organizational concepts in the field of purchasing and supply chain management have been developed. The professional development of the purchasing function in organizations can be analysed from different angles and/or aspects. Over the past years many authors have suggested conceptual models on this subject (see Van Weele *et al.* 1998 for an overview). Most authors assume a stage-wise or step-wise development of purchasing and supply management within organizations with the following characteristics:

- *Integrated final stage*. Most authors assume the existence of a final stage of excellence towards which all improvement efforts should be directed. Almost all models show a final phase where purchasing is integrated in the major lines of business. At this stage line management is actively involved in purchasing strategies and tactics. Also at this stage, it is assumed, purchasing processes are organized around multi-disciplinary, team-based structures.
- *Purchasing's organizational status*. Most models point out that purchasing firstly reports rather low in the organizational hierarchy. Next there may be some degree of centralization, which in a business unit structure will turn to some form of co-ordinated purchasing (where responsibility for purchasing policy resides within the individual business units).
- *Supplier management*. The development of supplier management is another similarity in the different development models. In the first stage, supplier management seems to be reactive ('opportunity driven'). In the next phase, it becomes more proactive ('supplier performance improvement'), and in the last phase it becomes relationship management ('partnership').
- *Supplier relationships*. Most authors assume that, as purchasing moves through the different stages of development, relationships with suppliers will change. Starting with a purchasing department handling many suppliers at 'arms length'. In the next stage, purchasing has reduced its number of suppliers considerably so that closer relationships with a smaller number of (preferred) suppliers are able to develop.

Major drivers, which influence how purchasing and supply management will develop over time, are considered to be:

- *Business context*. It is generally assumed that the more competitive the business context and the more mature the technology in the industry, in which the company is operating, the higher the pressure on purchasing to contribute to the bottom line will be.
- *Company strategy*. The more explicit the company is about the goals and objectives it wants to realize and the more formalized the planning process,

the larger the chance that purchasing issues are integrated into the overall company strategy.

- *Systems development.* Modern information and communication technologies are considered to be important enablers for the implementation of modern purchasing and supply management concepts.
- *Top management commitment.* This relates to the degree to which top management shows active interest in, and is actively involved in, purchasing strategy and supply issues.
- *Functional leadership.* This relates to the personality of the purchasing manager, his management style and prominence.

The approach that has been described by Keough (1993) is one of the most interesting ones. It is very detailed; it identifies five stages of development and assumes a direct causal relationship between the industry a company is in and the stage of development in purchasing. For the remainder of this chapter this model is taken as the point of departure. The author has tried, however, to integrate and combine some valuable insights from other contributors in order to arrive at an integrated purchasing developmental model.

Based upon these general parameters the following six-stage purchasing developmental model has been identified (see Figure 5.5):

Stage 1 'Transaction orientation; serve the factory'

In this first stage the primary task of purchasing is to find appropriate suppliers and ensure that the plant does not run out of raw materials and supplied components. There is no explicit purchasing strategy in place. Formulation of purchasing goals is very rudimentary and intuitive. The value added of the purchasing function is considered to be securing availability of the right materials and goods for production. The organizational structure can be characterized by a decentralized sub-department at plant level, mostly under the responsibility of a production or logistics manager. The purchasing function is strongly orientated on operational and administrative activities. Non-production buying is predominantly done by users themselves, and is considered by purchasing as of secondary importance. There is very little knowledge of what is exactly the total purchasing spend of the company. The culture is 'reactive'. Management is based on complaints. No complaints means purchasing does a good job. The information systems, if in place already, are developed by purchasing and very much administratively oriented. The purchasing staff consists usually of operational and administrative buyers, strongly task oriented, and with little education for the job.

Stage 2 'Commercial orientation; lowest unit price'

At this stage a pro-active type of purchasing manager is recruited who can negotiate credibly with suppliers for lower prices. Striving for the lowest unit

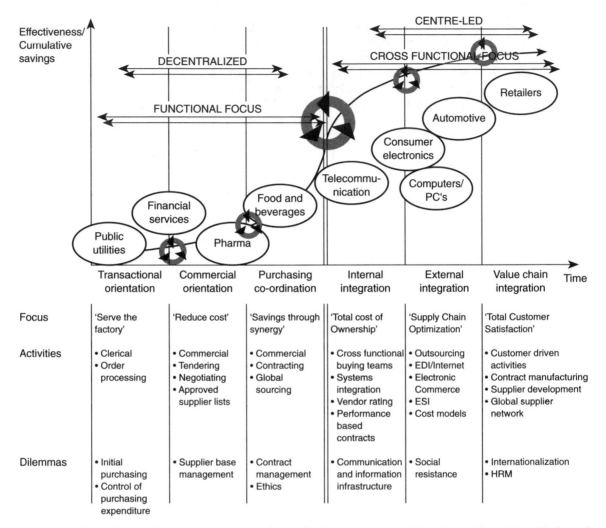

Figure 5.5 Towards a coherent purchasing and supply development model (adapted from Van Weele and Rozemeijer (1998)).

cost requires some independence from functions like product development, engineering and manufacturing. As a result purchasing, while reporting to a senior executive, has more autonomy at lower organizational levels (Lysons, 1996). Purchasing strategy at this stage is characterized by a sharp focus on low prices. The purchasing function has its own department at plant level, reporting directly to the plant manager, who is interested in the savings purchasing adds to the bottom line. At this stage the purchasing function more and more becomes a specialist function. Specialist buyers are organized around different product groups. Buyers are concentrating on negotiating and contracting 'good deals'. The culture is that of playing hard negotiations with many suppliers. Management monitors on low prices and savings. Performance measurement is focused primarily on price (-variance) and delivery performance of the suppliers. Cost savings are used as a prime performance indicator for assessing purchasing's overall effectiveness. Purchasing staff consists of operational and initial buyers with 'hands on' experience. Important skills are negotiating skills and the ability to make price comparisons.

Stage 3 'Co-ordinated purchasing'

Led by a strong central purchasing department to implement uniform buying policies and systems, the emphasis here lies on cross unit co-ordination and compliance with nationally negotiated contracts. This stage may lead to purchasing bureaucracy and lack of responsiveness from the decentralized business units. At this stage for the first time there is some kind of strategy formulation, aimed at capturing the benefits from internal co-ordination and synergy. Apart from price and costs, the purchasing function is seen as having an important influence on the quality level of purchased products. The importance of the non-production buying becomes recognized by purchasing. Slowly the purchasing function is getting some attention from top management. However, the rest of the organization is still not convinced of the value adding potential of the purchasing function. Supplier management is a central issue at this stage and is characterized by looking for synergy by bundling purchasing power of the different divisions and adoption of differentiated supplier strategy based upon portfolio-analysis techniques. The organizational structure of the purchasing function is a centralized purchasing department on divisional level. Formaliza-tion of the purchasing process and procedures is at full speed. The purchasing organization is (still) strongly product oriented. The culture is characterized by a great amount of attention for communication and the intention to co-operate more internally between business units. Computerized information systems are in place now, but still not linked to each other. The stand-alone databases are linked over the divisions, but not yet fully integrated. Purchasing staff has a specific purchasing background and training and there is a large number of different purchasing jobs in place. Training is aimed at analytical skills, total quality management and communication skills.

Stage 4 'Internal integration: cross-functional purchasing'

At this stage the emphasis is on cross-functional problem solving with the objective of reducing total systems cost and not just the unit cost of purchased components. These cross-functional efforts often include key suppliers as joint problem solvers and a move from confrontational to partnership sourcing (Lysons, 1996). Until this stage the purchasing function was very much functionally oriented, and trying to organize the company around the purchasing function. At this stage purchasing is becoming more process-oriented, trying to organize the purchasing function around the internal customers. In this stage there is serious attention for non-production purchasing. The strategic importance of the purchasing function comes to full recognition, and purchasing is involved in strategic issues like core / non-core questions and make-or-buy decisions. The structure is 'centre-led'; operational buying disappears in the line, i.e. is integrated with materials planning and/or scheduling or line planning. The culture is characterized by team-based management, often by means of cross-functional teams. Improvement actions are aimed at integrating the purchasing processes over the different divisions. In this stage the focus is still internal, however, process oriented. Information systems are integrated with that of other departments/functions and divisions, but not yet with those of the most important suppliers. Purchasing performance measurement is done in the form of internal customer satisfaction surveys and benchmarking. People involved in the purchasing process have a broad business perspective and a high educational level. Skills looked for at this stage are strong team-building abilities, strong communication skills.

Stage 5 'External integration; supply-chain management'

This stage is characterized by an outspoken outsourcing strategy combined with extra attention to co-operation with supply partners on product development and preproduction planning. The purchasing function concentrates on the effects the supply chain has on the resources of the company. Non-production buying is fully supported and/or executed by the purchasing function. Users order themselves against corporate contracts through advanced computer systems to which some major suppliers have been hooked up. This is especially true for the non-production area. Purchasing works hard to make things simple for their internal customers, by using systems contracting, purchasing cards, electronic business and catalogues and/or EDI. Supplier management becomes supply chain management at this stage. Companies invest a lot to really involve supply partners in different business processes, instead of just buying goods and services from them as efficiently and effectively as possible. Responsibility for initial purchasing resides with cross-functional teams (inter-divisional and inter-organizational) and is no longer executed by a separate department. There are residential engineering teams, and improvement teams with members from different disciplines, divisions and organizations (suppliers). Integration with other disciplines, divisions and especially suppliers is at full speed, to enable integrated supply chain management. The management style is results driven, though supportive and coaching at the same time. The culture is characterized by participation and consensus style decision making. Important skills are knowledge of total-cost-of-ownership principles, strategic supply chain management, and general managerial and leadership abilities. Information systems are not only integrated internally, but also with those of the partner suppliers.

Stage 6 'Value chain orientation'

The 'purchasing' strategy in this stage will be based on the recognition that most important for success is delivering value to the end customer. To satisfy the needs in end-customer markets, subcontractors seek for support among their suppliers. Suppliers are consistently challenged to support their customer's product/ market strategies and to actively participate in product development. The goal is to design the most efficient and effective value chain possible to serve the end-customer. Purchasing strategy is evaporated in the total business strategy. The orientation is both stream upwards as well as downwards. In fact the traditional marketing and purchasing functions are integrated, and have become 'virtual' in the company. The functioning is based on a shared vision carried by all organizational members. The culture is entrepreneurial. Information systems are integrated as much as possible.

Although this model may seem rather straightforward, some critical remarks must be directed towards it. First, the model has never been tested by thorough academic research. It is important to question and test the validity and reliability of this model. Is the process of development in purchasing a rational process, as the model suggests, or rather an irrational one? Does purchasing development really take place as a process of continuous change or is it in reality characterized more by step-changes and discontinuity? What change strategies underlie purchasing development processes in organizations? Do all organizations follow the stages identified or can some stages be skipped? To what extent are purchasing managers the most decisive actors in the process of purchasing development? Or are they rather receptive in general and are the real change agents coming from other disciplines? More research is warranted in order to use this model as a term of reference for guiding purchasing and supply's organizational and professional development.

Summary

In summary the argument is that most companies have a large potential for improvement in the area of purchasing management. A systematic approach of the purchasing policy can help make this potential visible and accessible.

The tasks, responsibilities and authority of the purchasing function must be established first: securing supply of required materials and services at consistent quality from reliable suppliers is the prime task and responsibility for purchasing. However, activities should not be exclusively limited to this. Purchasing and supply management has more to do. Purchasing and supply management should also strive for continuously improving the price/value ratio in the relationship with suppliers. Materials price control and cost reduction are therefore important policy areas. At the same time the risk exposure, in terms of the company's dependence on suppliers, should be minimized. Furthermore, the buyer should be alert to technological innovations that take place in his supplier markets, which may be beneficial to the company.

Professional purchasing requires effective communication both internally and externally. Purchasing procedures and policies should be approved by top management and communicated to the internal users. Simple brochures and leaflets, which explain how purchasing prefers to work with suppliers and what may be expected in terms of professional support may be helpful. The new electronic media also provide new and vast opportunities in this respect.

Managing purchasing implies that all elements of the purchasing management process are defined. Purchasing objectives need to be derived from the overall company policy and should support this. They need to be translated into detailed sourcing strategies and action plans, indicating what performance will be targeted for in terms of cost reduction, quality improvement, improving supply performance and internal efficiency. Finally, purchasing management should provide periodical, detailed management reporting.

Putting these elements of the purchasing management process in place takes time, however. This explains why differences exist in purchasing operations between companies, even if they operate in the same type of industry. The purchasing development model, which has been presented in this chapter, provides a picture of the stages companies may go through when they want to develop purchasing professionalism. However, this model should be used carefully, for all stages may not be relevant for all types of commodities, companies and industries, as some authors may want us to believe.

Assignments

5.1   In this chapter four major tasks and responsibilities have been described which can be attributed to purchasing and supply management. What are these? It has been argued that these four tasks and responsibilities should not necessarily be in line with each other. Provide at least four situations where two or more of these tasks and responsibilities may be conflicting. How would you solve these conflicts?

5.2   Why would communications both internally and to suppliers be so important for effective purchasing? Who would you see as the most important 'competitor' of a buyer? How would you prevent 'back-door selling' from a supplier's representative?

5.3   A reporting structure has been presented as an essential part of the purchasing management process. If you were a purchasing manager, what would you report to your superiors on a monthly basis? Would you report the same thing to your production and logistics manager? Discuss!

5.4   Reduction of the company's technological and supply risk was presented as an important purchasing task. What exactly is meant by these terms? Explain. What positive actions could companies take to reduce their technological and supply risk exposure in their relationships with suppliers?

5.5   Management has requested you to develop a cost-down programme for your organization related to non-production buying. What would such a cost-down programme look like? What structure would you give to it? How would you execute it? Describe and present.

PART TWO

PLANNING

PURCHASING MARKET RESEARCH

6

Learning objectives

After studying this chapter you should understand the following:

- The role and importance of purchasing market research in the purchasing management process.
- The most important characteristics and types of purchasing market research.
- How to organize for purchasing market research.
- How to conduct purchasing market research.
- Major areas for purchasing market research.

CASE STUDY
Supply market research through the Internet

Using the Internet to locate and evaluate suppliers just got easier. Finding a supplier and determining its adequacy, often two separate endeavors, can now be combined into one 'Net-based chore. Renowned business information company Dun & Bradstreet has teamed with SupplyBase, a San Francisco-based web-directory firm, to offer online supplier directories that include detailed information on supplier performance and manufacturing capacity.

According to PURCHASING's recent Internet-usage survey . . . researching potential suppliers is the number-one reason buyers log on to the Internet. Chris Golec, vice president of marketing at SupplyBase, noticed a similar trend. 'Manufacturers were looking for reliable third-party information to differentiate suppliers based on performance, risk, and other business factors,' says Golec.

Dave Otterness, director of supplier management for Flextronics International, an electronics contract manufacturer, has used the D&B/ SupplyBase directories. 'It is difficult to determine if a supplier's information is accurately portrayed on the Internet, or if the company has sufficient expertise to handle high-volume projects,' says Otterness. 'Integrating D&B's supplier-evaluation tools with SupplyBase's industry-capability information will reduce business risk and increase sourcing productivity.'

Finding and assessing a supplier on one of these sites is quite a seamless process. For example, a buyer . . . in search of recycled plastic materials might have an experience like this: from a list of five supplier categories, the buyer chooses 'materials,' and then from a menu of more specific industries, 'recycled plastics.' The buyer can choose to narrow the search by geography

Continued on page 118

and the next screen contains relevant suppliers. By clicking on one of the suppliers, the buyer comes to a profile page containing a brief company profile, product showcase, RFQ option, and contact information. Included prominently on this page is the supplier's standard D&B D-U-N-S number, hyperlinked to D&B's information store on that company.

According to Chris Golec, once the buyer has identified a prospective supplier, detailed D&B reports, including the supplier evaluation report (SER) and the supplier performance review (SPR), are available for purchase. The SER measures the financial stability of a supplier and quantifies the risk of doing business with them. The SPR determines how well a supplier performs in key areas, like quality, tech support, and delivery, relative to the industry average.

(Source: Vigoros (1998))

Introduction

Over the past years the Internet has become available to buyers as a professional tool for investigating supplier markets. A wide variety of supplier data bases is available nowadays, providing links between supplier directories and providers of financial and supply market information. Through this and the rapidly improving search facilities business-to-business markets have become much more transparent. The Internet even provides consumers and professional buyers with new tools which facilitate tendering, ordering, shipment and payment. Through these new tools the productivity of many purchasing departments has increased, whilst at the same time the quality of purchasing decision making has improved.

This chapter covers the subject of purchasing and supply market research. A major objective of purchasing market research is to ascertain sound decision making. Just as for other types of research, purchasing market research has to identify and analyse the risks related to important purchasing decisions. Purchasing market research will not reduce the risks related to decision making. However, it makes these risks more visible and transparent.

Some authors make a distinction between purchasing research and purchasing market research. Purchasing research, then, refers to subjects concerning the internal organization (such as research on the composition of the purchase assortment, its pricing, research on buyers' workload, the internal efficiency). Purchasing market research refers to the external suppliers' market. It contains analyses of macro-economic developments in supplier countries, analyses of supply and demand of important raw materials, and assessments of the (financial) strengths and weaknesses of the individual supplier organization. In this chapter the focus will be on purchasing market research only and will show what areas and aspects to consider. Also some research techniques that can be used will be discussed. At this point we will present the possibilities, opportunities and risks related to using the Internet for this purpose. Finally the subject of how to organize for purchasing market research will be discussed.

Why purchasing market research?

The need for systematic purchasing market research has been increasing in recent years. Many large companies, like IBM, Honda of America, Lucent Technologies and Philips Electronics have introduced corporate commodity teams which are responsible for the world-wide sourcing of strategic parts and materials. Relentlessly, these teams look for the best-in-class suppliers for their materials and service needs. Originally supported by specialized staff departments, the corporate commodity buyers increasingly commit to conduct purchasing market research themselves. The Internet increasingly provides better and more up to date information on supply markets in a faster and more convenient way. What factors have led to a greater need for active supply market research? The major ones are:

- *Continuing technological developments*. As was seen earlier, every company, whether industrial or trade, in order to stay competitive has to concentrate on product innovation and quality improvement. When investing in new technologies the question arises: should we develop new technologies ourselves or should we buy them? Strained financial resources often lead managers to the latter option. The make-or-buy decision demands a lot of research, as does the final supplier selection decision once the decision has been made to buy. Buyers have to refresh their knowledge constantly about new technological developments which are going on in their supply markets, through product and supplier research.
- *Supply market dynamics*. International supply markets are constantly on the move – export facilities can suddenly be limited because of changes in political arrangements between countries, suppliers can disappear as a result of bankruptcy, suppliers may be acquired by a competitor with several consequences for the price level and continuity of supply. Demand side changes may similarly occur – demand for a product can increase enormously (for example demand for Pentium microprocessors in the mid-1990s) resulting in a scarcity situation. Buyers, then, have to anticipate likely changes in a product's demand and supply situation and thus develop a better understanding of the price dynamics of their commodities.
- *Changes in Western society*. The relatively high wages level in Western Europe has led to changes in the suppliers' market. An example is the change in textile supply for most European retailers, who shifted from local to European suppliers and who now have shifted their primary supply base to the Far East due to much lower wages. The same trend can be recognized for many industrial products (varying from television glass to car tyres). For a lot of products, industrial production has shifted from Western countries to the Far East or the developing countries and this development probably will continue.
- *Monetary developments*. The ever increasing volatility of some major currencies poses new problems to internationally operating buyers. High inflation in some countries, large governmental budget deficits, rapidly changing currency exchange rates may require immediate action from buyers in terms of a reallocation of their materials requirements.

These are some of the factors which underline the importance of systematic purchasing market research.

Purchasing market research: definition

Fearon (1976) defines purchasing market research as:

> systematic gathering, classifying and analysing data considering all relevant factors that influence the procurement of goods and services for the purpose of meeting present and future company requirements in such a way that they contribute to an optimal return.

Some aspects of this definition warrant further explanation:

- Purchasing market research can relate to research which is conducted at regular intervals, such as monitoring market prices of strategic commodities. However, it may also be conducted on a project-basis. Examples of this type of research are: developing a detailed cost model for a strategic commodity, auditing suppliers or conducting a specific country study against the background of global sourcing initiatives.
- Purchasing market research can be qualitative or quantitative in character. **Qualitative research** is research based on gathering views on opinions on trends and developments going on in a specific industrial sector. Usually this type of research is based upon interviews with industry experts. **Quantitative research** is based on numerical data possibly derived from general statistics and other public sources. For example: what is the market share of a specific supplier? How do supply and demand develop over time? How can supply and demand patterns be clarified by other macro-economic indicators? Other examples are cost-breakdown analyses which explain whether the price charged by a given supplier is fair or not. Most supply market research covers both aspects. Supplier benchmark studies are examples of both quantitative and qualitative research.
- Purchasing market research can focus on short-term as well as long-term issues. Concentration tendencies and materials shortages, which are to be expected, in certain industries may require that the company covers its materials needs for a longer period and may foster long-term relationships with suppliers. Short-term supply market analysis may be required when a major supplier unexpectedly is suffering from production problems or goes bankrupt.

As demonstrated in Chapter 5, purchasing market research is an essential element of the purchasing management process. Its major benefit is that the data gathered through it may serve as a thorough and objective basis for key purchasing decisions.

How to structure purchasing market research

Figure 6.1 shows the most important steps to be made, when conducting purchasing market research. These are in more detail:

MEMO 6.1: Electronic sources of supply market information

Mid-size buying organizations with slim budgets and modest resources are not out of the electronic procurement game. Used properly, the Web offers even small-volume buyers the opportunity to streamline sourcing and cut costs with little or no monetary investment, according to operators of such sites.

Typical of such sites is e-Chemicals, Inc., based in Ann Arbor, Mich. From this site buyers can source and purchase from a multiple-supplier product database, with no financial obligations . . . Drawing buyers to these sites is the fact that free registration is often the only requisite to browse and to buy.

Since early 1998, e-Chemicals (www.e-chemicals.com) has offered chemicals buyers a one-stop e-sourcing solution on the Internet, designed to improve the procurement, sale, and distribution of industrial chemicals. After registering, buyers can search across a consolidated catalog and obtain what are said to be 'best prices,' without costly and time-consuming negotiation. 'Giving time back to the customer is a huge issue in this marketplace,' says e-Chemicals President Alf Sherk, a sales and marketing veteran from Dow Chemical.

Twelve suppliers have committed to feature their products on the e-Chemicals site–including chemical giants DuPont, Dow, and Elf Atochem–and supplier recruitment will be an ongoing mission. Catalog maintenance is handled by participating suppliers, who can make real-time pricing and availability changes electronically.

To handle logistics, e-Chemicals has partnered with carrier giant Yellow Freight. Buyers can check order status via a seamless electronic interchange between e-Chemicals and Yellow. 'Current research says that checking order status is one of the top reasons buyers call suppliers,' says Sherk. 'Now this can be done more efficiently and at any time of day.' . . .

Other electronic marketplaces:*

- Metal Suppliers Online (www.suppliersonline.com)–metals
- MetalSite (www.metalsite.net)–metals
- NetBuy (www.netbuy.com)–electronic components
- The Plastics Network (www.plasticsnet.com)–plastics
- BioSupplyNet (www.biosupplynet.com)–biomedical research supplies
- Chemconnect (www.chemconnect.com)–chemicals
- PurchasingGuide.com (www.purchasingguide.com)–multi-industry

(Source: Vigoros (1999))

* Other websites which are relevant for buyers can be found at the website of the Institute for Purchasing and Supply Development of Eindhoven University of Technology (www.tue.nl/tm/ipsd).

---

1 *Determine objectives.* What exactly is the problem to be solved? What information is desired? How accurate does the information have to be? These questions are not a problem if the research is carried out by the buyer himself. If, however, the research is delegated to others a good briefing is of great importance, in order to generate useful information from it. Are we talking about a global market review or is an extensive description of the

product assortment and the supplier's marketing policy required? When does the answer have to be available? These aspects should be covered in a concise briefing.

2   *Cost–benefit analysis*. What will be the costs of the research? How many man hours are required for the research? Will the value of the obtained information outweigh the expense?

3   *Feasibility study*. What information is already available on the company? What information is available from publications and statistics? There may be more information readily available than originally expected. A good (computer-based) documentation service can be invaluable. On many issues international (computer) databases exist (see Memo 6.1) – and specialized agencies may conduct market and product studies at limited costs. If a public database cannot be found directly, it is worthwhile asking for such a survey at services such as university libraries or economic information services. The next research step should only be taken once it is confirmed that the required information is unavailable in the form of publications or statistics.

4   *Design of a research plan*. Specific action is sometimes needed to obtain information, as for example in the case of auditing a specific supplier. Another example is a survey to analyse possibilities for a 'kitting' contract – a situation in which the buyer looks for opportunities to transfer a coherent assortment of products (e.g. fasteners, computer supplies) from many suppliers to only one supplier. In addition to desk research, interviews with buyers and suppliers will be required, followed by field research. It is important to prepare well for such research through a detailed project plan.

5   *Execution of research activities*. In the execution stage it is important to follow the project plan prepared earlier. Decision making is often dependent on a certain amount of information being available. Excuses for lapses in research activity cannot be accepted – potential problems should have been anticipated while designing the time plan and estimating the workload.

6   *Preparing research report and evaluation*. When the research is finished a report has to be prepared – this has to contain the assignment, as well as the obtained results. Did the buyer get an answer to his questions? Is the report drawn up in a comprehensive manner? What assumptions underly the obtained results? These are issues that require attention in the report; finally, what is the opinion on the research after it has been carried out? Have the method and the result been satisfactory? These questions have to be considered to prevent mistakes being repeated in the future.

In the case of purchasing market research it is common to differentiate between desk research and field research. **Desk research** is the gathering, analysis and interpretation of data that serve the research assignment, but which have already been gathered by others. In purchasing, this type of research is used the most. Philips Electronics has a special documentation service that continuously gathers general and market-specific technical information. Much of this information is published in the *Purchasing Bulletin*, sent to all buyers in the Benelux countries. Shell has a similar service which is provided by the Sources Planning Group, that

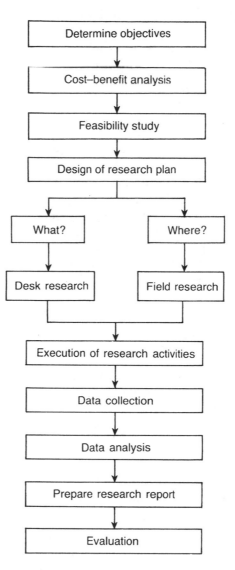

Figure 6.1 How to structure purchasing market research: a stepwise approach.

informs the buyer of suppliers, contracts, market forecasts, etc. Buyers can also address their specific questions and assignments to this service.

Field research is the gathering, analysis and interpretation of information that cannot be obtained by means of desk research. It tries to track down new information; visits to industrial exhibitions and suppliers are examples of field research methods (see Figure 6.2).

Not every research project will follow the phases described above exactly. The available time usually places restrictions on research design and each project will require its own approach so that a standard method is hard to provide.

Subjects of purchasing market research

It will be clear by now that purchasing (market) research covers a wide variety of subjects. Fearon (1976) distinguishes three main areas of investigation.

- *Materials, goods and services.* This kind of research aims at realizing savings or at reducing purchasing-related costs. It can also aim at reducing the risks incurred by the firm with regard to supply by searching for alternative supply sources.
- *Suppliers.* Supplier-related research is concerned with the long-term relationship with a supplier. Questions to be addressed here include, for example, 'Will the supplier continue to be able to satisfy both future technical requirements and our requirements concerning flexible supply?'.
- *Systems and procedures.* A good purchasing information system is of great importance to all buyers and efforts should be directed constantly at improving the supply of information. Information and communications technology offers great possibilities for this, but it has to be guided on the basis of buyers' needs. In connection with this, purchasing research can also focus on simplification of administrative procedures in the relationship between buyers and suppliers.

Another distinction is the one between macro-, meso- and microeconomic research (see Figure 6.3).

- *Macroeconomic research.* This refers to the general economic environment and focuses on factors that can influence the future balance between supply and demand. Examples of these factors are developments in (un)employment in a country, labour costs, inflation, consumer price index, order position.

- Plan visits to trade-fairs on an annual basis
- Request catalogues of the fairs to be visited in advance
- Combine visits, when useful and possible, to different fairs
- Select the stands/suppliers to be visited on the basis of the catalogue
- Think about the subjects to be discussed with the suppliers; what specific information are you after?
- Inform internal departments about intended fair visits; do they have additional subjects to discuss?
- Plan your time carefully; prepare a route before going to the fair
- Take time for the visit
- If going with others, divide tasks
- Report on your impressions; discuss your experiences with others in the firm

---

Figure 6.2   Planning for a trade-fair visit.

- *Mesoeconomic research.* This focuses on specific sectors of industry and at this level a lot of information is often available at central statistical offices and industrial agencies, established in many countries. They have specific information on profitability of the sector, technological developments, labour cost, indirect cost, capacity utilisation, order position, energy consumption etc.
- *Microeconomic research.* This focuses on assessing strengths and weaknesses of individual suppliers and products. Examples are: financial audits of suppliers, quality audits as part of a supplier certification programme, supplier cost analyses, etc. The objective here is to get a thorough understanding of the supplier's specific capabilities and its long-term market position.

Table 6.1 shows typical subject areas for each of the three categories of purchasing market research.

Purchasing market research and information technology[1]

Earlier in this chapter it was illustrated how Internet technology may be used to conduct purchasing market research. Currently, companies are discovering the

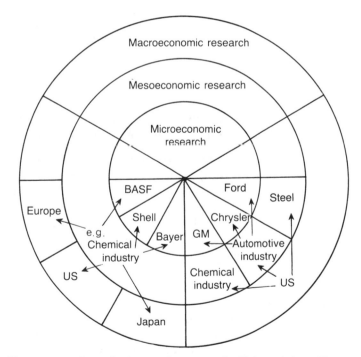

Figure 6.3 Three areas of purchasing market research. (Adapted from Faes and de Weerd, 1983.)

---

[1] This paragraph has been adapted from Van Weele and Rozemeyer (1998a)

Table 6.1   Main parameters to be addressed in purchasing market research (adapted from Van Eck and De Weerd (1981)

Level	Parameter
Macroeconomics	Business cycle and economic growth
	Development of industrial production
	Average utilization rate in industry
	Price development (e.g. currencies, inflation)
	Interest rate
	Development of Wages
	Productivity development
	Political climate
Mesoeconomic	Supply-and-demand analysis
	Utilization rate
	Order situation and sales
	Inventories
	Market structure
Microeconomic	Financial situation
	Organizational structure
	Quality of delivered goods
	Delivery performance
	Delivery lead time
	General conditions
	Service quality
	Ownership and shares
	Cost–price structure
	Price level

many ways in which this new technology may support their purchasing operations and strategies. The following examples further illustrate this point:

- Company's like Grasso, a medium-sized manufacturer of industrial cooling and heating equipment and part of a large German group with business units around the world, have installed a purchasing Intranet within three months enabling exchange of product, supplier and contract information among all sites. Investment: less than $ 35,000, for software (licenses) and three months' preparation. The system is based on Microsoft's Outlook software. Other manufacturing companies, ranging from automotive and computer industry to the beverage and food industry, have built similar systems based on Lotus Notes software.

- Data-suppliers like Yellow Pages, ABC, Kompass and Wer Liefert Was have now available through their Websites vast supplier bases covering supplier addresses in all major EC-countries enabling buyers to conduct market surveys in a very short time. For commodities, long lists of potential suppliers may be developed in just a few minutes. Supplier information (with regard to product assortment, references, financial stability) may be asked for through extensive database searches and directly through e-mail from the supplier. Requests for quotations may be submitted through simple, computer-supported ordering systems or directly through e-mailing the supplier concerned.

- Sony uses its Purchasing Website to attract new suppliers for certain commodities (see also Memo 5.3). Suppliers are requested to react for components which are short of supply. Suppliers may act through filling in the SQA-questionnaire and sending it through e-mail directly to Sony. In this way the Internet is actively being used for 'reversed marketing'. Also NASA and Siemens use their Purchasing Website this way.

- Companies like FedEx, DHL Worldwide Express and UPS provide linkages through the Internet which enable companies to keep track of their deliveries. Some of these sites enable cost breakdowns per port of destination enabling buyers to find their most competitive source of supply for shipment and transportation.

- Although electronic payment is still troublesome and far from safe, developments are going fast in this area. In the consumer goods business some companies have posted impressive turnover figures and financial results (such as CD Direct, Amazon and DELL). Although legally not yet approved, it is expected that Electronic Commerce and payment will grow rapidly in the years to come.

Other examples can be added to this list. Memo 6.2 summarizes how the Internet may be used in the purchasing area nowadays. It will be clear from this list already that the electronification of purchasing will develop very fast. New IT-supported tools will become available for the coming years, and not only for buyers. The same tools will also be available to all other disciplines in the company (who in general are computer-wise much better equipped than their counterparts in the purchasing organization), which will call for a sometimes drastic reorientation of the traditional purchasing function in companies.

Introduction of purchasing market research

Every purchasing department possesses a large amount of purchasing market knowledge and information. The issue for managers is how to make this knowledge and experience available to other departments in an efficient way. Fearon (1976) mentions three possible methods of establishing purchasing market research in a company.

- *Create a separate staff department*. One possibility is to locate all purchasing market research activities in a separate staff department or section. The big advantage is that purchasing market research can then be assigned to specialists, who have knowledge of specific research techniques. If this option is chosen, good communication between researchers and buyers must be ensured to prevent the research from becoming too detailed and/or theoretical.

MEMO 6.2: Internet and Intranet applications in purchasing supply market research

Purchasing market research and supplier selection. Examples are Wer Liefert Was, Yellow Pages, Industrynet, all of which may be used to find (new) suppliers.

Getting the right product specifications. Product descriptions may be derived from Purchasing Extranet.

Checking supplier references. Supplier financial and performance references may be checked from Dun & Bradstreet.

Sending requests for proposal. This may be done through e-mail directly to the supplier or through the websites of supplier data-providers.

Bid information is exposed through specialized intermediaries such as BidCast or Tender Daily.

Virtual auctions. Free Markets Online provides software to organize auctions among suppliers for individual buyers. Some large retailers (such as Wehkamp in The Netherlands) have daily auctions for merchandise on sale.

Reversed marketing. Some large subcontractors and manufacturers (such as NASA and Sony) have a special purchasing website on which they expose products for which they seek new suppliers. Initial screening is done through filling out a detailed questionnaire.

Commodity buying. Some major commodities can now be traced online through the Internet enabling buyers to manage their commodity buyers from hour to hour and enabling them to buy at the right moment.

Shipment tracking. FedEx, DHL Worldwide Express and UPS have extensive websites where tariffs may be asked for express freight and shipments and deliveries may be tracked and traced.

Electronic payment. Payment may be tied to credit cards or special Purchasing Cards, enabling paperless invoice handling.

Education and training. Some universities and professional organizations have websites which present training and educational programmes and virtual programmes in purchasing and supply management.

- *Market research conducted by the buyer.* The advantage of this arrangement is that research will only be done on issues which buyers consider relevant; this also enlarges their involvement in the activity. However, a major drawback is the buyers' lack of time to do the research systematically because they are constantly forced to spend their time on pressing issues. Other disadvantages are the lack of knowledge that most buyers have of market research techniques and potential sources of information, and the lack of a central collection point for all the gathered knowledge.
- *Work with research teams.* A compromise solution is that of forming *ad hoc* research teams, consisting of both buyers and researchers; after the assignment is finished the team is broken up. The advantage of this method is the involvement of the team in the research and, when required, other specialists can be invited to contribute, depending on the progress made. Another advantage is the task orientation of such teams, provided that a clear working plan has been prepared. Although this approach is preferable from a

costs point of view, there are some objections. In practice, it is difficult to work on a research project in combination with day-to-day activities because the latter receive priority, thus affecting the market research. It is for this reason that good project planning is essential. Experience shows that a small, specialist staff department is to be recommended for large companies; for smaller companies the team approach is best. When left to the buyer, market and supplier research will only be carried out during the buyer's spare time. Not surprisingly, companies with dedicated researchers carry out more market research (Fearon, 1976) and this undoubtedly has consequences for the knowledge of the supply markets in these companies.

Summary

The ever-increasing turbulence in global supply markets makes purchasing market research a crucial activity. Supply market research is required in order to keep informed about changes going on in technology, supplier markets, to assess the competitiveness of the current supply base and to keep track of changes in currency rates, to name just a few. These subjects can be investigated by using different techniques. A distinction has been made between qualitative and quantitative research. Purchasing market research can be aimed at providing data on short-term and long-term policy issues.

In setting up research a stepwise approach is recommended. First, the objectives of the research should be clearly formulated. What questions should be answered by this activity. Will the value of the information to be gathered probably outweigh the costs? What information is already known about the subject? In most cases desk research will be sufficient. In some specific cases field research and surveys may be necessary, although these will add to the costs of the activity and its lead time. Finally, the results should be presented in a concise report.

As discussed, the Internet provides ample opportunities to conduct purchasing market surveys. For some commodities and services, information may be found covering all aspects of the purchasing cycle, just by using Internet technology. And these opportunities and facilities expand every day! Therefore it is very important for buyers to keep informed about this medium, since it will make supply markets more transparent than ever before. This is not only true for macro-economic research, but also for branche-studies and individual supplier research.

Most research will probably be done by the buyers themselves. For specific subjects support staff will be convenient. In specific cases, purchasing market research may be done by a specialized outside market research agency. A specialized purchasing staff usually only is found at large, multinational companies.

Assignments

6.1   What would you consider to be the most important internal and external sources of information for purchasing market research. Name at least eight sources for each category.

6.2   Would you feel that purchasing market research is required for every purchased commodity? For what type of products would you feel it would be most appropriate? Link your ideas to the portfolio approach which is presented in Chapter 7.

6.3   Conduct a purchasing market survey, by using Internet technology, for the following commodities:

- 100 tons of steelplate (C1119 Mod. And C1144 free machining steelplates, 1 inch thick, 100 inch wide).
- 10 notebooks, minimum requirements: Pentium II 233 Mhz, 11.3" TFT screen, 2Gb Hard disk.
- A set of the following office supplies:

   - 50 perforators
   - 100 stapling machines
   - 1000 BIC ballpoints
   - 100 Post It noteblocks
   - 1000 A4 notepads (lined)

6.4   A distinction is made between macro-, meso- and microeconomic research. Name some sources of information to be consulted in each of these types of purchasing market research.

6.5   Internet technology is open to everyone. Not only to buyers, but also to users and budget holders within organizations. How would the Internet change the job of a buyer? Discuss.

PURCHASING AND BUSINESS STRATEGY

7

Learning objectives

After studying this chapter you should understand the following:

- The changing international business context and how companies strategically respond.
- The need for companies to focus on their core competencies.
- Major advantages and risks associated with strategic outsourcing.
- The increasing strategic role of the purchasing function.
- How purchasing can support the company's overall competitive strategy.
- How to develop a differentiated purchasing and supplier strategy.

CASE STUDY
Train manufacturing at ABB Traction

ABB Traction, one of the divisions of Asea Brown Boveri, develops, manufactures and sells trains. National railway companies can turn to this division for various types of locomotives and carriages. Business has prospered during the eighties. The company has been able to build a solid market position and has achieved a healthy profitability.

Some years ago, however, the market position of the division was threatened by competition from Yokohama, Japan. The threat was not one of lower costs because a complete train (including locomotive and carriages) could be obtained at more or less the same price in Europe. However, the Japanese competitor had a major advantage in terms of the delivery time, which was about 18 months, while the ABB division promised a delivery period of three years! This was unfortunately also true for other ABB divisions. It was one of the reasons for the 'T-50' programme initiated in the early nineties by ABB's chairman, Mr Percy Barnevik. The objective of this programme was to cut the total cycle time in all subsidiaries of the ABB group in half (hence the name T-50), to be achieved in three years' time. The interesting feature of this objective is that it is cross-functional, affecting all functions within the company, from sales to research and development, and from the administrative function to (of course) purchasing and suppliers.

First, all manufacturing and logistics lead times were benchmarked. The reduction of the total cycle time had to be established against the results of this initial benchmarking – an exercise that proved very interesting! In the case of ABB Traction it showed that 50% of the total cycle time was determined by the suppliers of subassemblies or parts. For example, the supplier of carriage

Continued on page 132

'bogies' had a delivery time of 18 months – the same amount of time that the competitor from Yokohama needed to deliver a complete train! – and this was no exception. A large number of suppliers were shown to be on the critical path and were thus responsible for a major part of the total cycle time. The conclusions were obvious: reducing the cycle time by 50% would require a considerable contribution from suppliers, and therefore from the purchasing function within the company. Reason enough for top management to take specific measures in this area, and not without success!

Introduction

The experience of this European company is not isolated, as evidenced by the automotive industry in Western Europe. A famous study conducted by the Massachusetts Institute of Technology (MIT) during the early nineties showed large gaps between Japanese companies and other automotive manufacturers in terms of competitiveness. Japanese manufacturers were not only able to turn out cars at lower costs but also at a much shorter development lead time! As a result many American and European automotive companies set out to aggressively improve their manufacturing operations. Examples are Chrysler, who initiated a new supplier relationship programme (see Dyer 1996; van Weele and Rozemeijer 1996). And, here, of course General Motors and Volkswagen should be mentioned as companies which hired Ignacio Lopez as their manufacturing and purchasing director. Through his unorthodox and aggressive sourcing and contracting strategies Lopez was able to post important cost savings for the companies he worked for. In both cases he turned a negative financial result, both in Germany and the US, into a positive one.

As companies like Chrysler and Honda of America have shown, suppliers are crucial to an effective and efficient supply chain. Suppliers should be involved, either directly or indirectly, in manufacturers' programmes that aim to reduce the time to market and materials-related costs. Chrysler illustrates this with the development of its 'Viper' (which had to compete with the Corvette of General Motors) (see case study in Chapter 10) using Japanese methods of working with suppliers. The time, which elapsed from the beginning of the development to the first production series took three years, instead of the usual five years. The budget was approximately US$700 million (45% of the budget of Mazda's 'Miata'). How did Chrysler accomplish this? One of the things was that Chrysler used suppliers to do most of the manufacturing; Chrysler contracted out most of the development and engineering work and 90% of all parts.

Increasingly, suppliers are being acknowledged as important sources for competitive advantage. This chapter discusses the strategic role that purchasing and supply management may represent to manufacturing companies and how to develop differentiated supplier strategies to support their overall product/ market and business strategies.

Purchasing and competitive strategy

Over the past decades the competitive situation of West European industry has changed dramatically. First, European manufacturers experience far more competition from countries that were not considered as major producers until some years ago (e.g. Korea, Hong Kong, Singapore, Thailand, Taiwan and China). Second, industry in Western Europe seems to be under-represented in the areas of new technologies and emerging new industries (e.g. the computer industry, telecommunications, chips). Looking at most industrial sectors in Europe it can be seen that many industries seem to be at the stage of saturation or decline (see Memo 7.1).

As a result of this situation, the long-term strategy of many companies nowadays focuses on 'selective growth', i.e. a combination of enhancing the core activity and starting up new, promising activities. One consequence of this

---

MEMO 7.1: How industry life cycles affect the role of purchasing and supply management

The competitive situation of West European industry has changed dramatically over the past two decades. As a result of improved transportation, the rapid progress in information technology and the increased **globalization** of markets, competition (from the Far East in particular) has increased. This competition is manifest in both conventional and new products, and their associated technologies.

Looking at the industrial structure of most European countries, a relatively large number of industries are in the phase of saturation or decline. There are relatively few European companies with a strong position in new, emerging industries, i.e. industries that are in the introduction or growth phase (see Figure 7.1). Most industrial activity (and employment opportunities!) in Europe seem to be situated in the latter two stages of the industry life cycle.

There are apparent differences in competitive strategy depending on the stage in the industry life cycle. In the stages of introduction and growth, companies obtain a market position through research and development, product development, the introduction of new models and varieties and improvement of existing products. Research and development and, of course, marketing, aimed at tailoring products and services to the requirements of specific market segments and target groups, are key success variables here. In the stages of saturation and decline, however, the company can only maintain or reinforce its market position if it is able to sell end products (of basically the same quality and service level) at very competitive prices. Technology in these stages is mature and not subject to significant changes. In other words, during these stages of the industry life cycle measures aimed at cost reduction, quality improvement and lead time reduction play a major role in maintaining or reinforcing the market position. Contracting out non-core activities to specialized suppliers can serve all these objectives. This explains the rising purchasing-to-sales ratio of many industrial enterprises (including Xerox, Electrolux, Philips Electronics, DAF Trucks, Alcatel, Volvo) over the past few years. This in turn results in an increased awareness among top-management of the strategic value of the purchasing function. This Memo also demonstrates the lasting nature of this interest, since no major changes in favour of European companies are expected in the international competitive situation over the next few years.

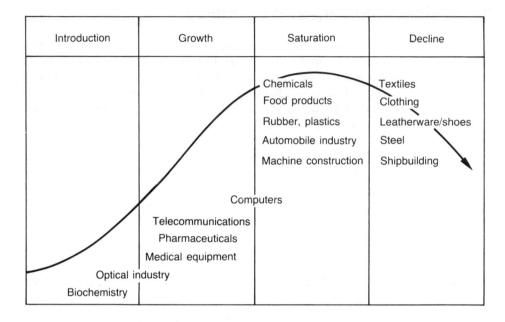

Figure 7.1   The industry life cycle.

strategy is that companies sell off those activities that are not considered to belong to their 'core business'.

In general, the following reasons may underlie this trend.

- *Increased subcontracting, as a result of make-or-buy studies.* Based on internal and external cost price studies, carried out in the context of a so-called 'competitive benchmarking programme', a manufacturer of office equipment discovered that particular manufacturing activities could not be carried out competitively any longer. The internal manufacturing costs appeared to be much higher than the costs of external suppliers. This prompted the manufacturer to start a 'make-or-buy' programme. As a result the company decided to focus its manufacturing on a higher level of assembly. At present, modular components are being sourced from a limited number of preferred suppliers. The company focuses on design, assembly, marketing and sales, and most component manufacturing has ceased. The same trend is observed in other companies. For example, a manufacturer of domestic appliances expects he will be making more use of flexible, universal production equipment in the near future and so specialized activities such as stamping, lathe work and plastic moulding will be contracted out in future (see also Memo 7.2).
- *Buying of finished products instead of components.* Due to the high labour costs level in some European countries, it is hard for some enterprises to compete. For example, the Benelux countries and Scandinavia are expensive for the clothing industry to operate in. This industry is experiencing heavy

> ## MEMO 7.2: Outsourcing pistons at Cummins
>
> The decision to outsource a strategic component is one of the most wrenching for any company. However, it is precisely this willingness to lose a battle in order to win the war that separates industry leaders from the followers. Managers at Cummins were faced with just such a choice in the mid-1980s. Confronted with a need to develop much more advanced piston designs to meet emissions legislation, they discovered the need to make enormous investments in order to upgrade capabilities. The financial payback appeared dubious since Cummins could buy pistons from several suppliers. On the other hand, pistons were the very 'guts' of an engine, and there was an understandable reluctance to relinquish control of this component to a supplier.
>
> An emotional debate raged for over three years. Should Cummins strive to rebuild its piston capability or turn to the best world-wide sources for piston technology? To quell the debate, senior management commissioned a team with representatives from engineering, manufacturing and purchasing to develop and implement an appropriate piston strategy. Engineers first identified the key technologies and capabilities that would be required to specify, design and manufacture pistons. The team visited the four leading piston suppliers and benchmarked internal capabilities relative to these suppliers.
>
> The team discovered that Cummins's internal design and manufacturing capabilities lagged behind those of two suppliers who were world-class technologists. Moreover, these two companies were aggressive innovators. Their scale allowed them to invest more than 20 times as much as Cummins did in product and process research and development. In fact, both suppliers had their own machine-tool divisions and foundries and developed highly specialized machines and metallurgical process. Cumulative volumes that were many times larger than Cummins's allowed them to ride down the experience curve much faster.
>
> Thus not only was Cummins's piston design and manufacturing capability low in relation to the suppliers; but so also was its relative rate of learning. In light of this disparity, it was unlikely that Cummins had any chance of matching the capabilities of these suppliers without substantial investments that were difficult to justify. This objective fact-finding mission confirmed that the right decision was for Cummins to outsource pistons.
>
> (Source: Venkatesan, 1992)

competition from 'low-wage countries' and in recent years there has been a shift of production capacity to developing countries. Large retailers buy the raw materials, which are then sent together with the design to low-wage countries, where the end products are made.

- *Turnkey delivery.* Manufacturers of specialized optical instruments often have to supply their products including sophisticated measuring devices. As a rule these costly devices need to be purchased by the manufacturers from specialized suppliers. To cite another example: manufacturers of industrial fences need to deliver their products' turnkey (at the buyer's request), which means that they have to take care of all installations including safety and surveillance equipment. These relatively expensive products also need to be obtained from specialist suppliers. As a result the purchasing share for these manufacturing companies in the project cost is gradually increasing.

- *Technological development.* In some industries the technology develops at such a pace that even large manufacturers cannot afford the investments needed to keep up. Take for example the computer manufacturers who obtain their microprocessors from specialized suppliers, or the manufacturer of compressors who has to rely on specialized foundries to be able to benefit from new developments in casting technology.

In summary, the changed competitive situation in many West European industries requires that management of many manufacturers focus on their core activities. Specialist activities outside the scope of these core activities are increasingly farmed out. As a consequence, purchasing's share in the cost price of many end products will rise. Hence, purchasing decisions will have a greater influence on the company's financial result. That is why management has become increasingly aware of the purchasing function. The consequences of these developments for integrating purchasing in the company policy will now be discussed.

Cost leadership and differentiation: consequences for manufacturing and purchasing strategy

Every company's goal is to develop a **distinctive, sustainable competitive advantage**. Only then will the company be able to guarantee its long-term survival. In recent years the question of how to obtain such a position has received a lot of attention in the literature. One of the most interesting books on this subject still is the classic written by Porter (1980). According to this author, there are three basic strategies that can lead to a distinguishing market position.

- *Cost leadership.* The main focus of this strategy is to continually work at reducing the cost price of the end product. If a company succeeds in marketing products at a lower cost price than its competitors, it will achieve a satisfactory return. Companies that employ this strategy usually have a strong financial–economic orientation, expressed in meticulous budgeting and reporting procedures and strict control of overheads. This type of strategy is usually only successful if a large market share can be obtained. This makes it possible to manufacture in large volumes, on streamlined production lines, with specialized production equipment.

    This strategy must also pay attention to aspects such as quality and service, but costs come first. Its application is illustrated by some automobile manufacturers (General Motors, Chrysler, Ford), a few computer manufacturers (manufacturers of IBM clones) and some manufacturers of domestic appliances.
- *Differentiation.* This strategy aims at marketing products which are perceived by the customer as being unique. Product individuality can be in the design (Swatch watches), the logo (Lacoste), the technology (Apple), service (American Express) and many other dimensions. Combinations are also

possible; in addition to a high quality technical product, most truck manufacturers have an after-sales service organization that can supply parts within 24 hours all across Europe. In this way these manufacturers anticipate and respond to the problem of downtime which is experienced by every haulier: every hour the truck does not run costs a lot of money! A differentiation strategy aims at creating customer loyalty and brand preferences, thereby reducing the importance of price. If the size of the target group that responds to the unique advantage of the product is limited, the company may have to settle for a smaller market share.

- *Focus strategy.* This strategy aims to serve a particular, clearly defined group of customers in an optimal way. Examples are to be found primarily in the industrial sector (relatively small paper finishing companies that concentrate on finishing the products supplied by printers), or in transportation (some hauliers are equipped specifically for the transportation of clothing, furniture or computers). A focus strategy means that the company studies the activities of the customer group, becomes familiar with the main problems, and provides specific solutions.

The importance of Porter's (1980) division is that the company will have to make a clear choice between these strategic alternatives. The consequence of not making a choice is that the company will be unable to build up a sustainable competitive advantage in the end-user markets. This will probably result in a mediocre return accompanied by a small market share!

This reasoning seems simple, but applying it in practice is something else again. Many entrepreneurs have a hard time in making a choice. They frequently want everything at the same time – very high quality and high customer service at the lowest price!

Limiting ourselves to the first two strategies, in Porter's view a company cannot realize both *simultaneously* because the necessary support in terms of organization and company culture is different for each of the strategies.

A company that strives for cost leadership will emphasize cost reduction. Since stocks raise costs, they are kept as low as possible; investments in automation are analysed with regard to their efficiency; strict budget systems and budget reports prevent cost overruns. The production tasks are prepared in detail and, to run as efficiently as possible, breakdowns must be prevented. Because everything has been prepared so thoroughly and high-quality technical production equipment is used, there is no reliance on improvization or human creativity. Production managers are judged on the capacity utilization of their machines and changes in production planning are not really acceptable, because they would result in production loss and therefore increased costs. Production companies that aspire to cost leadership are usually large, integrated companies that take advantage of effects of scale through vertical integration (textile industry, food products industry).

The company that applies a differentiation strategy operates in a completely different way and there is far less attention to costs (although they are not completely ignored). A company that wants to respond flexibly to customer requirements is constantly searching for opportunities to reduce internal lead times.

Production utilization may vary over time, which means that personnel must be able to perform different tasks. Flexibility, a high level of education, and a strong identification with the company are important here. Budgeting can be less detailed since it is known that capacity planning is never fully realized.

A company that wants to differentiate in the area of technology must invest continuously in its people and machines. A well-equipped development and design function guarantees the quality of the end product.

In practice, elements of both cost leadership and differentiation will often be found. However, the descriptions demonstrate that the choice between them has far-reaching consequences for the design of the production organization and production strategy. It goes without saying that the consequences for the production organization will have to be translated in terms of purchasing policy. Cost leadership and differentiation require different types of purchasing strategies.

In the case of cost leadership, price and costs are central in the negotiations with the supplier. An important criterion for supplier selection is not so much delivery time, but delivery reliability. Regular failure by the supplier to comply with delivery requirements results in production failures, which in turn means high costs. Rejection of incoming materials should be prevented for the same reason.

In the case of differentiation the emphasis is on close co-operation with the supplier. This co-operation can be in the area of process and product improvement, quality control, lead time reduction and exchange of information. It is important that there is a direct relation between the supplier and the user, which is why a central purchasing department can have a disruptive effect in this type of company. The buyer is more or less the intermediary between production and the supplier market.

In the cost leadership situation, communication with the supplier takes place via a formal, administrative route. Much time is invested in optimizing or developing the ordering routines.

Lean manufacturing

Porter's ideas on competitive strategy have influenced management thinking for a long time. Over the last few years these basic beliefs about competitive strategy have been put to the test by some major Japanese and US manufacturers, who seem to have been able to combine the elements of a low-cost strategy with the advantages of a differentiation strategy. The core concept through which they are able to do this seems to lie in what has been designated as **lean management**. This concept originated first in an extensive study on the automotive industry, conducted by the Massachusetts Institute of Technology (MIT) (Womack *et al.*, 1990). Lean management is a philosophy concerning how to run a manufacturing organization, which entails all aspects of the business system in general, and design, manufacturing and supply management in particular. The practices applied in these areas differ significantly from those applied in mass production by most American and European manufacturers. Significant changes in management style are also implied. Fundamental to lean management (Womack *et al.* 1990, p. 99) is that

> it transfers the maximum number of tasks and responsibilities to those workers actually adding value to the car on the line, and it has in place a system for detecting defects that quickly traces every problem, once discovered, to its ultimate cause.

Important features of lean management are

- Teamwork among line workers, who are trained in a variety of skills to conduct different jobs within their working group. These not only relate to manufacturing tasks; workers are also trained to do simple machine repairs, quality checks, housekeeping and materials ordering.
- Simple, but comprehensive information display systems that make it possible for everyone in the plant to respond quickly to problems and understand the plant's overall situation.
- Total commitment to quality improvement on the shop floor. Workers are encouraged to think and act positively on how to improve the effectiveness of their work, whereas their supervisors need to provide active support to bring these ideas to fruition.

Japanese manufacturers devote considerable time and effort to the design of new products. First, the manager in charge of new product development has far greater authority to make decisions than his Western counterpart. Second, product and process engineering are integrated responsibility areas. Third, the engineering manager decides on who he wants to involve in his engineering team and for what period. These are significant differences compared with how engineering projects are organized in Western manufacturing companies.

The most important differences are apparent, however, in the way that Japanese manufacturers manage their supply chain (see also Lamming 1993).

- The average supply base is much smaller than for Western manufacturers. Most Japanese manufacturers are dependent for a large part of their business on their suppliers and the power balance is definitely to the former's advantage. As a result OEMs have organized their suppliers into regional supplier associations which meet several times per year in order to learn about the future product/market plans of their customers.
- Most Japanese OEMs have a 'layered' supplier structure, which is often three or more tiers deep (see also Chapter 10 for more background information on this subject). Assemblies and subassemblies (such as seats, engines and gearboxes) are assigned to first-tier suppliers ('main suppliers'), who in turn rely on a team of second-tier suppliers for specialist components, and so forth.
- Suppliers are usually involved in new product development at a very early stage. It is not uncommon for Japanese OEMs to delegate half of the engineering hours to their first-tier suppliers. Engineers from the manufacturer and the supplier may work full time at each other's premises when solving technical problems and/or working out improvements.

- Suppliers are confronted with well-defined targets in terms of quality improvement, lead time reduction and cost reduction and are, by means of a simple though effective grading and performance measurement system, fully informed as to whether they meet their contractual obligations.

Since the principles of lean management extend to marketing, design, manufacturing and supply management, Japanese manufacturing companies have been able to obtain impressive results, which has put them at a safe distance from their foreign competitors. In the context of this book it is important to acknowledge that supply and supplier management is definitely considered to be the cornerstone of their competitive strategies! Most impressions on lean management are related to the (Japanese) automotive industry and we have to be careful about generalizing. However, for this type of manufacturing environment, the ideas of Porter clearly need to be refined.

In previous sections the influence of the corporate strategy on the purchasing policy has been discussed. It has become clear that the contents of the purchasing strategy depend on whether the company in question pursues a cost leadership strategy, a differentiation strategy or lean management. The next section shows how to obtain a view of a company's strategic vulnerability in relation to its purchasing markets.

Integrating purchasing into company policy

In designing their overall business strategy top management will have to make explicit decisions about the company's positioning *vis-à-vis* its three major stakeholders. Some authors have added a fourth group of stakeholders, namely 'employees' or 'unions'. As more and more companies see knowledge and human capital as key success factors for their organization, the Strategic Triangle may develop into a 'Strategic Quadrant' in the future. These stakeholders constitute what we would call the 'strategic triangle'.

1 *Primary customer groups or target groups*. This touches upon the issue of market positioning and segmentation. Products and services will have to be tailored increasingly to the needs of more differentiated customer target groups, which requires specific product/market strategies. This subject is not elaborated here but can be studied in the specialized marketing literature, for example Kotler (1997).

2 *Major competitors*. Companies must not only be able to respond to customer needs; they also need to respond in such a way that they achieve a so-called 'distinctive, sustainable competitive advantage'. This may explain why customers are turning to the company, instead of its competitors. As we have argued earlier, a competitive advantage may be derived from a superior cost position (South Asian car manufacturers), a superior brand image (many top consumer brands), superior product quality (Rolls Royce), superior logistics performance and customer service (DHL, UPS, Federal Express). To guarantee that customers will turn to the company, they must be able to

clearly differentiate the company's products and services from the offerings of their direct competitors. In order to be able to do so continuous benchmarking of the company's overall performance is required against that of direct competitors and those companies who are considered to be best-in-class in a specific activity.

3 *Major suppliers.* Developments within the supplier markets necessitate continuous review of the company's core activities. Management will have to ask itself continually to what extent core and non-core activities (both production activities and support services) are carried out competitively. If the conclusion is that current (production) activities cannot be carried out competitively in the long run, it will be necessary to investigate subcontracting options and/or possible partnerships with suppliers (in the shape of so-called 'focused sources'). As a result supply chain strategies and specific supplier strategies as an element of this need to be developed.

One example is a European automobile manufacturer who transfers the design and production of compressor valves for the new generation of cars to a specialized supplier. With financial support from the subcontractor, this supplier has built a factory to enable just-in-time deliveries based on call-off orders. Both parties are completely dependent on each other for the supply of this type of components; the relationship has developed from an adversarial, arm's length relationship into a long-term partnership relationship.

The conclusion from the foregoing is that the ultimate competitive position of a company is thus a result of (a) the company's positioning relative to its major customers, (b) its sustainable, distinctive advantage compared with direct and indirect competitors, (c) its positioning versus its major suppliers and its supply chain strategies.

This is expressed in Figure 7.2. Although many companies have an explicit customer orientation and competitive strategy has become a major theme, there are only very few companies that systematically benchmark the performance of their key processes against those of specialist suppliers. This may explain the growing interest currently seen for supply chain management and supplier strategy.

In shaping the relationship with suppliers two elements play a major role. The first is 'costs'. Large companies are looking increasingly for suppliers who can produce at minimum total cost of ownership. In trying to find the most competitive sources of supply most manufacturers have adopted a global sourcing approach at the expense of their traditionally 'nationally' oriented sourcing strategies. The second element is superior customer service. At the same time manufacturers are looking for suppliers who can support their logistics and just-in-time programmes. Some authors (for example Fisher (1997)) have demonstrated that in structuring their supply chain and supplier strategies, manufacturers need to differentiate between functional products (commodities) and innovative products ('specialities'). Functional products have a rather predictable demand and have a rather long lifecyle, whereas demand for innovative products barely can be predicted due to their short lifecycle. Managing supply chains for the latter requires a highly structured, local supplier

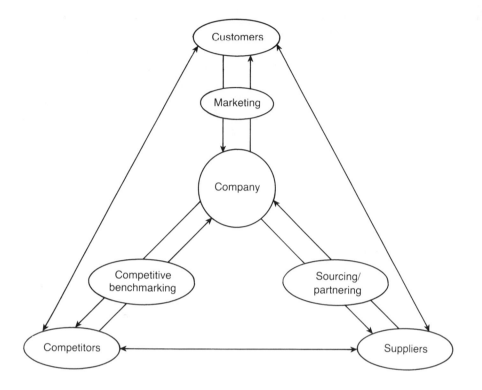

Figure 7.2 The strategic triangle.

network. Due to the fact that customer demand can be predicted much better for functional products, supply chains need to be less responsive. Hence, global sourcing for this type of product is an option.

In many cases manufacturers develop and sell a mix of both functional and innovative products. Therefore, they need to manage different supply chains at the same time. This obviously explains why most companies have adopted both a local and a global approach in their dealings and relationships with suppliers.

Towards leveraged purchasing strategies

In the previous paragraphs the relationship between business strategy and purchasing and supply management has been described. As companies pursue different types of business strategies, the role of purchasing will be different. It has been argued that purchasing strategies definitely need to be linked to overall business strategies. The following paragraphs describe how purchasing and supply strategies can be designed and what steps can be helpful in formulating them.

In doing so the author is following the ideas of Monczka and Trent (1991)(1992), who has published extensively on this subject. Based at Michigan State University he launched a Global Procurement and Supply Chain Benchmarking Initiative in the early nineties. The idea behind this initiative was that companies participating in it would be able to compare their purchasing and supply processes, to exchange experiences and to learn from 'best-practices'. A number of large manufacturing companies (such as Shell, Philips, Motorola and Coca-Cola) subscribed to this initiative and worked with the researchers from Michigan State University to leverage their purchasing and supply strategies. In doing so they went through several stages or cycles of the programme (see Figure 7.3).

- *Insourcing/outsourcing.* During the first step companies need to decide what activities to handle inside or outside the company. The decisive criterion is the question whether the activity concerned contributes to achieving a competitive advantage. If this is not the case the company should decide to bring that specific activity outside the company. The reverse, however, may also be true. Insourcing means that the company may decide to take over strategic activities that previously were performed by suppliers.
- *Develop commodity strategies.* At this stage the company needs to develop a clear and detailed picture of its purchasing spend. On what commodities do we spend the most money? And on what suppliers? How many suppliers do we have per commodity and are we happy about the outcome of this analysis? Commodity is used here in its broadest sense since it may relate to raw materials, technical and high-tech components and standard, off the shelf products. A commodity strategy should then be developed. Such a strategy provides guidelines on whether or not to pursue product standardization and reduce the product variety, whether or not to reduce the number of suppliers, what type of relationship should be developed, etc.

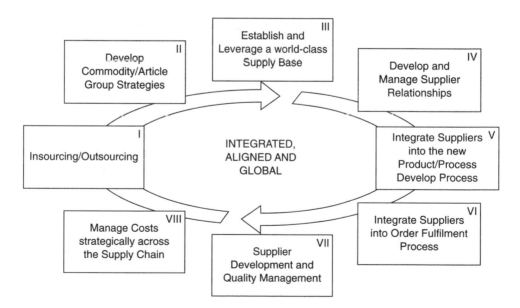

Figure 7.3 Leveraging purchasing and supply management (adapted from Monczka (1999))

Of course the strategy for each commodity should be in line with and support the company's overall business strategy. It should be absolutely clear what benefits should be expected when the commodity strategy is implemented. Therefore a commodity plan maps out who will be responsible for each activity, a detailed timeframe and how progress will be monitored.

- *Establish and leverage world class supply base management.* Supply base management is part of every commodity strategy. Supply base management covers how many suppliers will be dealt with for a certain commodity, what conditions and qualifications the best-in-class suppliers should meet and how the best suppliers will be selected. At this stage suppliers are investigated and benchmarked and, often, submitted to a detailed audit.
- *Develop and manage supplier relationships.* In order to do so suppliers need to be grouped into distinctive categories. Philips Electronics (see Quality Matters, 'Purchasing becoming Supply Chain Management', Issue 94, January 1999) may serve as an example here, as a company which differentiates between:

  (a) commercial suppliers: these suppliers just need to deliver the goods and services according to the agreed terms;
  (b) preferred suppliers: mutual objectives and improvement programmes are developed and agreed by both parties. The preferred status is reciprocal;
  (c) supplier partners: these suppliers work intensely with Philips to develop new technologies, products and business opportunities. Usually, it concerns a limited number of suppliers, who are considered to be crucial in supporting Philips' overall business strategies and core-technologies.

  As will be seen later, developing partnerships is a very difficult issue and takes a long time between parties to develop. In general a major step forward is reached when suppliers no longer suspect that their customer is simply trying to find out and cut back their profit margins.

- *Integration of suppliers in product development.* Having carefully selected the best-in-class suppliers, companies next should focus their efforts on building constructive relationships with suppliers in the area of new product development. This implies that technical experts from the suppliers will become part of the research and development teams and other project teams and vice versa. Often both parties are confronted with difficulties in collaborating effectively together, which relate to differences in working methods, management style and culture. This subject will be discussed in more depth in Chapter 10.
- *Supplier integration into the order fulfilment process.* Motorola is one of the few companies which integrates suppliers into their Customer Focus Teams. The idea behind this is that manufacturer and supplier in the end have one mutual objective which is to satisfy the final consumer as best as they can. Joint teams work on issues like how to increase responsiveness and customer service, how to improve asset utilization, how to reduce pipeline inventories in the supply chain and how to improve communications and transaction flexibility by applying modern ICT (information and communication technology).

- *Supplier development and quality management.* At this stage suppliers are challenged actively to provide new ideas for improvement. These ideas may relate to product design, manufacturing technology and other business processes. Ideas and suggestions from suppliers are carefully considered and action is taken to implement them. Suggestions from suppliers are no longer considered as criticism but as sources for innovation and improvement. Motorola refers to this process as the 'Open Kimono' approach. This is the reason why it often asks its suppliers to value Motorola as a customer to work for. As experience has shown, adopting such a practice is not without risk. If suppliers feel that ideas are not taken seriously or good ideas simply are not being implemented, they will no longer support this type of programme (see Van Weele and Rozemeijer 1998).
- *Strategic cost management.* This concept includes the identification of all costs, cost drivers and strategies aimed at reducing or eliminating costs throughout the supply chain (see Chapter 14 for more details on these subjects). Developing cost models and value stream mapping are important concepts and vehicles at this stage. The idea behind this is that both parties (or clusters of suppliers) work jointly with their customer to realize cost savings. Obviously, this will only work when each party may share some benefits of this exercise. Otherwise, this will lead to a clear lack of motivation for such initiatives in the future.

Through this eight-step process some leading-edge manufacturers have actually been able to integrate suppliers into their business processes. Based upon experience the author in general agrees with the approach as suggested by Monczka. However, in most cases the author feels that supplier development and quality management need to get a higher priority in the procedure. Preferably, it should be placed after the third part of the suggested programme.

Purchasing portfolio-analysis

When designing commodity strategies, the approach originally suggested by Kraljic (1983), who in a classic article presented a useful portfolio-technique, is recommended. Fundamental to his approach is the idea that, since suppliers represent a different interest to the company, purchasing managers need to develop differentiated strategies towards their supply markets.

Key in developing purchasing and supply strategies is the issue of influencing the balance of power between the company and its key suppliers. In the author's view the balance of power should preferably be in favour of the subcontractor. If the situation is the reverse, the subcontractor may suffer from an overdependence on a specific supplier, who may be able to pass on his requirements and conditions onto his customers. Obviously, when a company is too dependent on a supplier, something should be done to change this situation. In developing effective supplier strategies, the following questions may be helpful:

- Does the present purchasing strategy support our business strategy and does it meet our long-term requirements? Are opportunities for benefiting from synergies between divisions/business units fully exploited, for example by joint contracting for common materials requirements?

- What is the balance of power between our company and our major suppliers? For which products/materials does the company have a dominant position on the supply market and for which products/materials is the company dependent on one single supplier?
- Are the strategic products and services sourced from the best-in-class suppliers? To what extent have the purchasing requirements and volumes been evenly spread over several suppliers and geographic regions?
- What percentage of our purchasing requirements is covered by long-term contracts? What percentage is covered by spotmarket transactions or short-term contracts?
- To what extent are internal operations benchmarked against those of specialist suppliers?
- What difficulties or interruptions in supply can be expected in the near future and how can these problems influence the profit and growth objectives of our company?
- What opportunities exist for collaboration with suppliers with regard to product development, quality improvement, lead time reduction and cost reduction? Are these opportunities sufficiently being used?

An analysis of the company's purchasing spend per category and its supplier base in general will show that the 20–80 rule applies: 20% of the products and suppliers will represent about 80% of purchasing turnover. This analysis is a first step in identifying the company's strategic commodities and suppliers. It also reveals the often huge number of small expense items and small suppliers, who in general are responsible for 80% of the company's internal handling costs. After this step the analysis can be refined using Kraljic's (1983) purchasing product portfolio-approach. In this approach the purchasing turnover and the supplier base are analysed based on two variables:

- **Purchasing's impact on the bottom line** to the company – the profit impact of a given supply item measured against criteria such as cost of materials, total costs, volume purchased, percentage of total purchase cost, or impact on product quality or business growth. The higher the volume or amount of money involved the higher the financial impact of purchasing on the bottom line.
- The **supply risk** – this is measured against criteria such as short-term and long-term availability, number of potential suppliers, competitive structure in supply markets, make-or-buy opportunities, storage risks and substitution possibilities. Sourcing a product from just one supplier without an alternative source of supply represents a high supply risk. Supply risk is low when a (standard) product can be sourced from many suppliers, whilst so-called switching costs are low.

Combination of these variables yields a two-dimensional matrix with four quadrants; these represent the product groups or suppliers, each offering different interests to the company (see Figure 7.4).

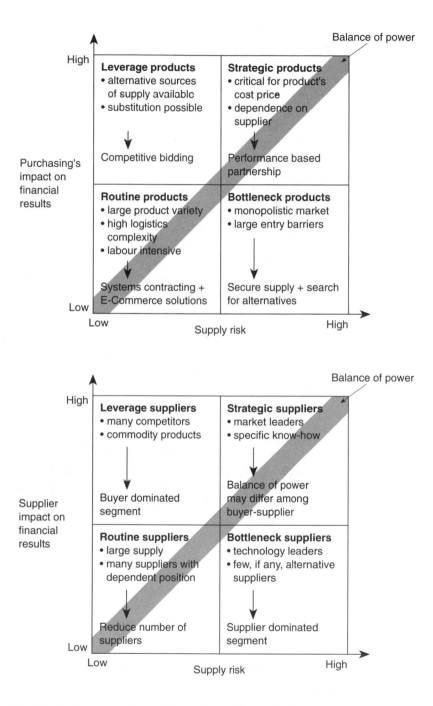

Figure 7.4 Purchasing product portfolio and supplier portfolio.

- *Strategic products.* These are high-volume products, which are often supplied at customer specification. Only one source of supply is available, which cannot be changed in the short term without incurring considerable costs. Usually this type of product represents a high share in the cost price of the end product. Examples are engines and gearboxes for automobile manufacturers, turbines for the chemical industry and bottling equipment for breweries.

  Communication and interaction between subcontractor and supplier are usually intensive, and, as they relate to different aspects of the relationship, complex.

  Looking at the balance of power between the parties involved one can differentiate between three different sub-segments:

  - *Buyer-dominated segment.* Here requirements are in fact imposed on the supplier by the subcontractor/manufacturer. Although some of these manufacturers have developed partnership programmes for their suppliers, suppliers will experience the relationship as rather one-sided. This situation is common in the automotive industry. The relationship between supplier and contractor is not a balanced one. The manufacturers dictate their demands to the suppliers, who just have to meet their requirements.
  - *Supplier-dominated segment.* Here the situation is different. Through its technology and carefully designed marketing strategies the supplier actually has the customer 'locked in' a relationship. This is often the case in business information technology industry, where IT providers have made their customers totally dependent on them in terms of supply of hardware, software and services. Customers buy their hardware and software at one single supplier, only to find that the same supplier charges enormously for these. Usually the performance guarantee is only valid if products and services are bought from that same supplier. The customer has little leeway in general; it only can accept the conditions of the supplier imposed on him.
  - *Balanced relationship.* In this situation neither of the two parties dominates the other. They have a mutual interest in keeping the relationship stable. In this situation a 'partnership relationship' may develop over time.

- *Leverage Products.* In general these are the products that can be obtained from various suppliers at standard quality grades. They represent a relatively large share of the end product's cost price. A small change in price has a relatively strong effect on the cost price of the end product. This is the reason why the buyer exerts aggressive sourcing and tendering among a small sample of prequalified suppliers. Examples are bulk chemicals, steel, and aluminum profiles, packaging, steel plate, raw materials and standard semi-manufactured commodities.

  Characteristic for this situation is that the contractor has freedom of choice regarding his selection of suppliers. There are various suppliers and the 'switching costs' are low. Abuse of this power however, can lead to co-operation between the suppliers. **Cartels** and price agreements may develop in these situations, shifting the commodity to the right side of the matrix.

- *Bottleneck Products.* These items represent a relatively limited value in terms of money but they are vulnerable in regard to their supply. They can only be obtained from one supplier. Examples are catalytic products for the chemical industry, pigments for the paint industry and natural flavourings and vitamins for the food industry. Spare parts for equipment also fall into this category. In general the supplier is dominant in the relationship with the contractor, which may result in high prices, long delivery time and bad service.

- *Normal Products.* These products produce few technical or commercial problems from a purchasing point of view. They usually have a small value per item and there are many alternative suppliers. In practice most items fall into this category; examples are cleaning materials, office supplies, maintenance supplies, fasteners, etc.

  The problem with this group of products is that the handling often takes more money than the value of the products itself. Usually, 80% of the time and energy of purchasing is used for these products; a reason why purchasing is often seen as an administrative job. The purchasing of these normal products should be organized efficiently, in order to spare time for the other, more interesting products.

Depending on the product segment of the portfolio, the supply strategy will differ. The emphasis should lie with the strategic and leverage products. Work related to normal products has to be limited as much as possible.

The purchasing product portfolio provides the possibility to identify and analyse the risks of the company in its purchasing markets. This is illustrated below.

Four basic supplier strategies

For every segment of the portfolio a different strategy is possible. The strategies are:

- *Partnership.* Strategic products together with the leverage products make up 80% of total turnover. Minor changes in price levels will have an immediate impact on the end product's costs so that the price and cost changes, as well as the developments in the supplier market, must be monitored closely. At the same time, the supply risks are high. These arguments justify a central or co-ordinated purchasing approach. Depending on the relative power position of the different parties involved, the purchasing policy for strategic products will be aimed at partnership or collaboration. The goal is to create mutual participation based on planned co-operation. A relationship based on 'open costing' is preferred. With the suppliers', efficiency programmes are developed to achieve cost reduction, quality improvement, process improvement, and improved product development. Such co-operation can in the end lead to the fading of borders between the different companies.

An essential aspect of this partnership strategy is the thorough selection of the supplier. Early in the development, the market is scanned for the 'best-in-class' suppliers. These suppliers are screened on their references, financial stability, the present research and development potential, production capacities, the quality of their logistics and their quality systems, and of course their research and development and engineering capabilities.

- *Competitive bidding*. For leverage products a purchasing policy based on the principle of competitive bidding or tendering will be pursued. Since the suppliers and products are basically interchangeable, there will be, as a rule, no long-term supply contracts. Long-term contracts and annual agreements will be combined with 'spot' purchasing. Buying at a minimum price while maintaining the required quality level and continuity of supply will take priority here. Small savings (small in terms of percentages) represent a large sum of money. This justifies an active market scanning through continuous market and supply research. Regularly, outsiders will be introduced so as to avoid price arrangements between the present suppliers.

Buying of leverage products justifies a corporate or co-ordinated approach where corporate agreements with so-called preferred suppliers are negotiated which can be used by decentral units. Price changes caused by, for example demand and supply changes, are monitored closely in order to estimate the effect on the cost price.

- *Securing continuity of supply*. The purchasing policy concerning bottleneck products has focused on securing continuity of supply, if necessary at additional cost. At the same time activities are conducted aimed at reducing the dependence on these suppliers. This is done by developing alternative products and suppliers. However, the costs involved in these actions (for example tests in laboratories) often exceed the price profits obtained, which is why management often has difficulty in approving this type of action.

A risk analysis to determine the most important bottlenecks in the short-, middle- and long-term supply is necessary. Based on this analysis contingency plans are made. With contingency planning, measures are prepared in case one of the established risks actually occurs. Examples of measures are consigned stock agreements aimed at keeping stock of the materials concerned at the supplier's or the company's own premises, preparing alternative modes of transportation and actively investigating product alternatives.

- *Systems contracting*. For reasons mentioned earlier, routine products require a purchasing strategy which is aimed at reducing administrative and logistic complexity. Buyers will have to work out simple but efficient ordering and administrative routines with the suppliers in the form of systems contracts or kitting contracts. A few aspects relevant to the policy for these products are: standardizing the product assortment (article catalogue), reducing the number of suppliers, pursuing systems contracts for groups of MRO items (office supplies, technical maintenance products, cleaning products, catering, etc.), working with electronic catalogues, ordering through Internet-technology, electronic payment or using the Purchasing Card (see Chapters 5 and 6 for a discussion of these subjects). A final example is to contract out the purchasing of these articles to specialized purchasing offices and/or trading houses.

The use of the purchasing portfolio leads to a differentiated purchasing strategy. It points out that suppliers represent a different interest for a company. The different supplier strategies that have been discussed are summarized in Figure 7.5.

In Chapter 8 it will be seen how the relationship with suppliers can be structured and developed. An illustration of how the purchasing portfolio can be applied is given in Memo 7.3.

MEMO 7.3: Purchasing Portfolio Management at Siemens

The Purchasing Portfolio as described in this chapter, is being used at several companies for some time now. Examples are Shell, Alcatel Bell, Philips, Océ van der Grinten, SmithKline Beecham and Siemens. In 1993 Siemens worked with 420 purchasing departments world-wide and three International Purchasing offices in Japan, Singapore and the United States. At that time 4100 people worked in purchasing.

Siemens used the purchasing portfolio in order to achieve a greater (international) co-ordination of the common components and suppliers. Figure 7.6 shows the results of the analysis made in the factories and purchasing departments of Siemens Germany (notice the switch of the axes!). The 20 - 80 rule becomes apparent here. The segment of routine products is 19% of the total amount of purchasing. However, this segment contains 82% of the total amount of different products and 83% of all suppliers. Compare this with the segment of strategic products, where only 2% of the products and 9% of the suppliers are responsible for 38% of the purchasing costs.

Siemens developed strategies for every segment in order to (1) reduce the purchasing costs and (2) reduce the workload for the purchasing departments. Siemens purchasing policy is aimed at a drastic reduction of the amount of suppliers, in order to create an intensive co-operation with the remaining suppliers focused on development, quality and logistics.

Summary

One of the reasons why purchasing management is being assigned a more prominent position in corporate policy is closely connected with the strategic reorientation that many companies are involved in. After the diversification strategy of the seventies, today's motto seems to be 'concentrate on your core business'. The advantages are self-evident: many activities can be carried out at lower cost by specialized suppliers, the company gains flexibility, and management's attention can focus on the 'core business'. These considerations are the reason why purchasing activity is receiving more attention from top management circles now than it did a few years ago.

Strategies / Characteristics	Partnership	Competitive bidding	Secure supply	Systems contracting
● objective	● create mutual commitment in long-term relationship	● obtain 'best deal' for short term	● secure short- and long-term supply ● reduce supply risk	● reduce logistic complexity ● improve operational efficiency ● reduce number of suppliers
● suitable for	● strategic products (gearboxes, axles, optics, engines)	● leverage products (commodities, steelplate, wire)	● bottleneck products (natural flavours, vitamins, pigments)	● routine products (consumables, supplies)
● activities	● accurate forecast of future requirements ● supply-risk analysis ● careful supplier selection ● 'should cost' analysis ● 'rolling' materials schedules ● effective change-order procedure ● vendor rating	● improve product/ market knowledge ● search for alternative products/suppliers ● reallocate purchasing volumes over suppliers ● optimize order quantities ● 'target-pricing'	● accurate forecast of future requirements ● supply-risk analysis ● determine ranking in supplier's client list ● develop preventative measures (buffer stock, consigned stock, transportation) ● search for alternative products/suppliers	● subcontract per product group/ product family ● standardize product assortment ● design effective internal order delivery and invoicing procedures ● delegate order handling to internal user
● decision level	● board level ● cross-functional approach	● board level ● purchasing	● purchasing ● cross-functional approach	● purchasing ● cross-functional approach

Figure 7.5 Basic characteristics of the four supplier strategies.

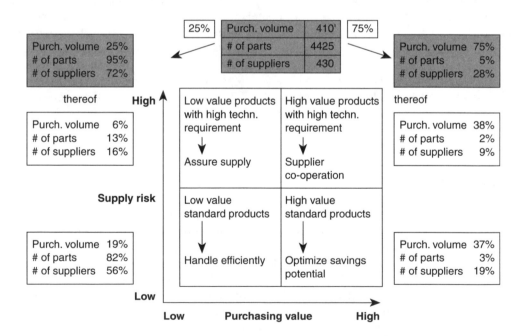

Figure 7.6 Siemens Purchasing Portfolio (© Siemens)(Kowalski (1993) (revised).

The purchasing strategy that is to be developed cannot be separated from the corporate policy or from competitive strategy. As we have seen the extremes of the strategic continuum are cost leadership and differentiation. These strategies cannot be pursued simultaneously, as their organizational requirements are completely different.

Whatever business strategy is developed, they need to position the company against its three major groups of stakeholders, i.e. its customers, competitors and suppliers. Over the past decade there has been a large interest from managers and academics for marketing management and competitive strategy. The interest for purchasing and supply (chain) management as a prime concern for top management is fairly recent. However, it is growing fast.

In the discussion on how to develop leverage in purchasing and supply management, the author has followed the ideas as developed by Monczka. He suggested a programme where companies would preferably go through eight different steps. Key to his ideas are that purchasing and supply management is recognized as a major area of business and is managed that way. Elements of his approach are to develop corporate commodity strategies and article group strategies, to develop a supplier base which is 'world class' and to actively manage this supplier base. Supplier integration in new product development processes and the operational processes of the company are part of this activity.

When developing supplier strategies Kraljic's purchasing product portfolio may be very helpful. It recognizes that different products require different supplier strategies. It starts with a thorough analysis of both product groups and supplier base based on two criteria: (1) purchasing's impact on company profitability and (2) the degree of supply risk associated with the purchase of a specific item. An analysis of these aspects provides the first clue for the purchasing strategy which has to be developed. The second step is to further analyse the four product categories: (1) strategic products, (2) leverage products, (3) bottleneck products, and (4) normal products. For each of these products different supplier strategies can be developed. The value of this approach is that it explains that partnership and competitive bidding should be seen as complementary strategies rather than mutually exclusive. It also shows that the four basic supplier strategies serve different objectives.

Assignments

7.1 This chapter has talked about the 'globalization of purchasing markets'. What is meant by this? To what products or goods does this phenomenon apply?

7.2 Consider a manufacturer of food products (macaroni and spaghetti products, dry soups and sauces). Analyse the purchasing portfolio based on Kraljic's portfolio analysis. Indicate which products can be characterized as strategic products, leverage products, bottleneck products, and normal products.

7.3 Global sourcing has become more popular among manufacturing companies. For what segments of the purchasing portfolio would you recommend a global sourcing strategy? Discuss the advantages and disadvantages of global sourcing.

7.4 The automobile industry is characterized by a limited number of large customers and a large number of smaller suppliers. Discuss which form the purchasing strategy adopted by these automobile manufacturers can take. Do you think a true partnership approach is feasible in this industry? How will the suppliers be able to respond adequately to this purchasing strategy? Use the purchasing portfolio approach to answer this question.

7.5 Some time ago the microprocessor market was characterized by considerable scarcity. The demand for products was enormous, and the supply was limited. Those manufacturers who were able to secure supply of essential parts could increase their production volume. As a result, these manufacturers realized a larger market share than their immediate competitors. Describe the optimal purchasing strategy in this situation. In answering this question, use the purchasing portfolio approach.

SOURCING STRATEGY: GETTING BETTER RESULTS FROM SUPPLIERS

8

Learning objectives

After reading this chapter you should understand the following:

- The position of supply management in the purchasing policy of the company.
- The reasons why suppliers do not always think and act in the interest of their customers.
- Sourcing-strategy and contract-strategy as basic elements of supply management.
- Measures that have to be taken in order improve the performance of suppliers.
- How to develop partnership relations with suppliers.

CASE STUDY
Océ purchasing strategy

Océ and its suppliers are entering a period in which we will work together in new ways. In this brochure we document the key elements of Océ's new purchasing vision . . .

Océ enables people to share information by offering products and services for the reproduction, presentation, distribution and management of information.

Because of the changing environment we are changing the scope and focus of purchasing activities. There will be a greater focus on the overall quality of our suppliers in terms of engineering capacity, the core competences of the suppliers, their role and attitude in the value chain and their capacity to support Océ in its future developments.

The impact of this changed orientation is that suppliers will be involved in new ways. Key words . . . will be long-term relationships, systems buying, simultaneous engineering and continuous improvement . . .

Continued on page 156

The main issues of our purchasing strategy are:

- We prefer to leave design and part of the industrialization to suppliers who can design to functional requirements.
- We are going to increase the strength of our supply base, raise supplier networks and find more world class suppliers.
- We are going to work more closely together with selected world class suppliers and we are going to establish more long-term relationships.
- We will be very selective in choosing suppliers and will do (more business) with less suppliers.
- The purchasing department will focus on value sourcing and strategic management of quality and logistics issues, will increase the access to know-how and technology from main suppliers, will analyse suppliers from a competitiveness point of view and will focus on overall cost . . .

We will continuously be looking for the best suppliers in the world and want them to perform better. We will constantly benchmark our suppliers' performances. We will set challenging targets on cost, quality, logistics and functionality. We have to reduce our total value chain related costs by double digit percentages. In doing so we will create a world class supply base from which we all will benefit.

(Source: Océ Purchasing Strategy, 1998)

Introduction

This case shows how Océ, a leading manufacturer of copying and design equipment, intends to integrate suppliers into its business strategy. Also other large European manufacturers have discovered the strategic importance of an effective purchasing and supplier strategy. In the early nineties, Ignacio Lopez, the flamboyant purchasing director of successively General Motors and Volkswagen, stirred up the European supplier industry. As a result of his unorthodox and aggressive purchasing approach, he realized 'double-digit' savings on the materials costs of the companies he worked for. The method of Lopez has not been undisputed, but it shows that a well-prepared purchasing strategy can reap significant benefits.

This chapter discusses the management of supplier relationships and will build on the purchasing portfolio technique, which has been described in Chapter 7. Active and professional management of supplier relationships is an important topic now that many companies have contracted out the greater part of their activities. The basic assumption is that when manufacturers are not capable of managing their supplier relationships, they without doubt will be managed by them! The author's experience with suppliers in many companies has shown that suppliers often do not think and act in the interest of their client. This chapter shows what the underlying reasons are and what companies can do about it. Therefore, the cornerstones of effective supply management will be described. In doing so we will also describe what companies can do to foster collaboration with their suppliers and how they may develop partnership relationships.

Why suppliers do not always think and act in the interest of their clients . . .

The cost down programmes that have been set up over the past few years by an increasing number of companies have resulted, almost without exception, in large cost savings. Impressive savings have not only been reported in the area of production-buying, but most certainly also in the area of non-production buying. This, notwithstanding the often long-established and often highly-valued relationships between the parties involved! How were these cost savings realized? What activities have generated these? What reasons may explain the slack that apparently exists in the prices paid of the purchased materials and services? In general most manufacturers and suppliers are reluctant to share this type of information with the outside world. Based on experience the following reasons why slack in materials costs and prices may exist are mentioned:

- *Price increases automatically passed on to the next in line*. This phenomenon has been referred to later as the 'french fries principle' (see Memo 8.1). According to this principle suppliers will pass on cost increases to their clients, who in turn pass these increases in costs on to their final consumers. This happens not only with materials cost increases; also increases in wages, social insurance and other labour costs ultimately will be passed on to the customer next in line. As recent examples in the automotive and consumer electronics industry have shown, this practice cannot go on for ever. In some cases this practice has lead to customer prices that simply were no longer accepted by consumers. As an example Mr Piech, the CEO of Volkswagen AG, complained in 1993 (when Volkswagen AG was suffering from a financial loss of 2 billion DM) that the cars produced by his company were too expensive. A drastic cost reduction programme was initiated aimed at reducing the costs of a car by 25%. Since materials costs amounted to 80% of a car, suppliers had to deliver 20% price reduction, which they ultimately did.

  Some visionary purchasing and supply directors have emphasized that manufacturers and suppliers in fact share a common goal: serving the final consumer in the best way possible (see among others Dave Nelson, Honda of America in Van Weele and Rozemijer (1996) and William Marx, AT&T in The Conference Board (1996), pp. 9–10). The more products are sold by the manufacturer, the more business will be generated from suppliers. This premise underlies the Total Customer Satisfaction Programme of Motorola (manufacturer of micro-chips and telecom equipment), where suppliers are working in integrated Customer Teams to improve customer satisfaction.

- *Overspecification*. As opposed to Japanese and some American companies, concepts such as 'concurrent engineering' and 'Early Supplier Involvement' are hardly developed in Europe. This is a consequence of the highly functional structure of European companies. As a result, technical specifications for purchased products are being defined by research and development departments only, without any input from purchasing specialists or suppliers.

In most cases this leads to 'overspecification'. In this situation technical requirements are imposed on suppliers, which are not necessary for the functioning of the product. An example are the boxes for food products, as used by a large food manufacturer, with full six-colour print, which only served for transportation to the retailer's distribution centre. In general, the more specific the requirements for a given product, the less suppliers can be found for delivery. In some cases it may even lead to monopolistic supply situations (i.e. single sources), where manufacturers are very dependent on one specific supplier. The disadvantages of overspecification are obvious:

- products become unnecessarily expensive;
- supplier knowledge for improving or simplifying product design is not used;
- it limits opportunities for competitive bidding amongst suppliers.

These disadvantages illustrate the need to work with cross-functional teams. However, this often requires a drastic change in the organizational culture.

- *Mechanistic competitive bidding amongst a fixed group of suppliers.* This means that purchasers regularly sound out competition amongst their often known suppliers by playing them off against each other. The procedure here is that out of five bids, you take the lowest one, just to start a negotiation to reduce the price even more. When applied regularly, it is clear that suppliers will anticipate behaviour. First, they probably will refuse to offer in their quotations their lowest possible price, since they will keep some leeway in the 'game' of give and take, which will follow. These ritual dances between purchaser and supplier usually deliver limited results. Moreover, this process consumes often valuable time. Second, when applied among a small group of suppliers, it promotes silent agreements among them and the forming of cartels. This type of purchasing behaviour is widespread in the construction industry. It explains why relationships in this industry usually are at 'arms' length' and why collaboration between construction firms and their suppliers often is ill developed.
- *Supplier cartels in (international) supply markets.* In spite of the agreements made on EC level and the EC laws concerning competition, cartels in most European economies are very common. In many industries like paper industry, packaging industry, some construction materials (concrete, bricks) and some food ingredients (like sugar and some fragrances) concentration is very high. There are only a very limited number of players around, which makes it easier to make some silent agreements on pricing behaviour and division of markets. Usually, such a situation results in product prices which are not in any way related to the underlying cost structure of the manufacturers.
- *Traditional purchasing.* In many companies, purchasing is managed in a traditional way. This means that buyers are only involved late, if at all, in the purchasing decision-making process and the company actually deals with a fixed group of familiar suppliers. Specific policies on purchasing or on how

to deal with suppliers are hardly developed. If available, purchasing plans usually are not very ambitious. It might be that products are purchased for years without any knowledge of the underlying cost structure of the suppliers involved. Supplier representatives have free access to the company. In such a situation much benefit can be gained from adopting a more business-like way of working with suppliers.

- *Suppliers' customer relationship programmes.* Many suppliers avoid the discussion to improve their performance for their clients. Rather, they spend time and money on 'customer management programmes' trying to influence the preferences of decision makers in their favour. The activities related to such programmes are abundant! Tactics vary from invitations for in-company seminars (banks) and product presentations (car manufacturers) and personal gifts and presents, to straightforward bribes. All these activities aim to influence personal preferences of decision makers on 'soft' aspects and to avoid an objective client testing the products and services. Given the often aggressive and personalized marketing and sales policies of many suppliers, most companies would benefit from company-wide policy on business ethics.

These points explain why in most cases suppliers have considerable slack in their price setting. Some of these points are related to the manufacturer. Other points relate to characteristics of the supply market and the sales and marketing activities as applied by suppliers. The next section deals with the issue of how to identify slack in supplier prices and how to capture this cost reduction potential.

MEMO 8.1: The 'french fries principle' in purchasing

The passing on of cost increases can best be described by the price developments of potatoes. A bad potato harvest has direct consequences for the price of a bag of chips. A good harvest has hardly any consequences. If the harvest of potatoes in a given year is bad, supply will decrease. However, demand usually stays the same. As a result of the stable demand and shortages of supply, the price per kilo will increase. As a result the prices per portion of french fries at the cafeteria will increase.

What happens in the case of an abundant harvest of potatoes the next year? Then supply, of course, will increase, whilst demand remains the same. As a result the price for potatoes per kilo will decrease. One would expect that this in turn will result in a price reduction for a portion of french fries. However, in real life this is rarely the case! The idea of this principle is that cost increases, which have been incurred by suppliers, immediately are passed on to the customer. However, materials prices reductions and productivity gains are to be kept from the customer in order to improve supplier profitability. In most European economies this phenomenon is very visible as can be seen from the tariffs charged for gas, oil and energy, or for paper and corrugated board, petrol and gasoline, etc.

Main elements of supplier management

In order to be effective a supplier strategy should be able to answer the following questions:

- For which commodities should the number of suppliers be reduced?
- For which commodities should the current number of suppliers be maintained?
- For which commodities should the number of suppliers be increased?

In answering these questions, conducting the purchasing portfolio analysis (see Chapter 7) can be a first step. Over the past few years many companies have focused their sourcing strategy on reducing the number of suppliers. However, obviously this cannot go on for ever. Reducing the number of suppliers should never be considered as a goal in itself. Rather, it should be seen as a vehicle to reduce costs and/or complexity.

Next, the supplier strategy should describe per commodity what type of relationship with the supplier needs to be pursued. Here, a distinction can be made between the sourcing strategy and the contract strategy, that preferably needs to be followed. Considerations concerning the sourcing strategy are:

- *Global vs local sourcing*. Is an international, global supplier orientation required for this product or can a local, national orientation suffice? The answer depends on the type of product. Factors in favour of local sourcing are when it concerns a high-tech product for which the product specification often changes, when a high flexibility and precision is required in terms of delivery, and when intensive personal communication is required in the relationship. Factors in favour of global sourcing are when it concerns bulk products or standardized products, when large price differences among suppliers exist for the same commodities, when products can be bought in large quantities in order to benefit from transport economies, etc. These examples show that decisions on global versus local sourcing should always be based on considering the total cost of ownership.
- *Single vs multiple sourcing* (see Memo 8.2). Does the company wish to purchase the product at one supplier or are several suppliers for that same product necessary? If the company purchases the product at one supplier, the company becomes dependent on that supplier. Supply risk is usually less when the same product is or can be sourced from more than one supplier.
- *Partnership or competitive bidding*? Does the company wish to buy the product from a supplier with whom a partnership relation is preferred, or is the supplier to be kept at a distance and focused by regularly sounding out competition? Entering a partnership relationship has far-reaching consequences for the ways of working of the companies involved, the openness and willingness to share sensitive information and the contractual arrangements. These aspects will be discussed later in this chapter. Competitive bidding means putting out a 'tender' amongst a limited number of previously approved suppliers. Depending on the propositions, the total volume is spread over the most attractive suppliers. For the

individual supplier the allocated volume may differ from year to year. This tactic is mostly used when commodities are purchased or when the products are purchased in large volumes.

A second aspect of supplier strategy is deciding on contract strategy. Developing a contract strategy requires a decision on the following aspects:

- *Buying on contract or buying on spot basis.* Is the total volume of purchased products to be covered by a contract or is part of the volume to be bought on a spot basis (at the current market prices). The advantage of buying under contract is that the volume is bought at a previously agreed price. The buyer is also certain of delivery. The disadvantage of covering the total volume under a contract is that the company loses his contact with the market. The suppliers who dropped out are aware that the company has secured the delivery of the products and therefore they will not continue to inform the company about the latest developments on the market. In case of expected price increases, a contract covering the greater part of the total purchasing volume is preferred. In case of expected price decreases, the opposite applies. As a rule, most companies choose a combination of both contract and spot buying.
- *Price agreement vs performance agreement.* What kind of a contract is preferred? How detailed should it be? Should it be confined to a price agreement only?

MEMO 8.2: Single sourcing

Single sourcing is the deliberate choice for one supplier. *Sole sourcing* refers to the situation in which the company could not make a free choice for any supplier because it concerns a monopolist. Generally, a company will prefer single sourcing when it concerns: (1) the production of a small series of complex components with high tooling costs, (2) contracting out small volumes of client specific products which are produced under licence or with specific know-how, (3) products that need to be delivered with very short lead times, (4) when the technological knowledge is simply not available within their own organization.

One advantage of single sourcing is the involvement of the supplier, which makes it easier for the supplier to open up to the customer since there is no fear of competition. Being dependent on the supplier, the contractor is often willing to involve the supplier more and more in his new product development process. However, this can result in losing contact with the supply market and a greater dependence.

For these reasons most large companies prefer a sourcing strategy based on multiple sourcing in order to have several alternative suppliers at their disposal for a certain product group. However, it is possible that within the product group, one specific supplier is responsible for one particular item. For example: Toyota has several suppliers for their automobile chairs; however, the chair for the Toyota Carina is delivered by one supplier, while the one for the Yaris is delivered by another.

Single sourcing does not automatically lead to a partnership relationship. This depends on the relative power between supplier and contractor. The concepts 'single sourcing' and 'partnership' therefore are by no means synonymous.

This may be sufficient when buying fabrics with certain standard qualities. Or is a detailed service level agreement (SLA) with specific arrangements on time of delivery, tests, maintenance, guarantees, etc. to be preferred? This is appropriate when contracting for specific process equipment or other investment goods. When buying services, SLA's have increasingly become popular. Another development can be found in automotive industry. Ford, as an example, uses a 'life of type' contract for the suppliers of components which states that the prices have to decline a certain percentage every year and that the supplier should be able to deliver during the total economic life span of the car.

These issues have to be well considered before searching the (international) supply market.

Getting better results from suppliers

How to secure superior service from suppliers? How to develop a relationship with a supplier? How to enter into a partnership relationship with a supplier? These questions are addressed in this section.

Usually, the following step-wise approach will provide a useful vehicle:

- *Contract review*. This step concerns a thorough analysis of current contract arrangements with existing suppliers. Often, this results in some search activities, since it appears that contracts are difficult to find and have not been accurately documented. This is particularly true for contracts which are made without the involvement of the purchasing department. Often the supplier has to be contacted to provide a copy of the contract. The contract documents are at this stage analysed and checked for completeness and functionality. The main objective is to determine which price agreements have been made, whether the actual performance and satisfaction with the supplier have been documented and to assess the risks and responsibilities involved. Usually, such an analysis leads to a new, up-to-date and complete contract outlining the product and service performance required from the supplier. The objective of this step is to conclude a performance-based contract. Experiences have shown that this activity alone can lead to substantial savings (5–10%). An example is a food company where such analysis revealed a maintenance contract which was still being paid for while the machines had been sold and scrapped years ago!
- *Competitive bidding amongst current and new suppliers*. This step focuses on analysing the (international) supply market and sounding out international competition. The objective here is to get a competitive bid from a large number of new suppliers. An important element is that the number of possible suppliers is not limited to well-known companies. Before the market research, the company must decide which requirements the suppliers have to meet (supplier profile). Then a shortlist is made of all the suppliers who conform to this profile. Some of these (15–25) are asked to present quotations;

a few international suppliers are deliberately included. The three most promising suppliers are invited for a number of creative sessions, which challenge them to come up with some creative ideas for cost reduction, improvement of the product design and quality improvement. An audit team will visit the supplier in order to determine possible means of improving the product process, using a detailed company audit. Lopez (see Memo 8.3) developed a specific workshop for this purpose. The ideas that grew out of this workshop are presented to the management of the supplier at the end of the workshop. Honda of America developed a 'Best Practice Programme' for this purpose (see Memo 8.4). After these ideas have been processed in a final purchasing order specification, the suppliers are invited to present their final quotations. The final choice for a supplier is based on these quotations. The objective of this step is to identify the 'best-in-class supplier' for the required product or service, on a performance-based contract.

- *Optimizing the supplier relationship and value chain mapping*. After the previous steps the company now has a perfomance-based contract with the 'best-in-class supplier'. From now on, the focus is on continuous improvement within the supplier relationship. The premise here is that in the balance of power there is a relationship, or that the balance of power is at the advantage of the contractor. At this stage concrete objectives and targets on price and cost reduction, quality improvement, lead time reduction and improvement of customer service are settled. These objectives and targets are often prepared by Supplier Improvement Teams or Supplier Alignment Teams, consisting of specialists from several disciplines from both parties. A major objective is to exchange ideas for improvement activities on both sides. Both parties exchange sensitive technical information and cost information. Often, contractors find out that the greater part of the homework has to be done on their side! Working this way leads to a situation where the supplier becomes gradually integrated in the customer's business processes. This is the reason why Chrysler uses the term 'Extended Enterprise Programme' (Dyer, 1996). They see their suppliers as an extension of their own company, that needs to be equally, or even better, managed than their internal operations. This approach can result in the early involvement of suppliers in the development of new products. During that period of time, specialists of the supplier are actually working within the organization of the contractor (residential engineering). Reversedly, engineers of the contractor can be present in the organization of the supplier when the first trial production runs take place, supporting them in solving start-up problems. This subject will be further discussed in Chapter 10. At this stage, some advanced contractors will analyse the entire supply chain with help from their suppliers. The instrument used is Value Chain Mapping: per component, the source of origin of every part is determined. Then, per subcomponent the purchasing contracts are analysed and possible simplifications for purchasing or logistics are identified. In many cases, this results in the contractor helping the supplier with improving his contracts with the next tier of suppliers. This approach is used at Japanese and some American manufacturers. In Europe this approach is still in its infancy. Characteristic for this stage is that the improvement activities are initiated and managed by the contractor and followed through progress meetings. Detailed vendor rating schedules showing the achievements of suppliers are discussed in these meetings.

The major objective underlying this way of working is to develop and optimize the operational relationship with the best-in-class supplier and to integrate him in the new product development processes and projects. In this way suppliers are systematically challenged and mobilized to support the company's overall business strategies and to secure business success!

The myth of partnership

This chapter would be incomplete if it didn't discuss the issue of 'supplier-partnership'. In recent years, large international manufacturers have spent a lot of time and money in the development of supplier-partnership programmes. One

---

MEMO 8.3: The Lopez Approach

In the early nineties, the European supply industry was stirred up by Ignacio Lopez, the flamboyant purchasing director of General Motors and, later, Volkswagen. Lopez demanded extreme price reductions from his suppliers and he got what he asked for. His approach, however, has been highly criticized.

His approach is based on what Lopez calls the Third Industrial Revolution. In Western Europe, this revolution is in full blast. European companies have to face competition with an ever-growing number of competitors coming from South-east Asia (Asian Tigers). The idea behind the Third Industrial Revolution is that these companies will only survive when they focus on their ultimate customers. In the eyes of Lopez, Volkswagen and their suppliers, therefore, share a common interest and that is serving the Volkswagen owners. If they both see to it that the present owners of a Volkswagen car will continue to drive a car of this brand or if they are able to expand market share, this will be to the benefit of both Volkswagen and its suppliers. According to the vision of Lopez, the whole supply chain has to be focused on providing the best product and the best service possible for present and prospective Volkswagen drivers. Lopez was strongly opposed to the earlier-mentioned passing on of materials and labour cost increases. He also disapproved of the hierarchical and bureaucratic structures in the companies he worked for and of the dominance of technical disciplines like product development and engineering. He was a great advocate for implementing cross-functional teamwork within the company and teamwork with suppliers. He created the necessary conditions for teamwork through his extended KVP (Kontinuischer Verbesserungs Programm) training programme aimed at continuous improvement.

Lopez knew how to sell his philosophy to the companies he worked for. He asked his employees to wear their watch on the right in order to remind them that the times had changed. He developed a special 'warriors-diet' for his employees, based on the familiar 'Fit-for-life diet'. Every week Lopez had a video-conference with the purchasing managers all over the world in order to expand his ideas and to monitor the progress of his plans.

MEMO 8.4: Working on supplier quality at Honda of America

Honda of America deals with suppliers. The co-operation with suppliers is characterized by simplicity. Dave Nelson, Vice President Purchasing says:

> When we receive a promising quotation from a new, unfamiliar supplier, we invite him to come and explain his proposal. At this meeting, a team of Honda specialists is present. If this meeting passed satisfactorily, one of Honda's younger engineers will visit the supplier's factory. The task of this engineer is to organize the working space of the supplier. He will start cleaning the machines and the tooling warehouse. Moulds and dies are inspected, cleaned and categorized so people will not have to search for them anymore. Then the factory is whitewashed so as to make it spotless. At first the engineer works alone, but after a while a few employees of the supplier cannot bear to see him working alone and will give him a hand. And that is precisely the intended plan. Eventually, we want to create a situation in which the supplier incorporates our management philosophy, which is based on respect for the individual and the full utilization of the creativity of employees. If that is accomplished, we are both working with common views and barriers between the supplier and us automatically fade away.

Honda of America works with their 'Best Practice Programme', which stands for 'Best Practice', 'Best Price' and 'Best Process'. The purpose of this programme is to show suppliers how to eliminate the seven wastes in their production organization: standstill of machinery, moving materials, defects and failures, production disturbance, over-production, lead time and stocks.

of the first companies in Europe which focused on partnership was Philips, which introduced the term 'co-makership'. Broersma (1991) defined this term later as: 'the building of long-term relationships with a limited number of suppliers based on mutual trust'. A major objective underlying this type of co-operation is to achieve significant improvements in:

- *Logistics.* By giving the suppliers insight into the supply needs and materials schedules for the coming months, they can anticipate much better the future requirements, which will lead to a higher level of service and lower logistics costs for both parties.
- *Quality.* Early mutual agreement on quality requirements enables zero defects deliveries, which in turn result in a reduction of quality costs for the contractor.
- *Product development.* By introducing product and process engineering knowledge and experience of the supplier early into the development process, the time-to-market and start-up costs may be reduced.

The subject of partnership has been widely covered by academic research. In recent years, many concepts have been developed. Interesting views come from the research done by Ellram and Hendrick (1993). In their investigations these authors used the following definition of partnership:

> A 'partner' is defined as a firm with whom your company has an ongoing buyer-seller relationship, involving a commitment over an extended time-

period, a mutual sharing of information and a sharing of risks and rewards resulting from the relationship.

Based on this definition, the researchers concluded that, within the examined companies, less than 1% of the total of supplier relations could be defined as partnership relationships. These suppliers however, were responsible for as much as 12% of the total purchasing volume of the examined companies.

Another interesting study on partnership was conducted in the British automobile industry (DTI, 1994). This study shows that the mutual trust between supplier and contractor is still out of reach. This research reports of many years of broken promises, abuse of trust, and conflicts, which made close collaboration in general and partnership between (car) manufacturers and their suppliers impossible. The researchers concluded: 'In developing new working agreements with their suppliers most vehicle manufacturers still appear to deal more in rhetoric than reality' (p. 5).

Reviewing the current practice of purchasing, these results do not come as a surprise. Co-operation with suppliers requires internal teamwork between all the disciplines. The functional structure in many companies interferes with an effective internal co-operation and as a consequence interferes with a close and effective co-operation with suppliers. Of course, there are some examples of successful partnership relationships. However, it must be acknowledged that these were the result of many years of muddling through, disappointments and perseverance. Developing partnership relationships with suppliers takes time. This is illustrated in Figure 8.1. It shows the large differences in the relationships with a supplier and design-partner.

The author considers partnership to be the result of the contractors' continuous effort to improve results in the relationship with suppliers, rather than a technique which can be adapted and applied in a short time. This probably explains the small number of really successful partnership relationships in practice.

Summary

Effective supplier management is another cornerstone for a successful business strategy. The way this policy is executed in organizations, increasingly determines its shareholder value. Companies like AT&T, Ford, General Motors, Motorola and Volkswagen use purchasing and supply strategies as an integrated part of their company policy. They are proof of the huge savings and significant improvements in operational processes that can be made through dedicated, effective supplier management.

The international competitive arena forces manufacturers to look continuously for ways to improve their customer value. Product costs need to be maintained at a competitive level. At the same time, they have to work continuously on product and process innovation. Suppliers are able to, and should, contribute to both objectives. The author's view is that this cannot be done automatically. In this chapter it has been explained why most suppliers do not automatically think in

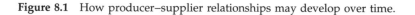

Aspects	Supplier	Preferred supplier	Supply partner	Design partner
Relationship characteristics	• operational	• operational	• tactical	• strategic
Time-horizon	• from order to order	• 1 year	• 1–3 years	• 1–5 years
Quality	• as requested by producer • quality control by producer	• as requested by producer • quality control by producer and supplier	• 'sign-off' by supplier • quality assessment by supplier (process quality)	• 'sign-off' by supplier • early supplier involvement in design • quality assessment by supplier (design quality)
Logistics	• orders	• annual agreements + call-off orders	• periodical scheduling of materials requirement by producer	• electronic document interchange
Contract	• from order to order	• annual agreement (1 year)	• annual agreement (> 1 year) • quality agreement	• design contract • life of type responsibility (product liability supply)
Price/cost	• price	• price + rebate	• price + cost-reduction targets	• price based on open calculation • continuous improvement (design, quality, cycle time).

Figure 8.1 How producer–supplier relationships may develop over time.

their clients' interest. Reasons are due to both the contractor's organization and the suppliers' marketing and sales policies. It is fair to say that if contractors are not able to manage their suppliers, the suppliers without doubt will manage their customers. Successful companies tie their purchasing and supplier strategies to their overall business strategies. Suppliers basically should support their customers' business strategies in the best way possible. This is the basic principle behind the Third Industrial Revolution as described by Lopez. If the manufacturers do well in terms of growth and volume, so will the suppliers. Successful contractors will try to overcome conflicting interests in the relationship with their suppliers which may have developed over the years. This is done by developing carefully designed sourcing programmes which focus on where to go for single sourcing, global sourcing and/or partnership. These sourcing programmes always result in detailed action programmes which will highlight contract review, competitive bidding and co-operation with suppliers at the same time.

The road to partnership is long and difficult. There are no easy ways or short cuts to success. Supplier strategies should be supported by the top management. Activities are to take place in cross-functional teams from both sides. This often requires a complete change of view on traditional purchasing practices. Purchasing needs to become more and more integrated into line management and the major business processes. The buyer, then, becomes just one of the team's players. Firm rules on ethics and on how to deal with suppliers are needed in order to limit the effects of their often aggressive marketing and sales programmes.

Assignments

8.1 In the case as described at the beginning of Chapter 5, AT&T (a company with a purchasing share of 55%) states: 'Purchasing is by far the biggest activity at AT&T. Nothing else is more important.' How do you feel about this statement? Do you agree with AT&T?

8.2 This chapter focuses on the necessity of cross-functional teamwork during the stage of product development. What do you think are the benefits of such co-operation? Why does cross-functional teamwork often require a complete cultural change?

8.3 This chapter states that the reduction of the number of suppliers should not be a goal in itself; it should be seen as a means for other goals. Which objectives are served with the reduction of the number of suppliers? Why does the reduction of the number of suppliers mostly result in cost decreases?

8.4 What is the difference between single and sole sourcing and partnership? Give examples. Discuss how these terms interrelate.

8.5 What do you think of the approach used by Lopez? When can it be useful? How do you feel about the critique on this approach?

PURCHASING AND SUPPLY STRATEGY, ELECTRONIC MARKET PLACES AND E-PROCUREMENT

9

Learning objectives

After studying this chapter you will be able to:

- Explain the differences between E-Procurement as defined in its broadest sense and its narrowest sense.
- Identify the different kinds of electronic market places that are relevant for purchasing and supply managers.
- Outline how electronic market places and E-Procurement may support purchasing and supply strategies and what savings can be generated from these.
- Cite possible electronic solutions that are open to purchasing and supply managers and categorize them.
- Delineate the risks associated with implementing E-Procurement solutions and the conditions that should be met within organizations in order to do so effectively.

CASE STUDY

Business-to-business, or b2b, markets have been quite turbulent over the years. In the year 2000, 50 competing multinational companies in the food industry announced they were going to make joint purchases via the Internet. By means of joint purchase and distribution via www.Transora.com, they believed it would be possible to save millions of dollars. The founders

Continued on page 170

included large multinational companies such as Procter & Gamble, Unilever, Heineken, Coca Cola, Pepsi, Johnson & Johnson and Kraft Foods. This initiative was a response to the action taken by a large number of retail companies who announced collaboration via a World Wide Retail Exchange earlier that year.

Retail companies and food manufacturers are not the only parties taking such initiatives. At the start of this millennium car, consumer electronics and computer manufacturers, to name but a few, published similar plans. The common denominators on which these initiatives are based are: reduction of costs through global sourcing, better control of purchasing expenditure and a considerable reduction of transaction costs in b2b relationships.

Introduction

Modern information technology is the great enabler behind plans to set up electronic market exchanges. By using Internet technology, large manufacturing companies can communicate and trade both with their customers and suppliers faster, more efficiently and on a larger scale.

After the initial euphoria during the start of the new millennium, we have witnessed a turnaround. It seems that investors are becoming increasingly realistic in appraisals for their portfolios, with a sharper eye for what is and is not possible regarding E-Business applications.

Within the various Internet applications, those in the field of purchasing are especially important. There is a growing interest on the part of purchasing and supply managers and of top managers. Is all this attention justified? Which electronic applications are we talking about exactly? Are they of equal use to all businesses? What electronic purchasing solutions should enterprises invest in and how sustainable will these investments be? What are the risks and what kinds of losses can be expected? This chapter reviews the most important insights into the field of purchasing management, supplier relations and the Internet.

Investing in purchasing: now or never?

An international company quoted on the stock exchange was approached some time ago by an equally international consultant who planned to work with similar companies to set up a joint electronic market place for purchasing. The idea was that their joint forces would lead to considerable purchasing savings. In addition, transaction costs would be lowered by forcing suppliers to use the standardized protocols of the electronic market place for their transaction processing. As a result, transaction processes would be faster and would suffer from fewer problems. The initiative was not only to the advantage of the manufacturers involved; suppliers could also profit from the arrangement. It was to be a win–win situation. It seemed a plan that was too good to be true. Each participant had to be prepared to invest a couple of million Euros. In fact, setting up the market place required an investment of about 100 million Euros in total.

If you were a purchasing manager, what would your decision be? Would you ignore the proposal and run the risk of missing an important development and the accompanying purchasing advantages? Or would you invest and run the risk that this sketchy initiative would turn into hot air and produce only a fraction of the savings it proposed to do?

First, we shall indicate how enterprises in such situations could respond. Top executives and purchasing managers, as we see it, would need to take several aspects into account. In our opinion the initiative must first support the procurement strategy of the enterprise and the procurement processes and accompanying information systems will have to be brought up to date. This finding is quite significant. It is assumed that enterprises do indeed hold a strategic view concerning the field of purchasing. If such a view does not exist however, investments in an electronic market place may become isolated without being adequately embedded in the purchasing processes of the enterprise. Hence, a basic question is: to what extent should participation in such an electronic market place differentiate the corporation from its competitors? If the competition gains more from such a project, is it wise to participate?[1]

Next, it is necessary to consider what investment one is prepared to make, what yields are set off against this investment, and within what period one expects to see profit being realized. This aspect focuses on the cost–benefit ratio of the initiative. In practice, this proves to be an extraordinarily difficult exercise, which makes it all the more important to use a scenario analysis for it (best case–worst case scenario). One of the difficulties is that supplier relationships are much harder to change than is generally assumed. Another issue is that, when reducing transaction costs, it will appear that most of these costs are fixed, since they relate to labour and investments in information systems which are, again, difficult to influence.

In addition, one needs to know what type of technology platform is chosen for implementing an electronic market place. More important than the technology platform is the question of what purchasing functionality is sought. Are solutions to be sought in the field of global sourcing, auctioning and tendering, or are solutions needed that simplify the transaction flows between the enterprise and its suppliers? Combinations are possible too, of course. Does the proposed initiative sufficiently deal with the needs and issues of the enterprise?

Once these questions have been answered, the purchasing manager is left with the question of how to take the first step. How can you get the ball rolling? Memo 9.1 summarizes the most important initial questions.

It is our impression that most enterprises do not make a true effort to systematically answer these questions, with or without pressure from shareholders. We have the impression that the notion that rapid action has to be taken so as not to miss out ('it's now or never') dominates in most cases. Investments involving millions of Euros are made without a clear foundation and without the perspective of solid yields in the future. Therefore, there is little doubt that a large number of these initiatives are bound to fail.

---

[1] This finding was reason enough for General Electric (see *Purchasing*, 15 June, 2000, p. 14) to go its own way regarding electronic market places.

MEMO 9.1: Initial questions related to investing in an electronic market place

- To what extent does electronic purchasing support current purchasing and supplier strategies?
- To what extent will electronic purchasing contribute to the realization of a sustainable competitive advantage?
- What are the technological implications of the initiative for the enterprise and how dependent will the company become on its IT provider?
- Which investments are necessary and how long will it take to earn them back, and what are the chances of success?
- Which electronic solutions can be imagined in the field of purchasing and which are the most suitable for the enterprise?
- How can one obtain a view on these questions and what is the first step one needs to make?

Electronic market places and electronic procurement: definitions and concepts

There are various types of market place that can be found on the Internet. Here, an electronic market place is defined as a place on the Internet where actual transactions can take place between buyers and sellers. A visitor to such a market place may find one of the following variants (see Figure 9.1):

- *Website*: a place where a buyer finds a single seller or vice versa (1–1). A web site is characterized by a one-to-one relationship between the buyer and seller.
- *Buyer-centric portal*: a market place set up by several sellers with the objective of offering the potential buyer an integrated product line (n–1). The buyer is not aware of the presence of the other buyers (n–1). Shopping malls and market plaza's are examples of this kind of portal.

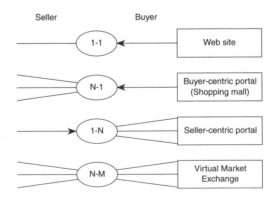

Figure 9.1   Websites, portals and electronic market places.

- *Seller-centric portal*: a place where a seller finds several buyers at the same time (1–n). The buyers are aware of the presence of other buyers. Examples here are auctioning sites run by large departments stores where individual consumers can bid. Other examples are the auctions run by independent providers such as FreeMarketsOnline and E-Breviate.
- *Electronic market exchange*: a market place where several sellers and buyers are present at the same time (n–m).[2] These may be organized by type of industry (ChemConnect.com, Covisint.com) or by type of commodity (MRO.com, AtYourOffice.com).

A distinction can be made between vertical and horizontal market places (also referred to as E-Hubs by some authors). *Vertical market places* aim to encourage, facilitate and realize transactions between parties that belong to the same value chain. One such example is www.Transora.com, set up by food manufacturers to facilitate communication with their suppliers. Other examples are Covisint.com, E-Steel.com, ChemConnect.com and PlasticsNet.com. *Horizontal market places* focus on facilitating relations between parties which operate in different value chains. Examples here are MRO.com and AtYourOffice.com, which both aim to facilitate transactions between sellers and buyers in the field of office articles. Horizontal market places are an electronic version of the *buying consortia* that arose in the United States in the late 1990s, in which various large companies worked together to close joint contracts for a particular purchasing product category. These consortia can be found in the fields of energy and healthcare, where a number of hospitals combined their forces in the area of purchasing.[3] The *buying community* is a less strict variant of a consortium, in which a number of buyers join forces only temporarily to purchase certain products. Examples of buying communities can be found in business-to-consumer relationships. Early attempts were www.letsbuyit.com and priceline.com. However, these initiatives have not been very successful in most cases. An interesting classification of electronic market places has been presented by Kaplan and Sawhney (2000). Memo 9.2 gives more details about this interesting scheme.

To conclude, Memo 9.3 provides a description of some frequently used terms within the area.

Possible ICT strategies for purchasing

Companies may follow different strategies when implementing information technology for E-Procurement. Here are some examples:

- Purchase of a separate ('front office') application that is integrated into the 'back office' systems already present (e.g. PurchasingNet).[4]

---

[2] In the following we will use the terms 'portal' and 'electronic market place' interchangeably.
[3] See Corsten and Zagler (2000) for a detailed discussion of this subject.
[4] 'Front office' relates to the actual ordering cycle between the requisitioner and the buyer. 'Back office' relates to all transaction processing activities between buyer and supplier.

MEMO 9.2: Classification of electronic market places according to Kaplan and Sawhney (2000, pp. 98–99)

These authors differentiate between *manufacturing inputs* and *operating inputs* on the one hand, and how the products were purchased on the other. Here they made a distinction between *systematic sourcing* and *spot buying*. Systematic sourcing involves negotiated contracts with qualified suppliers. The contract tends to be long-term, so the buyers and sellers often develop close relationships. In spot sourcing the buyer's goal is to fulfil an immediate need at the lowest possible cost. Commodity trading for things like oil, steel and energy exemplifies this approach.

Based upon these two criteria a matrix is presented in which the following electronic market places can be identified (see Figure 9.2):

- *MRO hubs:* horizontal market places which enable systematic sourcing for indirect, non-production-related goods and services.
- *Yield managers:* horizontal market places which enable spot buying for indirect goods and services.
- *Catalogue hubs:* these market places allow systematic sourcing for direct, product-related goods and services.
- *Exchanges:* vertical market places allow spot buying for direct, product-related goods and services.

systematic sourcing	**MR Hubs** Ariba WW.Grainger MRO.com BizBuyer.com	**Catalogue Hubs** ChemConnect.com SciQuest.com PlasticsNet.com
spot buying	**Yield Managers** Empolyease Adauction.com Capacity.Web.com	**Exchanges** e-Steel.com PaperExchange.com Altra Energy IMX Exchange
	Operating inputs	Manufacturing inputs

Figure 9.2   Business to business matrix, adapted from Kaplan and Sawhney (2000, p. 99).

- Extension of the available back office (Enterprise Resource Planning) system to include an E-Procurement function, which stops integration from being an issue. Known ERP suppliers such as SAP, Oracle, Peoplesoft and Baan have already developed this functionality.

MEMO 9.3: The jargon within E-Procurement

Application Service Provider (ASP): a firm which operates a technology platform and allows users access for a pre-arranged licence fee and/or an allowance per transaction. Examples in the purchasing area are: Ariba, CommerceOne, Netscape. Companies may place their own product catalogues on these platforms or use those provided by the ASP.

E-Commerce: encompasses all business actions carried out electronically to improve the efficiency and effectiveness of market and business processes. In practice, however, E-Commerce is usually understood to be 'Marketing, sales, and purchasing of products and services via the Internet and/or other open electronic information networks'. The term E-Business is used for the collection of activities aimed at the improvement of business performance through the application of electronic solutions in and between value chains.

E-procurement: there is a distinction between E-Procurement in its narrowest and broadest senses. In the broad sense it is a collection of web technology-based purchasing solutions aimed at simplifying commercial transactions within and between organizations. In a narrow sense it entails information technology solutions for ordering, logistics and handling systems, as well as for payment systems. Examples include electronic ordering systems and catalogue systems.

EDI (electronic data interchange): this is related to the exchange of information between the information systems of trade partners by means of standardized communication protocols and data entities.

Intranet: this term relates to an internal computer network within a given organization, which is only accessible to employees of that organization, and is primarily intended for internal communication and message exchange. An intranet is often connected to the Internet via a so-called 'gateway'.

Extranet: an extension of the Intranet that allows external parties (customers, suppliers, dealers, etc.) to make use of the same facilities as internal employees of the organization. Thus, electronic message exchange is possible between parties using communication standards set by the organization in question.

OBI (open buying on the Internet): a communication standard that was developed on the initiative of a number of large American purchasing organizations together with their suppliers. It is especially focused on facilitating electronic transactions of indirect or non-production-related goods.

- Use of a front office application that is available within the market place (e.g. Ariba, Netscape or CommerceOne).

Essentially, E-Procurement systems must enable their users to specify their purchasing requirements, to conduct purchasing market research, to pre-qualify suppliers and if possible allow for the running of tenders. Besides remarkable differences in the functionality offered by the various applications currently available, the efforts necessary for integration differ greatly. To realize the savings claimed by the providers of these applications, a high degree of integration is required between the front office and back office on the one hand, and between the back office and the supplier's systems on the other.

The applications discussed here can be acquired by the user in various ways:

- Purchase and implementation of E-Procurement software. Take for example Philips, where in 1999 the decision was made to base the E-Procurement solution on Ariba. Philips actually decided to buy the software from Ariba and install it on their own servers and systems. Their biggest hurdle in this case was the implementation, integration, maintenance and management of the application in compliance with their different ERP systems.
- Hosting of the E-Procurement application by the ASP on behalf of the user. In this situation, the user puts his or her product catalogues on the ASP system, which takes care of the technical management. Content management and development are in the hands of the user. One example is WorldWideMarketExchange, in which Ahold participates. Supplier and product databases and files, as well as transactions Ahold carries out with suppliers, are visible only to Ahold and not to its competitors.
- Making use of an application including its content. The user not only makes use of the technological platform of the ASP but also the product and supplier catalogues that are in its care. Naturally, a company's own catalogues can be integrated into those of the ASP and tailored where necessary.

These examples make it clear that, when choosing a specific electronic platform, a company may become very dependent on the ASP. Purchasing managers therefore need to verify at a very early stage the technological stability and financial strengths of their future partner. We shall return to this point later in the chapter.

Different purchasing solutions for different purchasing objectives

Our description makes it clear that a great diversity of electronic tools are available already in the field of purchasing. These tools can be used for different purposes. Electronic market places facilitate the searching of and actual tendering among suitable suppliers. One important advantage is that supplier markets, as a result, become more transparent. Another is that large firms can move away from traditional supplier relationships and find new suppliers. The present broadening of their supplier markets has major consequences for the balance of power and pricing mechanisms in b2b markets. Modern information technology also makes new types of purchasing possible: consider electronic auctions (in the shape of upward or downward auctions[5]), computer-supported tendering and best-bid analysis. ERP systems and catalogue systems may offer efficient solutions in the field of more efficient order control, goods logistics and payment systems. Present information technology already makes it possible to deal with transaction flows between organizations without human intervention. Cisco claims that 55% of its customer orders (stemming from more than 34,000 customers for a sum of about 4 billion dollars) are handled without intervention

---

[5] The latter are also referred to as reverse auctions.

from Cisco employees. Next to considerable savings this also results in a major reduction in order throughput time (from 6 to 8 weeks down to 1 to 3 weeks).[6] Examples like Cisco, however, are rare. For most enterprises this picture may remain utopian.

Which solutions are available for which type of product or supplier? Using the purchasing portfolio[7], we have attempted to provide a systematic view on this topic (see Figure 9.3).

The purchasing portfolio shows that different solutions can be imagined for the various purchasing segments. For more commodity-oriented products, which can be specified easily and are bought against standard qualities, such as the well-known MRO articles,[8] we would suggest catalogue systems and electronic payments solutions (i.e., a Purchasing Card). This segment focuses particularly on the lowering of transaction costs. For strategic products and services, which are often tailored to customer needs, EDI is often favoured as a solution, due to the frequent transactions and interactions, and the fact that automatic materials requirements planning systems trigger purchasing orders. The yield from electronic auctions is largest for so-called leverage products, which does not lessen the fact that these can be equally applied to routine articles. However, we expect that catalogue systems and E-Procurement solutions will be used mostly for the latter segment of the market (see also Memo 9.4). For the bottleneck segment, usually, there is little to choose from for the buyer. Given the dominant position of the supplier *vis-à-vis* the buyer, the former will impose his/her ordering systems on the latter.

On the basis of Figure 9.3, we believe that most companies in the area of purchasing need to apply a variety of electronic solutions. In other words, we do

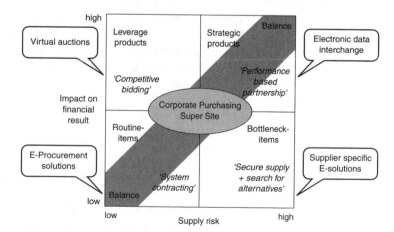

Figure 9.3 Different electronic solutions for different purchasing purposes.

---

[6] Source: Elisabeth Fee, Supply Chain Management at Cisco, E-Motion Conference, Eindhoven, October, 2000
[7] For more details please see Weele (1999), Chapter 7 or Weele and Rozemeijer (2000).
[8] MRO stands for maintenance, repair and operating supplies. See also Croom (2000) on how Internet technology could support MRO buying.

not place great stock on an all-encompassing information system that supposedly offers every possible type of functionality in the field of purchasing. The reason is that because of the position of suppliers in the portfolio it is highly unlikely that they will all be willing to cooperate in integration. Powerful suppliers with strong positions will force their systems upon their customers. Customers in such cases will unfortunately have to adapt to their suppliers rather than the other way around. Obviously, the story is completely different for purchasing segments where the customer holds a dominant position with respect to the supplier.

Consultants and suppliers of these solutions have great expectations of possible profits resulting from these solutions. The following is claimed:

- Important advantages can be gained from electronic sourcing through electronic market places. Increased market transparency and the accompanying improved options in the field of competition can lead to considerably lower purchasing prices. The advantages for direct and indirect goods differs. For direct goods the percentages are between 1% and 15%; for indirect goods potential savings are estimated at between as much as 15% to 30%.
- By using electronic catalogue systems, more purchasing transactions can be contracted so that the percentage of maverick buying[9] can be drastically reduced. This again would lead to considerable savings.
- Transaction costs can be reduced (from a mere hundred to just tens of Euros per transaction) by using integrated ordering and goods handling systems. Here we see the third source of potential savings.

These estimations sketch a picture that will catch the eye of any reasonable manager. However, perhaps some warnings should be given also. With regard to the first issue, it is true that a broader market orientation and greater competition can be expected to lead to lower prices.[10] However, this only applies to enterprises that have had a poor and unprofessional purchasing policy in the recent past. In our opinion this is the reason why a number of enterprises with very professional purchasing policies have been rather reluctant to participate in electronic market places. In addition, we believe that advantages gained in this way will be of a temporary nature; after an initial period all participants will level out to the same price regarding their purchasing. Based on this argument we do not believe market places exclusively aimed at pricing will survive for very long. But there is more, surveys[11] show that top managers generally are more positive about the options offered by electronic procurement and electronic market places than their purchasing managers. The latter continue to refer to the importance of good suppliers, who score well on the basis of a good business relationship founded on total cost of ownership. The purchasing managers resist the opportunistic attitude and short-term advantage that can be achieved.

---

[9] This refers to the share of the purchasing volume that is bought without a contract (often a considerable share of the total purchasing expenditure).
[10] See also Chapter 10.
[11] See also the special issue of *Purchasing*, 15 June, 2000, which is exclusively dedicated to E-Procurement (pp. 6–13).

MEMO 9.4: What problems are solved by E-Procurement systems?

E-Procurement systems[12] enable users within organizations to order directly from an electronic catalogue without interference from a purchasing department. Orders are acknowledged automatically by the supplier. The user can verify the order status on-line when desired ('When will the order be delivered?' 'What terms and conditions apply?'). There is no need for any contact with the purchasing department regarding such questions. Many suppliers nowadays offer detailed tracking and tracing facilities which enable their customers to monitor order, follow-up and delivery in real time. Besides this, E-Procurement systems enable electronic invoicing, invoice matching and payment. As a result the traditional purchasing cycle is reduced considerably and simplified (see Figure 9.4).

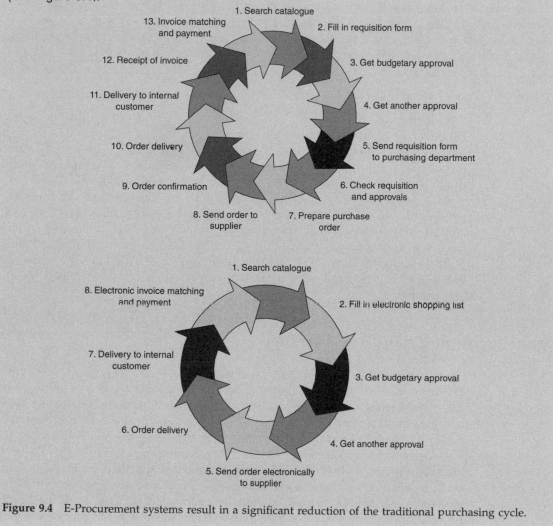

Figure 9.4 E-Procurement systems result in a significant reduction of the traditional purchasing cycle.

[12] Here the term is used in the narrow sense. See also Kalakota (1999), Chapter 10, for a detailed discussion.

Continued on page 180

> **Memo 9.4: continued**
>
> Implementing E-Procurement systems allows companies to reap significant benefits in terms of both lower materials prices and lower organizational costs. E-Procurement systems represent an important productivity tool for both purchasing managers and departments, since these will lead to a significant reduction in administrative workload. At the same time customer service levels will improve because internal customers will now have the responsibility and authority for ordering the materials they need through pre-arranged and efficient order routines. Finally, savings may result from the fact that common material requirements are grouped in homogeneous product families, which are ordered from electronic catalogues from fewer suppliers. Concentration of a larger volume among fewer suppliers, again, may lead to better prices. However, implementation of E-Procurement systems is a far from simple matter. It requires a high level of purchasing professionalism, clearly spelled out purchasing procedures and a seamless integration with the general ledger system and other systems within the company. Next, these systems need to match with the administrative systems of suppliers, which in many cases is a big problem!

Reducing maverick buying is a good resolution and nearly always pays off. However, it is hard to realize due to all sorts of political considerations and sensitivities in the field of purchasing within enterprises. The introduction of electronic ordering and catalogue systems requires a properly defined purchasing structure, which is still lacking in many companies.

With regard to the potential savings that can be obtained in transaction processing, we would like to point out here that the costs related to this mainly consist of personnel and system costs, which are very inflexible in most European countries. Cost advantages in either field can only be realized slowly within the European social structure and legislation. This means the advantages listed are only realized after a far longer period than that sketched by most consultants.

Agent technology and the Internet

So-called software agents are expected to play an important role within E-Procurement in the near future. A software agent is a piece of software that can operate more or less independently, is capable of learning (intelligent agents) and in some cases can move across the Internet (mobile agents). These agents are presently used to locate web sites that offer the best price for a given product. They are also used in auctions, where the agents independently participate in the bidding process within the boundary conditions specified by a given buyer and/or seller. A well known example is a Spanish academic experiment with an electronic fish market, where homemade agents can participate in the bidding process (http://www.iiia.csic.es/Projects/fishmarket). Agents reduce the workload for users, who would otherwise have to spend considerable time carrying out Internet searches or standing by to participate in the bidding processes. Some infamous viruses are perhaps the most known example of software agents. Their effects may be very negative, but they are an illustration of the new opportunities which are constantly arising on the World Wide Web.

Summary

Independent of the question whether the various phenomena in the field of E-Procurement[13] will prove successful, it is obvious that the traditional b2b landscape is undergoing fundamental changes.[14] Anticipating and using these means is far from easy and requires a carefully designed corporate strategy, which should give priority to how to result in an integrated supply chain. In this chapter we have demonstrated that neither entrepreneurs nor purchasing managers should rush into things. Rather, they should make a thorough study of what electronic solutions have to offer in terms of realizing and helping to support their overall business objectives. Much attention should be paid to the question of to what degree the introduction of the solutions mentioned will contribute to the realization of a sustainable and defendable competitive advantage. As we see it, the Internet is not a miracle cure for poorly working purchasing organizations. Before making large-scale investments into E-Procurement solutions and electronic markets, it is necessary to check whether the conditions for their successful application within the organizations are present. Using the points listed in Memo 9.5 may be useful. Even if the conditions for a successful introduction are present, the introduction of E-Procurement will nevertheless be a tough process. In general it will take much time and effort to ensure the compatibility of the systems involved.

MEMO 9.5 Are you ready for E-Procurement?

- Does the organization have a fully understood purchasing and supply strategy that matches and supports the business strategy of the corporation?
- Is article or commodity management adequately structured through cross-functional buying teams?
- Is an objective procedure available for the selection of suppliers?
- To what extent are operational purchasing/order systems compatible with the electronic solutions that are under consideration? Is flawless integration possible with current general ledger systems?
- Are structured and documented purchasing procedures in place and adhered to?
- Is purchasing authorization organized?
- Are there clear ordering and handling procedures available supported by Work Flow Document Control?
- Are supplier and purchasing contracts regularly revised?
- Etc.

---

[13] Here the term is used in the broad sense.

Only a few enterprises have the luxury of putting their house in order, of making effective use of E-Procurement. However, in our opinion there is little choice. Purchasing and supply managers will be forced to invest and to gain experience with new electronic tools in the field of purchasing. We advise managers to keep their investments low and to control them.

Assignments

9.1   Conduct a global sourcing, 'best deal' assignment, using the Internet, aimed at buying consecutively: (1) 20 tons steelplate (C1119 Mod. and C1144, 1 inch thick and 100 inches wide); (2) rental of a mid-size car in New York for three days; (3) car insurance, full cover, for a car with a catalogue value of 35,000 Euros; (4) 140 tons bunkeroil. What supplier provides the best value for money? Assess how each of the stages of the purchasing process model (specification, supplier selection, contracting, ordering, expediting, evaluation and follow up) is supported by the Internet.

9.2   This chapter describes how electronic market places develop within different types of industries. Electronic market places can be initiated by different parties: sellers, buyers and/or intermediary organizations. What factors explain the success of electronic market places? Which of the three market places mentioned here (initiated by sellers, buyers or intermediaries) will be the most successful in your opinion? Discuss!

9.3   A large manufacturer of handtooling equipment considers whether to implement an E-Procurement system in one of its manufacturing locations. Describe what it will take to be able to do so effectively. What role would the purchasing department have in such a process?

9.4   Find European examples for each of the types of electronic market place that have been identified by Kaplan and Sawhney (2000).

9.5   Implementing electronic solutions in purchasing should, according to some leading consultants, lead to impressive savings. From what sources are these savings derived? Mention at least three possibilities. How easily can these savings be realized?

PURCHASING, ENGINEERING AND QUALITY CONTROL 10

Learning objectives

After studying this chapter you should understand the following:

- The possibilities and impossibilities of integrating the purchasing function in technical design and development processes.
- The most important concepts concerning purchasing and quality control.
- The purchasing function's role in and contribution to quality management.
- The elements necessary for an approach aimed at improving supplier quality.
- The consequences of the implementation of total quality management for the purchasing organization.

CASE STUDY
Chrysler's Viper

Car buffs got their first look at Chrysler Corp's Viper in January, 1989, at the North American International Auto Show in Detroit. The curvaceous show car drew huge crowds, and Chrysler President Robert A. Lutz quickly gave the preliminary OK to develop a mass-production version. But he set strict guidelines. Get the Viper ready in three years, he ordered – two years faster than usual for Chrysler. And he set the development budget at just $700 million, 45% less than MAZDA Motor Corp. spent on its Miata roadster. Now, with the first Vipers starting down the assembly line on Nov. 18, the car looks like something of a milestone. The $50 000-model's sales won't be large – Chrysler plans to build only 200 Vipers next year, rising to 3000 annually in the mid 1990s. But the sexy two-seater should draw car buyers into showrooms – which is crucial, because Chrysler can't live off hot minivan sales forever. Chrysler's car market share fell again in the 1991 model year to 8.9%. And for the first time, Japan's Honda Motor Corp. passed its US car sales. However the Viper sells, Chrysler used the car as a laboratory for learning efficient new development techniques. With the company's losses through Sept. 30 estimated at about $1 billion, that could be a key to helping troubled Chrysler stay independent. "There just aren't the money, the people, or the time to do it the old way", says David E. Cole, director of the University of Michigan's Center for the Study of Automotive Transportation.

Continued on page 184

Chrysler is already adapting some of the lessons it learned on the Viper to its new LH line of midsize cars, due out next year. But Lutz admits that "by Japanese standards there's still a lot of waste" in the LH-program. On later models, he says, using Viper development will cut costs dramatically . . .

What's the secret to the savings? In developing the Viper, Chrysler fully embraced the simultaneous engineering techniques pioneered in Japan. This meant forming a small team composed of specialists in engineering, manufacturing and marketing as well as outside suppliers. The teams performed the development tasks together, avoiding for example the need for designers to keep making changes after manufacturing engineers couldn't produce what had been asked for . . . Chrysler also cut costs by having Viper suppliers engineer key components such as the transmission. More than 90% of the Viper's parts will come from suppliers versus 70% for a typical Chrysler . . .

To cut bureaucracy the Viper was developed as a lean 'skunkworks' project. The model had a development team of just 85, hundreds fewer than most Detroit projects . . .

(Source: *Business Week* (1991) 4 November, pp. 42–44)

Introduction

The Viper case description reflects several issues. First of all it reflects that to be able to remain in a competitive position, Chrysler must pay considerable attention to reducing the 'time-to-market'. This is the time period between the moment the development of a product is started and the moment it is introduced to the market. Japanese companies need considerably less time for this than European companies. And this situation, unfortunately, is not limited to the automotive industry! In the second place this case description illustrates the importance of suppliers' contributions in the development stages of new products. Suppliers are a major source of ideas at this stage: working together instead of working at arm's length not only leads to a considerable result in terms of engineering lead-time reduction, but also to important cost benefits. For if suppliers are involved in the product design at an early stage, they can provide their suggestions about simplification of the design and substitution of materials with types that are easier to process, etc. This chapter addresses the role and significance of development processes in companies. The role assigned to the purchasing function in this context will be identified and the contribution that purchasing can and/or should make to the company's quality policy will be discussed extensively. It will become clear that the implementation of total quality control generally has far-reaching consequences for the purchasing organization.

Purchasing and engineering

In Chapter 5 were listed four primary tasks or responsibilities that the purchasing function must cover. The fourth task was to contribute to product and process development by spotting technical developments which take place at suppliers, and to translate them in terms of the company's own needs. To give substance to this task, it is reasonable to suggest that the purchasing function must be involved from the early stages of development. In addition, purchasing should continuously strive for improvement of the suppliers' quality performance. These subjects are now further expanded.

Purchasing's early involvement in the engineering process

Many companies attempt to track down new technologies and products through systematic market research. The results of this research are usually translated by the marketing department into several new product ideas which are then discussed with research and development, and the engineering department. These discussions are often the starting point for projects aimed at improving current products or the development of new products.

Depending on the nature of the product and the type of company, the development process, starting with conceptualization and ending with introduction on the market, will pass through several stages.

- *Product development*. In this phase the ideas supplied by the marketing department are translated into a few concrete, but still relatively abstract **functional designs**. Such designs describe the functions that the product to be developed will have to fulfil for the user. From these functional designs, the most promising design is selected to be elaborated further.
- *Product design*. In this phase the functional design is worked out in detail – proposals are made about the materials to be used, the physical properties that the product must satisfy, etc. Often, several product designs are produced which meet the functional design and these can be presented to potential clients at an early stage, in order to get their first reactions and impressions (**concept testing**). This information enables the engineers to focus on the most promising design. Subsequently, the product design is elaborated in the form of a **prototype** or **mock-up**. If necessary this prototype can also be presented to potential users.
- *Preproduction planning*. The manufacturability of the product has already been considered during the product design stage. At this stage the production requirements are taken into account. After the prototype has been approved, preparation for production can be started. If it concerns a technically complex product, this phase may take a lot of time and it may be necessary to purchase new production equipment. The requirements of this new equipment will have to be determined based on (among other things) the market exploration and the sales forecasts. Preproduction planning frequently ends with a number of **preproduction series**.
- *Start of the production*. Products from the preproduction series are subjected to thorough examination; based on the results of this examination the product design or the settings of the machines might be adapted so as to limit future production problems to a minimum. One of the problems that might occur in this phase is changing the specifications. Every change is documented in a

change-order sent by the engineering department to the purchasing department in order to discuss this with the supplier. This phase means a lot of work for the purchaser involved in this project. Every change in the specification has to be approved by the supplier, the consequences for the total costs have to be analysed, the changed product needs to be tested again, etc. This is one of the reasons why it takes so long for a new product to become available for customers. After all the problems have been taken care of, actual production can commence.

It goes without saying that it is possible to refine this sequence of steps, depending on the nature of the product and the type of company. As the product development process advances, the specifications become more rigid and it becomes more difficult to introduce changes. The consequence for purchasing is that its latitude decreases and the costs of technical changes introduced at a later stage in the process become higher (see Figure 10.1).

Many engineers and developers usually play it safe: their primary interest is in materials and components that solve the technical problem they are faced with. Once a suitable material or construction has been found, tested and approved, the willingness to consider any alternatives (in the form of a different material, component or a substitute product from another supplier) will be limited at a later stage. This is because an alternative will have to be tested and approved again, which implies not only a lot of work, but also risks. This attitude of the engineer, to reduce technical risk, may result in specific components being specified in the direction of one particular supplier because of positive

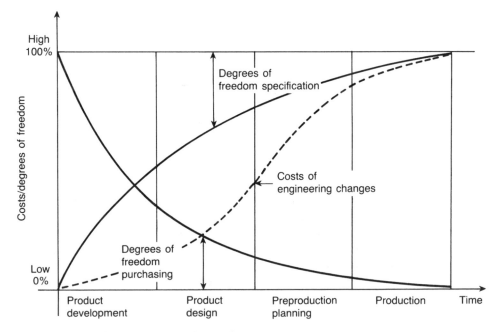

Figure 10.1 Purchasing's relationship to the engineering process.

experiences with this supplier in the past (see Memo 10.1). This puts the buyer in a difficult situation since it is very difficult to negotiate with such a supplier, if one can speak of negotiating at all. Based on his job perception, a buyer will always attempt to have more than one supplier to fall back on. So, for the buyer to be able to go out into the market, the product preferably must be described in terms of functional specifications (rather than in terms of supplier or brand specifications). There exists, therefore, a kind of natural conflict in the way designers and buyers operate (Figure 10.2) which can only be solved by means of **cross functional development teams**.

How do large manufacturers communicate with their first tier suppliers in product development projects? Possibilities are:

- *Purchasing engineering.* This is a specialist function to provide the liaison between the engineering department and the purchasing department. Purchasing engineers are members of the design teams, where they will evaluate designs against purchasing-specific criteria. It is their task to bring in specific supply market knowledge at an early stage of design.
- *Early supplier involvement (ESI).* Those suppliers, who have proved in the past to be 'best-in-class', are invited to participate in the company's development projects at an early stage. In this way they are able to criticize future designs, suggest alternative materials, come up with ideas for more efficient manufacturing, etc. at a stage where engineering changes can be made without severe cost consequences.
- *Residential engineering.* A next step is to locate engineers from the other party on a more or less permanent basis within the organization, in order to work on design or manufacturing problems which appear during the successive stages of development. Examples are seen at large manufacturers who have placed engineering specialists at their suppliers' premises in order to resolve a variety of problems (sometimes referred to as supplier support teams).

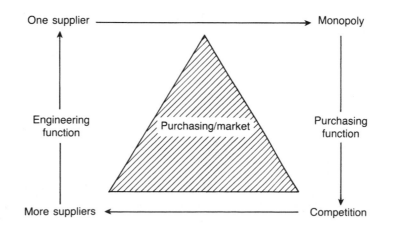

Figure 10.2 Interaction between purchasing and engineering activities. (Adapted from Schijvens, 1985.)

However, there are also cases where engineering specialists from suppliers are located at the customer's organization.

Buyers are important scouts for any organization when it comes to spotting new technical developments; in their professional capacity they come into contact with suppliers, products and technologies much more frequently than engineers and developers. Buyers are **generalists**, while engineers are **specialists**. Involving buyers in development processes at an early stage can result in the contribution of new knowledge and a better understanding of construction, suitable materials, suppliers, and also the early introduction of supplier knowledge. Practice has shown that **early supplier involvement** can result in considerable cost reductions and product improvements (see Table 10.1) This is the reason why, for example, Philips Electronics speaks of **co-design** in addition to co-makership.

Table 10.1 Involving the supplier in new product development can result in considerable savings

Stage of product design	Degree of design complexity or product uniqueness (%)		
	Low	Average	High
Initial design	2–5	10–25	30–50
Changing existing design	1–3	3–15	15–25
Redesigning to improve quality	10	15–30	40–60

The figures indicate the percentage of savings on the cost price (see de Rijcke, Faes and van Weele (1982)) see also Wijnstra, (1999) for more research on this subject.

MEMO 10.1: Suppliers' catalogues

Some suppliers cleverly take advantage of the uncertainty that engineers experience in their design activities. They make it easy for them by providing a catalogue with all the information about the product assortment they carry. Examples are European distributors of technical components who provide (electronic) catalogues to their clients which list all their products. These concern small articles, such as switches, condensers, resistors, fasteners, etc. The most important technical data are presented for all these articles, together with the article number which can be used to order them.

To specify the technical description of these articles is, of course, a very labour intensive task and, for the sake of convenience, many designers just list the article number from the catalogue on their design. The result is that the articles, described in that way, can only be ordered from that specific distributor.

Through this practice some distributors have been able to build captive customer relationships against handsome margins. Electronic catalogues prove to be very successful. They often go with handy terminals, from which orders for materials can be placed directly at the distributor. Obviously, this type of relationship and ordering procedure is facilitated by Internet technology.

Development projects require careful project management. Targets on design-to-cost and time-to-market need to be carefully translated in detailed action plans and cost-budgets. Ideally, the project planning for a new product development project will identify at what time suppliers will be involved in the project. Memo 10.2 shows how Océ has solved this problem: this company differentiates between four possible relationships with their supplier during the design and development process. A distinction is made between co-design (where a supplier engages in developing specifications), co-development (joint development of a prototype that meets the specifications) and co-making (manufacturing the product according to specifications and production schedule). In this case the term Early Supplier Involvement relates only to the first two concepts.

MEMO 10.2: Early supplier involvement at Océ

Océ's range of products contains copying, printing, plotter and document handling systems. Océ develops and produces the main part of these products by itself (see also case at beginning of Chapter 8). The company is heavily research-oriented: annually about 7% of the turnover is invested in research and development. For its new line of copiers Océ has started a technological co-operation with KMWE Precisie Eindhoven and Nedal Aluminum in order to develop a new photocarrier cylinder. This part is one of the high-tech, key-components of any copier.

Nedal Aluminum is the supplier of the basic aluminum and KMWE shapes this into the cylinder with high precision. KMWE has been a supplier for Océ for many years, but this new product has many new and much higher technical requirements. For this reason KMWE was selected after a thorough and careful selection process.

For the supplier selection Océ has developed a special questionnaire: the Questionnaire for Preventive Supplier Evaluation. Through this the engineering capacity and capabilities of potential suppliers are assessed and documented. The questionnaire covers the following subjects:

- *Identification details*: relates to subjects like ownership and shareholders of the company, organizational structure, major clients, breakdown of turnover, investments made recently and major suppliers.
- *Technical competence*: relates to the production process, type of machinery and equipment available, transportation equipment and type of manufacturing systems in place, type of materials requirements planning systems used.
- *Financial situation*: here Océ want the supplier to provide detailed financial figures and records.
- *Quality control*: questions here relate to the quality control systems in place, quality certificates, organization of quality function, manuals which are available, method of evaluating suppliers.
- *Price information*: here questions are asked on method of cost price calculation, allocation of overhead costs, and the willingness to co-operate based on open calculations.

Océ has a very clear strategy on product development and the involvement of suppliers in the new product development process. Prior to actually developing a new product, all parts, key-components and subassemblies are plotted down into a matrix (see Figure 10.3). The technical

Continued on page 190

Memo 10.2: continued

aspects and costs of every part are analysed. Furthermore the supply risk and the availability of each specific component is assessed. Based on this analysis, four quadrants usually apply:

- *Strategic components.* In this quadrant Océ pursues a relationship with prospective suppliers based upon **co-development**. The example of the photocarrier cylinder fits into this category. Suppliers for this type of components are selected at a very early stage in order to be able to let them participate in the development teams as early as possible. Part of the development and design work is done by the suppliers.
- *Leverage products.* Here Océ pursues a relationship with the supplier based upon **early supplier involvement.** Actual development of the component is done by Océ itself. The suppliers involved are contacted in the engineering phase, before starting pre-production. At this stage suppliers bring in their ideas on how to manufacture the parts involved in the most efficient way. This may lead to some minor technical changes in the original design of the parts. Next, suppliers will provide prototypes which will be tested by Research and Development.
- *Routine components.* Suppliers of routine products are involved when all design and development work and engineering activities have been finished. In fact they need to submit their proposals based on detailed designs and specifications, as provided to them by Océ. Relationships with suppliers here can be characterized as jobbers or routine suppliers.
- *Bottleneck components.* This type of component normally causes a lot of trouble given the large dependence on the supplier. When identified early during the design and development process it is assured that sufficient alternatives are considered.

Through this Development Portfolio (see also Wijnstra and Ten Pierick, 1999) the joint purchasing and R&D teams are able to decide for what component at what time which supplier to involve. Experiences are that only a very limited number of suppliers is invited to participate in the new product development process at a very early stage. However, their activities may easily cover 80% of the targeted cost price of the new product!

2. LEVERAGE PRODUCTS EARLY SUPPLIER INVOLVEMENT coatings, sub-frames, motors, couplings	1. STRATEGIC PRODUCTS CO-DEVELOPMENT TL-lamps, lenses, stapling heads, mainframe, photocarriers
4. ROUTINE PRODUCTS –BUILT TO SPEC– simple, moulded parts, mechanical components	3. BOTTLENECK PRODUCTS EARLY SUPPLIER INVOLVEMENT/RISK MANAGEMENT rubber transport materials, reflectors, special surface finishings

Figure 10.3   Development Portfolio as used by Océ.

Purchasing and quality control

Definition of terms: quality and quality assurance

After the product specifications have been released the purchasing department must assure that they will be met by the supplier. The products that are to be manufactured must remain within these specifications. In addition, the purchasing department has to ensure that the suppliers will honour their agreements on other points, such as delivery time, delivery quantity and price. In this way buyers need to reflect total quality management approaches in their ways of working.

What exactly is quality? The literature on the subject contains almost as many definitions as there are authors who have written about it. A distinction is made between concepts such as 'functional quality', 'physical quality', 'fitness-for-use', etc. One common definition of **quality** is:

> the total of features and characteristics of a product or service that bear on its ability to satisfy a given need. (American National Standards Institute, quoted in Moffat *et al*. 1993: 40)

Without wanting to do any injustice to these terms, the author would opt for IBM's simple definition of quality:

> Quality is the degree in which customer requirements are met. We speak of a quality product or quality service when both supplier and customer agree on requirements and these requirements are met.

The requirements mentioned in this description can relate to the technical properties of a product. However, they can also relate to user-friendliness, ease of maintenance, delivery agreements and packaging instructions. Here, the author proposes to take a broad view in that the quality concept is related to more than just the physical properties of the product!

Most large companies initiate quality programmes for the purpose of effecting a change in attitude towards quality. These programmes also address the issue of quality control. **Quality control** is defined as 'making sure that the requirements are met' and being able to demonstrate this objectively. This implies that for every transaction between customer and supplier, they will agree on

- the basic requirements of the transaction;
- the way in which the requirements are to be realized;
- how to check that the requirements are (being) fulfilled;
- the measures to be taken when the requirements/expectations are not met.

These steps form the four basic elements of the **requirement–verification** cycle, which is shown in Figure 10.4.

In summary, quality control entails all activities and decisions aimed at taking the organization's products and services to the desired quality level and to maintain that level. Quality control therefore requires intensive consultation and sound tuning between the various departments in the organization and with outside suppliers and customers. After the desired quality level has been established, the complete production process must be organized in such a way

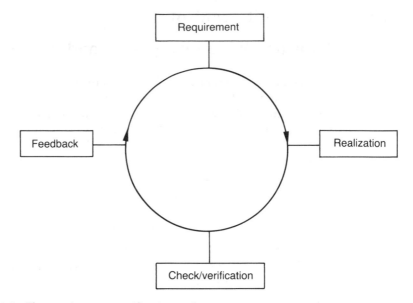

Figure 10.4   The requirement–verification cycle.

that this level of quality is reached and maintained in a controllable manner. To accomplish this, quality management has at its disposal four interrelated functions: setting standards, assessment, control, and assurance. This last function will now be addressed in more detail.

Quality assurance is an important criterion for supplier selection. What guarantees can the supplier give with regard to design and technical specifications? According to what quality standards is it proposed to operate?

Quality assurance concerns **keeping up the methods and procedures of quality control**, i.e. systematically checking that they are efficient, that they lead to the desired objective, and that they are applied correctly. Internal company assessment of these issues is often called **auditing**; external assessment is referred to as **verification**. An external assessment establishes the degree to which the methods and procedures used satisfy the conditions which have been recorded in national and international standards. The best known are the ISO-9000 standards, which are accepted in many European countries. These will be discussed later.

The collection of methods and procedures used for quality control is called the **quality system**, which is usually recorded in a **quality handbook**. This handbook should be the (formal) reflection of the way in which quality control, including quality assurance, actually functions in practice.

The costs of quality

Crosby (1984) pointed out that it is not so much quality, as the lack of it that costs money. The concept of quality costs can be used to initiate quality improvement initiatives. In many companies a considerable number of man hours are spent on the inspection of incoming goods and on solving acute quality problems (troubleshooting). The costs involved are often invisible and many companies have absolutely no idea what the lack of quality is costing them. Making these costs identifiable starts with classifying them. In practice three types of quality costs are distinguished:

- prevention costs – the costs of preventing errors;
- assessment costs – the costs related to the timely recognition of errors;
- correction costs – the costs that result from (rectifying) mistakes.

Prevention costs are all costs that are related to actions in the context of preventing quality errors. Prevention costs therefore include the expenses related to the development, implementation and control of the system of total quality control. This concerns matters such as

- conducting systematic product inspections;
- executing process controls;
- ensuring that product inspections and process control (auditing) are conducted systematically and periodically;
- investigations to uncover the causes of errors and mistakes;
- establishing the internal organization of quality control;
- drawing up specifications, procedures, instructions and regulations for the total quality control system;
- the development of special testing and measuring equipment and other tools in support of quality assessment;
- education, training and motivation of personnel on quality management.

Assessment costs are incurred to minimize the consequences of errors. Examples are:

- incoming or acceptance inspection of purchased goods;
- inspection of intermediate and semi-manufactured products;
- sorting the production (100% inspection) to track down faulty products and to separate them from good products;
- final inspection of products and quality assessment of finished products;
- registration and processing of and reporting on the measuring data.

Quality can be present in various degrees. This must be taken into account during the inspection procedure of a product series. Some of the rejected items may be made suitable for the client's production process by minimal treatment. However, these corrections come with a price-tag. The so-called **error costs** are usually divided into internal and external categories.

Internal error costs (including wastes and losses) emerge as a result of mistakes which are noticed in time, i.e. before the product is delivered to the customer. These include

- the costs of corrective measures;
- losses due to product downgrading;
- losses due to a reduced speed or even standstill of production, to the extent that they are caused by quality deviations in materials or components.

External error costs are a result of flaws identified by the customer. This group includes

- the costs of processing complaints;
- costs made for settling customer claims and disputes;
- costs of processing return shipments from customers;
- loss of 'goodwill'.

For many years the emphasis has shifted from **correction** to **prevention**. In an attempt to reduce the total quality costs, preventive quality control has been enhanced. This is illustrated by Figure 10.5 which shows the quality costs model.

Supplier quality assurance

An important role in the implementation of total quality management is reserved for the purchasing department. This is because the quality of the finished product is determined to a very large extent by the quality of the basic and raw materials! Working on improving the quality offered by the suppliers is therefore a main task for buyers. For this reason many large manufacturers in Europe have established supplier quality assurance (SQA) programmes (see Memo 10.3).

To improve the quality of their products, many companies opt for an approach based on prevention. Co-operation is required from every department in the company, and this also applies to the purchasing department. With regard to purchasing, the **objective of prevention** is to maintain and/or improve the

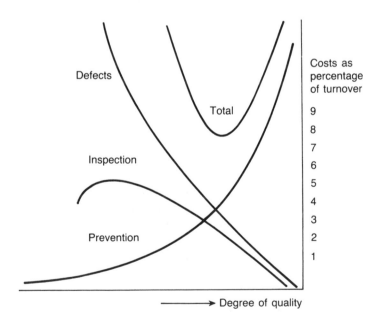

Figure 10.5   The quality costs model.

MEMO 10.3: Inter-functional co-operation at IBM

Large companies give a lot of attention to improving co-operation across business functions. In this context IBM started developing a programme to achieve 'zero defects' in co-operation with Philip Crosby. Top managers in all IBM branches took quality courses. These managers developed zero-defects programmes in every production plant. The first initiatives were aimed at shifting attention from the detection and correction of errors to the prevention of errors.

The suppliers were invited to participate in the seminars, for the purpose of acquainting them with IBM's objective of zero defects, and to convince them of the importance of this objective. The role of the suppliers in all this was strongly emphasized. The supplier's employees were the next link that had to be made aware of the quality message.

Potential suppliers were selected on the basis of a checklist. The total quality performances of the supplier were considered: conformance, quality of production, the supplier's attitude towards quality and response to quality problems, facilities and personnel.

The quality performance (in a broad sense) of existing suppliers is evaluated continuously. One important parameter is the so-called quality-conformance of the supplier. Conformance in percentages is the ratio of the number of accepted deliveries divided by the total number of deliveries in one month. A delivery is accepted when inspected samples meet the standards. The suppliers are audited periodically. In addition, delivery reliability is measured and assessed, as are the price and cost behaviour and the administrative accuracy of the supplier!

Most production plants inform their suppliers about their performance on the subjects mentioned on a monthly basis. Every year the best supplier receives an award (the IBM Supplier Award). All of these measures are aimed at one objective: motivating suppliers towards continuous product and process improvements.

quality of goods and services to be purchased. This is based on selecting the supplier who can guarantee a sufficient level of quality. It is important that the supplier can also guarantee this quality level for the future. The preventive approach is expressed by the following measures.

- *Preparing the purchase order specification.* A sound preparation is half the battle. Many problems can be prevented if there is an up-to-date, complete purchase order specification and it goes without saying that this specification contains a technical description, supplemented with the designs. It will also contain an estimate of the materials requirements for the short and middle term, and additional logistic requirements such as packaging and transportation needs. At this stage clear **sign-off procedures** are important. The release of designs to suppliers cannot take place without the purchasing department's approval. This procedure also encompasses (future) engineering changes.
- *Preliminary qualification of (potential) suppliers.* Here the distinction between potential and existing suppliers must be made. Potential suppliers are sent a questionnaire before they can qualify for an order. The purpose of this questionnaire is to gain insight into the delivery possibilities of these suppliers. After a positive evaluation of the responses, a second round takes place. A team consisting of a buyer, a quality expert and a production

manager visits the supplier and subjects the quality system in particular to an investigation **(quality audit)**. A statement is then made about a possible order. As a rule, manufacturers document the results of their investigation and report on these to the supplier's management. Weaknesses found in the supplier (quality) organization and process are discussed. Corrective measures are suggested and agreed upon. These are to be written down by the supplier in a quality improvement programme. The activities recorded in this programme are checked in periodical progress meetings. Based on the observed progress it is determined whether a supplier qualifies for orders related to new (development) projects or if he can only supply for existing projects. Of course there is a third possibility, that the relationship will eventually be terminated.

- *Sample inspection procedure.* The next step on the road to acceptance of a new supplier is the sample inspection procedure. The supplier is requested to manufacture a sample product in co-operation with the design department. This product will then be assessed on its conformance with the requirements as agreed beforehand. Suggestions to achieve improvement of the product can be elaborated by the supplier as well as by the design department. This type of co-operation results in a certain degree of co-design. A number of large manufacturers use the number of times that the sample has to be offered for final approval (the **initial sampling reject rate**) as a measure for the supplier's design quality. The most important objective at this stage is to establish the degree in which the tools (moulds, templates) that will be used to produce the products, will meet the requirements.
- *Delivery of first and subsequent preproduction series.* The next step is to have the prospective supplier manufacture a preproduction series. Specialists from the customer company will be present during production to audit the process. Attention is paid specifically to the degree of process control and the functioning of the quality control organization. Afterwards the strong and the weak points of the process are analysed and agreements are made about adjusting the process. In the end this co-operation can result in a partnership agreement.
- *Manufacture of the first production series.* This is the moment of truth. Has the supplier lived up to his agreements? Is he capable of really meeting the zero-defect requirement? The customer checks the process completely: all products are inspected for quality (100% inspection). If everything is satisfactory, then the level of inspection is reduced. The ultimate goal is to reach a situation of direct acceptance of delivered products, i.e. without prior inspection. In this way the customer avoids the incoming inspection, which is a major source of costs.
- *Quality agreement and certification.* As a rule, a quality agreement is closed when the objective of zero-defects has been reached. This agreement determines that the supplier will manufacture the products involved in the way agreed upon with the manufacturer. It also describes the change procedures, which are so very important: i.e. in what way should the manufacturer and the supplier act if it is necessary to deviate from the

agreements (for example if there is a change in the technical design). The quality agreement usually involves one product (article code).

The supplier who proves able to supply, without any defects or mistakes, all deliveries of all products which are purchased from him by the manufacturer is awarded a certificate by the client. The certified supplier is placed on the final list of preferred suppliers which means he is also eligible for new, future projects. If there are no problems, these suppliers' deliveries are subjected to inspection only a few times each year.

- *Periodic verification*. The extent to which the tasks which have been agreed on with the supplier in the context of product and/or process improvement are being realized, must be checked periodically. Should it turn out that the tasks were set too high, adjustments can be made. If the tasks are fulfilled, then this results in new tasks being formulated. In this way the concept of continuous quality improvement (or *Kaizen*) in the relationship with the supplier is given substance.

At this stage many large manufacturers work with computer-supported **supplier rating systems**, which are used to record and report on the suppliers' performances on several points (see Memo 10.4).

A few closing remarks in conclusion of this section now follow.

- *Supplier selection*. Selection of new suppliers is a cross-functional issue. Ideally, the following functions should be involved: purchasing, design, quality, production, production planning. Considering Ford, for example, the cross-functional product development teams request two or three qualified suppliers to make a proposal for the design of new components. Following analysis, the buyer negotiates with the supplier. If this negotiation leads to acceptance of the proposal, this supplier usually remains solely responsible for the delivery during the lifecycle of the product ('life-of-type responsibility').
- *Functional design*. Industrial customers must enable their suppliers to study the design of the complete subassembly beforehand. This is in line with the growing trend of drawing up only general specifications. Based on these specifications, the supplier can submit a design proposal. The customer's designers should concentrate on the design of essential parts and not on designing, for instance, valves and switches.
- *Feedback and recognition*. Feedback and recognition are prerequisites to motivate suppliers towards a better performance. Looking at a company such as Hewlett-Packard, it is seen that they assess their suppliers every 3 months, every 6 months and every 12 months, depending on the nature of the delivered components. In the assessment they judge technology, quality, response time, reliability and costs. In addition there are consultations between members of the Hewlett-Packard purchasing teams and the major suppliers, in which the results and possibilities for improvement are discussed in detail. Just as for IBM (see Memo 10.3) and other large manufacturers, Hewlett-Packard provides an annual award to the best-performing supplier.

MEMO 10.4: Supplier rating at Alcatel Bell Antwerp

'Alcatel Bell only buys from sources which have been selected on the basis of their ability to meet requirements' (ISO 9001, par. 4.6.2.). These sources are registered in the Procurement Management Systems Database as 'approved', 'potential', or 'discontinued'. Any buyer can purchase from the approved sources. Purchase from suppliers with the status of 'potential' or 'discontinued' are subjected to the approval of senior buyers.

The quantity and identity of purchased goods is always verified at the receiving gate. Whether or not additional incoming inspection is performed, depends on the nature of the purchased materials and the confidence Bell Alcatel has in the supplier; this confidence is indicated by the Incoming Inspection Category (IIC) which once again features in the Procurement Management System Database.

The IIC ranges from 0 to 9. The IIC provides us with a steering mechanism enabling us to optimize the incoming inspection resources. We judge quality performance of a supplier by comparison with others who supply similar components. This comparison is based on two indices:

1   The IIC, which is a measure of the amount of incoming inspection we still have to perform and which consists of an average of the evaluated IICs.
2   The Quality Index (QI) based on the quality of actual deliveries. This QI takes into account the percentage of deliveries with a problem and the percentage of delivered products with a problem.

For each percentage point, 5 points are deducted from a level arbitrarily set at 1000. Based on this score suppliers are at present considered to be:

very good	$QI > 990$
good	$990 > QI > 950$
poor	$950 > QI > 900$
bad	$QI < 900$

(Source: Bell Alcatel, *Quality On Time Magazine*, 1st Quarter (1991))

- *Dependency.* Raising quality requirements leads to a reduction of the number of suppliers. For many buyers, this development has resulted in the fear that suppliers might be gaining a more powerful position *vis-à-vis* the buyers. This fear is not completely justified because, as a result of the new co-operative relationships, many suppliers are also becoming more dependent on large manufacturers. Companies that start to function as 'single source' suppliers get involved in a product policy they have no control over, and as such they have no guarantees that the life cycle of the product is long enough for them to recover the investments they make. Large manufacturers must not lose sight of the fact that it is of vital importance to the suppliers that they keep making profits. Both parties would suffer if the supplier's financial means were insufficient to invest in R&D, process innovation, training, etc.

● *Testing relationships*. To uncover the suppliers' needs, Ford Supplier Relations conducts a confidential survey annually. Several suppliers are asked to describe in detail how they experience their co-operation with Ford. The information gathered in this way is passed on to all management levels of the departments of Quality Control, Design, Production Control and Purchasing. To motivate suppliers towards just-in-time deliveries, Ford also organizes regular seminars in areas such as statistical process control and total quality management.

Assessing supplier quality: diagnostic methods

Several methods are available for the evaluation or assessment of suppliers' quality policies. Earlier, a distinction was made between internal and external assessment. As a rule, the following methods for assessing a supplier's resources are at the buyer's disposal:

● product audit;
● process audit;
● systems audit.

The **product audit** provides an image of the degree in which a company succeeds in making everything run perfectly, i.e. according to the standards and demands established by the company itself. The product is judged and every flaw is registered, the cause located and removed. Frequently, the observed deviations are awarded defect points in terms of reject rates. The total score provides, to some extent, an image of the quality level of the entire production process.

The **process audit** is a systematic investigation of the extent to which the (technical) processes are capable of meeting the established standards in a predictable way. It is also checked whether the raw materials, semi-manufactured materials, etc. are satisfactory, and whether the job instructions and process instructions are complete and clear. In short, the process audit investigates whether the process operators have at their disposal all the facilities (including expertise) to ensure sound and controlled production. This is also sometimes called a 4M audit (man, materials, machines, methods).

The **systems audit** compares the quality system to external standards. A standard, or norm, is used which is a generally accepted guideline. Standards can be either general standards or company-specific standards. Examples of general standards are the Allied Quality Assurance Publications (AQAP), originating from the military, and the European NEN-ISO standards. The latter are presented in Table 10.2.

One major company-specific system standard that is used for auditing suppliers is the Ford Q101 procedure. The supplier is required to answer questions related to some 20 subjects. Questions are answered by means of awarding a score between 0 and 10. The total score gives an indication of the quality of the production process. Volvo employs a systems audit which is based on the Ford Q101 system. Table 10.3 shows the subjects that are addressed in such an audit.

Table 10.2 The ISO 9000 series of quality assurance standards

Standard	Title
ISO 9000	Guidelines for selection and application of ISO 9000 through 9004
ISO 9001	Requirements concerning quality control in purchasing, development, production and sales (equivalent to AQAP 1)
ISO 9002	Requirements concerning quality control in purchasing, production and sales (equivalent to AQAP 4)
ISO 9003	Requirements concerning quality control of final inspection and testing (equivalent to AQAP 9)
ISO 9004	Guidelines for the organization of a quality system
ISO 8402	Terminology and definitions

Table 10.3 Structure of systems audit automobile manufacturers

	ACTION PLAN
NR. SUBJECT	Jan Feb Mar Apr May Jun Jul Aug Sep Oct Nov Dec

1. Organization
2. Planning
3. Documentation and management of technical changes
4. Manufacturing equipment control
5. Production – procedures
          – instructions
6. Inspection – procedures
          – instructions
7. Standards
8. Means of inspection
9. Quality assurance purchased components
10. Process parameters
11. In-process inspection
12. Final inspection
13. Sampling instructions
14. Nonconformance
15. Quality and inspection status
16. Materials handling
17. Training personnel
18. Documentation and registration
19. Corrective measures
20. Volvo inspections at suppliers

Classification		Required points
A1	Qualified	825–855
A2	Qualified, with comments	755–820
B1	Acceptable	645–750
B2	Acceptable, with reservation	535–640
C	Not acceptable	

External verification contributes to the assurance of the quality system or, as the case may be, to keeping up the quality system, and it also demonstrates that the system meets the standards.

Many suppliers strive to live up to the standards, especially the NEN–ISO standards. A supplier who meets the standards becomes eligible for certification. Whether or not the candidate-supplier possesses one or more certificates plays a major part in purchasing's decision to use this particular supplier.

Many companies have their organization assessed by an independent organization in the context of a quality certifying programme. In most European countries Certification Councils have been founded during the last 10 years. These councils are the central (national) institutions that confer competence on certifying organizations to give out NEN–ISO 9001, 9002 or 9003 certificates to the organizations that meet the relevant standards. Such a certificate is evidence of the company's capability with regard to the quality of the system, at least for the period of its validity.

Not all manufacturers attach the same value to these general standards and accompanying certificates. Some continue to use their own company-specific standards, which suppliers must meet to qualify for co-operation. Examples are the military AQAP standards and the Ford Q101 standards mentioned earlier. Even during a long-term agreement between supplier and manufacturer, periodical checking (especially of the system, the process and the product) against the standards, is necessary. Based on the results of the audits, the decision is made to either continue the agreement or to start looking for an alternative supplier.

Implementing supplier quality assurance: consequences for purchasing

As a rule, the implementation of total quality management requires considerable adjustments in terms of structure, systems and patterns of communication. The same applies to the purchasing department that wants to pursue a specific policy with regard to supplier quality assurance. Some of the most important changes that will have to be prepared for are now discussed.

- *Clear task descriptions*. There is not much point in formulating a general policy without formulating clear and unambiguous tasks. For that reason it must be very clear what supplier quality assurance is expected to yield in terms of, for example:

  - maximum rejection percentages per article code or per supplier;
  - the average term in which rejection reports must be dealt with (per buyer);
  - number of quality agreements closed with suppliers;
  - number of certified suppliers, etc.

- *Clarity concerning supplier selection*. As the demands made on suppliers increase, there are also higher demands on the manufacturer's entire organization, and on the purchasing department in particular. It must be clear who within the company is competent to enter into relationships with suppliers. In particular it must be clear who is responsible for the ultimate selection of suppliers. Requirements must be communicated to the suppliers from one central point so as to prevent misunderstandings.

- *Quality first*. Taking responsibility for quality also means being accountable and being judged on it. If the ultimate selection of suppliers is made by the purchasing department, then it must also be possible to call this department to account on the quality these suppliers deliver. This means that rejection percentages, the number of quality agreements, etc. are becoming part of the buyer's annual assessment.
- *To measure is to know*. It is essential that suppliers receive feedback on their performance. This is done in the form of a report on the findings of the audit which has been carried out, but is also needed in the form of a supplier rating score on subjects such as rejection, too late or too early deliveries, administrative errors, etc. This requires the appropriate administrative procedures, which should be computerized where necessary. Producing such data is not necessarily a simple matter, because the basic information is often stored in different systems and in various locations within the company.

The implementation of quality control in organizations is frequently a process of trial and error, with many ups and downs. The same goes for introducing a supplier policy based on quality principles. The extent to which problems occur regarding these aspects provides an indication of the extent to which suppliers are really seen, or experienced, as an essential link in the business chain.

Summary

In this chapter the interfaces between purchasing, engineering and quality assurance have been shown. As the competitive environments of organizations become more turbulent, issues such as 'time-to-market', flexibility and product and service quality become more important. In those circumstances it is crucial to do things right the first time, because every error leads to time loss and extra costs.

It has been shown that co-operation between engineering, purchasing and suppliers offers considerable opportunities. As the product development process advances, the product specifications become more and more fixed, and it therefore becomes more difficult to introduce changes. Furthermore, changes made at a later stage will make the costs rise exponentially. Buyers are important scouts when it comes to spotting new technological developments that occur in the supplier market. Buyers are generalists, while designers and engineers are predominantly specialists. To them, the technical solution is often more important than supply. To prevent technical problems in the future, designers will tend to operate as specifically as possible and to record their designs in detail. This may go against the buyer's interests: he would like to see the product design drawn up in functional terms, so he can use different sources of supply in the future.

The product design is the basis for product quality. The term 'quality' has been taken in a broad sense, i.e. as 'the degree in which the requirements are met'. It has been seen that this concept entails more than just the technical properties. Quality control contains all activities and decisions whose purpose is to bring the organization's product to the desired quality level and to keep it there. These terms were central in the discussion of supplier quality assurance. The purpose of supplier quality assurance is improvement of supplier quality in the broadest sense. Some elements involved in a quality approach towards suppliers are:

- preparation of the purchase order specification;
- preliminary qualification of (potential) suppliers;
- sample inspection procedure;
- inspection of first and following preproduction series;
- inspection of first and following production series;
- quality agreement and certification;
- periodic verification.

Several methods used by manufacturers to assess the qualities of their suppliers were considered and the distinction between the product audit, the process audit and the system audit was explored. With regard to the latter it is general practice to follow the ISO standards. The most widely known and followed systems audit developed by manufacturers is Ford's Q101.

Assignments

10.1 In this chapter the author contends that quality control must be regarded as an integrated business function – indicate why. Which departments in particular are involved in the quality control? Illustrate your answer.

10.2 Which types of quality costs can be distinguished? Provide at least two examples of every type. To what extent can the purchasing department contribute to a reduction of the quality costs?

10.3 The purchasing manager can undertake preventive activities to maintain or increase the quality of the goods and services which are to be purchased. Supplier selection is the most important activity in this context. Indicate which steps can be distinguished in the selection procedure.

10.4 Some large manufacturers have a supplier quality assurance section in their purchasing department. This section is responsible for the improvement of supplier quality. Other organizations have no such section and their buyers work in co-operation with specialists from the central department of quality control. Which of these constructions do you prefer? List the advantages and the disadvantages of both.

10.5 What do you feel supplier evaluation means? And what in your opinion is supplier rating? Can you indicate the most important similarities and differences?

10.6 This chapter talked about a corrective and a preventive approach to quality issues in organizations. What is the difference between the two? How would you recognize these approaches when applied to purchasing?

PURCHASING AND SUPPLY CHAIN MANAGEMENT

11

Learning objectives

After studying this chapter you should understand the following:

- The definition of logistics and the basic logistics concepts;
- The most important steps in the materials planning cycle;
- How logistics activities can be structured within organizations;
- Characteristics of just-in-time scheduling and purchasing;
- The most important elements of a purchasing information system.

CASE STUDY
Changing supply chains in the chemical industry

More chemical buyers are reducing the cost of buying chemicals by consolidating as much volume with as few distributors as possible, and asking the chosen few to provide a variety of value-added services. National distributors are scrambling to meet the demands of this new market niche, while regionals are starting to form co-operative relationships that enable them to compete.

Buyers want distributors to help them cut costs in several ways:

- Through simplified billing and payment processes, especially electronic commerce.
- By managing inventory to the point of total inventory management, in some cases.
- By performing value-added services, including toll and custom manufacturing and bar coding, as well as more traditional services like blending.
- By providing some form of price protection.

Typically, these types of arrangements involve two or three national distributors serving major chemical customers. More recently, smaller buyers with only one or two plants are consolidating distributor chemical supplies. Some relationships are sole source, but those are the exception rather than the rule.

National distributors like Van Waters & Rogers, Ashland Chemical's Industrial Chemicals and Solvents (IC&S) Div., Chemcentral Corp., and Soco Chemical are the major players thus far,

Continued on page 206

according to several industry sources. However, regional distributors are now attempting to work together to offer all the benefits of integrated supply while taking advantage of the close, long-term local relationships they have with customers.

In chemicals the term 'integrated supply' is rarely used by distributors, and almost never used by buyers. But what's in a name? There's no question that this trend is alive and growing quickly in chemical buying. But the ride is still a bumpy one. Both buyers and distributors agree that implementing the plan is much more difficult than creating it.

(Source: www.purchasing.com)

Introduction

This chapter addresses the role and significance of the purchasing function in the materials planning process. In this context the focus is on several important concepts and developments in the field of logistics management. The materials planning cycle is described, which will make clear how materials planning processes affect the ordercycle and the incoming materials flow. In discussing this subject the chapter will differentiate between different logistics structures that can be encountered in industry. Hence the distinction will be made between order-based materials processes and forecast-based materials processes. Given its importance there will be ample discussion of the subject of just-in-time manufacturing, lean supply and the impact of these concepts on purchasing and supplier relationships. Finally, this chapter discusses the major elements and principles in designing effective purchasing information systems.

Purchasing and logistics: definitions

The term 'logistics' stems from military organization and was in use in the days of Louis XIV of France. Even then it was clear that the effectiveness of the military organization did not depend solely on the weapons, the fighting strength and the fighting spirit of the soldiers. It was also affected by the possibilities of transportation and the efficient supply of ammunition and food. The rationalized consideration of the transportation and supply of materials, food and ammunition was called **logistics**. The French military successes of that time were mainly due to the importance attached to logistics.

Logistics and flexibility go hand in hand. Flexibility is getting a lot of attention in many companies today where **functional thinking** still dominates. In a functional organization individual departments such as sales, production, product development administration, purchasing and personnel, come directly under the board. Each department has very specific tasks which are established in annual departmental budgets. Realization of these budgetary tasks is an important factor in departmental assessment and managers often strive to realize their own budget targets, even at the expense of other departments.

This practice can easily lead to departments operating fairly autonomously so that co-ordination of the whole is left to the interplay of forces between the departments themselves. Logistics management aims to counterbalance the shortcomings of functional thinking and thereby provide a better service to the customer.

A description of logistics, which covers most characteristics mentioned in management literature, is the following. Logistics management encompasses all materials flows, from the flows of purchased materials into a facility, through the manufacturing process, and out to the customer (see, for example, Vollman, Berry and Whybark, 1984, p. 571). The starting point is the short-term sales plan and the related product plan. The total logistics function therefore involves short-term materials planning, the supply of raw materials and other purchased goods, internal transportation, storage and physical distribution.

Speed and flexibility demand very close co-operation between these materials-related functions. Logistics management therefore applies to a very broad area of activities and is sometimes also referred to as **materials management** and/or **integrated business logistics**. Figure 11.1 illustrates the relationship between these and other materials concepts.

The following features are relevant to an understanding of the importance of a holistic view of the company's materials processes.

- Design, engineering and development activities can strongly affect materials management, for these activities determine the structure of the (future) manufactured products. The tolerances and specifications of products and the components they are made up of, can be defined in such detail, that they can only be obtained from a few suppliers. One question in the context of the design activities is to what extent one strives for **standardization** of components. If new components are specified for each new end product being developed, then this irrevocably leads to a very extensive article assortment. This will have considerable consequences for the degree of sophistication of the materials planning and control systems.

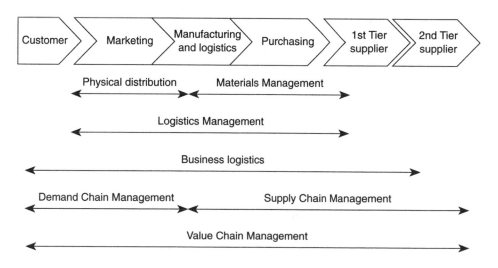

Figure 11.1 The business chain and some related terms.

- The production department also determines the effectiveness and efficiency of the logistics function to a large extent. The production department will usually aim for a high-capacity utilization. Disruptions of the production process as a result of rejection and shortages of materials are undesirable. A production manager will take certain measures to prevent such disruptions, for example by building up buffer stock. Although these measures may reduce the threat of production stops, the cause of the problem remains. In other words, these 'solutions' (which used to be applied in many companies) actually represent **suboptimization** – although the measure is a solution for one department, it is not for the entire organization.
- Logistics management starts with the customer. If the sales organization, for the sake of landing an order, promises a delivery time within the internal production lead times, materials problems are likely to occur! This frequently results in 'rush work' in production planning, production, and . . . purchasing. It leads to a situation in which purchasing must exert considerable pressure on suppliers to get the required materials earlier . . . and often at considerable extra costs!

Some authors (see, for instance, Schmidt 1986) describe logistics management as:

> the management (i.e. the planning, execution and control) of all factors that affect the materials flow and the information about it, seen from the perspective of customer requirements, for the purpose of achieving: high delivery reliability, a high degree of delivery completeness and a short delivery time.

This author clearly differentiates between materials management and integrated business logistics. This broader description is interesting, because the relationship between the supplier and the customer is also included in this logistics concept. It has become clear that suppliers can make important contributions to the improvement of the materials flow management. The same applies to the involvement of customers: if they are willing to give up or adjust certain requirements (for instance with regard to packaging and minimum delivery quantities) considerable savings or simplification of the materials management structure can be the result. For these reasons this book will henceforth use the integrated business logistics concept in its discussion.

Some authors and managers differentiate between materials management and **physical distribution**.

As a rule, materials management encompasses the materials flow between supplier and final assembly. Physical distribution focuses on the optimization of the materials flow from the moment that the goods are 'released' by production up until the moment that they have been delivered to the customer and/or have been installed.

Over the past decade more and more attention has been given to the concept of supply chain management (SCM). Stevens (1989) looks at the supply chain as the connected series of activities which is concerned with planning, co-ordinating and controlling material, parts and finished goods from suppliers up to the customer. This author extends the concept of business logistics to other tiers in the supply chain. This is also recognized by Cooper and Ellram (1993) who present supply chain management as an integrative philosophy to manage the total flow of a distribution channel from suppliers to the ultimate user. Like vertical marketing systems SCM is a systems approach to viewing the channel as a whole rather than as a set of fragmented parts. SCM differs from traditional approaches on inventory control and focuses on the management of inventory control through the entire supply chain (ibid: p. 2). Successful SCM relies on forming strategic partnerships with trading partners along the supply chain, with one partner playing a key role in coordinating and overseeing the whole supply chain . . . (ibid: p. 3).

This last description proves that supply chain management should be considered as a logical extension of the logistics concepts, which have been described. It says that in order to be able to manage cost throughout the supply chain, effective and co-operative supplier relationships are required. Hence, purchasing and supply management (including supplier management) can be seen as an integrated part of supply chain management. In fact, the latter concept encompasses both the logistics and the purchasing and supply function.

Materials requirements planning

Materials requirements planning (MRP) starts in the sales department with drawing up a sales plan. This plan provides an estimate of the volume that management thinks can be sold in the following months or the year to come. Data are presented both at product-group level and at the product/article level. Comparison of the sales plan with the available finished product stock yields the volumes to be produced. This information is the input for the manufacturing planning and control system (see Figure 11.2) in which the following elements can be distinguished.

- *Master planning*. In the master plan the manufacturing plans at the level of the product families (product groups) are established in consultation between the departments of sales, product development, manufacturing, finance and administration and logistics. In the master plan the customer orders, the sales plan, the planned stocks of finished products and the production and purchasing plans are linked together.
- *Manufacturing resources planning (MRP-II)*. The resources needed to realize the master plan are recorded in the manufacturing resources plan, from which the required composition of manufacturing resources is derived. In the process it may become clear that particular production series are not feasible because production capacity is insufficient. This necessitates adjustment of the master planning and/or adjustment of the manufacturing capacity. In the latter case an investment plan needs to be prepared for adding additional production capacity.
- *Master production scheduling (MPS)*. The master production schedule translates the master plan into specific materials requirements. The MPS is also the basis for computing the quantities of materials, semi-manufactured

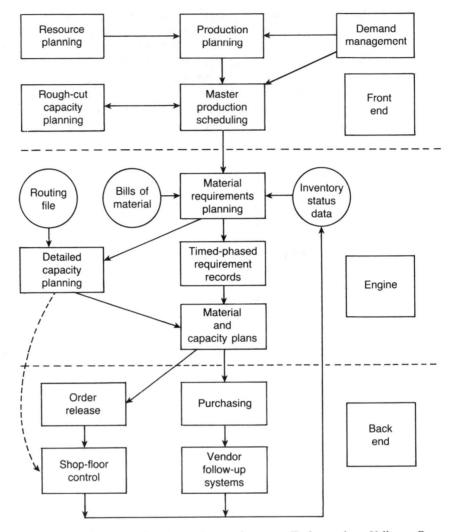

Figure 11.2 Manufacturing planning and control system. (Redrawn from Vollman, Berry and Whybark, 1984, p. 25).

products and components which must be manufactured. In this way the MPS provides the input for calculating the net materials requirements

- *General capacity testing*. The MPS must also be tested for capacity limitations. This should be done for all potential bottleneck capacities. Such a check may reveal that the internal capacity is insufficient to produce certain components. If that is the case, the possibilities of contracting out the production of these components, or buying them, must be investigated.
- *Materials requirements planning (MRP)*. The materials requirements planning 'explodes' the requirements of the MPS level, step-by-step, in accordance with the bill of materials. It determines the materials requirements at the

different levels of product structure and, finally, at the materials (item) level. If at some level identical requirements emerge from different MPS items, then these are grouped and added up per period. These needs are called the gross requirements and are converted into net requirements per period. This is accomplished by deducting the stock in hand from the gross requirements and subsequently deducting the manufacturing orders and purchasing order volumes that have already been placed. The net requirements are then plotted, taking into account the ordering procedures that have been developed. In this way the materials requisitions are built up. These requisitions must be available in time, to be ordered from the supplier or to be manufactured by the company's own manufacturing departments.

- *Capacity requirements planning*. Capacity requirements planning is conceptually comparable with materials requirement planning. The current and planned manufacturing orders from the materials requirements planning provide the input for the detailed production line planning. The required capacity is compared with the available capacity per production line (machine). The capacity requirements planning spots, at an early stage, where and when utilization problems will occur, so that preventive/ alternative measures may be taken. If it is impossible to solve these problems, then the MPS must be adjusted.

- *Order release*. Order releases change the status of the manufacturing orders and purchase orders from 'planned' to 'released'. The decision to release is based on the availability of the required materials and capacity. If a manufacturing order is released by a planner, the information system automatically allocates the required materials to this order. This prevents these materials being allocated to another process or manufacturing order. The system generates documentation for issuing the materials and components required to feed the manufacturing orders; in case stock is insufficient it generates materials requisitions for purchasing (i.e. purchasing requisitions).

- *Priority management*. The priorities are derived directly from the master production schedule. Each unit receives a priority sheet which lists all manufacturing orders for that production line or machine centre. Orders with the highest priority should be given preference; regular 'overdue' reports indicate which manufacturing orders and purchasing requisitions will not be executed on time.

- *Capacity management*. The issue of managing lead times, work-in-progress (WIP) and capacity is a complex one. To prevent under-utilization, manufacturing always tends to take on more work. However, when the expected workload (the input) exceeds the available capacity, long waiting periods ensue. The various manufacturing orders will be waiting longer, the lead times increase, the amounts of work in progress grow and delivery reliability decreases. This is why it is of the utmost importance that the waiting times per processing group are controlled. Input/output reports have an important function here; to compare the realized output for a production unit against its planned output.

The literature makes a distinction between MRP-I and MRP-II. MRP-I stands for materials requirement planning; this type of management system aims at releasing manufacturing orders and purchasing requisitions and at managing them. MRP-II stands for manufacturing resources planning and entails more than MRP-I. It is an integral system that controls relevant materials flows and production capacity, while also taking into account the relationship between these materials flows and the required capacity.

Basic logistics structures

The systems described above are characterized by the fact that they are forecast-based. The more accurate the sales forecasts, the more accurately production planning and materials requirements can be determined. It will be clear that in practice the unpredictability of sales orders is the stumbling block in the application of these systems. Furthermore, industrial manufacturing and logistics practice often shows much more variation than we have outlined here. Many companies have **order-based production** (as in the shipbuilding industry) instead of a **forecast-based production** (as is the practice in the processing industry). In customer-order-controlled manufacturing companies, production and materials plannings are derived directly from the customer order. Every order is **customer specific** and therefore requires individual handling. Each sales order in fact represents a unique project. The customer's requirements tend to become known only at the last moment, which results in high time pressure. In such a situation the project approach to production is much more effective than an approach based on the MRP method. In other words, the application of MRP systems is limited to (small and large) series and process production.

In practice there are numerous hybrids between those production companies managed solely on the basis of customer orders and those based on forecast alone. Most manufacturing companies, unfortunately, have to deal with both types of manufacturing and goods flows. The **order decoupling point** (or **order penetration point**) concept is of major importance when organizing for efficient manufacturing and logistics. The order decoupling point indicates how deeply the customer order penetrates the firm's materials flow (Hoekstra and Romme, 1985, p. 80). It defines from what moment on a production order becomes customer specific. The order decoupling point separates the activities based on order information from the forecast-based activities. This is important because these two types of activity require totally different planning techniques. Hoekstra and Romme (1985) distinguish the following situations.

- *Making and sending to stock (MSS).* Products are manufactured and distributed to various distribution points which are dispersed and located close to the customer. Manufacturing is based upon forecasts and on the expected stock turnover at the points of distribution. Examples are the manufacture of sweets, foods, beverages.

- *Making to stock (central stock) (MTS).* Finished products are kept in stock at the end of the production process and from there are shipped directly to many geographically dispersed customers, as in the manufacture of dairy products.
- *Assembly to order (ATO).* Only systems elements or subassemblies are in stock at the manufacturing centre and final assembly takes place based on a specific customer order. In other words, manufacture of components takes place based on forecasts and final assembly takes place based on customer orders. Examples are the manufacture of cars, computers, materials handling equipment.
- *Making to order (MTO).* Only raw materials and components are kept in stock. Every customer order is a specific project. Examples are the manufacture of beer and lemonade cans, basic construction materials.
- *Engineering and making to order (ETO).* In this situation there is no stock at all. The purchase and order of materials takes place on the basis of the specific customer order and the entire project is carried out for this one specific client. Examples are construction companies and shipyards.

Figure 11.3 presents these situations in diagrammatic form.

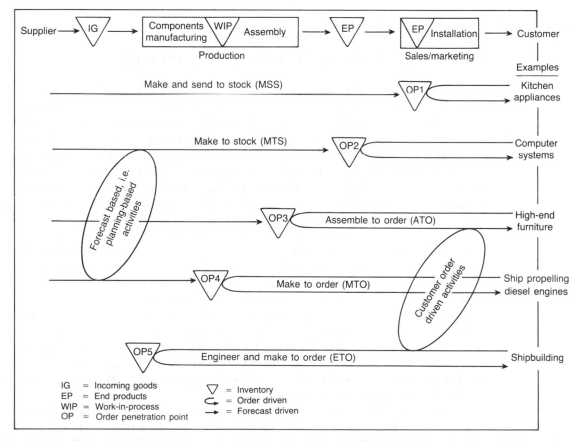

Figure 11.3 Order penetration point – the deciding factor for an effective logistics structure. (Redrawn from Hoekstra and Romme, 1985.)

The question of where the order decoupling point should be located in the company's primary processes is a major issue when designing the manufacturing and logistics organization. The answer to this question also determines where in the process inventories should be located and in what quantities. The role and position of the purchasing function will differ in each of the situations described above. In the first situation the planning of the quantities to be purchased per period is fairly predictable. Based on expected volumes, annual (bulk) agreements can be negotiated with suppliers or price agreements with a long period of operation can be made. Based on the production planning, delivery schedules can be drawn up and made known to the supplier.

In the last situation purchasing strongly resembles project purchasing. Every project is new – new suppliers have to be found for every production order, the products that are to be manufactured must be discussed in detail with suppliers, and intensive consultation between the design and/or engineering department is necessary. On-time delivery and quality are more important than price! Purchasing must be able to respond to changes in design and project planning quickly.

Just-in-time management (JIT)

Characteristics of just-in-time management

The principle of just-in-time management (JIT) means that all materials and products become available at the very moment when they are needed in the production process, not sooner and not later, but exactly on time and in exactly the right quantity. The major objective underlying this approach is to continuously tackle and solve manufacturing bottlenecks within, and interface problems between, consecutive steps in the manufacturing processes. Incoming inspection, buffer stock, and extensive quality control procedures on incoming materials are primarily considered as 'waste'. The basic idea is to strive continuously to reduce these often 'hidden' costs in the factory.

Just-in-time management implies that nothing is produced if there is no demand. The production process is in fact 'pulled' by customer orders. The 'customer' is in fact the organizational entity which is 'next-in-line'. This concept, therefore, may relate to other departments within the company itself. However, it may also relate to external customers, outside the organization. When no customer orders have been received, manufacturing activities will come to an end and the spare time is used to do minor repairs/maintenance, housekeeping and/or prepare for materials planning. The spare time may also be used to discuss how to improve on the work currently being conducted within the organizational entity ('small group activities'). No production, therefore, does not imply that the time is used unproductively.

Because they contract out a considerable amount of work, many large Japanese producers work closely with a limited number of suppliers (which are sometimes organized in supplier networks or supplier associations). The bulk of the materials requirements are supplied from these suppliers. It is not uncommon that one manufacturer is responsible for more than 50% of a supplier's turnover. At the same time this same supplier may deliver 80% of the manufacturer's specific materials requirements. This leads, contrary to many European manufacturers, to a large interdependence between manufacturers and suppliers. As a result Japanese manufacturers are able to benefit much more from the supplier's expertise and capabilities. Another aspect is that Japanese manufacturers in general focus on assembly only. All component manufacturing is outsourced to specialized suppliers. Since the producer frequently represents a large share of the supplier's turnover, a maximum effort by the supplier is ensured. Obviously, there is some risk involved for suppliers when engaging in this type of relationship: if there is no market demand for the customer's product, there will be less work for the supplier. In this way part of the business's economic risk is transferred to the suppliers. However, if the producer can guarantee a certain production volume for a number of years, it becomes appealing for the supplier to invest in new technology. Japanese supplier relations are characterized by their long-term orientation (three to five-year contracts).

Order quantities and batch sizes

Continuity in production demands a constant availability of the required materials. Manufacturing managers continuously need to decide when and how much should be ordered from their suppliers. There are several models that can be used for optimizing the incoming materials flow. One very well-known model is **Camp's formula**. The variables used in this inventory model are.

S fixed usage per period
t delivery period
Q order quantity
C_0 costs per order
C_i inventory carrying costs for one unit during one time unit.

The **economic order quantity** is where the sum of inventory costs and ordering costs per unit is lowest. Ordering large quantities from suppliers has the advantage that the ordering costs (fixed costs) can be spread out over a larger number of products. Hence, large order quantities will lead to a lower order cost per unit. The disadvantage of ordering large quantities, however, is that larger quantities of the product must be kept in stock for a longer period of time, which naturally implies higher inventory carrying costs per product.

Starting with the order quantity Q and a usage rate per period S means that in a given period S/Q orders are required. The order costs for that specific period therefore will amount to $S/Q \times C_0$.

The average inventory level, measured over one period, is $1/2\ Q$ and the total inventory costs for the considered period are $1/2\ Q \times C_i$.

The total ordering and inventory costs will be

$$\frac{S}{Q} \times C_0 + \frac{1}{2} Q \times C_i$$

The economic order quantity can now be calculated (Camp's formula) as

$$Q_0 = \sqrt{\frac{2S \times C_0}{C_i}}$$

Although this formula has received significant interest from practitioners, it is only of significance under the following conditions:

- the consumption of the component at hand is fairly stable;
- the consumption of the component is evenly spread over the course of time;
- the delivery time of the product is fixed and not due to fluctuation;
- the ordering costs per order are fixed;
- the inventory carrying costs do not depend on the ordered quantity, etc.

The just-in-time approach basically challenges each of these assumptions. For example, order-related costs are analysed in terms of costs related to:

- negotiations with the supplier;
- administrative processing;
- follow-up and expediting of orders;
- incoming and quality inspections.

Suppliers are now classified in categories, depending on the degree in which they represent work for the buyer. Suppliers who comply with the stringent JIT conditions require no more investigation. This saves costs on the four items mentioned above. By systematically considering how savings can be accomplished for each separate cost item, the buyer succeeds in reducing the optimal order quantity. A graphic representation is provided in Figure 11.4.

The reasoning used for determining the economic order quantity can also be applied to determining the (optimal) batch size in production. This issue arises when one production line is used to produce different products or product varieties. Changing production from one product to another means that the production line needs to be reset, a process which usually costs time and money. In general, four steps in the process of setting up a production line may be identified.

- *Preparation*. This includes gathering tools, moulds, spare parts, work instructions, etc. and transporting them to the machine or production line concerned.
- *Conversion*. This is the dismantling and rebuilding of the machine or production line, mounting the appropriate tools and moulds, and, if necessary, cleaning.
- *Setting up*. This refers to setting the machine in such a way that the desired quality and speed is achieved; a trial run may be necessary.
- *Finishing*. Finishing may consist of removing, cleaning and storing the used tools and spares, and removing the finished product.

While the machines are being reset nothing is produced. Many companies therefore regard setting-up production lines as a necessary evil. In practice the easy solution is frequently chosen: the production line is used to make the same product for a longer period of time, so that less frequent re-setting is required. In other words, the batch size is enlarged to benefit from economies of scale

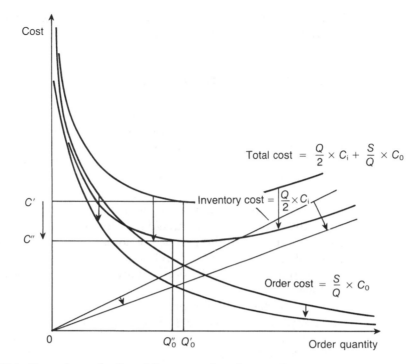

Figure 11.4   Towards a reduction of the economic order quantity.

achieved as the result of a lower set-up cost per unit produced. Moreover, this practice leads to a much better capacity utilization in production (yield). Clearly, one disadvantage of this way of working is that the size of the stocks related to semi-manufactured products and finished products and the associated **inventory carrying costs** increase. The decision about the optimization of batch sizes must therefore be based on balancing set-up costs against inventory costs. The **optimal batch size** is achieved when the sum of the inventory costs of work in process and set-up costs per unit produced is lowest.

Thinking based upon economies-of-scale and production yields, which still can be observed in many manufacturing organizations, limits production flexibility and fast response to customer requirements. This poses a problem for manufacturers when customers demand short lead times, which happens in many markets nowadays.

By systematically striving for reductions in set-up times, the optimal batch size can be reduced considerably. Often, when calculating the optimal batch size, the set-up costs of the production machinery, among other things, are considered fixed. These costs can be very high. Japanese production thinking has continuously focused on the question of whether these fixed costs can be made variable. Japanese producers have constantly looked for ways to minimize their set-up costs and times. Much has been achieved by means of organizational measures, and new machines have been designed that are easier to handle and set up. As a result, optimal batch sizes have been reduced considerably, enabling

Japanese producers to benefit from low costs per unit together with a high product mix flexibility in their production.

Quality and zero defects

A second characteristic of the just-in-time principle is related to quality awareness. Smaller batch sizes make it necessary to detect quality defects at an early stage. In most Japanese companies every employee is responsible for the quality of his/her work. If a production employee notices that a particular part does not meet the specifications, he/she immediately notifies his/her colleague in the previous link of the production process. It may be that the conveyor belt has to be stopped. The advantage of this procedure is the fast response time – corrective action is taken immediately following a complaint. This situation is in sharp contrast with the practice of some European companies, where defective material is first put aside, then handed over to the quality department, which in turn contacts the production department in question in order to solve the problem.

It is clear that the JIT approach must be supported by all functions within the company. Top management should actively support foremen and shop floor workers in providing the resources necessary to improve manufacturing operations. Adopting a JIT approach will take considerable time; it took Toyota 15 years to implement its famous KANBAN philosophy. There is considerable attention to quality in Japan because there is almost no slack in the production process. This means that a defective product may threaten the continuity of the whole production process.

Traditional quality control procedures were often based on inspection after a set number of parts had been manufactured. The rejected parts were dismantled and, when appropriate, repaired. Just-in-time management requires that everything goes right the first time. In Chapter 10 this principle has been referred to as the 'zero defects' principle. It will be clear that just-in-time production and scheduling cannot be successfully implemented without a 'zero defects' philosophy.

Having discussed the major characteristics of just-in-time management, the question of what its introduction means for the purchasing department and for the performance of suppliers is now addressed.

JIT and the purchasing function

The JIT concept cannot be limited to production only. It must be supported and implemented in every functional area in the organization. Applied to purchasing, JIT is a philosophy that aims to make exactly the required materials and products available at exactly the time they are needed, so that value is added only to the product which is to be manufactured, and indirect costs are avoided.

What does the introduction of JIT mean for the purchasing function? JIT has a major impact on both the quality and the quantity of the materials to be purchased. Table 11.1 lists the main differences between the traditional purchasing approach and the JIT approach.

The JIT approach is characterized by regular but flexible supply. Ordered materials are delivered frequently (sometimes, in an assembly environment, several times a day) in different quantities. To facilitate this the supplier is informed of the production planning and the related purchasing requirements on a daily, weekly and monthly basis through delivery schedules which are available on-line. In this way he is able to anticipate on his customer's future requirements. Hence, he will be able to plan his production and materials requirements more effectively. Apart from this, there are some other definite advantages of working with suppliers in this way. The producer uses in general long-term contracts, against which periodic call-off orders are placed. Once (or more often) a year the conditions are renegotiated with the supplier. Targets for productivity improvement and cost reduction, as required by the producer, are also part of these negotiations. Agreements on these issues are documented and communicated to the supplier. In essence, they are the standards against which the future performance of the supplier is going to be monitored and measured.

As far as quality is concerned, the guiding principle is zero defects. Imposing quality targets upon suppliers may represent large savings to the producer, both in terms of a reduction of the number of incoming quality inspections and a reduction of buffer stock. In this way the supplier is educated towards a better quality performance.

Table 11.1 Differences between the traditional approach and the JIT approach in purchasing

Purchasing activity	Traditional approach	JIT approach
Supplier selection	Minimum of two suppliers; price is central	Often one local supplier; frequent deliveries
Placing the order	Order specifies delivery time and quality	Annual order; deliveries called off as needed
Change of orders	Delivery time and quality often changed at the last moment	Delivery time and quality fixed, quantities are adjusted within predetermined margins if necessary
Follow-up of orders	Many phone calls to solve delivery problems	Few delivery problems thanks to sound agreements; quality and delivery problems are not tolerated
Incoming inspection	Inspection of quality and quantities of nearly every delivered order	Initial sample inspections; later, no inspections necessary
Supplier assessment	Qualitative assessment; delivery deviations of sometimes up to 10% are tolerated	Deviations are not accepted; price is fixed based on open calculation
Invoicing	Payment per order	Invoices are collected and settled on a monthly basis

The practices described above are still different from the traditional purchasing practices of most European companies. Traditionally these are aimed at creating optimal **competition** between suppliers. Relations with suppliers are, in this approach, mostly focused on the short term; dependency on a single supplier is considered to be fundamentally wrong. Traditional purchasing theory prescribes multisourcing, i.e. obtaining materials from various suppliers. The underlying idea is that a company must not become too dependent on one single supplier. Therefore, many manufacturers prefer multiple sourcing in their supplier relationships. Where possible, single sourcing (see also Chapter 8 on this subject) should be prevented.

Looking at the characteristics of JIT it is clear that traditional buyers must alter their views and policies radically, in order to adopt this approach:

- willingness to consider single sourcing as an appropriate strategy;
- willingness to arrange longer term contracts instead of 'one-shot' deals.

The criteria used to select and assess suppliers must also be adjusted. The demands made on suppliers are different and (generally) considerably higher. These refer to both product and process quality (zero defects) and delivery reliability (just-in-time). The purchase price, traditionally a prime issue in the negotiations, usually will get a lower ranking within the selection criteria used.

The JIT approach was initially introduced to the United States and Europe by subsidiaries of Japanese companies. Nowadays, many European companies are attempting to follow their example. Philips Electronics and Alcatel Bell were among the first companies to introduce the just-in-time approach in their European plants in the relationships with their suppliers (see Memo 11.1).

Consequences for suppliers

Advantages and disadvantages for the supplier

The JIT concept has some specific advantages and disadvantages for the supplier. This section will start with the advantages.

With the JIT approach the supplier is regularly informed about the quantities to be delivered. The supplier is able to plan his future production volume much better because of this information. The same holds for the planning of materials. As a result the pipeline inventory may be reduced. This advantage will be even larger when the supplier succeeds in implementing JIT principles in the relationship with his own suppliers.

JIT can, besides better planning, lead to administrative savings for the supplier. All handling of transaction documents is done through electronic information systems. Suppliers are able to connect their production and materials planning systems with those of their customers. This requires, of course, some sophistication of the computer systems which are available on both sides – this is why some large manufacturers shun those suppliers from their business, who do not have sufficient EDI capabilities. When the supplier is notified in case of quality defects, he immediately should take corrective action. Claims and bills will being avoided.

MEMO 11.1: Supplier relationships at Philips

The relationship with suppliers is a central issue in the purchasing policies of many companies. Philips introduced the term **co-makership**:

The Philips companies in Belgium and The Netherlands operate in an international and dynamic market. A characteristic of this market is that there is a demand for a variety of products which are subject to rapid technological change. In addition, demands for delivery lead times and customer service are greater than ever. Only an organization which can respond quickly to this fast-evolving and changing market – in which there is intense competition – will be able to maintain its position. For this reason Philips organization has decided to introduce an integrated Manufacturing Resources Planning (MRP) concept. This management system produces quick feedback from the market to product development, manufacture and logistics planning, thereby ensuring a flexible supply capability to our customers . . .

The purchasing organization will have to make its own contribution to the achievement of the required results by means of more intensive co-operation with its internal and external suppliers. We call this approach to suppliers 'co-makership'. This co-makership must produce the following results:

- improved product quality
- increased flexibility of response to market demand
- shorter delivery lead times
- quicker implementation of product changes
- increased reliability of orders and deliveries
- reduced stock levels
- lower integral cost prices

We also find programmes, that focus on the ideas described, in other companies, such as IBM's 'First Time Right' programme, Rank Xerox's 'Leadership through Quality' programme and Alcatel-Bell's 'Quality on Time' programme.

(Source: Philips Electronics (1989), Co-makership (internal brochure))

The constant communication between supplier and manufacturer on quality and cost improvements, can lead to product and process innovations. These innovations can be very profitable for the supplier in other markets.

A last advantage for the supplier is his investment policy. JIT contracts are signed for a long period of time. A certain volume and turnover are guaranteed. This makes it easier to decide whether and when to invest in new production technology and equipment.

However, engaging in JIT relationships with a manufacturer obviously also has some disadvantages for the supplier. These types of relationships have affected in Japan not only supplier relationships, but also the industrial structure of this nation. In many industrial sectors a strong hierarchy can be observed in the different links of supply chains. In general the large manufacturers, at the top of the supplier pyramid (see Figure 11.5) have imposed their demands and requirements rather ruthlessly on the often much smaller suppliers. Given the

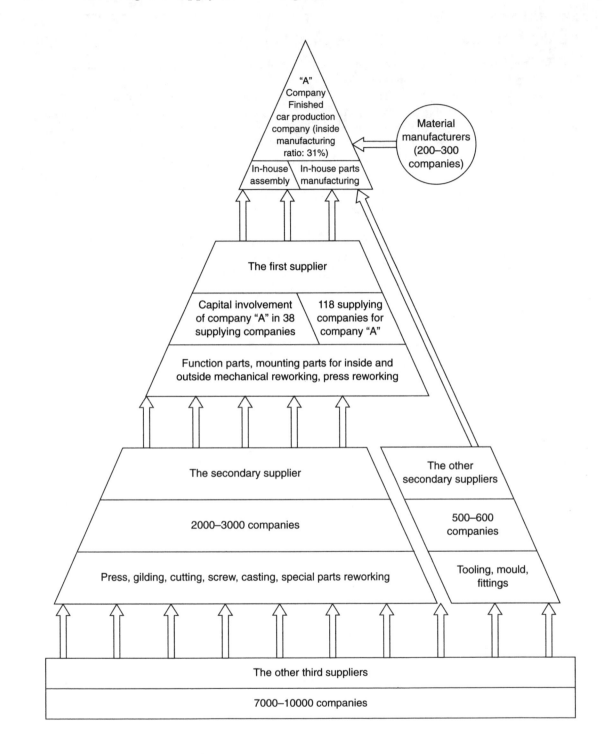

Figure 11.5 The supplier pyramid.

large dependence on these large manufacturers, suppliers have had to comply with these demands, at the risk of losing their entire business.

In general, it may take some time for a supplier to deliver at zero defects, or to produce zero defects. In the beginning the supplier has to conduct many quality checks and many products fail the test. To deliver just-in-time with zero defects takes great effort and therefore initially requires high costs. These investments are not being paid for by the large manufacturers; they come at the expense of the supplier.

Another disadvantage is that the supplier can become very dependent on only one manufacturer. If the supplier focuses too much on the business of one or two manufacturers, this can become a threat to its continuity. After a long-term contract has ended, circumstances could have changed which can result in the end of the relationship. Given its large dependence on that one manufacturer the supplier will go to great lengths in order to get a new contract. Obviously, when a supplier is not able to keep up with competition and has missed the contract, it will not be easy to regain the lost territory.

Some more words here on how JIT principles in supplier relationships may affect the industrial structure of a nation. In Japan it resulted in a pyramid shaped supply structure (see Figure 11.5). In this structure OEMs (Original Equipment Manufacturer) work closely together with main suppliers, responsible for the development and delivery of complete subcomponents (dashboard units, transmission systems). These system suppliers buy their own materials from a second tier of suppliers. These suppliers, in their turn, do business with smaller suppliers who work on components. At the bottom of the pyramid are the often large and powerful suppliers of basic, raw materials.

This structure is criticized by both Japan and Europe. OEMs often make extreme demands on the system suppliers who shift these demands to their own suppliers and so on. In the end the smaller companies have to work very hard to be able to survive (therefore the smaller suppliers at the bottom of the pyramid often are referred to as 'sweatshops').

The system suppliers are in many cases strong specialized and international companies who work closely with their customers. In some cases this co-operation means not only delivering systems or components, but also assembling these into the end product. The system supplier is made responsible for the planning of delivery and the logistics involved. This principle is also referred to as JIT II (see Memo 11.2). Another principle, which is applied in dealings with those systems supplies, is 'Pay for Production'. The equivalent of this principle is 'Pay for Consumption'. The manufacturer only pays the supplier for the components which actually have been consumed during the production of a given day or batch. At Whirlpool and Xerox suppliers of key-components and packaging are no longer paid for the products they deliver, but for the products that actually have been consumed in a day at a certain production line. Through EDI a supplier can monitor every day which components have been consumed at the production lines of the manufacturer. At the end of the day the balance is made and the amount due paid electronically. Pay for production is closely related to JIT.

Manufacturing organizations in Europe do not wish to follow the example of the Japanese industry. The main objection to the Japanese situation is the

---

MEMO 11.2: JIT II

JIT II is a concept pioneered by the Bose Corporation. In Sales, Purchasing & Material Planning applications, the customer planner, buyer and supplier salesman are replaced by an 'Inplant' supplier employee who is empowered to place customer purchase orders on his company. Supplier access and linkage to customer computers is also utilized. The inplant also performs concurrent engineering with customer engineering department from within the customer company. 'Vendor managed inventory' and 'automatic material replenishment' are features of JIT II.

JIT II has been featured in front page articles in the US and European Wall Street Journal, Harvard Business School Case Study and ongoing world-wide business periodicals. US corporations such as IBM, Intel, AT&T, Honeywell and many other major corporations have implemented nationally in scores of supplier relationships. Business Week named Bose one of the 'World Class Champs' in supplier management. Many corporations have adopted JIT II as a sales and customer support programme.

(Source: various articles in *Purchasing*)

---

dependence on too few suppliers. In Japan exclusiveness is demanded from suppliers: a supplier may deliver a product only to one company. Most organizations in Europe do not encourage a too large dependency of the supplier. Philips for example wishes suppliers to be dependent on Philips for less than 30% of their turnover.

JIT and supplier selection

In the context of supplier selection, suppliers located close to the client organization are in an advantageous position. Toyota, for example, demands that their main suppliers have production plants within a radius of 30 kilometres! Business is based on open calculations, and agreements about the supplier's quality and delivery performance are reached in advance. If there are no suppliers in the immediate vicinity, then the company will try to do business with suppliers who are concentrated in particular geographical areas. In that way transport can be combined and the associated costs reduced.

Suppliers are required to deliver with zero defects, so that incoming inspection can be omitted. The reduction of incoming inspections is a gradual process of increasing quality and reliability, which takes time. The right products must be delivered at the right quantities at exactly the right moment. Quality and 'on time' are the two main criteria on which suppliers are assessed when applying JIT-purchasing and the following classification of suppliers is used often:

- on time delivery
  A = excellent
  B = good
  C = inadequate

- quality delivery
  1 = excellent
  2 = good
  3 = inadequate

These scores are a simple way to rate the supplier's performance. A C1 supplier, for example, provides high quality, but does not always deliver on time. At worst this can cause interruptions in the manufacturing process. An A3 supplier, however, delivers on time, but the quality of products is poor. This means that incoming inspection remains a necessity, which is in conflict with the JIT concept.

In their discussions with their suppliers, buyers consistently emphasize that, preferably, all suppliers have to get into the A1 category, and remain there. A problem can develop if the buyer occupies a weak negotiating position (*vis-à-vis* the supplier). It will be very hard for a small producer, for example, to induce large suppliers to provide JIT deliveries. In that situation, the producer should try to find more accommodating suppliers, even if this means a higher purchase price.

In conclusion, it is argued that the implementation of JIT principles automatically leads to (more) single sourcing, closing long-term contracts and engaging local suppliers. The central issue affecting supplier selection is not so much the purchase prices, as the magnitude of the total costs, i.e. the costs including the 'waste' that results from poor supplier performance, safety stocks, quality and incoming inspections and (possibly) production standstills. Hence, this kind of supplier relationships should be embedded in agreements based on Total Cost of Ownership (TCO).

Scheduling problems between purchasing and logistics

This chapter has made clear that production planning and materials planning in most companies are far from simple matters. The large amount of data to be processed, the huge differences in the demand structure of products and the related differences in predictability of expenditure, render these subjects extremely complicated in practice. It is therefore not at all surprising that, in practice, many problems are encountered. Some typical problem situations are discussed below.

- *Lack of well-defined specifications*. Specifications are sometimes described ambiguously and bills of materials can be incomplete. In a recent investigation of a manufacturer of food products, it was found that specification sheets were absent or incomplete for 50% of the raw materials that were being purchased. This made it very difficult if not impossible to purchase materials at the right quality (because actually it was not clear what the right quality was); each stakeholder in the discussion (production, laboratory, quality control, supplier) appeared to use its own definition. The result was a very high reject rate on incoming raw materials and a lot of useless discussion among the persons involved.

- *Lack of standardization.* Needlessly complex specifications are sometimes used where standard products would suffice. These limit the buyer's latitude and lead to an expansion of the article assortment. The result is increasing administrative and logistic complexity and often an excessive dependence on one supplier.
- *Frequent changes in materials planning.* Frequent changes in the materials planning due to changes in the production planning disrupt the delivery schedules with suppliers. The consequence is that delivery agreements have to be cancelled or that deliveries have to take place before the agreed delivery dates. This increases the number of rush orders and the cost of non-quality to an unacceptable level.
- *Unreliable planning information.* MRP systems must be provided with sound information. Keeping basic but fundamental logistics information up-to-date is an important task. Working with incorrect stock and delivery information causes (unnecessary) orders to be placed, too frequently, and inside the suppliers' lead times, which generates extra work and raises transportation costs.
- *Insufficient integration of purchasing in materials management.* When it is decided to automate the production and logistics systems, purchasing often lags behind. The problems which result often become clear when logistics managers want to add a **purchasing control module** to their electronic materials planning systems. For then it turns out that descriptions of materials and articles must, for example, be available in four languages, that the units in which purchases are made (for instance in metres, kilograms) differ from the units which are invoiced (units, volume), etc. Implementation of purchasing systems may then take years instead of months.

Up to now the focus has been on the most important elements of production planning and materials planning. The next section describes the most important elements of the purchasing system.

Elements of the purchasing system

The administrative complexity in purchasing can be very high. In a study conducted in the mid-1980s among 48 industrial companies, it was found that the companies had on average 16,600 different article items (Stock Keeping Units), which were obtained from 1155 suppliers. On average 19,980 order signals (or purchasing requisitions) had to be processed, which resulted in 18,900 orders. The deliveries had to be made payable by processing 26,980 purchasing invoices (see Van Weele and Van Hespen, 1986). These numbers show that a solid and efficient administrative organization is a prerequisite for the functioning of any purchasing organization, if it is to focus on its commercial and strategic tasks.

Figure 11.6 shows the most important elements of a purchasing information system. These are now briefly described.

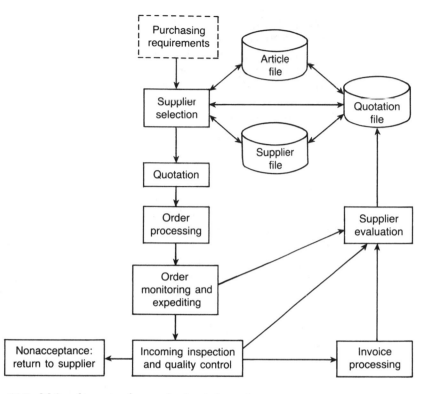

Figure 11.6 Major elements of a purchasing information system.

- *Requisitioning and ordering.* By means of **purchasing requisitions** the internal users within the company express their requirements regarding goods or services to be purchased. These requisitions can be generated directly by the materials planning system (p. 169), but they can also be generated manually. This is often the case when it concerns non-recurring purchases (for example investment goods). The purchasing requisition lists the article code (Stock Keeping Unit number), provides a general description of the item, the quantities required, the desired delivery date plus the data necessary for Finance and Administration (budget number, account number, etc.)

- *Product and supplier database.* The data on the purchasing requisition then are transferred by purchasing to a purchase order document. Here, specific supplier and product data are added, as the price per unit and the address where the order should be delivered. In case of a frame agreement the purchase order also mentions the contract number. All purchase orders get a unique purchase order number, which should be used by suppliers in future correspondence and documents. The purchase order is the basis for delivery. Without it, a supplier should not deliver. Some manufacturers require their suppliers to confirm their orders prior to delivery (by means of an **order confirmation**).

- *Order follow up*. Subsequently the order must be monitored (**order follow up** or **expediting**). Delivery of the goods by the supplier in accordance with the agreement must be checked. To ensure effective monitoring, the buyer uses numerous **exception reports**. One of the most important of these is the **delivery overdue list**, which lists the purchase orders that should be delivered by a certain date but which have not been. Another important list here is the incoming inspection report, which lists the purchase orders which at delivery have been rejected by Quality Control. Of course, in these cases the buyer will need to take immediate corrective action (this activity is referred to as 'trouble shooting'). Some advanced purchasing systems allow the buyer to assign a code to purchase orders, strategic materials and unreliable suppliers. This code is used for generating several signalling-reports, through which the buyer can take preventive action: those suppliers usually are requested through fax or e-mail to confirm and restate that they will meet the required delivery dates (this enables a differentiated approach to order-expediting as described in Chapter 3). In case of delivery of complex investment goods it may be necessary to visit the supplier several times during production and assembly. This type of expediting is referred to as field-expediting. This way of working is common in the defence and aircraft industries.

- *Delivery*. Normally, the supplier will deliver the goods which have been ordered at the right time and at the right quantity. At delivery the supplier will produce a delivery document (freight bill), which needs to be signed by personnel of Incoming Inspection. They will check the delivered goods against the (electronic) order copy. Both quantity and quality are inspected. When approved, a copy of the delivery document is sent to Finance and Administration. At the same time the goods are released and shipped to Warehousing or the user. When the shipment by the supplier does not match the original order, a complaint form is filled in. Complaints may relate to quality, delivered quantity or packaging. These data are, again put into the system. These are the basis of any vendor rating systems, which records the performance of a supplier in a given period. Complaint reports are sent to Purchasing who will discuss the problems with the supplier to prevent them being repeated in the future. When handled by Purchasing, the form will be sent back to the Quality Control department, which will authorize the report and file it.

- *Invoice handling and payment*. Some time after the delivery the supplier will send an **invoice**. Normally, the invoice will be sent to Finance and Administration who will match it with the original order and the delivery document. When matching is possible, the invoice will be paid to the supplier according to the agreed payment terms. Sometimes matching is not possible. In that case the invoice is sent for approval to Purchasing, who will investigate why the invoice does not match with the order. After the differences are cleared, the invoice will be sent to Finance and Administration for final handling.

In recent years various computer systems have become available to buyers and purchasing managers which can support the activities described above.

Examples are: SAP, Triton, MAPICS, XA and MFG-PRO (see for a detailed description of purchasing information systems Van Stekelenborg (1997)). These systems have been found appropriate for supporting purchasing transactional processes. However, these systems still are not capable of producing the required purchasing management information. Most systems have difficulty in providing overviews of turnover figures ranked by product, supplier, purchaser, country or currency. Furthermore, they lack facilities to support advanced vendor rating. A final aspect is that they do not provide sufficient opportunities to provide management reports on the performance of the purchasing department. Obviously, in this area there is still a lot of work to be done by the large ERP (Enterprise Resource Planning) systems providers.

In many smaller and medium-sized companies automation in purchasing is limited to the administrative processing of the purchasing requisitions. Many purchasing systems are isolated and not linked to materials planning systems. This implies that the ordering data must be entered manually into the purchasing system, and this increases the risk of mistakes. It also makes the work of buyers very laborious and time consuming. Therefore, introducing advanced purchasing systems into an organization is a prerequisite for improving both efficiency and its professionalism.

Summary

In this chapter the relationship between purchasing, materials planning and logistics has been discussed. The co-operation between these functions should result in an efficient and uninterrupted flow of products. This requires an integrated approach to managing materials planning processes. Apart from materials management and physical distribution, we have described the role and importance of business logistics. Business logistics is aimed at the optimization of the total flow of goods, up from customer demands to the supplier. Supply Chain Management looks upon how to optimize materials processes through the whole supply chain. These are no simple matters, since in reality customer demands seldomly fit exactly to the capabilities of the firm. Therefore many advanced materials planning methods have been developed, the most important being Materials Requirements Planning and Manufacturing Resources Planning. Both systems are basically forecast driven and require the use of advanced computer-supported planning systems. Apart from forecast-based planning systems, companies may use order-based planning systems. JIT scheduling is a third type of planning system. Basically, it is forecast based; however, it is aimed at continuously reducing cycletimes and lead times, so that planning horizons may be shortened. Suppliers play a vital role in implementing JIT. They need to be challenged constantly to look for ways to improve their operational processes. In the end this may result in a situation where suppliers are requested to fully integrate their activities with those of their customers. This principle has been referred to as JIT II.

This chapter has also presented five different structures or ground forms which may underlie a company's production and logistics activities. A central element in the discussion has been the order penetration point. Downstream from this point all activities are customer order driven; upstream of this point activities are forecast based. Understanding this principle is necessary to understand how purchasing processes may vary in an organization.

Managing suppliers as described in this chapter requires lots of very detailed logistics data and management information. Therefore, the most important elements of a purchasing information system have been discussed. The conclusion is that most available ERP systems are capable of supporting the operational, transactional purchasing activities. However, they do not sufficiently support the needs of generating management information and reports.

Assignments

11.1 What is the difference between logistics management and materials management? Name some examples of activities for both types of management.

11.2 What does 'functional thinking' mean? Can you give examples of functional thinking in:

- the purchasing department;
- the production department;
- the sales department.

11.3 It is sometimes said that: 'Integrated materials management starts with sales!' Do you agree with this statement? Explain your answer.

11.4 In this chapter a distinction was made between order-based production systems and forecast-based production systems. What is the difference between both types of systems? What is the relevance of this distinction for the purchasing organization?

GETTING ORGANIZED FOR PURCHASING

12

Learning objectives

After studying this chapter you should understand the following:

- The structure of the purchasing function within organizations.
- The underlying factors that determine the role, position and organizational structure of purchasing.
- The major tasks, responsibilities and competences of purchasing and how to organize these.
- How to get organized for purchasing in single-unit companies.
- How to get organized for purchasing in multi-unit companies.
- Which criteria to use in deciding on centralized versus decentralized purchasing.

CASE STUDY
Purchasing condition at Hershey Foods Corporation

Over the past four years, Hershey Foods Corp. has reengineered its purchasing operations in a major effort to get full value from the supply base. The results? A centralized purchasing group that has moved away from transaction processing and toward strategic supply management and a supply base that is deeply integrated into Hershey's operations and business strategy. Keys to Hershey's supply strategy were:

- Centralization—and consolidation—of purchasing, which had been operating with individual purchasing departments, at each operating business unit and at the corporate level.
- Major consolidation of the supply base, in order to maximize Hershey's leverage and develop closer supplier relationships.
- Shifting purchasing resources toward strategic supply activities and away from transaction processing, while simultaneously educating the Hershey organization to the reasons behind the shift.
- Vertical integration of key suppliers into Hershey's operations, which includes open sharing of process and business information and, in some cases, supplier units that are 'dedicated' to Hershey's business.

Continued on page 232

Frank Cerminara, vice president of procurement, says it was a simple decision to change purchasing's basic structure at Hershey. 'Four years ago we decided to centralize it all: commodities, packaging, capital purchases, and services,' he says in reference to the purchasing function.

Until that point, Hershey Foods, headquartered in Hershey, Pa., had many small purchasing departments including its several commodity groups at the corporate level as well as in divisions. Between Hershey's core confectionery business and its pasta and grocery division, the number of groups or departments sourcing raw materials and MRO was too large to be effective . . .

. . . All the core competencies and skills were consolidated into one group of procurement professionals. The team that emerged included Cerminara at the helm, two commodities directors, a capital and services director, and a packaging director. The intention was to leverage the volume of Hershey Foods' buy to cut costs . . .

Although centralization was a major initiative of Cerminara's efforts, purchasing at Hershey now works closely with all individual business units in a variety of activities, including new-product development.

'Procurement is on every operating division staff—sales, marketing, manufacturing, and other supplier chain operations,' Cerminara says. 'We get involved at the concept stage [of development] in order to find the right suppliers.' For instance, procurement reps may work on new-product development teams that also include research and development, food technologists, engineering, manufacturing, and marketing personnel.

Cerminara emphasizes that commodity managers focus on strategy rather than number of contracts. 'We wanted the cocoa bean buyers, for instance, to spend less time working on transactions and more time tracking the market,' he says . . .

For this effort to succeed, procurement enlisted support from all its units—which took some time. Cerminara notes that any time there is consolidation, 'there's a certain amount of anxiety that goes along with it.' To alleviate concerns, the procurement group embarked on an education process. 'There's no formula; we just looked for opportunities to communicate directly with plant managers and others at Hershey plants who had been involved with sourcing,' says Cerminara. He and other members of the procurement team visited some plants, called others, and spoke to plant managers at one point when the managers were in town for a conference. 'We addressed them to tell them why we were changing,' he says . . .

For long-term savings, procurement established cross-functional teams to work with suppliers. With certain suppliers, 5–7 Hershey representatives sit down regularly with counterparts from a supplier and 'they don't negotiate, they look to take cost out of the system,' says Cerminara.

To ensure that the teams find solutions that are acceptable to Hershey, Cerminara says that packaging director Thomas Bowman 'coaches' the team to set goals and achieve them. The results have been solutions such as labels that lower costs for Hershey, improve manufacturing efficiencies, and add value to the supplier's product . . .

(Source: Murphy, 1998)

Introduction

As this case shows changing customer demands forced Hershey to turn around its purchasing organization. Key decision making on strategic commodities was centralized, whereas at the same time cross-functional co-operation on new product development across the disciplines involved was fostered. The more strategic role of purchasing within Hershey's led to some drastic changes in the way buyers needed to operate. They needed to move away from their operational and transactional tasks into more strategic and policymaking tasks. In order to be able to perform these tasks effectively, higher demands were imposed onto them in terms of communication with the business units and plant managers.

This chapter discusses the major changes which companies are experiencing nowadays in restructuring their purchasing and supply organizations. The descriptions will be focused on purchasing within manufacturing companies.

Also discussed is how to get organized for purchasing and supply management. In particular, the question of how to define primary purchasing tasks, responsibilities and competences in the relationship with other departments will be addressed. Furthermore, this chapter will describe how to organize for purchasing and supply management in a single and multi-plant environment. In this respect the relationship between purchasing and engineering on one hand, and logistics management on the other, are discussed. Next, some time is spent on the issue of centralization/decentralization in purchasing and supply management, and the issue of purchasing co-ordination. Finally, the profiles of some important jobs in purchasing and supply management are presented.

Purchasing organization structure

The location and structure of purchasing is very much dependent on business characteristics and situational factors. For example, the buying of raw materials in chemical industries is often executed by a small group of specialists, which reports directly to the board of directors. Some very large companies, such as Dow Chemicals, have created a separate department or even a separate business unit for this purpose. In small and medium-sized enterprises, however, this could be the exclusive responsibility of the general manager. The same pattern can be seen for the buying of investment goods. As shown in Chapter 2, small companies may buy these goods with only marginal interference by the purchasing department.

However, in bigger companies (such as AKZO Nobel or Procter and Gamble), these types of buying decisions are prepared by a corporate purchasing department. It is not uncommon to find the purchasing of raw materials, commodities and production-related materials on one hand, and technical equipment and spare parts on the other, to be organizationally separated (this traditionally was the case in the aircraft and chemical industry). The organization of purchasing, therefore, is highly dependent on the characteristics of the company and the characteristics of the products bought.

The survey conducted by Fearon and Leenders (1995) in the US and Canada provided some relevant data on how purchasing is organized. This survey was based on an in-depth analysis of international purchasing practices at 302 large multinational industrial and service companies. The results of this survey were compared with a similar survey which was conducted in 1988 (see Table 12.1). A more detailed analysis of these data showed that a substantial amount of

Table 12.1   Centralized versus decentralized purchasing (Source: Fearon and Leenders (1995) pp. 15–16) (adapted)

Organization Structure	1995 Study < 10 $ Billion $	%	> 10 $ Billion $	%	Total $	%	1988 Study $	%
Centralized, in which all, or almost all, purchasing is done at one central location for the entire firm	61	24	8	18	69	23	83	28
Centralized/Decentralized, in which some purchasing is done at the corporate headquarters and purchasing also is done at major operating divisions/plants	161	62	35	80	196	65	175	59
Decentralized, in which purchasing is done on a division/plant basis	36	14	1	2	37	12	38	13
TOTAL	258	100	44	100	302	100	296	100

organizational restructuring had taken place. A more detailed analysis of these data showed that only 45% of the companies which reported a centralized purchasing structure in 1988 were still centralized; 48% of this group had moved towards a hybrid centralized/decentralized structure. Of those who reported to have a centralized/decentralized structure 78% reported to still have the same structure. However, 72% of the companies who reported to have a fully decentralized structure in 1998, moved towards a more co-ordinated purchasing structure. It is fair to conclude, based on these figures, that purchasing activities in international companies among business units become more and more co-ordinated.

Table 12.2 shows what purchasing techniques, approaches and activities are used. Also is indicated to what extent respondents expected that the use of these subjects would increase in the near future. This table shows that at the time the research was done respondents expected that use of cross-functional teams and teams involving suppliers would increase most. On the whole, participative approaches were expected to increase in the future according to these data.

Factors influencing the location of purchasing in the organization

The organizational location of purchasing is very much dependent on the view management holds towards the purchasing function. When management considers the purchasing function mainly as an operational activity, this will result in a position of the purchasing department relatively low in the organizational hierarchy. If management considers purchasing to be an important competitive factor, however, and of strategic importance to the organization, then the purchasing manager might very well be reporting to the board of directors. Management's view of purchasing is, to a large extent, related to the following factors:

Table 12.2 Use of various purchasing techniques, approaches, activities, and expected use over next 12 months (source: Fearon and Leenders (1995) p. 46)

	Number of Firms Responding	Percent of Firms Using Technique/Approach/Activity					Percent of Firms Predicting Increase over the next 12 Months
		% None	% Slight	% Moderate	% Substantial	% Extensive	% Increase
Purchasing Councils (purchasing managers only)	305	17	22	30	20	11	26
Supplier Councils (primarily key suppliers)	305	27	30	30	10	3	38
Commodity Teams (purchasing personnel only)	303	11	23	25	25	16	35
Cross-functional Teams	307	3	11	30	37	19	54
Teams involving supplier(s)	306	9	27	39	20	5	58
Teams involving customer(s)	304	21	30	28	15	6	43
Teams involving both supplier(s) and customer(s)	304	33	35	20	10	2	43
Co-location of purchasing personnel with users/ specifiers	303	28	23	26	16	7	27
Consortium buying (pooling with other firms)	306	65	25	7	2	0	33

- *Purchasing' share in the end-product's cost-price.* The higher the purchasing content, the more strategic the purchasing function is considered by the management
- *The financial position of the company.* In times of severe financial losses, management will become more demanding on its purchasing operations and purchasing related costs, resulting in a greater accountability being demanded
- *The extent to which the company is depending on the suppliers' market.* Supply markets with high concentration ratios usually get more attention from management.

The implementation of materials requirements planning or just-in-time principles leads to a greater need for integrating purchasing and supply management with logistics management. As a result the purchasing manager in those companies will often report to the logistics manager.

In technically oriented companies, however, which are confronted with rapid changes in product and/or process technology, the purchasing manager may report to the production manager. Table 12.3 shows how some of these factors may influence the reporting relationships of purchasing managers.

Table 12.3 Factors influencing purchasing's reporting relationships

	Purchasing reports to			
	General management	Production management	Logistics management	Financial management
Purchasing turnover ratio				
High	x			x
Low		x	x	
Technical complexity				
High		x	x	
Low	x			x
Logistics complexity				
High		x	x	
Low	x			x
Strategic impact				
High	x			x
Low		x	x	

Levels of tasks, responsibilities and authority

With regard to the allocation of purchasing tasks, responsibilities and authority, three different levels may be differentiated:

- strategic;
- tactical;
- operational.

Strategic level

The strategic level covers those purchase decisions that influence the market position of the company in the long run. These decisions primarily reside under the responsibility of top management. Examples of purchase decisions at this level are:

- The development and issuing of operational guidelines, procedures and task descriptions, which provide authority to the purchasing department.
- The development and implementation of auditing and review programmes in order to monitor and improve purchasing operations and performance.
- Establishing long-term contracts and contacts with certified and/or preferred suppliers (for example long-term purchasing agreements, license agreements, partnership agreements, co-design agreements).
- Decisions related to adopting a supplier strategy based on multi- versus single sourcing.
- Major investment decisions (in buildings, equipment, computers).
- Major make-or-buy decisions, through which manufacturing activities, which were conducted in-house, are shifted to outside suppliers.

- Decisions with regard to backward integration i.e. decisions to participate financially in supplier organizations in order to safeguard future supply of critical materials.
- Decisions related to policies concerning transfer-pricing and intercompany supplies.
- Decisions related to policies on reciprocal arrangements, countertrade and barter-deals.

This list illustrates the long-term, strategic impact that purchasing and supply decisions may have on the company's competitive strategies.

Tactical level

The tactical level encompasses the involvement of the purchasing function affecting product, process and supplier selection. Examples of purchasing decisions at this level are:

- Agreement on corporate and/or annual supplier agreements.
- Preparing and developing value analysis programmes and/or programmes aimed at design-review and/or simplification.
- Adopting and conducting certification programmes (including audits) for suppliers in order to improve the quality of incoming goods and materials.
- Selection and contracting of suppliers in general and programmes aimed at supply-base reduction in particular.

Decisions on these issues often have a medium-term impact (one to three years). They are cross-functional in the sense that dealing with them effectively, requires the co-ordination and co-operation of other disciplines within the company (including engineering, manufacturing, logistics, quality assurance). Earlier, in Chapter 1, these activities were referred to as 'initial purchasing'.

Operational level

The operational level addresses all activities related to the ordering and expediting function. This level of activities incorporates the ordering of materials, monitoring the deliveries and settling quality disputes on incoming materials. More specifically the operational activities of the purchasing function include:

- The ordering process (release of orders corresponding to already concluded agreements with suppliers).
- All expediting activities related to released orders.
- The monitoring and evaluation of supplier performance.
- Troubleshooting: solving daily problems in the relationship with the supplier.

Table 12.4 presents the relationships between the three defined task-levels and a number of purchasing functions.

Table 12.4 Relationship between the three managerial levels of purchasing and some management positions

	Managerial level				
Task	Top management	Logistics management	Purchasing management	Senior buyer	Buying assistant/ materials planner
Strategic level	x	x	x		
Tactical level		x	x	x	
Operations level				x	x

Organizational structures within purchasing

This section describes some alternative structures on which to organize the purchasing function within companies. For this purpose the discussion differentiates between multi-unit companies and single-unit companies.

Structure of purchasing in multi-unit companies

For the organization of purchasing in multi-unit companies a number of alternatives are available:

- decentralized purchasing structure;
- centralized purchasing structure;
- line-management organization;
- pooling structure;
- cross-functional sourcing teams.

Decentralized purchasing structure

This structure can be found in companies with a business-unit structure. A major characteristic is that every business-unit manager is responsible for his own financial results (see Figure 12.1).[1] Hence, the management of the business unit is fully responsible for all its purchasing activities. One of the disadvantages of this structure is that different business units may negotiate with the same supplier for the same products, and as a result arrive at different purchase conditions. When supplier capacity is tight, business units can operate as real competitors to each other.

This structure is particularly attractive to conglomerates that have a business-unit structure, where each business-unit purchases products that are unique and markedly different from those of the other units. In this case economies of scale would provide only limited advantages and/or savings.

---

[1] The term 'business unit' is used here as equivalent to operating unit or operating company. With this term the author refers to a situation where the unit management is profit-responsible and operates with a large degree of freedom.

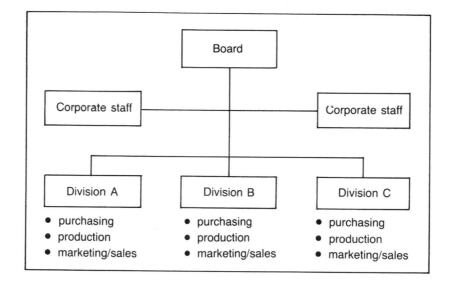

Figure 12.1   Decentralized purchasing organization structure (example).

Centralized purchasing structure

In this situation at the corporate level, a central purchasing department can be found where corporate contracting specialists operate at the strategic and tactical level (see Figure 12.2). Decisions on product specifications are made centrally (often in close co-operation with a central engineering or R&D organization), and the same goes for supplier selection decisions; contracts with suppliers are prepared and negotiated centrally. These contracts are often multi-year agreements with prequalified suppliers stating the general and specific purchase conditions. The operational purchase activities are conducted by the operating companies.

General Motors Europe and Volkswagen may serve as examples of companies which have centralized their strategic and tactical purchasing operations to a high degree. Other examples are Rank Xerox, Ford Motor Company and Caterpillar. The main advantage of this structure is that, through co-ordination of purchasing, better conditions (both in terms of prices and costs and in terms of service and quality) from suppliers can be achieved. Another advantage is that it will facilitate efforts towards product and supplier standardization.

The disadvantages are also obvious: the management of the individual business unit has only limited responsibility for decisions on purchasing. Often the problem is that the business-unit managers are convinced that they are able to reach better conditions on their own, and will act individually; in this way they will gradually undermine the position of the corporate purchasing department.

This structure is appropriate in cases where several business units buy the same products, which at the same time are of strategic importance to them.

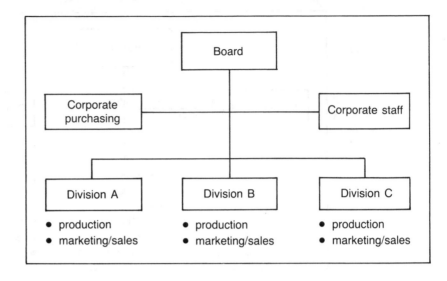

Figure 12.2   Centralized purchasing organizational structure (example).

Centralized/decentralized purchasing organization[2]

In some major manufacturing companies a corporate purchasing department exists at a corporate level, while individual business units also conduct strategic and tactical purchasing activities. In this case a corporate purchasing department usually deals with the design of procedures and guidelines for purchasing. Furthermore, it may conduct audits when requested to do so by the management of the business units (see Figure 12.3).

Often, the central department also conducts detailed supply market studies on strategic commodities, the results of which are made available to the purchasing departments of the business units through periodical brochures, bulletins and/or Intranet. Furthermore, this corporate purchasing department may serve as a vehicle to facilitate and/or solve co-ordination issues between divisions or business units. However, no tactical purchase activities are conducted here. These all reside within the divisional purchasing organizations or the purchasing organizations at the business units. Finally, the corporate purchasing department in this structure may be responsible for human resource management in purchasing and supply.

From this description it follows that this type of structure is in general limited to very large international companies, for example the Electrolux Group AB in Sweden. General Electric Company and Raytheon Company in the US used to have a line-staff organization, but changed their structure some years ago.

Figure 12.4 lists what activities may be conducted by a corporate purchasing staff in a centralized/decentralized structure.

[2] Sometimes referred to as a hybrid structure or line-staff structure.

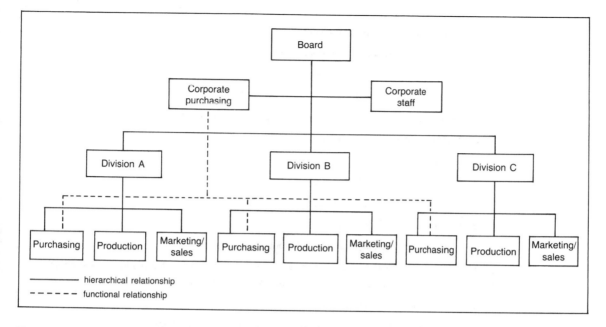

Figure 12.3 Centralized/decentralized purchasing organization (example).

Pooling structure

As explained earlier, a pooling structure represents a combination of the previous three organizational structures. The terms 'pooling' and 'co-ordination' are used interchangeably. Both concepts relate to 'efforts aimed at combining common materials requirements among two or more operating units with the objective to improve the leverage of the company in order to reduce overall materials costs and/or to improve the service obtained from outside suppliers'. However, a lot of variety still exists in practice – depending on the type of commodity, pooling may be forced upon the business units or may have a more voluntary character. In order to illustrate the major characteristics of this structure, some examples of pooling structures are now described.

- *Voluntary co-ordination.* In this case a considerable exchange of information takes place between the purchasing departments of the operating companies. Based on this data every business unit is free to decide whether to take part in a (corporate) contract or to operate individually. Contracts are prepared by purchasing co-ordination committees (or commodity teams), in which the largest users are represented.
- *Lead buyership.* In this case the business unit that has the greatest volume for a specific type of commodity is made responsible for negotiating a corporate agreement with the supplier involved. This business unit collects all relevant data from all other units and negotiates with the supplier. Each individual

- Contracts for common requirements
- Purchasing of headquarters requirements
- Establishes policies and procedures
- Develops supply systems (EDI, purchasing cards)
- Participates in system-wide purchasing/supply personnel decisions/actions
- Develops and/or provides training
- Collects and provides purchasing information
- Evaluates/audits unit/divisional purchasing performance
- Performs special studies and reports
- Interfaces with government
- Interfaces with industry/professional groups/associations
- Provides input to and supports services for special corporate initiatives in areas such as quality, cost, timeliness, productivity, customer satisfaction
- Measures supplier satisfaction
- Participates in interplant purchases and/or goods or services transfers . . .

Figure 12.4 Corporate headquarters role and activities (Fearon and Leenders (1995), p. 45 (adapted)).

business unit periodically releases orders directly to the supplier referring to the appropriate contract conditions.
- *Lead design concept.* The guiding principle underlying this form of pooling is co-design – the operating unit or division, which is responsible for the design of the specific product or component (the 'lead-house') is also responsible for contracting all materials and components from suppliers. An example would be a division of a major automotive company responsible for developing a new fuel-injection system. After approval of the new product, the system is offered to the other divisions which may incorporate it in their new models. Materials and components, however, are obtained from suppliers which have been approved and contracted by the 'lead-house' division. This practice is also apparent at some electronics manufacturers with regard to the design of new semiconductors. Usually supplier relationships are rather intense. Suppliers are involved in discussions on development and design at an early stage, so that the assembler may benefit optimally from the supplier's technical knowledge.

Pooling may occur at different levels of aggregation:

- at article level;
- at supplier level;

- at business-unit level;
- at division level; and
- according to geographical characteristics of the purchase market.

As mentioned earlier purchasing organizational structures are influenced by a large number of variables, which makes manufacturing companies difficult to compare. Most companies, however, will have mixed patterns of organization based on the basic structures presented here.

Cross-functional sourcing teams

This organizational form is relatively new within purchasing. It can be best described by an example from IBM. As a result of enormous financial loss in 1992, the purchasing function at IBM was reorganized. IBM's new purchasing structure provides a consolidation of needs on components for the whole organization with one single contact point (the commodity team) for the supplier. Contracting is done centrally on corporate level. However, in all cases the operational purchasing activities are decentralized.

Purchasing components and other production related goods is organized through Divisional Global Procurement Executives (see Figure 12.5). These managers are responsible for purchasing, sourcing and supplier policy for a certain group of components. They report to the Chief Purchasing Officer and to their own business-unit manager. The business-unit managers meet the CPO during various Corporate Business Councils where purchasing and supplier issues are discussed and decisions are being made. The CPO communicates with every business-unit manager separately in order to match the corporate purchasing strategy with the needs of the individual divisions and business units. This guarantees a thorough integration of the purchasing and supplier policy in the organization. This way IBM uses its enormous purchasing power in combination with maximum flexibility.

For purchasing of production-related materials IBM pursues uniform purchasing procedures all over the world. Supplier selection and choice should follow a uniform pattern. They focus more and more on selecting and contracting main suppliers, which offer products and services at a world-class level and which have global presence. This leads to lower price and cost levels, higher quality, shorter delivery cycles and therefore lower stocks. This approach results in less suppliers and a growing mutual involvement because the purchasing turnover is spread over less suppliers. Therefore more attention can be given to the relationship with an individual supplier in the value chain and a relationship based on continuous performance improvement can be developed.

Key factors to realize and improve a global sourcing process are: strong leadership, active involvement of management, aggressive supplier management, corporate commodity plans, cross-functional teams (see Memo 12.1) and standardization of logistics and delivery processes.

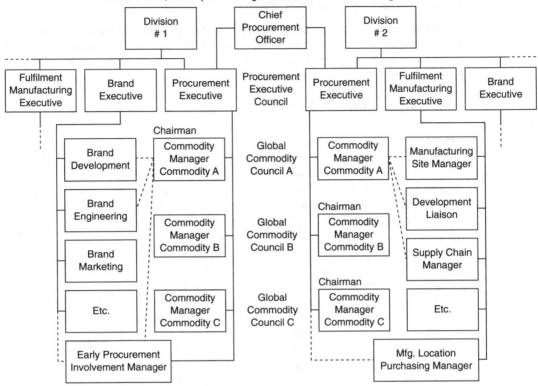

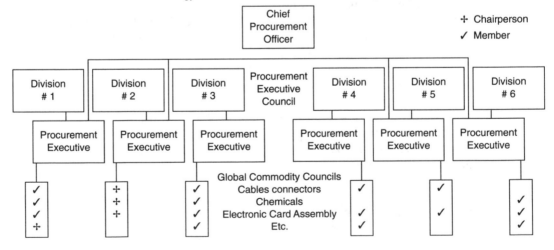

Figure 12.5   IBM's Commodity Team structure (Van Weele (1996), p. 75).

MEMO 12.1: Cross-functional teams in Purchasing

Corporate commodity plans are made by cross-functional commodity teams. These teams consist of professionals in product development, Research & Development, marketing, production, distribution and finance, together with purchasing professionals. The leader of this team is a commodity manager, who is not necessarily a purchaser. This manager reports to the Vice President Purchasing and Supply. The structure of the team is virtual because most professionals work all over the world. They communicate through e-mail, fax and video conferencing. These commodity teams have the authority to select suppliers and contract them for a specific commodity.

Centralized versus decentralized purchasing: some criteria to consider

The question as to what extent to centralize or decentralize purchasing cannot be easily answered. Most companies balance between the two extremes: at one moment of time they will have a centralized purchasing organization, whereas some years later they may opt for a more decentralized purchasing organization. In recent years many automotive companies have decided to centralize their purchasing operations. The same goes for some major office equipment manufacturers (such as Rank Xerox) while other companies, such as KLM, have changed from a functional to a divisional structure. As a result the central purchasing department was split up into five decentralized purchasing departments within each of the divisions and business units that were formed.

The following factors or criteria are commonly used when deciding to opt for centralization or decentralization in purchasing.

- *Commonality of purchase requirements*. The greater the commonality of the purchased products required by the business units, the more benefits can be obtained from a centralized or co-ordinated approach. This is why the buying of raw materials and packaging materials in large companies is often concentrated at one (corporate) location.
- *Geographic location*. When business units are situated in different countries and/or regions this may hamper co-ordination efforts considerably. In practice there appear to be significant differences in trading and management practices between Europe and the United States. Even within a European context significant cultural differences exist and some large companies have changed their co-ordination strategy from a global to a regional approach.
- *Supply market structure*. Sometimes the company is confronted in some of its supply markets with one or a limited number of very large supplier organizations. In such a situation the power balance is definitely to the advantage of the supplier and it makes sense to adopt a co-ordinated purchasing approach in order to arrange for a better negotiating position *vis-à-vis* these powerful trading partners.

- *Savings potential.* Prices of some types of raw materials are very sensitive to volume: in such circumstances buying higher volumes may immediately lead to cost savings. This is true both for standard commodities and high-tech components.
- *Expertise required.* Sometimes, very specific expertise is required for effective buying, as in the purchase of high-tech semiconductors and microchips; prices are also strongly related to the laws of supply and demand. As a result most manufacturers of electronics goods have centralized the buying of these products. The same goes for the buying of software and hardware.
- *Price fluctuations.* If materials (e.g. fruit juices, wheat, coffee) prices are highly sensitive to the political and economic climate, a centralized purchasing approach is favoured.
- *Customer demands.* Sometimes a customer will dictate to the manufacturer which products it has to purchase. This is typical for the aircraft industries. These conditions are agreed upon with the business unit that is responsible for manufacturing the product. This practice will clearly obstruct any efforts aimed at purchasing co-ordination.

In practice these considerations appear to be decisive when deciding on buying products centrally or otherwise.

In summarizing this section, the advantages and disadvantages of decentralization are shown in Figure 12.6 – for centralization, the reverse of the arguments may be used.

Purchasing organization in single-unit companies

In a single-unit organization the issue of centralized versus decentralized purchasing relates to the question as to what extent purchases need to be made through the purchasing department. This refers directly to what authority should be assigned to the purchasing department and, in general, depends on the following variables.

Advantages	Disadvantages
• direct responsibility for profit centres	• dispersed purchasing power, lack of economies of scale
• stronger customer orientation towards internal user	• no uniform attitude towards suppliers
• less bureaucratic purchasing procedures	• scattered market research
• less need for internal co-ordination	• limited possibilities for building up specific expertise on purchasing and materials
• direct communication with suppliers	• probably different commercial purchase conditions for different business units

Figure 12.6 Some advantages and disadvantages related to decentralized purchasing.

- *Management's view towards purchasing*. This clearly affects the tasks, responsibilities and authority assigned to the purchasing department (see Chapter 5).
- *Information technology*. This directly affects the possibilities for co-ordination of all materials-related activities within the company. Generally, implementation of MRP systems will alter the traditional ways of working within purchasing. In general, it will require better discipline and more systematic communication from purchasing operations. As a result purchasing procedures will need to be changed and adapted and changes within the materials organization may even be necessary. Information systems also enable better management information and reports. As a result of a greater transparency of purchasing operations, its reporting relationships may need to be reviewed.
- *Personal relationships*. As in any organizational issue, personal relationships often play an overriding role in discussions on how to structure reporting relationships. If the purchasing manager is to report to the logistics manager, it is important that the latter shows some affinity with the purchasing job. Otherwise, conflicts may occur.
- *Total cost approach*. A better understanding of some important logistics parameters, such as inventory turnover, supplier delivery reliability, the supplier reject rate, etc. will diminish the relevance of purchase prices only. As a result purchasing decisions will become more cost oriented instead of price oriented, which has been the tradition in many companies. Knowledge of these additional 'performance indicators' often leads to a less autonomously operating purchasing department and to a better integration with the logistics function.

Based on these variables purchasing's reporting relationships may take different forms, as differentiated in the structures given below (Miller and Gilmour, 1979).

- *The fully integrated logistics structure*. Here, purchasing reports directly to the logistics manager at the same level as production planning and physical distribution (see Figure 12.7).

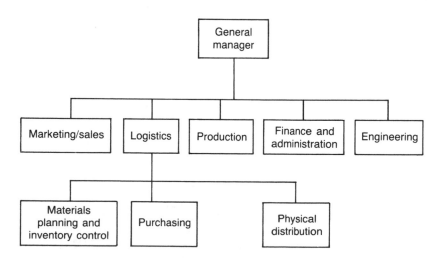

Figure 12.7   Example of a fully integrated logistics structure.

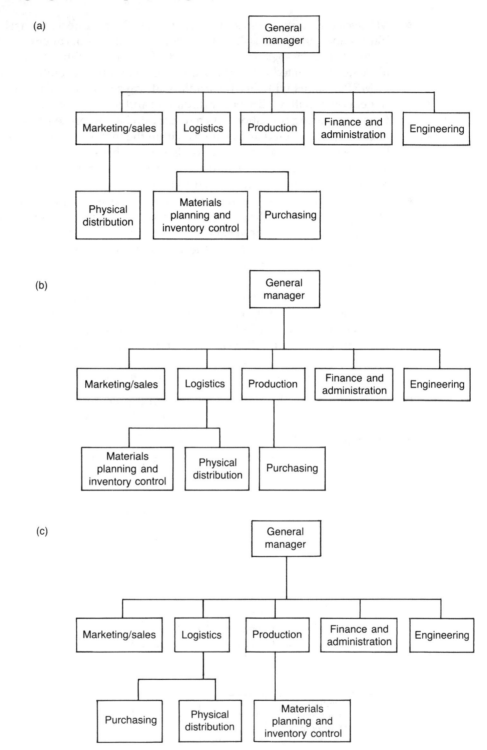

Figure 12.8 Example of a partially integrated logistics structure.

- *The partially integrated logistics structure.* In this structure purchasing, production planning and physical distribution report to the logistics manager in various ways. Figure 12.8 (see p. 248) shows three possible configurations.

In the preceding chapters, some important changes have been discussed which affect the role and position of the purchasing organization. These changes can be divided into external and internal changes. External changes are related to changes outside the company. They are not to be influenced by the company. Internal changes are related to changes inside the company. In most cases they result from rethinking the value chain, i.e. the company's primary processes and its relationships with suppliers.

It may be clear, that all of these changes influence the tasks, responsibilities and authority of the purchasing function. And, hence, they will affect and change the structure of the purchasing organization (see Figure 12.9).

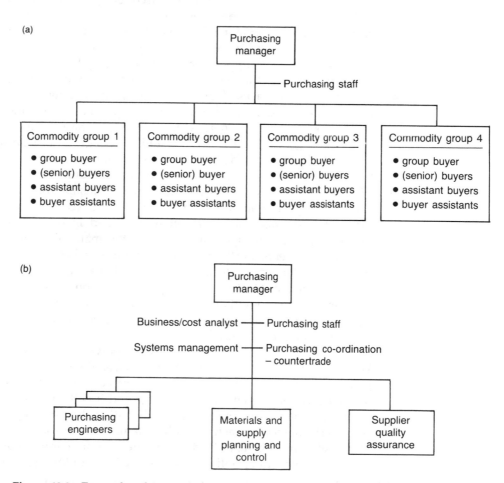

Figure 12.9 External and internal changes may lead to significant changes in purchasing's organizational structure in a business unit: (a) traditional structure, (b) revised structure.

Consequences for purchasing professionals

The developments described above will also lead to significant changes in the necessary skills and abilities required by the purchasing department. In most large companies the following positions can be found.

- *Corporate buyers*. These are generally focused on very specialized tasks. It is their job to negotiate for large volumes (in the case of raw materials) or large investment projects (e.g. in the case of manufacturing equipment and computer hardware and software). Their counterparts are often account managers, who are highly educated and experienced. For this reason corporate buyers preferably have a similar educational background, often at university level.
- *Purchasing engineers*. These buyers, often working at a decentralized level, normally have a shorter planning horizon and a more operational task. As they have to meet and converse frequently with engineers and other technical specialists they require an adequate technical background, combined with commercial skills. These aptitudes relate to the most importants tasks and activities of the purchasing engineer, most of whose time is spent on supply market research, selection of suppliers, and preparing and conducting contract negotiations with suppliers.
- *Project buyers*. The tasks of the project buyers are somewhat similar to those of the purchasing engineer. However, the purchasing engineer deals with production materials, whereas the project purchaser deals primarily with investment goods. For this job a technical background of university level is required. Since these decisions always require a team approach, project buyers should possess effective communication and presentation skills.
- *Materials planners*. Materials planners are responsible for materials planning and ordering. In companies with a high degree of computerization within the materials area, both tasks are often combined in one function. Here, the materials planner focuses on calling off the materials required against the annual agreements. Furthermore they monitor and control suppliers on their quality and delivery performance. For this job a secondary educational level will be sufficient. Most important here are personal abilities, such as stress-resistance, service orientation and the ability to organize the work effectively. Apart from this, this job provides a good opportunity for future buyers to become acquainted with the work.
- *MRO buyers*. For an MRO buyer a general, polytechnic education will suffice. With regard to the purchasing of spare parts, the delivery of these items in general will be covered in the original contract for the investment good. The MRO assortment is generally very large and it is the task of the MRO buyer to manage these assortments effectively, rather than striving to optimize the price performance for each individual item. Therefore, a good understanding of logistics management and techniques (of inventory management and order management specifically) would be basic to this type of buyer.

Table 12.5 summarizes the most important skills and abilities of the functions which have been described above.

Table 12.5 Buyer profiles and their most important responsibilities and skills

Function	Responsibilities	Skills required
Corporate buyer	Strategic commodities	Specialist commercial skills Long-term planning horizon Communication skills Broad business orientation
Purchasing engineer	New materials and components New suppliers	All-round technical background Medium-term planning horizon Commercial skills Communication skills
Project buyer	Equipment and services	Specialist project management skills 'Team player'
MRO buyer	MRO supplies	Generalist Efficient order handling Assortment manager Service oriented Commercial skills
Materials planner	Materials and order planning Order handling Vendor rating	All-round 'common sense' Stress-resistant Service oriented Problem-solving skills

Summary

In this chapter some issues related to purchasing organization have been discussed. Purchasing structures appear to vary to a great extent among companies. This is due to the different views which top-managers hold towards purchasing and some company-specific characteristics. Among these, purchasing's share in the end products' costs, the financial position of the company and the company's dependency on the supplier market have been discussed. These factors, to a significant degree, determine purchasing's reporting relationships.

When analysing the tasks, responsibilities and authority of the purchasing department, we differentiated between the strategic level, the tactical level and the operational level. When (re)designing purchasing structures managers should make sure that each of the task levels is given sufficient attention. The result will probably be different for multi-unit companies and single-unit companies. In a multi-unit environment it should be decided to what extent the purchasing function should be (de)centralized. In this respect five types of organizational structures have been discussed: the centralized structure, the decentralized structure, the line-management organization, the pooling structure and cross-functional sourcing teams. The last two are the most complicated ones; however, their popularity is growing. Pooling structures may have different forms, i.e. voluntary co-ordination, the lead buyer concept and the lead design concept. The decision whether to centralize or decentralize the purchasing operation usually depends on a number of parameters.

It is fair to conclude that there is no single best way to get organized for purchasing in a multi-unit environment.

Purchasing structures appear to be highly volatile: a period of centralized purchasing is often followed by a change to the other way around. Due to increasing international competition and the maturing of many end-user markets, the present trend is towards co-ordination and more participative approaches. Many companies try to reap the benefits of joint purchasing of common materials requirements, whilst preserving the advantage of entrepreneurship low in the organization.

When designing purchasing structures in a single-unit environment a number of parameters need to be considered. As computerization in the materials-related functions progresses, purchasing activities become more integrated with logistics management. In this respect various options are open to managers. They may choose a totally integrated organizational model or decide on a partially integrated model.

Major organizational changes need to be reflected in future roles of those purchasing positions. Of these, the chapter discussed in outline the profile of the corporate buyer, the purchasing engineer, the project buyer, the materials planner and the MRO buyer – the purchasing area provides significant challenges to those with an engineering and MBA background.

Assignments

12.1 With regard to purchasing tasks, responsibilities and authority, three different levels can be distinguished. What are these three levels? Why do you consider this differentiation useful?

12.2 The policies concerning intercompany business and counter purchase are regarded as strategic decisions. What does this mean? What might the contribution of purchasing be, in dealing with these two issues?

12.3 A manufacturer of candy consists of four business units. These business units respectively produce chewing gum, chocolate, candy bars and sweets. Purchasing activities are all located within the business units. Describe the possibilities of this company for changing the organization of purchasing to a centralized organization or a pooling structure. What would you prefer? What factors would you consider in arriving at a decision?

12.4 In the preceding text it was stated that information technology increases the need for greater integration of the purchasing and logistics functions. Do you agree with this statement? Explain your answer.

12.5 To what manager should purchasing report in the following companies:

- a manufacturer of basic chemicals;
- a wholesale company in construction materials;
- an automotive manufacturer.

Explain your answer.

PURCHASING PERFORMANCE MEASUREMENT

13

Learning objectives

After studying this chapter you should understand the following:

- The factors that influence the way performance measurement is executed and evaluated.
- The key areas that should be considered when measuring and evaluating purchasing performance.
- The methods, techniques and performance measures that can be used.
- How to conduct a purchasing audit as a tool to improve purchasing performance.
- The value of benchmarking in purchasing.

CASE STUDY
The introduction of a quality programme by an industrial components manufacturer

The major policy decision of a large manufacturer of industrial components is to become a quality leader in his business area. According to management's view, quality improvement is the only way to survive in the highly competitive environment. Management is aware of the direct relationship between product quality and process quality and that good products can only be manufactured if the manufacturing processes are controlled accurately. In this case it was decided to adopt the ISO 9001 standards and a quality manager was appointed to help the organization make the necessary transitions.

The task of the quality manager is, more specifically, to support the company's departments in developing their own quality programmes. Furthermore, he has to ensure that the targets, as agreed by the departmental managers, are realized.

The purchasing department is actively involved in the company's quality programme and, like his colleagues, the purchasing manager has developed a quality programme for his department. However, as time goes by, he meets with little enthusiasm from his buyers to support the plan.

Continued on page 254

Gradually he gets the impression that they regard implementation of the plan to be a responsibility of the quality manager. Furthermore, the purchasing manager discovers, through complaints from production, that the buyers remain primarily interested in price, rather than quality. When discussing this matter with the quality manager it emerges that targets concerning quality improvement have been translated insufficiently into individual targets. It is not clear to the quality manager how each individual buyer should contribute to the overall quality objectives of the company. On the other hand, objectives with regard to price reduction are readily available and specified in a fair degree of detail. Every month individual buyers are assessed on their budget results at which time actual prices are compared with budgeted prices. Variance reports are prepared on each purchaser's activity and discussed in the monthly meeting of the purchasing team. The purchasing manager eventually sees that the buyers respond to what they are expected to do, not what they are inspected on. He thinks about ways in which to change this situation . . . but what parameters should be used?

Introduction

This case illustrates the fact that measuring and evaluating purchasing performance at the present time is a fuzzy issue, yet it is one of major concern for many industrial companies. The question of how to measure and evaluate purchasing performance is not easily answered. A major problem is that to date no practical approach that produces consistent results in different types of companies has been found. It is highly uncertain whether such a yardstick or method, of universal application, could be developed. This chapter will explain why. The consequence is that managers typically rely on their own insight and experience when establishing procedures and systems to monitor the effectiveness and efficiency of their purchasing organizations.

The intention of this chapter is to develop a consistent approach to the subject; specific questions to be addressed are:

- Why should purchasing performance be measured and evaluated? What are the major benefits to be derived from such an activity?
- What problems are involved in assessing purchasing performance?
- What should be measured and evaluated?
- What measures and techniques exist in order to perform such an evaluation?
- How could an evaluation system be implemented?
- How to benchmark purchasing processes?

Factors influencing purchasing performance measurement

One of the most important factors that influences the way in which purchasing results are measured, is how management looks upon the role and the importance of the purchasing function. As early as 1962, Hayes and Renard in the United States suggested that management's expectations of the purchasing operation have a significant influence on the methods and techniques that are used in its assessment.

Results from a survey among industrial companies revealed that differences between companies, in their approaches to measurement and evaluation in the purchasing area, are to be traced much more directly to differences in management style, degree of formalization, and responsibilities delegated to purchasing than to specific company characteristics such as type of industry, type of production operation, and so on. Four different management views are prevalent.

- *Operational, administrative activity.* In this case management evaluates purchasing operations primarily on parameters such as order backlog, purchasing administrative lead time, number of orders issued, number of requests for quotations issued, adherence to existing procedures, etc.
- *Commercial activity.* In this situation management is aware of the savings potential which purchasing may represent. Targets are agreed upon with the purchasing department on price and/or cost reduction. Purchasing should issue competitive bids to suppliers in order to keep them sharp. Parameters being used here are the total savings reported by purchasing (often per product group and per buyer), number of quotations issued, variance reports, inflation reports, etc.
- *Part of integrated logistics.* Management becomes aware that price hunting has its drawbacks and may lead to sub-optimization. Putting too much pressure on prices may seduce buyers to buy 'penny wise and pound foolish'. Demands on lower prices appear always to be met by suppliers to the detriment of quality and delivery reliability. At this stage management introduces targets to buyers on quality improvement, lead time reduction and improving supplier delivery reliability.
- *Strategic business area.* Here, purchasing is actively involved in deciding the company's core business and reinforces the company's competitive position. It is actively engaged in make-or-buy studies. Local suppliers are put to the test of international competition. Here, management evaluates purchasing on a number of aspects including the number of changes (often reduction) in its supply base, the number of new (international) suppliers being contacted (and contracted), and its contribution to the bottom line in terms of savings realized.

Depending on the prevailing view, the position of the purchasing department within the organizational structure will differ, and the measures used for purchasing performance measurement and evaluation will differ significantly. As shown in Figure 13.1, when purchasing is seen as an operational function, performance measures are largely quantitative and administrative in character. On the other hand, when purchasing is considered to be a strategic business area, performance measures are more qualitative and judgmental. In this case, a complex framework of procedures and guidelines typically are used to monitor progress against specific plans to improve purchasing effectiveness.

Which factors determine the prevailing purchasing mode? Firms that consider purchasing as a strategic business area are frequently forced to do so by external factors, such as strong pressure on prices and margins, loss of market share, the need for severe cost reduction on incoming materials, and severe price fluctuations in the supply market. These issues often force managers to focus attention on the need for high-level purchasing performance. In addition, internal

Alternative viewpoints	Hierarchical position of purchasing	Performance measures
Purchasing as an operational administrative function	Low in organization	Number of orders, order backlog, purchasing administration lead time, authorization, procedures, etc.
Purchasing as a commercial function	Reporting to management	Savings, price reduction, ROI-measures, inflation reports, variance reports
Purchasing as a part of integrated logistics management	Purchasing integrated with other materials-related functions	Savings, cost-reduction, supplier delivery reliability, reject-rates, lead time reduction
Purchasing as a strategic business function	Purchasing represented in top management	'Should cost' analysis, early supplier involvement, make-or-buy, supply base reduction

Figure 13.1 How management may look at purchasing. (Adapted from van Weele, 1984a, p. 17.)

factors may also affect or change the view that management holds towards purchasing. Among these are things such as management style, the degree of integrated logistics the company has adhered to, the degree to which modern quality concepts have been introduced and applied, the degree of computerization in the materials area, etc.

In summary it can be said that the way purchasing activities are measured and judged will differ for every company considered; this makes it almost impossible to develop one uniform yardstick, methodology or system for performance measurement in purchasing.

Why measure purchasing performance?

What benefits can be derived from a systematic performance evaluation? Many purchasing managers were asked this question during one of our surveys and their answers are summarized in the following statements.

- Purchasing performance evaluation can lead to **better decision making** since it identifies variances from planned results; these variances can be analysed to determine their causes and action can be taken to prevent their occurrence in the future.
- It may lead to **better communication** with other departments: e.g. analysing the number of invoices which need an extra check may lead to better arrangements in payment procedures and improve mutual understanding between the purchasing department and administration.

- It makes things **visible**: regular reporting of actual versus planned results enables a buyer to verify whether his or her expectations have been realized. This provides constructive feedback to the buyer and it also provides information to management about individual and group effectiveness, and hence contributes to the recognition of the purchasing department.
- It may contribute to **better motivation**: properly designed, an evaluation system can meet the personal and motivational needs of the buyer. It can be used effectively for constructive goal setting, and motivational and personal development programmes in purchasing.

Collectively, these comments indicate that purchasing performance evaluation should result in a higher added value of the purchasing department to the firm. This might take the form of operating cost reductions, lower material prices, fewer rejects, better sourcing decisions, etc.

Purchasing performance should be evaluated regularly for two reasons. First, performance evaluation should be conducted to rate the individual buyer. In this sense, measurement is used primarily to serve the purposes of functional and individual performance assessment. Second, systematic performance assessment should serve the purpose of self-appraisal. In this sense, improvement of purchasing activities can be achieved most effectively by enabling each buyer to assess the results of his or her own purchasing activities. Hence, the evaluation activity is directed towards support of the individual buyer in doing a better professional job.

Problems in measuring and evaluating purchasing performance

Thirty-five years ago, it was concluded that the purchasing department was one of the more difficult departments to evaluate. From the author's own experience I would say that, certainly in comparison with other business areas, things have progressed only in a limited way. The major problems that make it difficult to evaluate purchasing performance are summarized below.

- *Lack of definition*. Although frequently used in practice as well as in theory, terms like purchasing performance, purchasing effectiveness, and purchasing efficiency have not been precisely defined; some authors even use these concepts interchangeably.
- *Lack of formal objectives and performance standards*. As some authors have indicated, the objectives of the purchasing function often are not clearly defined; likewise, most purchasing departments operate without the guidance of well-defined performance standards.
- *Problems of accurate measurement*. Purchasing is not an isolated function; purchasing performance is a result of many activities which, due to their intangible character, are difficult to evaluate. In general, direct input–output relationships are difficult to identify; this seriously limits the possibility of measuring and evaluating purchasing activities in an accurate and comprehensive way. Memo 13.1 illustrates this problem.
- *Difference in scope of purchasing*. As was argued in the second section of this chapter, purchasing tasks and responsibilities differ greatly from one

> ## MEMO 13.1: About accurate measuring of purchasing performance
> A large, multinational company was looking for a young, ambitious purchasing manager. The candidate, when given the job, was required to accept the assignment to reduce purchasing costs by 5% within one year. When asked if he felt uncomfortable with this target, the appointee said 'Not at all; management still has to decide how it is going to measure my performance.'

company to another. This precludes the development of broadly based, uniform evaluation systems.

These four problems seriously limit an objective and accurate assessment of the purchasing function.

What should be measured?

In order to decide what should be measured, it is necessary first to define purchasing performance. For the purpose of this chapter, purchasing performance is considered to be the result of two elements: purchasing effectiveness and purchasing efficiency.

Purchasing effectiveness is defined as the extent to which, by choosing a certain course of action, a previously established goal or standard is being met. It is important to recognize that effectiveness essentially refers to the relationship between actual and planned performance of any human activity. Purchasing effectiveness relates to the degree to which previously established goals and objectives have been met. A strategy or activity is either effective or not: a goal is reached or not. However, the goal can be expressed in terms of aspiration levels; the strategy or action that realizes a higher level may then be considered as more effective than another.

Purchasing efficiency is defined as the relationship between planned and actual sacrifices made in order to be able to realize a goal previously agreed upon. Purchasing efficiency is related to the resources which are required to realize the previously established goals and objectives and their related activities. Essentially it refers to the relationship between planned and actual costs.

Purchasing performance thus can be considered as the extent to which the purchasing function is able to realize its predetermined goals at the sacrifice of a minimum of the company's resources, i.e. costs.

The given definition is very important. It assumes that any evaluation of purchasing activities would include both measures related to effectiveness and to efficiency.

Effectiveness thus is related to the goals and objectives of the purchasing function. The classical statement summarizing the overall objectives of the purchasing function is that it should obtain the right material, in the right quantity, from the right source, for delivery at the right time and right place, with the right service and at the right price. Next, purchasing should contribute to product and process innovation and reduce the company's overall supply risk. Purchasing efficiency relates, as has been said before, to the resources which are required in order to meet the objectives which have been set for the purchasing function. Therefore efficiency relates to the purchasing organization.

Hence, four dimensions are suggested on which measurement and evaluation of purchasing activities can be based:

- a price/cost dimension;
- a product/quality dimension;
- a logistics dimension;
- an organizational dimension.

The relationship between these dimensions is illustrated by Figure 13.2 and discussed in detail in the following sections.

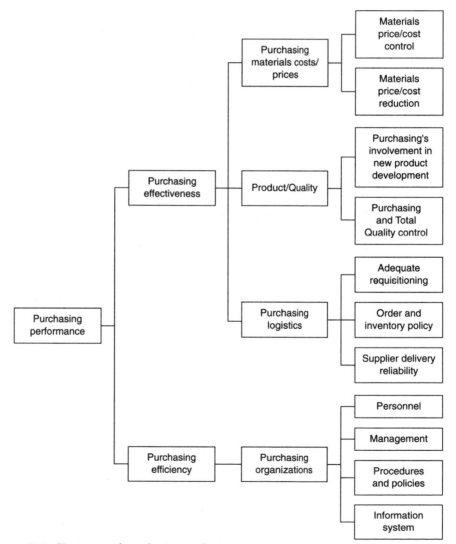

Figure 13.2 Key areas of purchasing performance measurement.

Purchasing Price/Cost Dimension

This dimension refers to the relationship between standard and actual prices paid for materials and services. Here, a distinction is made between:

- **Price/cost control**, which refers to the continuous monitoring and evaluation of prices and price increases as they are announced by suppliers. Examples of parameters and measures to be used are ROI measures, materials budgets, price inflation reports, variance reports, etc. The main objective here is to monitor purchasing prices in order to control them and to prevent them getting out of hand.
- **Price/cost reduction**, which relates to the continuous monitoring and evaluation of activities initiated to reduce costs in a structured way associated with purchased materials and services. Examples of these projects are searches for new suppliers or substitute materials, value analysis, co-ordination of purchasing requirements among business units, etc. The main objective here is to monitor activities, which have been initiated to structurally reduce materials costs.

Budgets are important instruments for performance planning and monitoring with regard to the price/cost dimension. A description of purchasing budgets is to be found in Memo 13.2.

Purchasing Product/Quality Dimension

Purchasing's responsibility with regard to the quality of purchased materials should not, as was seen earlier, be defined too narrowly. Here, the chapter differentiates between purchasing's role in new product development and purchasing's role in total quality control securing that products are delivered by suppliers in conformance of the organization's specifications and requirements:

- *Purchasing's involvement in new product development*. This relates to purchasing's contribution to product innovation. Obviously, it is important that the organization's new product plans in terms of target cost and time to market are being met by all disciplines involved, including purchasing and suppliers. Measures to be used here are the number of man hours spent by purchasing on innovation projects, the number of engineering hours spent by suppliers, the project's overall lead time. Specific measures are the number of technical change orders (indicating the number of engineering changes that have to be communicated to suppliers) and the initial sampling reject rate (i.e. the number of times a sample needs to be presented by the supplier to have it approved by engineering). Measures on these activities will indicate why new product development projects may get out of hand both in terms of costs and time-to-market.
- *Purchasing's contribution to Total Quality Control*. After product specifications have been released by engineering it is purchasing's job to ensure that goods ordered are delivered according to the company's specifications. Here,

MEMO 13.2: Budgets in purchasing management

In order to control purchasing costs many companies use budgets. These can be divided into budgets aimed at controlling materials costs and budgets aimed at keeping control of purchasing departmental costs. With regard to the former the following types of budget are used.

- **Purchasing materials budget.** These reflect, often per product item, the volume which is expected for the next planning period (usually a year) and the expected price level for that specific product. The volume estimate is to be derived from the production plan. The estimate for the price to be paid has to come from the buyer. Often the final estimate is decided after a thorough discussion with the senior buyer and/or the purchasing manager in order to make sure that price targets are set at a challenging level.

  However, the price targets are sometimes set by manufacturing management. Many manufacturing companies nowadays are being confronted with severe cost cutting; this means that they need to plan for specific cost reductions (say 8%). When purchasing contributes to (say) 60% of the overall cost price this implies that purchasing materials cost needs to be reduced by 4.8%. This target, then, is imposed upon the purchasing department. Every buyer in that situation should submit plans and targets per product in order to meet the overall goals of the purchasing department.

  Performance against budget is closely monitored through periodic variance reports which indicate, at buyer level, deviations from the plan for specific products. Variance reports are therefore an important factor when it comes to evaluating the performance of the buyer. Some companies have refined their reporting procedures by eliminating the effect on prices caused by external factors (such as fluctuations in currency rates, inflation), which are then reported separately.

- **Tooling budget.** This budget indicates the expected expenditure related to specific tooling (for example casting moulds), required by the supplier to manufacture the product. Large companies often want to pay for any specific tooling, so as to maintain legal ownership of this equipment. In some companies buyers must indicate what tooling budget they require, and for what product or supplier; these budgets may not be overrun.

  The purchasing departmental budget is most often used since it is easily determined. This usually shows what costs are related to salaries and wages, social security, automation and systems, travel and development and training; here, variances are also monitored regularly.

parameters are being used such as reject rates on incoming goods, line reject rates, number of approved suppliers, number of certified suppliers, number of reject reports handled, etc. These measures indicate to what extent the company is able to secure a flawless incoming materials flow from suppliers.

Purchasing Logistics Dimension

A third key performance area is purchasing's role to contribute to an efficient incoming flow of purchased materials and services. This area includes the following major activities:

- *Control of the timely and accurate handling of materials requisitions.* Measures used here are average purchasing administrative lead time, number of orders issued, order backlog. Important measures to improve performance in this area are electronic ordering systems, introducing E-Commerce solutions to internal customers and suppliers, and EDI.
- *Control of timely delivery by suppliers.* Measures which can be used here are supplier delivery reliability, materials shortages, over/under delivery, number of JIT-deliveries. These measures indicate the level of control over the incoming materials flow.
- *Control of quantities delivered.* In some cases, purchasing has the responsibility for determination and control of cost effective inventory levels. Measures used here are inventory turnover ratio, number of over/under deliveries, average order size, pipeline inventory, etc.

Supplier evaluation and vendor rating are techniques used to monitor and improve supplier performance in terms of quality and delivery reliability. Many of the performance indicators, which have been mentioned here, will be part of the company's supplier rating system.

Purchasing's Organizational Dimension

This dimension includes the major resources that are used to achieve the goals and objectives of the purchasing function, namely:

- *Purchasing staff.* This relates to background, level, training and development and motivation of purchasing personnel.
- *Purchasing management.* This refers to the way the purchasing department is being managed. It encompasses the quality and availability of purchasing strategies, action plans, reporting procedures. It relates also to management style and communications structure.
- *Purchasing procedures and guidelines.* This refers to the availability of procedures and working instructions for purchasing staff and suppliers in order to make sure that work is done in the most efficient manner.
- *Purchasing information systems.* This subject relates to the efforts made to improve the information systems, which are required to support purchasing staff and other employees in their daily activities and to generate necessary management information on purchasing activities and performance.

Table 13.1 provides an overview of the key areas of purchasing performance evaluation and some examples of performance parameters which can be used per key area. A comprehensive assessment of any purchasing organization should focus on each of these areas, individually and collectively. Hence, it follows that a comprehensive performance measurement system in purchasing should monitor effectiveness as well as efficiency and therefore should include, preferably, measures of each key-performance area.

Interrelationships exist among all four dimensions. For example, if purchasing pushes too hard for lower prices, this action may ultimately affect material

Table 13.1 Examples of purchasing performance indicators. (Source: van Weele, 1991)

Area	Measurement aimed at	Continuous/ Incidental	Examples
Purchased materials prices and costs	Purchased materials cost control	C	Materials budgets, variance reports, price inflation, reports, purchasing turnover
	Purchased materials cost reduction	C	Purchasing cost saving and avoidances, impact on return and investment
Product/Quality of purchased materials	Early purchasing involvement in design and development	I	Time spent by purchasing on design and engineering projects, initial sampling reject rate (%)
	Incoming inspection quality control and assurance	C	Reject rate (%), line reject rate (%) quality costs per supplier
Purchasing logistics and supply	Monitoring requisitioning Delivery reliability (quality and quantity)	I/C	Purchasing administrative lead times, order backlog (per buyer) Rush orders, delivery reliability index per supplier, materials shortages, inventory turnover ratio, just-in-time deliveries
Purchasing staff and organization	Training and motivation of purchasing staff Purchasing management quality Purchasing systems and procedures Purchasing research	I	Time and workload analysis of purchasing department, purchasing budget, purchasing and supply audit

quality. The reverse may also be true: the requirement of a zero-defects quality level may ultimately result in higher material prices. However, the result may be a lower total materials cost or lower cost of ownership.

Finally, each of the four dimensions can be measured and evaluated at different levels of aggregation, such as:

- line-item level;
- individual supplier level;
- level of the individual buyer;
- departmental level;
- overall company level.

It is therefore clear that performance measurement systems in purchasing will show a large degree of variation, in that measures are tailored to the specific needs of the company.

Purchasing audit as a management tool

Through a purchasing audit, management may assess the extent to which goals and objectives of the purchasing department are balanced with its resources. The latter relate to the elements of the organizational dimension. The purchasing audit is a form of action research whose effectiveness depends on the expertise with which it is conducted. More important, however, are the actions which are derived from it at a later stage. The audit must therefore be conducted in such a way that people do not feel threatened, and in a way which builds trust and generates professionalism.

Audits can be preventive or corrective in nature. Preventive audits are to be compared with periodical check-ups – with the aid of a limited number of standard checks, the department is checked to see whether it meets the expectations of its most important stakeholders. Corrective audits focus on acute problems apparent in the functioning of the department – the situation can be sufficiently grave that immediate treatment is imperative. Based on a quick scan, the (internal) auditor determines the treatment, which is then to be carried out with vigour. This is known in management consulting as turn-around management. After such an operation, the purchasing organization often will go through a substantial metamorphosis. Purchasing management and personnel are reorganized, new managers are recruited, the product assortment and supply base are reorganized and so on. Audits for turn-around situations should be conducted by experts.

Figure 13.3 shows the points of reference which must be included in a purchasing audit. This figure shows that final purchasing performance is affected by several factors:

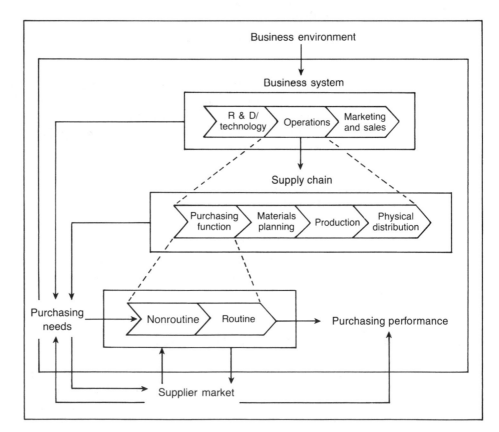

Figure 13.3   Elements of a purchasing audit. (Redrawn from van Weele, 1991, p. 131.)

- *Commercial data*: sales turnover, cost of materials, ratio of materials cost to sales turnover

- *Personnel and organization*: total number of employees, number of purchasing employees (classified according to educational level, functioning level, years of experience), ratio of purchasing employees to total employees

- *Purchasing's place in the organization* (organizational diagram)

- *Reporting relationships*: top management, materials management, etc,

- *Job description*: primary tasks, authority and responsibilities of the purchasing department

- *Purchasing data*: number of articles (production related, non-production related), number of suppliers, number of purchasing requisitions, number of requests for quotations, number of orders, number of purchasing invoices, Pareto analyses of purchasing turnover according to article, order quantities, supplier, country of origin, etc. Purchasing department budget, divided according to nature of costs

- *Relationships with other departments*

- *Action plans*: in the areas of cost reduction, quality improvement, automation, etc.

- *Purchasing procedures and systems*

Figure 13.4   Examples of key data relating to the purchasing function.

- *The requirements that the corporate system lays down for the purchasing function.* Purchasing policy must be tuned to overall company policy; changes in the business system will affect purchasing objectives or the required performance of the department.
- *Changes in the company's supply chain.* The purchasing function must react optimally to the requirements of its internal customers. Changes in the supply chain manifest themselves in changing materials requirements. The purchasing department will have to react to these changes or anticipate them flexibly.
- *The opportunities provided by the supplier market to fulfil the materials requirements, as defined.* Changes in the supplier's technology and/or organization or in the supplier market can strongly affect materials availability and prices (suppliers determine, to a large extent, internal customer satisfaction).

The purchasing audit will have to map the major requirements that the stakeholders assign to the purchasing department, as well as the changes which occur in these requirements. This implies that the audit must pay attention to the quality of the interfaces between purchasing and other departments. Regarding the internal performance of the purchasing department, a distinction can be made between non-routine purchasing activities (purchasing engineering, purchasing market research, supplier selection, etc.) and routine purchasing activities (e.g. order processing, expediting, supplier rating, etc.).

The starting point is the intake interview, in which the auditor clarifies the goals and structure of the audit. This is done in a meeting with the purchasing manager and his superior. The auditor explains what can be expected of the audit as well as the methods to be used. Ideally this is followed by an introduction to the purchasing department, during which the purchasing manager explains the functioning of his department. The rest of the organization is informed about the audit and the auditors will set to work. First of all they will gather factual information concerning the purchasing department, with the aid of a structured checklist; Figure 13.4 shows several subjects on which data could be gathered. A selection is then made of the key personnel to be interviewed; confidentiality towards the respondents must be guaranteed, a factor that frequently constitutes a reason for using external consultants in this kind of research. Figure 13.5 shows some questions which may serve as terms of reference for the investigation.

Based on the information gathered the auditor will prepare a report, the initial findings of which are first checked with the purchasing manager. This provides the opportunity to find out to what extent the results are recognized. Also at this stage some ideas about improvement measures can be exchanged. A meeting with top management will then follow, after which a final report is drawn up containing recommendations in the form of a policy plan or action programme. An important part of the final report is taken up by the documentation of performance indicators, which will serve in the future as a means to monitor progress.

Establishing a purchasing performance evaluation system

There are different methods which can be used to arrive at proper performance measures and norms and standards in purchasing. The more common methods of establishing performance standards are as follows:

- *Subjective by management*. Objectives and targets are defined and imposed on purchasing by management.
- *Expert opinion*. Targets for purchasing performance are provided by experts, who have a broad experience with purchasing issues.
- *Time series analysis*. Past performance is extrapolated to the near future. Targets for purchasing performance are based on historical data, assuming that trends which have appeared in the past will continue in future years.
- *Intercompany and interindustry comparison (benchmarking)*. As has been argued this cannot be done without understanding the specific background of the purchasing organizations which serve as a terms of reference for the comparison. However, benchmarking in purchasing becomes more and more popular and accepted (see Memo 13.3).

The most common method is to keep track of specific measures over time – standards and norms may be derived from analysis of trends, i.e. by extrapolating historical data. The initial steps involved in the development of a systematic performance measurement system are typically those noted below.

Goals and objectives

Goal orientation

- What are the purchasing department's goals?

- What are the purchasing department's responsibilities?

- To what extent are the purchasing department's tasks stated in objective and verifiable terms?

Client orientation

- Does the purchasing department communicate efficiently with its internal customers?

- Is there adequate reaction to the requirements and wants of the internal customers?

- Is the purchasing department sufficiently aware of new internal developments and changes in the supplier market?

Risk

- What are the major risks with regard to price behaviour of high-value items and with regard to availability of critical materials?

- Is purchasing sufficiently aware of these risks and what measures have been taken in order to cope with them?

- In general, is continuity of supply and purchasing operations sufficiently guaranteed?

Resources

Results and resources

- To what extent does purchasing meet its tasks and objectives?

- Is the purchasing department adequately equipped in terms of people and systems to be able to meet expectations?

- What measures are taken in order to improve on results on the one hand and systems and human resources on the other?

Flexibility

- Does purchasing adequately react to changing materials requirements and internal customer needs?

- Is purchasing sufficiently interested in and pursuing new technology?

- What important changes have taken place in the service and organization of the purchasing department?

Management

- Is teamwork within the purchasing department sufficiently developed?

- Is the purchasing department a well-respected partner for discussion of internal customer problems?

- What measures have been taken in order to keep the quality of human resources up to date?

Figure 13.5 Aspects to be considered in a purchasing audit.

MEMO 13.3: Benchmarking in purchasing

More and more companies are interested in comparing their purchasing performance against those of their competitors or those companies who are considered to be best-in-class. Through benchmarking initiatives one tries to assess the effectiveness and efficiency of purchasing organizations. An example is Philips Electronics who during the early nineties conducted a benchmarking study into the purchasing and supply strategies of some leading-edge companies (such as Motorola, BMW, Marks & Spencer). In particular Philips wanted to get a thorough insight into how these companies acted in the areas of:

- global purchasing market research;
- supplier management;
- purchasing co-ordination among business units;
- negotiation and contract management;
- managing the supply process in the relationship with suppliers;
- purchasing and supplier involvement in new product development;
- collaboration with marketing and services.

Through this study Philips gained a thorough understanding of the strategic role of purchasing and supply management. As a result every divisional manager was summoned to develop a purchasing action plan to bring Philips into the league of leading-edge companies. It is fair to conclude that this study has generated significant awareness on the role that purchasing and supply management should have within the company.

CAPS (Center for Advanced Purchasing Studies) in the USA periodically reports on a score of purchasing performance indicators per industry. Every year questionnaires are sent to the purchasing managers of large, multinational companies, covering a large number of subjects. Items which are investigated and reported are, among others:

- total purchasing dollars spent as a % of corporate sales;
- purchasing operating expense as a % of total purchasing dollars spent;
- total purchasing headcount as a % of total company headcount;
- total purchasing department purchase dollars per purchasing employee;
- average purchasing spent per supplier;
- per cent of active suppliers that account for x% of total dollars spent;
- per cent of company purchase dollars spent with small suppliers;
- per cent of total purchase dollars processed through EDI;
- per cent of total goods purchases handled by the purchasing department.

This type of research may provide some feeling whether the purchasing function is moving in the right direction. Comparison with companies on just one aspect is less useful. However, comparing all aspects provides a picture of the relative position of the company in the area of purchasing among competitors.

- First, after careful analysis, management must determine which activities are most important and justify the effort of evaluation.
- Next, it is necessary to determine the frequency and format for data reporting, as well as which personnel will assume these responsibilities.
- Once the preceding decisions have been made, it is necessary to develop a systematic procedure for collecting a great deal of historical and statistical data that may be used in the evaluation programme.
- The next step in the process typically involves analysis of the data. Managers must look for interrelationships between various types of data and also attempt to establish relationships between means and ends. At the same time, the manager must differentiate between purchasing effectiveness and purchasing efficiency.
- Following the analytical stage, various measures are developed, implemented, and subsequently refined. A danger to avoid at this stage is the possibility that the measures may become too complex and too numerous. Simplicity is the key.
- The final step in the operating process is timely reporting of the results to those who should use them, along with appropriate follow-up.

The entire process is self-reinforcing. After standards and plans are initially developed and implemented, results are reviewed and used for further refinement of measures and standards. Hence, the process of data collection, analysis, and programme refinement continues in a cycle characterized by increasing precision and sophistication.

Summary

Performance measurement in purchasing cannot be considered in isolation. Rather, it is part of the purchasing management process. Planning and control go hand in hand. If the purchasing function lacks a clear vision, when purchasing strategies and action plans are ill developed and management reporting is absent, systematic performance measurement and evaluation will be difficult if not impossible.

This chapter has shown that the degree of sophistication in measuring purchasing performance differs among companies. A major factor influencing the parameters used to assess purchasing is the view which management holds towards purchasing. When purchasing is considered primarily as an administrative function, this will be reflected in administrative parameters that are used. If purchasing is considered as a strategic business function, which is deeply rooted in the overall business strategy and processes, this will result in an extensive management reporting.

Purchasing performance measurement is important since it may lead to a greater recognition by all other business functions. When applied effectively, it may lead to better communication with other disciplines, better decision making, a higher motivation of staff involved and a greater transparency of the company's dealings with suppliers.

Objective performance measurement is, however, in many cases a difficult matter since it is hampered by poor definitions and poor planning. Moreover, information systems may not support the data gathering and reporting structures required.

When measuring purchasing performance, it is suggested to focus both on purchasing effectiveness and efficiency. Purchasing effectiveness is covered by three key areas, i.e. purchasing materials costs and prices, new product development and Total Quality Control, and purchasing logistics. Purchasing efficiency is related towards the resources which are needed to realize predetermined targets and plans. Therefore it encompasses the purchasing organization. For each of these key areas a number of tools, monitoring reports and performance indicators can be selected, which enables a holistic view on how purchasing actually has performed. Actual performance needs to be compared with standards. These may be derived from various sources, such as time-based series analyses or future plans and budgets.

The purchasing audit can be used to thoroughly analyse the purchasing organization. Conducting such an audit in general meets with resistance from the organization, which is why it needs to be carefully prepared and introduced to the organization.

Apart from the purchasing audit, managers may also turn to benchmarking as a tool to assess their position. Comparing performance with that of other companies requires, however, a thorough understanding of the way in which the data concerned has been gathered. Therefore, benchmarking in purchasing should be applied with care and criticism.

Assignments

13.1 The general manager of a manufacturing firm uses the ratio purchasing departmental costs as a percentage of purchasing turnover to assess the performance of his purchasing staff. Would you consider this a valid procedure? Discuss pros and cons.

13.2 What parameters would you use when benchmarking the performance of your purchasing department against that of other companies? Explain.

13.3 How would you measure cost savings realized by the purchasing department? How would you define purchasing savings?

13.4 What are the major differences between purchasing performance measurement and vendor rating?

13.5 If you were asked to perform a purchasing audit, how would you proceed?

PART THREE

PRACTICE

SUPPLIER ASSESSMENT: COST APPROACHES AND TECHNIQUES

14

Learning objectives

After studying this chapter you should understand the following:

- How prices are set by suppliers.
- How to use the learning curve technique as a basis for price negotiations.
- Supplier evaluation and vendor rating techniques.
- How to evaluate the financial position of suppliers.

CASE STUDY
Designing and building a new headquarters

The management of an international company is considering building a new headquarters. As this is a major project, management approaches several architects and, based on the submitted provisional designs, a choice is made. Only then does the real work start, beginning with the basic specifications. The structural design is prepared meticulously: the foundation of the building is specified in detail, the strength of the structure is calculated based on the various types of materials that are going to be used. Once the basic design is complete, quotations are solicited from a few selected contractors.

Naturally, management will have indicated the available budget at an early stage. Based on empirical data and price information, the design department prepares a cost estimate of the project. At this stage, without detailed specifications being available, the estimate is only approximate. As the design is elaborated, it becomes possible to estimate the costs at a more detailed level. However, the final price will depend to a large extent on the buoyancy of the construction industry. If there is a need for work, the sum contracted for will be related directly to the estimated costs. If the contractors' order books are filled, however, the price will be influenced considerably by the supply and demand situation. An intimate knowledge of the local market, an insight into the order positions of individual contractors, and an idea of the expected building costs, are therefore of crucial importance in preparing for the negotiations with the contractor.

Introduction

As has been seen earlier, materials make up a large part of the cost price of industrial end products, and decisions relating to the purchasing price determine the cost price of the end product to a high degree. The importance of purchasing as a function increases if rises in materials prices cannot be automatically passed on to the customer. Price is therefore one of the most important elements in the purchasing decision.

Industrial salesmen will always attempt to hide their prices and cost structures as much as possible. It is in their interest that the pricing method remains obscure to the buyer. However, it is the buyer's task to unveil his suppliers' pricing methods and cost structures and, if this cannot be done directly, he should try more indirect methods. The buyer must constantly and systematically gather information that will yield some insight into the seller's pricing methods and his cost structures.

Cost-analysis techniques provide tools to check whether price increases announced by the supplier are justified. Insight into the cost price, and comparison of this cost price with those of the supplier's competitors may help the buyer decide whether or not to agree to the suppliers' request. The buyer often works with several suppliers, so he can compare the most effective manufacturing techniques, track down inefficiencies in the production process of a specific supplier, provide the latter with suggestions for improvement, and therefore get better prices. In dealing with suppliers, the following questions should be asked.

- Does a particular supplier belong to the 'best-in-class' companies?
- What is the supplier's ratio of direct to indirect costs?
- What is the supplier's cost breakdown in terms of overheads, labour and materials?
- Does the supplier experience learning curve effects in his production?
- What are the costs of non-quality for this particular supplier?

The answers will indicate whether a particular supplier is among the most advanced and respected companies in a particular industry.

Pricing and cost-price information are of course insufficient to answer all of these questions. It is also essential that the buyer knows how to use financial–economic analysis techniques. From annual reports and additional financial information, a complete picture of the supplier's credibility can be built up. This chapter will discuss several costing methods and in this context will also address the learning curve, particularly from the buyer's perspective. It will also touch upon a few analytical techniques used in the area of financial auditing.

How is the purchase price determined?

Basically, the price ultimately paid for materials and services is the result of environmental factors – both internal and external. Figure 14.1 shows the relationship between these factors.

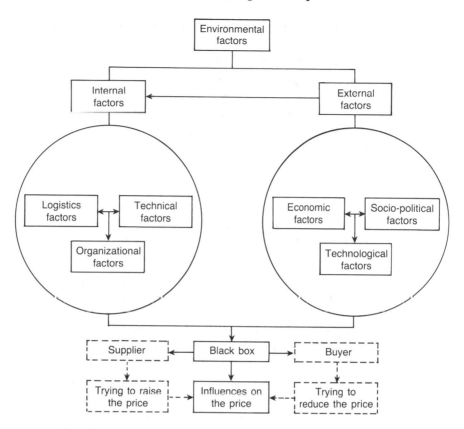

Figure 14.1 The influence of internal and external factors on purchasing price. (Redrawn from van Eck, de Weerd and van Weele, 1982.)

Internal factors can bring about a change in the materials before the finished product is placed on the market. These factors may be logistical, technical or organizational in character; examples are changes in delivery time, quality, or product specifications.

External factors are those factors that change the availability of a product in a given market and they can be divided into economic, socio-political, and technological developments. Examples are changes in general economic conditions, changes in the structure of the supply market, legislation, product technology, etc. External factors in general influence internal factors, although the reverse never occurs. The price of a product can be influenced by external factors in two ways (see Figure 14.2), due to direct changes in the cost structure of a particular product or, indirectly, due to changes in market structure and shifts in supply/demand relationships.

If the change in cost factors is identified by the symbol $f\,(c)$, and the change in market factors by the symbol $f\,(m)$, with f as a weighting factor, then the formula is

$$\Sigma\,(f\,(c) + f\,(m)) = 100\%\ \text{of the price}$$

According to this formula, a change in the price paid is to be considered as the sum of the changes in the cost factors and/or changes in the market factors. Changes in cost factors can stem from

- $f(c1)$: change in labour costs;
- $f(c2)$: change in materials costs;
- $f(c3)$: change in energy costs;
- $f(c4)$: labour productivity;
- $f(cn)$: etc.

Changes in the market structure can stem from

- $f(m1)$: change in demand;
- $f(m2)$: change in supply;
- $f(m3)$: change in supply side inventory;
- $f(m4)$: change in supply side capacity utilization;
- $f(mn)$: etc.

Some products react almost entirely to changes in cost factors, others to changes in market factors. Still others react to changes in both cost and market factors; see Memo 14.1.

The classification described here agrees to some extent with the concepts discussed by Corey (1978), who considers prices to be based essentially on three different models.

- *Cost-based pricing.* In this case the supplier's offering price is derived directly from his cost price; what most systems boil down to is that a particular profit margin is added to all costs, including the costs of sales (mark-up pricing).
- *Market-based pricing.* The price of the product is determined on the market, and is generated exclusively by market circumstances such as demand, supply, stock positions, the economic situation and political factors.
- *Competitive bidding.* The price of the product is influenced by market factors as well as cost factors. This situation is the most common.

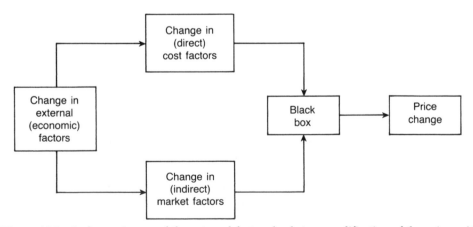

Figure 14.2   A change in one of the external factors leads to a modification of the price paid. (Redrawn from van Eck, de Weerd and van Weele, 1982.)

MEMO 14.1: Variations in determining purchase price

For plastic components, $\Sigma f(c)$ is nearly 100. In other words, the price modification can be attributed almost exclusively to a change in the cost factors. For example, an increase in labour costs will cause the price of these components to increase in proportion with the share of labour costs in the product's price.

For copper, $\Sigma f(m)$ is almost 100, but only in the short term. In other words, the price paid for copper is almost completely determined by the market situation, and cannot be influenced by the individual buyer. For instance, if economic activity declines, market circumstances will change and the price will fall. Clearly, the purchase price for derivative products is strongly related to the market price for the raw material.

For petrochemical raw materials, the sum of the cost factors is about the same as the sum of the market factors, i.e $\Sigma f(c) = \Sigma f(m)$. In other words, the ultimate market price is determined both by cost elements and by general market conditions. Relative to time, the price level will tend to move, both upward and downward, at a given distance from the predictable cost line. In this case, the purchase price is neither determined entirely by the market price nor by the cost price.

Raw materials and semi-manufactured products are traded mainly in a relatively free market in large quantities. The purchase price paid at a given moment strongly depends on market conditions at a given point in time.

As far as technical components are concerned, one must differentiate between components made to the supplier's specification (standard), and those made to the customer's specification (non-standard). In the latter case, the buyer will know precisely the cost of the material to be purchased; in the first case, the buyer can only obtain a rough indication of the product's cost by means of market research. For this reason, prices for non-standard components are typically determined on the basis of competitive bids or negotiation.

What has just been said about non-standard components also applies, for the most part, to finished products.

MRO products comprise such a heterogeneous group of materials that no general statement can be made about the methodology utilized in setting prices. Their prices are determined neither by market circumstances alone, nor on the basis of cost factors only.

The most heterogeneous group, however, is that consisting of the various services rendered by external companies. The price for services can usually be based on cost, assuming that the activities to be performed have been specified with precision and that the hours and hourly rates have been previously agreed upon. For cases such as software design and implementation, however, the price typically is based on market factors. In this case, the cost structure is so difficult to determine and the demand so large, that usually the price quoted by the firm must be paid.

Table 14.1 reflects the relationship between the pricing methods and the various purchasing product groups.

Table 14.1   Relationship between various purchase product groups and methods of price setting (source: van Eck, de Weerd and van Weele, (1982)

	Method of 'price setting'				
Purchase product group	Primarily based on cost factors	Based both on market and cost factors			Primarily based on market factors
		With the emphasis on cost factors	50/50	With the emphasis on market factors	
Raw materials				x	x
Semi-manufactured goods			x	x	
Components					
Standard		x	x	x	
Non-standard	x	x	x		
Finished products	x	x	x		
MRO		x	x	x	
Services	x	x	x	x	x

Pricing methods

Fixing the selling price is no simple matter. The supplier has to take into account many factors, a few of which are listed below.

- The **expected demand** for his product – if demand is high, the supplier will normally set the price a little higher than when demand is low. In addition he will not be willing to make price concessions easily.
- The **number of competitors** in the market – the monopolist's situation is, of course, ideal. Buyers have to go to him for a specific product. He therefore has a high degree of freedom in determining the selling price. This situation is rare in practice and, as a rule, suppliers will look to their competitors' prices when setting their own prices.
- The **expected development of the cost price per product unit** – large-scale production makes low prices possible. If the supplier expects his production volume to increase in the future, he will take this into account. He will anticipate his cost development based on potential learning-curve effects (see next section).
- The **customer's order volume** – suppliers are often willing to make price concessions in exchange for the promise of 'more business' in the future. This principle is often recognized in pricing methods, also when extra discounts for larger purchased quantities are awarded. Many suppliers employ a sliding scale to indicate which price applies to which quantities.
- The **importance of the customer to the supplier** – from a commercial point of view the supplier's position may be strengthened by good references. For this reason he will be eager to do business with certain large, well-reputed companies. In order to gain access to this type of customer, suppliers often charge 'special prices'. However, after some time has passed they will try to re-establish the price at 'normal' levels.

- The **value of the product to the customer** – some products (for example spare parts for manufacturing equipment) have a value to the customer that bears no relationship to the production cost price. In some circumstances supply of spare parts is critical for continuity of production. It is not uncommon for suppliers to charge prices for their critical parts, which are a multiple of the original cost price.

All of these factors affect the selling or purchasing price. In practice the following pricing methods can be distinguished (Kotler, 1984, pp. 515–522):

- *Cost-plus pricing.* The most common way of setting a price is by adding a fixed percentage mark-up to the cost price. If the cost price of a product is £100, and a mark-up of 50% is used, then the selling price will be £150. This method of pricing does not take competitors' prices into account, nor does it acknowledge developments in the demand for the product. Nevertheless, this method is frequently used in practice because of its simplicity. Another important reason is that it is often difficult for the seller to estimate the demand for the product. But he does know the cost price, so why not take this as a starting point for his sales price?

- *Target-profit pricing.* In this situation the price is determined based on profits that should be made. Based on the fixed and variable costs and the expected selling price, the required sales volume is calculated. This is done in two steps: first, the break-even volume is determined through a break-even analysis; then, based on the profit that is to be made, the required extra volume is determined; finally, a check is made as to whether this required sales volume can be realized at the estimated price. If this is not the case, then the calculation is repeated based on a lower price.

    In this situation, it is essential that the buyer finds out the potential total volume of sales of the product involved, as well as the supplier's sales target. If the sales representative has realized his goal, chances are that he will probably honour extra pressure on the price in negotiations. He will be less willing to do so if he hasn't made his profit and sales targets yet.

- *Pricing based on the buyer-perceived value.* A general rule in marketing is that you do not base your selling price on the cost price of the product, but rather on what the market can bear. In this reasoning the price that the buyer is willing to pay is related primarily to the value he attaches to the product. This pricing method is often used for consumer products (well-known branded articles), and also for industrial products; as explained earlier, the prices of spare parts for production machinery are often not directly related to the costs of the product; they are usually related to what they are worth to the buyer in particular emergency situations.

- *Pricing based on competitors' prices.* Some oligopolistic markets are characterized by price leadership. Smaller companies follow the market leader's pricing behaviour, often at some distance. Fuel prices in many European countries are examples of this pricing method.

- *Tender-based pricing.* One special variety of the method discussed above is public tender (also known as the tender system). This method is common in public procurement and some industries (such as the construction and defence industries). Based on a request for quotation from the principal, contractors are invited to submit bids for a specific job. These bids are handed over in a sealed envelope to the principal by all bidders simultaneously (sealed bidding). The job is awarded to the contractor who submits the lowest bid.

One special characteristic of pricing policies for industrial products is the discount policy which is applied. Some authors differentiate between the following discount practices:

- *Cash discount.* This discount usually depends on the industry (e.g. 2% discount with 10 days payment). The advantages are, among other things, acceleration of payments, advantages for quick payers and reduction of the amounts of accounts receivable.
- *Quantity discounts.* Small orders often require the same amount of work, in terms of production and administrative and physical processing, as big orders. This means that small orders have a higher cost per product. To stimulate larger quantity orders, many suppliers use quantity discounts in which the advantage for the buyer is that he can realize a lower price per unit. However, this price advantage must be considered against the extra costs as a result of longer storage and the risk of the product becoming obsolete.
- *Bonus agreement.* This discount is linked to the amounts purchased from a specific supplier for a specific period (usually one year). The supplier often employs a sliding scale, in which the discount percentage increases in proportion to the turnover. The advantage of this procedure for the supplier is that it reinforces customer loyalty.
- *Geographical discount.* This discount is given to customers who are located close to the supplier's factory or distribution centre, making the transportation costs much lower than average: part of the cost benefit is passed on to the buyer.
- *Seasonal discount.* This discount is applied to improve capacity utilization in periods when sales decline. If the buyer orders out of the season, he gets a lower price. By means of the winter discount system bicycle manufacturers, for example, stimulate dealers to place their orders in the winter (when consumer sales are rather low due to weather conditions), after which delivery takes place in spring. In this way manufacturing volume is spread evenly throughout the year.
- *Promotional discount.* This discount is provided to temporarily stimulate the sale of a product, or, if it concerns a new product, to lower the entry barrier (special offer discount).

It is not easy for the buyer to track down the pricing method used by the supplier, and the discount policy makes this matter even more difficult. To get a grip on the prices used by the supplier, a distinction should be made – in line with what has been discussed before – between the cost price analysis and the **pricing method**. The following list can help the buyer gain some insight into the supplier's cost structure:

- materials costs – to be itemized according to the major components;
- direct labour costs – information about labour costs can often be obtained by consulting the collective labour agreements for that particular industry;
- transportation costs;
- indirect costs – these can often be divided into general management costs and sales costs.

As a general rule, the higher the share of the fixed costs in the cost price of the end product, the greater the price elasticity; by enlarging the order volume, the buyer achieves a decrease in the fixed costs per unit, and this should result in lower prices.

Products whose prices are mainly determined by variable costs are affected by price. In this situation, a price increase at the supplier's purchasing side must be closely monitored to prevent the supplier issuing unwarranted price increases.

The learning curve

The learning curve is an important instrument in the development of purchasing strategies. The learning curve was originally developed in the American aircraft industry. It was discovered that the cost price per unit decreased at a fixed percentage as experience, i.e. the cumulative production volume of a particular type of aircraft, increased. This decrease of costs per unit had nothing to do with effects of scale; the result could be attributed to the **learning effect**. The learning effect in general results from the following factors:

- reduced supervision as experience with production of a particular product grows;
- increased profits, from improved efficiency through streamlining the production process;
- reduced defects and line reject rates during the production process;
- (as a rule) increased batch size, which means that less time is spent on resetting machines;
- (after a while) improved production equipment;
- improved process control: reduced loss of time as a result of emergency measures;
- reduced engineering changes (initially required to deal with unforeseen manufacturing problems).

The basic principle of the learning curve is that 'each time the cumulative production volume of a particular item doubles, the average time required to produce that item is approximately x% of the initially required number'. An 80% learning curve means that if the cumulative number of produced goods is doubled, only 80% of the original amount of hours is needed for producing one unit (see Table 14.2).

These data can also be reproduced graphically; regular graph paper yields a curve (see Figure 14.3), while log–log paper produces a straight line (see Figure 14.4).

Table 14.2   Learning effect results in cost price reduction (example)

Cumulative amount produced	Required time in hours per unit
1 000	20
2 000	16
4 000	12.8
8 000	10.24
1 6000	8.2

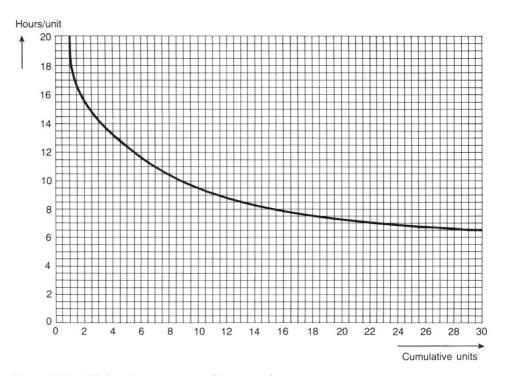

Figure 14.3   80% learning curve on ordinary graph paper.

This knowledge is clearly of vital importance to the buyer. Anticipating the supplier's learning experience, he can negotiate price reductions in the future. The learning curve is preferably used in the following situations:

- When it concerns customized components, manufactured by a supplier at the customer's specification.
- When large amounts of money are involved (so that the costs which must be incurred to apply the technology in question can be recovered).
- When the buyer cannot request competitive quotations because, for example, a considerable investment has to be made in moulds and specific production tooling, which leads the buyer to single sourcing.

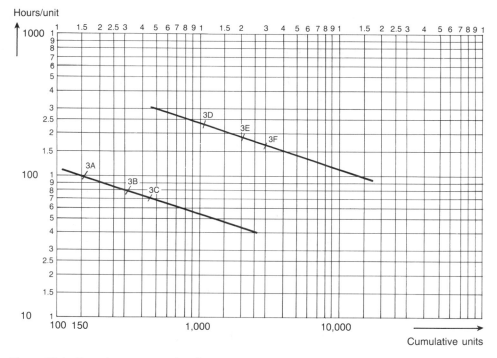

Figure 14.4 Learning curve on log–log paper.

- When direct labour costs make up an important part of the cost price of the product to be produced.

Supplier assessment

Levels of assessment

The growing role of suppliers in the company's business chain (see Chapter 8) increases the need for objective assessment of performance. In many cases it is not sufficient that the supplier is able to meet the materials and service requirements of today. The buyer also wants to determine whether a supplier is sufficiently equipped to live up to the company's longer-term requirements and needs. This requires knowledge of the strong and weak points in the supplier's performance. Furthermore, it is necessary to know whether the supplier can guarantee sustained continuity of supply. The systematic gathering of supplier performance data enables the buyer to negotiate strict agreements about improving reject rates, reducing total lead time and cost reduction.

Supplier assessment may take place at four different levels of abstraction.

- *Product level*. This level focuses on establishing and improving the supplier's product quality; incoming inspections and quality inspections are conducted, which result in establishing the degree of quality conformance of incoming materials.
- *Process level*. Here it is not the product which is the subject of inspection, it is the production process that is closely investigated. The underlying idea is that the quality of the product strongly relates to the supplier's manufacturing process. If this process is under control through consistent application of quality procedures, this will result in a product which conforms to the expressed quality standards and specifications. In this approach the state of the supplier's machinery and the quality control system are subjected to in-depth auditing.
- *Quality assurance system level*. Quality assurance means checking the way in which procedures regarding quality inspection are developed, kept up to date/maintained and refined. In other words, not only the procedures and guidelines are investigated, but the entire quality organization is the subject of investigation by the customer.
- *Company level*. This is the highest level of investigation. In this approach auditors not only focus on quality aspects; they also take financial aspects into consideration. And finally, they want to get an idea of the quality of the management. In this way the customer tries to establish how competitive that particular supplier will be in the near future.

Most supplier evaluation is limited to the first two levels.

Assessment methods

The methods used to assess supplier performance may vary from company to company; two types may be differentiated. **Subjective methods** are used when companies evaluate suppliers through personal judgements, for example by combining various departments' experiences with the supplier; **objective methods** attempt to quantify the supplier's performance. In general the following tools and techniques can be used for supplier assessment:

- *Spreadsheets*. These are used to systematically compare and assess quotations obtained from the suppliers. The most important criteria for evaluation are listed on one axis, the supplier quotations on the other. This gives a matrix with fields that can be filled in. Applying this very simple, but often extremely illuminating method is made easier when the suppliers have drawn up their quotations in a similar way. For this reason buyers are advised to use well-structured requests for quotations, which provide clear guidelines to suppliers on how to submit their quotations.
- *Personal assessment*. This method is used for those suppliers with whom close business relationships exist. Various specialists, who have experience with this supplier (e.g. quality control, engineering, manufacturing, production planning, purchasing) are asked to 'rate' him according to a previously agreed checklist.

- *Vendor rating.* This is limited to quantitative data only. It entails measuring the aspects of price, quality and delivery reliability per supplier. The supplier's price history is investigated and compared with the development of his competitors. Quality is measured in terms of the rejection percentage or the number of production-line stops as a result of faulty materials. Delivery reliability is measured by means of registration of the number of late (or early) deliveries.

  This may appear simple, but such systems are very difficult to establish, due to the enormous amounts of administrative data which need to be extracted from internal company records. To do this economically, an integrated computerized materials planning system should be in place.
- *Supplier audit.* This method entails that the supplier is periodically visited by specialists from the customer. They subject his production process and quality organization to a thorough investigation. Faults and weaknesses are reported and discussed with the supplier. Measures for improvement are negotiated and established. During a subsequent visit it is checked to see to what extent progress against targets has been made (extensively discussed in Chapter 10).
- *Cost modelling.* This is a very detailed approach. Specialists at the buying company estimate by means of shadow calculation, based on the production technology, which currently is being used by the supplier. A detailed analysis is made of the supplier's direct and indirect costs: materials consumption, materials prices, storage costs, waste, personnel costs, costs of supervising, overhead, etc. Usually this analysis leads to some interesting insights, which then can be discussed with the supplier. Based upon this information, some professional buyers go one step further and conduct a should-cost analysis. Based upon what they consider to be the most advanced state-of-the-art production technology and structure it is calculated what the supplier's cost price of a particular component really should be. The difference between the two then becomes, of course, the subject of discussion between buyer and supplier. There is an intensive exchange of ideas on how the should-cost position might be achieved. These discussions frequently result in the supplier having to invest in the existing manufacturing equipment. To compensate, the client is often prepared to offer long-term purchasing contracts.

  The use of cost-models and should cost-techniques usually deepens the relationship between both parties. These cannot, however, be implemented overnight since the supplier needs to develop trust in the other party. The supplier should be convinced that the buyer is not after a next round of cutting into his margin but that both parties equally will benefit from the efficiency improvements gained. The issue of developing trust in buyer-seller relationships actually takes a lot of time!

Memo 14.2 illustrates how to proceed when developing a cost model for purchasing.

Laseter (1998, p. 51) provides an interesting framework that may help buyers identify the most important cost drivers for their commodities (see Table 14.3).

MEMO 14.2: Developing cost models for purchasing

Cost models should provide a clear picture of the total cost of ownership of a purchased component. Since these models require a lot of analysis and many data, these still are not widely used. As experience shows, only some leading-edge companies are applying this technique. However, its popularity will increase steadily for the years to come.

In developing cost models a few principles can be used. First it is important to build cost models not only on cost-elements (such as labour, materials) but also around the actual cost drivers. Capturing the cost drivers produces a model that answers the question 'what if?' instead of 'what is?' (Laseter, 1998, p. 37). Examples are production lot sizes, set-up times, labour rates.

Cost models should expose at least three elements: materials purchase prices, the actual acquisition costs that the company incurs in buying the materials, and the cost of use. Taking copying equipment as an example, it is seen that the purchase price of this type of equipment in general only represents a small part of the total usage cost. Building a cost model for copying machines would then require a detailed breakdown of (a) the actual supplier cost price of the equipment, (b) the company's acquisition costs and (c) the cost related to accessories, maintenance and other services, costs and supply of spare parts, etc. Building a cost model for an aluminum die casted product would require a breakdown of the following cost elements: tooling, quality, logistics, purchasing administration, scrap, supplier inventory, supplier overhead, supplier indirect and direct labour, energy consumption and materials costs. In each of these cases these cost elements should next be related to the actual cost drivers.

Table 14.3   Identifying cost drivers

Category	Description	Examples
Design	Costs attributable to product design trade-offs	• Materials specifications • Product line complexity
Facility	Costs related to the size of the facility, equipment and process technology employed	• Facility scale • Degree of vertical integration • Use of automation
Geography	Costs associated with the location of the facility relative to the customer	• Location related wage rate difference • Transportation costs to customer
Operations	Costs that differentiate a well run facility from a poorly run facility	• Labor productivity • Facility utilization • Rejection rates

(Source: Laseter, 1998, p. 51)

The techniques mentioned above cannot be applied in all circumstances. Naturally, the costs and the benefits must be weighed. The last two methods are extremely labour intensive and will only be used with 'strategic' suppliers and products. Application of all methods requires co-operation between specialists in the areas of engineering, manufacturing, calculation, quality control and purchasing.

The first three methods, being less time consuming, are more broadly applicable. Table 14.4 indicates the major differences between supplier auditing and vendor rating. Vendor rating will be used to judge existing suppliers. It has a more quantitative focus than auditing techniques.

Financial assessment

The financial assessment of suppliers is carried out on the basis of annual financial reports. These can be obtained from the supplier. In most European countries legislation requires companies to file a summary of their financial reports at the local Chamber of Commerce where the supplier is registered. Dun & Bradstreet, Graydon and other information brokers provide on the world wide web detailed electronic databases nowadays from which up-to-date financial and other information can be obtained (see for example www.dnb.com/purchase). Based on these financial reports the supplier's financial performance can be evaluated. When conducting this analysis, one should keep in mind that this analysis is based on historical data. However, quite often it is possible, using financial forecasting techniques, to judge the potential future opportunities and threats based on these data. That makes the financial analysis an interesting instrument to the buyer. A financial analysis can only be carried out if one has access to the supplier's annual reports. The results give a first impression of the quality of the supplier's management. Such an analysis enables the buyer to visit the supplier well-prepared, and to ask pointed questions.

A financial analysis provides insight into the development of the quality of the supplier's results. If information is available about other companies (either directly, or indirectly in the shape of the industrial statistics of the Central Statistical Office), comparison with competitors becomes possible. This knowledge can be used in discussions with the supplier to achieve improvements in his organization.

Table 14.4   Major differences between supplier auditing and vendor rating

Aspect	Supplier auditing	Vendor rating
Orientation	Focus on future	Based on historical data
Application	New and current suppliers	Current suppliers
Nature	Mainly qualitative	Mainly quantitative
Scope	Broad, many aspects	Limited, few aspects
Work	Time consuming	Standard data
Data processing	Subjective, manually	Factual, computerized
Relation with suppliers	Co-operation required	Based on internal administrative data

Summary

Pricing and cost structure are always interrelated, but the effect they have on one another is not always clear. Pricing policies of industrial products are subjected to both external market factors and internal cost factors. The prices of goods and services can be based on market factors, on cost factors, or on a combination of both. The latter situation is the most common.

The supplier will take numerous additional (frequently political or strategic) factors into account when deciding on his pricing policy. The supplier's pricing policy is in most cases already obscure, and it may even be aggravated by the discount system he uses.

It is crucial to buyers to be able to lift the veil that covers the supplier's pricing policy. The buyer can achieve this by closely monitoring the developments in the supply and demand situation on the purchasing market. He can also monitor the individual supplier's financial performance and can make an analysis of the supplier's cost price, either with or without specialist assistance. Experience shows that the basis for negotiations becomes considerably more professional as a result of this knowledge. It furthermore facilitates reaching agreements on product and process improvements.

Finally, the buyer should monitor developments in the supplier's performance. Price behaviour, quality and delivery performance should be closely monitored. This information justifies the development of computerized vendor rating systems. It should be noted, however, that vendor rating can only be applied to existing suppliers who deliver goods on a more or less regular basis. For new suppliers and suppliers delivering critical items on an 7 basis other techniques must be used.

Assignments

14.1 This chapter discusses a number of methods in the field of supplier assessment. In addition to objective and quantitative methods, such assessments can also be made in a more subjective manner. The objective of supplier assessment is to determine the extent to which a particular supplier will be able to meet his delivery obligations, both now and in the future. Name a few issues which may indicate that a supplier's performance is deteriorating, and which can be observed by the buyer during a visit to the supplier.

14.2 A supplier of components announces that he has to raise his prices by 10%, because he has lost a major customer. He states he is now forced to spread his overheads across a smaller production volume. What costing method does this supplier use? What do you think of that? Assuming that this supplier is important to you, how would you deal with the supplier's request? What steps would you take?

14.3 In this chapter vendor rating was named as one of the methods that can be used to measure supplier performance. Delivery reliability and quality performance of the supplier are two aspects of vendor rating. How can a supplier's delivery reliability and quality performance be measured in a practical way? What criteria are used? Name some examples.

14.4 Last year you purchased 100 units of product X from a supplier at £50 each. You estimate that you will purchase 300 units of this product from the same supplier this year. You are now preparing for the price discussion with the supplier. What price are you willing to pay, assuming that an 80% learning curve applies to this product?

14.5 Name examples of products of which the price is set by means of cost-based pricing, market-based pricing and competitive bidding. What are the consequences of this distinction for the purchasing policy, or for the buyer's attitude during negotiations with the supplier? Which arguments will the buyer use in each of these cases to obtain the lowest possible purchase price?

NEGOTIATING TECHNIQUES AND RULES OF CONDUCT

15

Learning objectives

After studying this chapter you should understand the following:

- The main characteristics of purchasing negotiations.
- How to recognize actual negotiating situations.
- Factors that can affect the course of the negotiating process and the buyer's negotiating position.
- How to prepare and plan for purchasing negotiations.
- The tactics that can be used during purchasing negotiations.

CASE STUDY
Negotiating a car purchase

Two gentlemen enter a car dealer's showroom. After looking for some time at several of the cars on display they approach the salesman. They tell him they are interested in a particular type of car. However, their willingness to do business depends on the price they will get for the car they want to trade in. The salesman goes outside to inspect their car.

The salesman decides to take it for a test drive and leaves both customers at the dealer's site. There is some heavy consultation between the two gentlemen during the salesman's absence. A little later, the salesman comes back. They all go inside and settle around the table.

The discussion proceeds laboriously. The salesman asks what price the two gentlemen had in mind for their used car, but they don't want to tell him. The salesman has to take the lead. After some discussion and calculation, he writes down a figure on a piece of paper, folds it, and hands it over. A few seconds later, both customers know the price offered.

One of the gentlemen acts as spokesman. His reaction is one of incredulity: such a price for their car is impossible; a pure swindle! Other dealers offered much more! The discussion turns hostile. The prospective buyers stand up, and sit down again. At one point the person who has done all the talking so far tells his colleague: 'Come on, John, this isn't going anywhere. Let's go!'. He makes ready to leave. The other customer remains seated. In a confidential tone of voice he

Continued on page 292

resumes the discussion with the salesman, and tells him that his colleague is a bit excited, but he has his reasons. If the salesman will improve his offer, then maybe he can talk some sense into his colleague . . .

Introduction

Negotiations as described in the case study occur daily. Execution of the purchasing function without negotiation is unthinkable. Experiences with buyers show that at least 20% of their time is taken up by preparations for and the actual negotiations with suppliers. Knowledge of the negotiating process and negotiating skills are necessary for the buyer to be able to offer resistance to the frequently well-trained salesman.

In a study conducted in England in 1974, Farmer found that 80% of the salesmen in the industry he studied had received some kind of formal negotiating training. Of the buyers in that same industry, on the other hand, only 1% had received similar training!

When thinking of negotiating, we usually picture the commercial process that occurs in every buy-and-sell transaction. However, the subject can be viewed in a much broader sense, for, aside from negotiations with suppliers, the buyer often also has to negotiate, including within his own organization. An effective buyer must be able to maintain good contacts with his internal users. He must be able to judge the feasibility of certain ideas. He must also be able to make product designers change their minds if they have overlooked an alternative that is better for the organization. This chapter addresses the general principles that underlie negotiating processes. (The context of this book, unfortunately, does not allow elaboration on the impact of culture on international negotiations.) The chapter starts by describing the major differences between negotiations for industrial purposes and negotiations for retail. Next, the various stages that can be distinguished in a negotiating process are discussed. Finally, the various tactics that can be used in negotiations are addressed. All of these subjects will be investigated from the buyer's perspective.

Characteristics of purchasing negotiations for industrial purchases

Very little attention is given to the basic differences between industrial buying and retail buying, both in the relevant literature and in training courses. However, it is important to appreciate these differences, because they strongly affect the nature of the negotiations, as shown below.

- The purchasing policy of a trading company is closely related to its sales policy, because the purchase price directly influences the saleability and profitability of the product. This is much less so in industrial companies. In comparison with a trading company, the purchasing share in the cost price of the end product is lower. Therefore, the prices of purchased products have a less direct impact on the sales price of end products.

- Retail buyers generally have more freedom in decision making than industrial buyers. The latter are limited by production planning, technical specifications (small tolerances), call-off schedules, etc. This makes them less autonomous than their colleagues in the retail sector.

- The buyer of industrial goods usually has a longer term, more intense relationship with his suppliers than do his colleagues in the retail company. This is particularly so when it involves products which are manufactured to design. The retail buyer often buys products which were developed by the supplier. This means that it is easier for him to change suppliers than it is for the industrial buyer. For the industrial buyer, a change of supplier is often preceded by a long screening process with regard to technical reliability and delivery reliability.

- Price is often less important for the industrial buyer than good quality, delivery reliability and service. Although these aspects are also important in retail buying, price is even more important.

All of this means that the retail buyer will usually be able to take a more autonomous and independent attitude towards a supplier than the industrial buyer. He is reasonably autonomous in his work, and has to deal with fewer people in his own organization. This is reflected in his attitude towards the supplier. Negotiations in retail will generally be 'harder' and more focused on price than on industrial purchasing negotiations. This means that a number of the negotiating techniques used in trade negotiations are less suitable to industrial purchasing negotiations.

Recognizing negotiating situations

One of the most important elements in negotiation, irrespective of whether it takes place in a commercial or a non-commercial context, is being able to recognize when the situation is a negotiating situation. If your neighbour comes over on a sunny afternoon to ask you if he can borrow your lawn mower, many of you will answer his question with a 'yes' or a 'no'. The experienced negotiator immediately spots an opportunity in his neighbour's request. Maybe you also want your neighbour to do something for you. Then the request is a good opportunity to make a counter request. For example you noticed earlier that day that there is almost no fuel left in the machine and you ask your neighbour to fill it up. Or perhaps you will agree on the condition that your neighbour also will mow your lawn.

The essence of this type of situation is that somebody else asks for or wants something you are basically willing to provide. A request can be transformed into a negotiating situation when you discover that this person can also be of use to you. **Negotiating situations** are aimed at bringing together the parties through **concessions** in such a way that both parties can look back on the negotiations with satisfaction.

In the example of the lawn mower, the negotiating situation emerges spontaneously. In a business context often negotiating situations emerge long before the first contact with the other party takes place.

It is important to observe that negotiations concern more elements than price alone. Negotiations concern all elements that are important in reaching the agreement; this observation is of special significance for industrial products. Experience with purchasing departments in many companies shows that issues like quality and delivery reliability, as well as after-sales services are frequently more important elements in the purchasing decision than price and terms of payment.

Negotiations are focused on arriving at a good deal for both parties. If one of the negotiating parties is so powerful that they can impose their will on the other, there is no negotiating situation. In this context negotiating would be defined as 'a process, aimed at solving problems experienced by two or more parties, in such a way that the interests of all parties involved are served.'

From the definition it may be concluded that good negotiating requires a co-operative attitude, characterized by receptivity to the other party's interests. Furthermore, willingness to reach an agreement that is beneficial to both parties is indispensable.

Factors which can weaken the negotiating position

If a person does not have a clear picture of his target, the negotiating process will be affected. This occurs frequently in situations between industrial buyers and sellers. It is well known that, in general, salesmen have a more solid training than buyers. As a result of the numbers of suppliers the buyer has to deal with, and the size of his purchasing portfolio, he is frequently unable to prepare for all negotiations sufficiently. An insufficient knowledge about the subject of the negotiations can easily lead to being snowed under by detailed information provided by the other party. Buyers have identified many aspects which may weaken their negotiating position (see Memo 15.1).

These issues can be summarized in three main points which must be predetermined for every negotiation.

- *Goals and objectives.* Is it clear what the negotiations should accomplish? What is the minimum result that must be achieved and what are the maximum concessions one is willing to make?
- *Authority.* What authority does the negotiator have to make a deal? Does he/she have the necessary support from higher management levels?
- *Expertise and knowledge.* Do the people who are going to conduct the negotiation have the required expertise and knowledge? Are they experts on the subject? Do they actually know the business?

These items are essential prerequisites to entering into any negotiation.

MEMO 15.1 Factors which may weaken the buyer's negotiating position

- Lack of preparation time.
- Lack of knowledge with regard to market developments, the market position of the supplier, and own company's relative position.
- Lack of knowledge of the supplier's cost structure.
- Insufficient information on the supplier's organization (authority).
- Too little listening and too much talk on the buyer's side.
- Insufficient command of foreign languages.
- No or very few alternative sources available.
- Few valid arguments to support the buyer's point of view.
- A negotiating partner on the buying team speaks out of turn.
- Insufficient authority to close an agreement.
- The supplier uses arguments that were not anticipated.
- Lack of experience with a supplier.

Preparing for negotiations

Planning and preparing for negotiations starts long before the actual negotiation takes place. It is important to find out at an early stage what the other party's view of the negotiations will be: what exactly are they hoping to achieve? In exceptional cases a supplier doesn't want to sell at all, but keeps the discussion going to collect basic information about changing usage patterns and/or competitors. What interests are possibly shared, and what are the expected potential subjects of opposing interests (conflict)? To get some idea, a useful tactic can be to ask what subjects the other party wants on the agenda (this in itself can prompt preliminary negotiations – consider the disarmament negotiations between the Americans and the Soviets in Geneva in the late 1980s).

It is important to find out as much as possible about the other party. If it is a new supplier, examination of annual reports and bank references is a prerequisite. If it is an existing supplier, it is wise to analyse the past deliveries – have there been problems in the past with this supplier? (e.g. low delivery reliability, quality defects, unexpected price increases, etc.). There is no harm in trying to quantify the scope of these problems. Furthermore, it is also important to know who will represent the supplier in the negotiations. Are they people you know? If not, then the authority of the negotiating partners must be investigated. How far does their power of decision go? Do they have the authority to conclude an agreement? At first sight this may seem too detailed an approach; however, the buyer must take into account that sales people have an eye for detail and come very well prepared.

It is important, after having gathered the necessary information, to have an idea of possible points of agreement between you and the other party. If there are few, you might reconsider the wisdom of negotiating.

Planning negotiations

When the homework has been done, planning of the negotiations can begin. Clayton (1984) proposes a ten-step approach.

1 *Establish the objectives of the negotiation for yourself*. What exactly do you want to accomplish by means of the transaction with the supplier? What is it you want him to do? What are you willing to do in return? Make a distinction between the short-term benefits you want to achieve, and the long-term benefits you see. Sometimes it is necessary that you tone down your short-term expectation a little for the benefit of the long-term interests. Take the manufacturers of copying equipment, who, for example, are often willing to let something off the sales price, only to compensate for this reduction at a later stage through higher service rates, spare parts and supplies.

2 *Gather facts that can have a big impact on the negotiations*. If a supplier wants to come and talk about a price increase, it is worthwhile finding out how this increase relates to his competitors. Alternatively, a supplier might be willing to moderate the announced price increase if we are willing to consider larger purchases in the near future. These are examples of what we call objective facts which can influence the negotiation. However, there are also subjective facts that can affect the course of the negotiation. It is important to know what the other party thinks of us. Will they be influenced by possible bad experiences they have had with our company in the past? Do the negotiators on both sides get along on a personal level? It is worthwhile keeping a file of major negotiations with suppliers.

3 *Assess the power position of each of the parties*. A power position in a negotiation can be derived from various aspects (see Figure 15.1). It is important to realize that power is a relative concept. It also depends on how the position (power) is perceived by the other party (think of the poker game in which the player's power position is often based on bluff).

It is important, therefore, to determine the foundation of the other party's power position, and whether this is a reason for concern. In price negotiations sales people sometimes hide behind the price list or the company's guidelines. Do you accept this type of argument or don't you?

4 *Determine the points of common interest*. In many negotiations most of the time is spent on issues one cannot agree on. If these are the only issues that receive attention, it will be very difficult to reach an agreement. It is more important to establish (in advance) the points of agreement. Focusing attention here leads to a more positive atmosphere. The question of 'how do we solve our conflicts?' then becomes 'how can we turn the points of common interest into the largest possible mutual advantage?'.

Keep the negotiating atmosphere as positive and open as possible.

5 *Make a list of questions*. A systematic approach is important in negotiations. Resist the temptation to respond immediately to details or new information presented by the other party. If this new information sheds a completely different light on matters, it is better to discontinue the negotiations and redo your homework. So, draw up a list of questions and stick to it.

Competition
Letting the supplier know he's not the only option

Written word
Often applied by suppliers 'according to our list the price is . . .', or 'in view of your order we regret the maximum discount is . . .'

Trust
The other party will be more willing to make concessions if they trust you

Knowledge
Insight (about products, markets, alternatives) enhances your negotiating position and prevents surprises

Time
Time constraints will put negotiations under pressure and may lead to unexpected concessions

Money
The person who pays has the initial lead

Negotiating power
The person who is more skilled in negotiating and/or has prepared his work more thoroughly, clearly has the advantage

Figure 15.1 Aspects of a power position – factors which may lead to a better power position in negotiations.

6 *Define your tasks.* Both parties will probably make concessions during the process of negotiation. It is unrealistic to expect the other party to do it all (and this doesn't fit in the negotiating concept presented here). You can plan your concessions in advance. To be able to do this, it is important that you establish what for you would be the best possible result (what do you think is the feasible maximum result the other party would agree to, given the circumstances?). What for you would be the most likely result (what do you think is realistically feasible, and would that result be acceptable to you?). What for you would be the worst possible result (what is the minimum you would settle for, if there is no other possibility?)

7 *Decide on the composition and division of roles in your negotiating team.* The composition of the team will depend on the subject of the negotiations. Who are the best people to use? Do you need help from outside the purchasing department (this will often be the case in major negotiations)? Who will be the spokesperson for your company? Who will take notes? Who watches the other party's reactions? In the early 1980s, Lockheed had negotiating specialists for major negotiations, who, together with buyers, financial analysts and production managers, discussed the negotiating tactics (see Figure 15.2).

8 *Plan your concessions.* What will be your opening bid? When will you make it? Never make a concession without asking for something in return; but also,

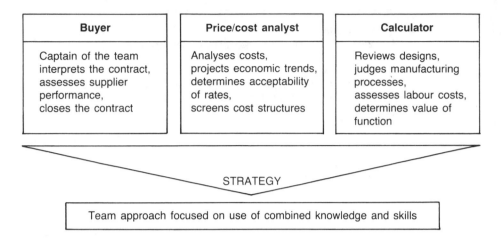

Figure 15.2 Composition of a purchasing negotiating team.

never ask for a concession without offering something in return. Discuss with your team members which concessions you are willing to make, and which concessions you absolutely will not make under any circumstance. You can do the same for the opposition: what concessions do you think they are willing to make and what is absolutely unrealistic to expect?

9 *Agree upon the negotiating tactic you will follow.* This subject is discussed in the next section.

10 *Indicate how you think you will conclude the negotiations.* What working agreements do you think you can reach with the other party? Is it necessary to schedule the next discussion? Summarize the results and agreements for the other party, to prevent misunderstandings.

These ten steps are essential in every significant negotiation process. It is obvious that effective negotiating requires appropriate preparation in order to arrive at a satisfactory outcome.

Tactics in purchasing negotiations

It has been indicated that determining the tactics to adopt during purchasing negotiations is an important aspect of the preparation. The literature which covers negotiating tactics (Karass, 1970, 1977, 1979) identifies the following approaches.

- *Take-it-or-leave-it.* One party wants to impose its terms on the other party, without making concessions. This tactic is contrary to the author's idea of negotiating and is less suitable in an industrial setting. Nevertheless, it is sometimes used by buyers who are aware of their power position *vis-à-vis* the supplier and is intended to lower the other party's aspiration level.

- *Bogey.* In this tactic the buyer approaches the supplier in a very friendly way and comments on his proposal positively. However, the buyer lets the supplier know that, if there is to be any business, the proposal 'will have to be slightly adjusted in view of the very specific situation'. With this tactic the negotiating atmosphere remains open and the supplier can utilize all his talents to develop a better deal.

- *Chinese crunch.* In this situation it is declared that an agreement with the supplier is possible, as soon as he solves just one little problem. Obviously, this little problem is interpreted differently by the seller! This tactic is to effectively sink the agreement, which was as good as settled in the seller's mind, just before it reaches home; for example, there is an agreement about the price, but the buyer then informs the seller that transportation is the latter's responsibility.

  Practice shows that sales people are ready to make considerable concessions in this stage of the negotiating process.

- *Auction,* also referred to as *Dutch* or *Chinese auction.* In this situation the buyer makes the supplier explain why they should do business together. If the buyer also applies this tactic to the others, a lot will be learned about the competition. Information is obtained without too much effort. It is, of course, desirable to check the accuracy of the information.

- *Good guy–bad guy.* This was very popular among the Germans during World War II. A prisoner was first interrogated by a tough officer. When he had almost lost courage, a second, much friendlier, officer would appear. He would reprimand his colleague and subsequently draw out the prisoner. This tactic is frequently employed by used-car dealers. The purpose of this tactic is to dim the other party's expectations about the outcome of the negotiations.

Several other tactics are feasible based on different considerations. For example, does one take the initiative in the negotiation, or leave this to the other party? Does one build in a recess or is this not desirable? In the context of this book, the discussion of the tactical components of purchasing negotiations can only be limited.

Stages in purchasing negotiations

If the preparations have been concluded and agreement is reached about the tactic to be used, the negotiations can be started. In practice, negotiation processes follow a certain pattern and, in general, four stages can be discerned in the course of the negotiation process.

- *Exploration.* During this first stage both parties try to get acquainted. Next they try to discover the mutual interests and intentions. They also try to assess the importance of the negotiations for the other party. This is done by exchanging information: everybody listens, both parties explain or ask for clarification of particular statements, and they continually check whether they understand each other. It is important to listen closely to the other party, and not make a first offer. Furthermore, one should not respond specifically to questions from the other party. The objective of this stage is to establish the context of the negotiations.

- *Reflection*. This stage consists in digesting the information received from the other party. Does this information necessitate a revision of your objectives? Did you overlook certain things in your preparations? Were your assumptions about the other party's willingness to reach an agreement correct, or do they now turn out to be wrong? Receiving new information can cause you to request a short break so you can consult with your partner.
- *Negotiation*. In this phase true negotiation takes place. Concessions are made on both sides. It is important to check how the other party responds to concessions made by you (through both verbal and non-verbal reactions). Don't jump to conclusions during this stage; avoid insulting remarks and, most importantly, don't concede more than your planning allowed for.
- *Closing*. Repeat and summarize the agreements that have been made. Is the other party satisfied with the results? Take your time to round off the negotiations well, so there is no possibility of misunderstandings about the results that have been achieved.

This list can be helpful to buyers. It is important to be aware of the stage the negotiations are at, all of the time. Practice shows time and time again that the first stage is the most time consuming. This leaves less time for the actual negotiations and the closing part and one common result is misunderstandings about who is supposed to do what. Both parties will then dispute (parts of) the agreements afterwards.

Negotiating is a difficult job, because it can involve so many different subjects. This work furthermore requires a certain disposition, namely a willingness to co-operate to reach an agreement that will benefit both parties.

Rules of conduct and purchasing ethics

It is in the interest of the buyer, but even more in the company interest, that the purchasing negotiations achieve the best possible results by using means and paths that are proper and responsible, not only in the business sense, but also in terms of ethics. A buyer is exposed to many temptations. These vary from Christmas presents which are sent to his/her home address at the end of the year, to vacations, which are offered disguised as a business trip to an overseas office. In sales practice lots of activities are undertaken to put the customer in the most positive frame of mind about a possible purchase. The question of course is what can and what cannot be accepted from the supplier. In business, this question is not easily answered. Questions can also be raised on the side of the buyer as to how far one should go in a relationship with a supplier. In this context the following questions may occur

- How should confidential supplier price information be handled?
- How to deal with quotations: should we only use quotations if we are seriously considering requesting a firm bid from a supplier, or do we also use them to check our current supplier's prices?

MEMO 15.2: The Ethical Code of IFPMM

1   *Precepts.* Members shall not use their authority or office for personal gain and shall seek to uphold and enhance the standing of the Purchasing and Materials Management profession and the Federation by:

- Maintaining an unimpeachable standard of integrity in all their business relationships both inside and outside the organizations in which they are employed.
- Fostering the highest standards of professional competence amongst those for whom they are responsible.
- Optimizing the use of resources for which they are responsible so as to provide the maximum benefit to their employers.
- Complying with the letter and the spirit of:
  - The laws of the country in which they practise.
  - The Federation's 'Principles and Standards of Purchasing Practice' and any other such guidance on professional practice as may be issued by the Federation from time to time.
  - Contractual obligations.
- Rejecting and denouncing any business practice that is improper.

2   *Guidance.* In applying these precepts, members should follow the guidance set out below:

- Declaration of interest. Any personal interest which may impinge or might reasonably be deemed by others to impinge on a member's impartiality in any matter relevant to their duties should be declared to their employer.
- Confidentiality and accuracy of information. The confidentiality of information received in the course of duty must be respected and should not be used for personal gain; information given in the course of duty should be true and fair and not designed to mislead.
- Competition. While considering the advantages to the member's employer of maintaining a continuing relationship with a supplier, any arrangement which might, in the long term, prevent the effective operation of fair competition, should be avoided.
- Business gifts. To preserve the image and integrity of both the member and the employer, business gifts should be discouraged. Gifts, other than items of very small intrinsic value should not be accepted.
- Hospitality. Moderate hospitality is an accepted courtesy of a business relationship. However, the recipients should not allow themselves to reach a position whereby they might be or might be deemed by others to have been influenced in making a business decision as a consequence of accepting such hospitality. The frequency and scale of hospitality accepted should not be significantly greater than a recipient's employer, through the recipient's expense account, would be likely to provide in return.
- When in doubt of what is acceptable in terms of gifts or hospitality, the offer should be declined or advice sought from the member's superior.

(Source: International Federation of Purchasing and Materials Management)

- What is the maximum share we as customers want to have in the supplier's turnover, in order to prevent excessive dependency on us?
- Do we always strive to have at least two suppliers (dual sourcing) or are single sources allowed in particular circumstances?
- How far do we go in negotiations with suppliers? Are we willing to buy at prices we know for a fact aren't sufficient to cover the supplier's cost price?

To increase uniformity in behaviour towards suppliers, a number of large companies have drawn up and subscribed to several **rules of conduct** for the purchase of large investment goods. Rules of conduct have also been drawn up by the International Federation of Purchasing and Materials Management (see Memo 15.2).

Summary

Negotiating is an important aspect of the buyer's activities. It takes up a large part of his time. Every negotiation is an interactive process between two or more parties. Negotiating demands a co-operative attitude, and a receptivity to the other party's interests.

Before starting negotiations with a supplier, it is important to determine

- the goals and objectives of the negotiations (preferably formulated in terms of different aspiration levels);
- what authority the negotiators have to conclude an agreement with the supplier's representatives (and vice versa);
- what information is required to negotiate effectively.

Sound preparation is half the job! This chapter presented a ten-step method; of course it is not necessary to go through each step in every negotiation. One important aspect of the preparations is deciding on the negotiating tactics. Purchasing practice shows a wide variety of methods and techniques. A relatively fixed four-stage pattern can be distinguished in every negotiation process: exploration, reflection, negotiation and the closing stage.

The buyer will have to observe several rules of conduct in his communication with the supplier. The ethical code of the International Federation of Purchasing and Materials Management can serve as a guideline here.

Assignments

15.1 You are the buyer in a machine factory. Management is considering the purchase of a CNC milling machine, representing an investment of more than €350,000. You have selected one supplier from a number of potential suppliers, with whom you have had an explorative discussion. A second discussion is scheduled for next week about the terms and conditions of a possible order. What issues would you pay attention to in preparing for the discussion with the supplier? Present an overview.

15.2 The preparations of negotiations should mention the location of the negotiations. One can basically choose between the buyer's office, the supplier's office and neutral territory. List the advantages and disadvantages of each of these locations.

15.3 Name some factors that can limit the supplier's negotiating power.

15.4 What do you think are the major differences between negotiations with European suppliers and negotiations with suppliers from the Far East?

THE PURCHASING FUNCTION IN TRADE AND RETAIL COMPANIES

16

Learning objectives

After studying this chapter you should understand the following:

- The main characteristics and importance of purchasing and supply in trade and retail companies.
- The most important developments going on in the purchasing policies of trade and retail companies.
- The way in which the purchasing function can be organized in trade and retail companies.
- The profile of the trade and retail buyer.

CASE STUDY
Direct product profitability at Procter & Gamble

To date, direct product profitability (DPP) has been used most in analysing the performance of individual items.

In the United States Procter & Gamble have gone so far as to use the 29 cents per case saving, achieved by repackaging its Ivory shampoo in advertising. The use of a cylindrical plastic bottle, rather than the characteristic curvy shape, resulted not merely in reduced distribution, handling and storage costs, but also in an increase in sales because people perceived the new shape as symbolizing value for money. Similar savings were achieved by Scott by the repackaging of Andrex toilet tissue. 11% more merchandise is now packed per case, and 6% more cases per pallet. Repackaging has also eliminated pallet overhang and resulted in less damage and returns. With a distribution volume in excess of 16 million cases per year the savings are significant.

Continued on page 306

The trend towards smaller delivery quantities reflects pressure from retailers for improved product profitability. Many manufacturers are receiving requests for mixed pallets to be delivered to central distribution warehouses, and many retailers are now operating break pack facilities which supply individual stores with single units in display packaging only.

The prompt delivery of fashion garments poses a particular challenge for the retail industry. If goods can be delivered ready for display, valuable time can be saved in making them available to customers as well as allowing a reduction in store labour from the removal of the ironing task. Marks & Spencer and many of the high street fashion multiples have shown their commitment to this approach. However, there is a trade-off in the equipment investment and warehousing space required . . .

(Source: Aston (1989), as quoted by Christopher (1992) p. 76)

Introduction

The situation described in the case study is still relevant. It demonstrates that there are a number of differences, but also a number of striking similarities with the purchasing function in industrial companies. The purchasing function in trade and retail companies is much closer to sales. Although the term 'buying' is more used in retail companies, the terms 'buying' and 'purchasing' are used interchangeably in this chapter. As will be seen in this chapter, the purchasing and sales functions are highly integrated in these companies. In retail, buyers are responsible for decisions related to running a whole product assortment. Sales and purchasing decisions are weighed against each other so that an optimal financial return can be achieved. It goes without saying that to be able to do this, buyers in trade companies need to have a broad business orientation, in which price is only one of the elements of the decision-making process.

Trade and retail companies in most European countries account for a considerable share of the total number of transactions. The purchasing-to-sales content is rather high, since these companies do not add significant value to their products. A purchasing-to-sales ratio of more than 80% is not uncommon. This means that functions such as purchasing, logistics and sales are core activities. Buying for trade companies means 'bottom line' thinking. Margins on products (especially in the retail business) are usually very small. This means that the buyer must take into consideration all the costs that are made in the trajectory from manufacturer to end-customer. Effective cost control is a prerequisite for the continued existence of trade companies. Costs related to materials handling, transportation and storage cannot be ignored. This concept is at the root of the development of advanced cost management (such as direct product cost and direct product profitability) and shelf or display simulation systems, which will be explained in this chapter. These information systems are nowadays important management tools for the modern retail buyer.

This chapter describes the role and importance of the purchasing function in trade and retail companies (from now on referred to simply as 'trade companies' for convenience). In doing so the issue of how to organize for purchasing in these kinds of company will be addressed. The chapter will also discuss the major developments taking place in the relationships between buyers and sellers in this important sector; however, definitions of some important concepts are required first.

Definitions

Trade companies are characterized by the absence of a production process. There is no transformation in the technical sense. At most there are some packaging or 'bulk-breaking' activities. The value added in trade and retail companies, when compared with manufacturing companies, is therefore rather low. The mere existence of the trade company is based primarily on the exchange of value, i.e. products between different parties in the market. Essentially the **trade function** can be described as 'bridging time, place, quantity, assortment and knowledge'.

Figure 16.1 shows the primary process of a trade company, with the materials flow as the point of departure. The products must travel the road from manufacturer to the final consumer. The primary process of the trade company takes care of this. The purchasing function, together with (inbound) logistics, is of major importance. In addition, outbound logistics (physical distribution) is a major activity in trade companies. Due to the lack of a production function, the time which elapses between the purchase and the actual sale is very short. This is one reason why in some retail companies buying and selling are integrated into one function, since buying decisions may to a large extent determine the sales potential for a specific product (and vice versa). Where this occurs, this integrated commercial function is often referred to as **category management**.

Trade companies can be divided into two different levels, the **wholesale** level and the **retail** level. Companies that operate on the **wholesale** level deliver their products to other companies. Their customers are the retail, industrial and service companies, which in their turn may deliver directly to the final consumer (see Figure 16.2).

Wholesale companies differ from retailers in several ways. As a rule they devote less effort to promotion, shop layout and selection of location since their contacts are mostly the industrial companies or retailers, rather than final

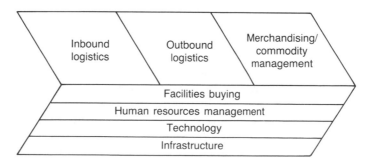

Figure 16.1 The value chain in trade companies. (Adapted from Porter, 1985, pp. 45–48.)

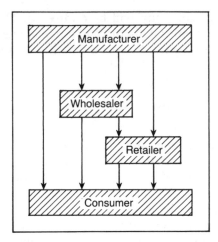

Figure 16.2   Wholesale and trade in the business chain.

consumers. Furthermore, wholesalers often make large transactions with a limited number of (retail) companies. The retailer, however, derives his income primarily from small purchases from a large number of consumers.

Role and importance of purchasing in trade and retail companies

Added value

Trade companies fulfil the function of intermediary between producer and end user. They are able to execute several activities more efficiently than the manufacturers. Their added value, and therefore the rationale of their existence, may be found in the following activities.

- *Sales and promotion.* Trade companies can reach many small customers at relatively low costs. Through their marketing and advertising activities, which are often considerable, they can create a brand image that is experienced as more positive than the image of the (for the consumer, often distant) producer.
- *Purchasing and building up a product assortment.* Trade companies select products and build up an assortment based on the needs of a specific target group. In this way they make the market offer transparent and more easily accessible for the customer.
- *Bulk breaking.* By buying products in large quantities and then selling them in smaller units, the trade companies reduce costs for the producer and improve the accessibility of his products for the public.
- *Storage.* By maintaining stocks they reduce the costs for both manufacturer and end user. At the same time they realize a high degree of availability for the end user.

- *Transportation*. There is also added value of trade companies in the fact that they take over the transportation function from the manufacturer. As a result of a higher loading level they are often able to execute this function more efficiently.
- *Carrying the risk*. Some products are perishable or carry a high risk in terms of pilferage, damage and obsolescence. Trade companies take over part of these risks from the producer.
- *Market information*. Thanks to the continuous advances of information technology, many trade companies have an excellent picture of the characteristics of their target groups and of the sales opportunities and problems with regard to the assortment they carry. This aspect is becoming more and more important in the relationship with producers who can use this information to improve existing or develop new products.
- *Management and marketing services*. Intensive interaction between trade and manufacturers results increasingly in new ideas and concepts in the area of shop layout, shelf layout, displays and the improvement of inventory management systems. Quite often trade companies take the initiative here.

Trade companies may handle an extensive range of products. In the wholesale business these products can vary from raw materials for numerous manufacturing companies and bulk food products for the catering industry to office supplies for government institutions. With regard to the retail trade, various types of shops can be distinguished in the area of consumer products, such as:

- specialty store;
- department store;
- supermarket;
- convenience store;
- combination store, superstore and hypermarket;
- service business.

The wide variety of enterprises in the trade sector, and their widely different modes of operation, make it impossible to generalize on purchasing policy and the 'ideal' structure of the purchasing organization. The scope of this book necessitates a decision on this issue, so for the remainder of this chapter the focus will be on the purchasing function in retail organizations.

Main differences with industrial companies

In comparing trade purchasing with buying for industrial companies, several differences may be recognized.

- *Bottom-line thinking*. The primary reason for buying in trade companies is to sell. No matter what, it must be possible to sell that which is bought. Business policy is primarily aimed at improving turnover and margin. The main objective is to realize the largest possible difference between sales price and total cost (net margin). Turnover, margin and (logistics) cost information are basic information to sound purchasing decision making.

- *Broad assortment.* Trade companies generally have a very broad product assortment. Carrying more than 25,000 items is no exception for a medium-sized trade company. Orders, prices, qualities and supplier conditions must be monitored for all these articles, in addition to the sales information. Managing these product groups, i.e. assortments well, again poses great demands in terms of the management information system.
- *Buying against supplier specifications.* Trade companies frequently buy what the market offers. A large part of the assortment consists of standard products. This can be quite different from industrial companies where many components may be manufactured to customer specification. In terms of purchasing this means that a trade company is usually able to change suppliers more quickly and more easily, and current products may be replaced by substitutes from other suppliers more easily. Relations with suppliers are generally less durable. This is also expressed in negotiations; trade negotiations often are much more businesslike and 'tougher' than industrial negotiations.
- *Short feedback loop.* Because the moments of buying and selling are closer together in a trade company, the sales results become visible more quickly. This means that fast feedback to buyers (and suppliers) is possible. Products can be eliminated from the assortment quickly if it becomes clear that they are less well received by the target group than expected. Such fast feedback loops are much less common in industrial companies.

These differences show that purchasing for industrial companies and purchasing for trade companies are two different worlds! The retail buyer is more sales-marketing oriented: in order to be effective he/she should monitor both the supply market and the end-user markets of his/her company. There are also similarities; for instance the purchasing decision-making process will, to a great extent, evolve according to the same steps as for an industrial context. This subject is now discussed in more detail.

Structure and organization of the purchasing process

Structure of the purchasing process

As has been seen, the purchasing and sales-marketing functions are closely related in trade companies. This is especially true in the case of products with short life cycles, such as fashionable clothing and particular leisure goods. Moreover, most trade products have very short lead times: auction products (such as vegetables, fresh fruit) may find their final destination on the same day that they were purchased by the retailer. As a result the effectiveness of purchasing decision-making is easy to assess. In the words of the purchasing manager of a retail chain store: 'We know on Friday whether Monday's purchases were good or not.'

The following stages in the buying–selling cycle can be distinguished.

- *Estimating the demand for a particular item.* In this stage the sales opportunities of the product concerned are estimated based on either market research or 'market intuition'. These sales opportunities are translated into sales forecasts and budgets for the coming period, preferably detailed at a monthly or weekly level. This information provides the basis for the next stage.

- *Determining product assortment policy and distribution strategy.* The next step is to determine the product's assortment policy. Important decisions here are to decide how **deep** (number of product items per product line) and how **broad** (number of product lines per product group) the assortment needs to be. With regard to the distribution policy, important elements are to decide which products will be kept in stock, for which products the method of stock consignment at the buyer's premises will be used, which products are to be delivered through the company's own distribution centre, and which products are to be delivered directly from the manufacturer to the customer.

- *Selection of the most suitable supplier.* Based on the information indicated above, a list of potential suppliers can be drawn up. In general the circle of (potential) suppliers is limited. Quite often the ideas for new products are presented to the retail buyer by the manufacturers. In that situation the buyer will have to judge whether the new product fits into the assortment policy, or whether the latter must be adjusted. If the buyer has personally developed a viable product idea, he or she will have to start looking for a supplier. The procedure that can be followed in this case is identical to the procedure described in Chapter 3. That risks are also run by retailers during this stage of the purchasing process is demonstrated in Memo 16.1.

- *Contractual agreements.* When the most suitable supplier has been selected, a contract is drawn up. This contract records all rights and obligations of both parties, as well as terms and conditions applying to, among other things, price, method of packing, order size, payment, delivery and quality. Another important issue is the product liability. Especially when the trade company has its own brand **(private label)**, recording the product liability in a contract can prevent many problems. In the food industry some products are bought on a contract basis, based on the annual quantities the buyer is obliged to purchase and the seller is obliged to supply. This is often the case with so-called harvest products (canned and pickled products), of which the buyer wants to secure a particular quantity. Other products often have no firm agreements about quantities. The buyer only provides an estimate of the amounts to be purchased, based on historical information and sales forecasts. Based on this information the parties try to arrive at a price. In general, negotiations between retailers and suppliers have become more complex over the years, as more and more requirements, apart from quality and price, are being put forward (see Memo 16.2).

- *Ordering.* The ordering process is kept as simple as possible in view of the philosophy that the outlets should focus primarily on selling products. Because the retail outlets often have limited space for storage and materials handling, frequent delivery is required, which is why most retail companies have developed sophisticated ordering techniques: with the aid of a pen that

---

MEMO 16.1: Problems surrounding the purchase of new soft drink bottles

Soft drinks suppliers in the Benelux countries have standardized their arrangements about bottles (contents and material), crates, deposits and prices. One of the results of this agreement has been that one manufacturer can take in the bottles of another. The following case concerns plastic soft drink bottles.

A large retail organization in food products wanted to expand its assortment with a low-cost soft drink, and intended to sell it under a private label. The retail buyer asked for quotations from several bottling companies with the result that all suppliers quoted almost the same price. The buyer, however, also requested an outsider in another European country to prepare a bid. This supplier was an affiliate of a large conglomerate located in Southern Europe. Negotiations were started and it soon turned out that this supplier could provide the required quantities at a much more favourable price. However, the bottles were different from those normally used in the Benelux countries. The crates were also different and were covered with the Southern European company's name. Another problem was the deposit. The retailer had to invest a considerable sum of money in deposits, the money being returned by the bottling company only when the bottles and crates had been received. Before signing the contract, the retailer had requested a bank guarantee from the Southern European company's bank. This guarantee did not arrive in time, and the buyer decided to go ahead without waiting for the bank guarantee.

Sale of the company's new soft drink (under its own private label) started. The turnover was high. However, a year after signing the contract, the retailer learned that the bottling company had gone bankrupt. This was a setback, because at least £750,000 worth of crates and bottles were in the pipeline from distribution centres to consumers. These crates differed from the other crates on the market, so the retail organization had no way to reuse them. None of the money could be recovered through the lawyers or the trustee from the Southern European firm.

The problem was later solved when a new supplier of soft drinks proved willing to fill the empty bottles and sell them to the Middle East.

---

reads the bar codes of the various products (**order entry**) and a portable computer, orders are placed directly at the central purchasing department and from there directly at the supplier. Another possibility is that the order is placed directly at the distribution centres, which subsequently make the delivery. The distribution centres are responsible for maintaining their stocks at the desired level. Their ordering systems are directly coupled to the receiving orders systems of the suppliers (often through EDI). Invoicing takes place at the central level. For some products, such as fresh foods, central order handling is not suitable. These products, then, are ordered by the retail outlets directly from the supplier, who also delivers the order directly.

Advanced information systems have enabled 'automatic replenishment'. Based upon cash-register scanning retailers now know what has been sold on a specific day. This information is through electronic linkages transferred to suppliers, who are requested to ship exactly these volumes of the products to the retailer's distribution centre during the night. Early in the morning the

MEMO 16.2 More substantial negotiations in retail trade

At present, negotiations between buyers for supermarket chains and their suppliers are very tough, not only because of the buyers' increased power, but also due to the pressure on their profits. The suppliers have to prove themselves repeatedly, and the outcome of negotiations is less predictable than it used to be.

Typical characteristics of modern discussions about terms and conditions include the following:

Element of marketing mix:	Topics:
Product mix	• assortment portfolio-analysis (performance in terms of turnover and DPP)
	• market research data (concerning consumer behaviour, brand performance, competition)
	• exclusivity in sales and new products
	• arrangements on returnable items (slow movers, new product introductions, seasonal products)
	• shelf filling packaging (in order to use shelf space to the maximum)
	• uniform article codes (to optimize product scanning)
Price mix	• price and delivery conditions (a classic area of negotiation)
	• recommended selling prices (in order to provide retailer with terms of reference)
	• pre-pricing of products (to reduce handling in stores)
Presentation mix	• detailed shelf layouts and displays
	• cost saving materials and packaging (ready for sale packaging and displays, etc.)
	• optimal use of transport packaging (in line with shelf systems)
Personnel mix	• effective use of supplier sales staff for in-store activities, commercial advice and training
	• rack jobbing for difficult and labour intensive categories (improved operations)
	• training and development (providing knowledge to sales personnel and other staff)
Promotion mix	• incentives for in store personnel (turnover and display contests)

stores are replenished with the requested volumes. This practice is often referred to as 'Quick Response Logistics'. In fact, suppliers are able to monitor on a daily basis what has been sold by their customers. Through these advanced information systems, logistics (planning) tasks are increasingly shifted to the (food-) manufacturers and their suppliers.

- *Expediting and evaluation.* As has been discussed, the ordered goods are delivered by the supplier either directly to the retail outlets, or to the distribution centres. Monitoring the delivered quantity and quality and time of delivery takes place there where the goods are delivered. The delivered quantities are also entered into the inventory control system. Some large retailers have sophisticated vendor rating systems in place in order to monitor and improve the overall supplier performance.

Based on this description the following additional observations are worth making.

- The purchasing decision-making process in trade companies is roughly similar to that in industrial companies. The most important differences are in the initial stages. Retail buyers definitely need to give more attention to marketing and sales aspects of the products they buy than their counterparts in industry. Furthermore, the technical complexity of most retail products is rather low. As a result retail buying is definitely more commercial in nature.
- The function of the retail buyer gradually evolves from straight buying to commodity or category management, where cross functional category teams are responsible for managing all aspects of a category in order to generate a maximum return for the retail company.
- The descriptions above illustrate that ordering and purchasing are often separate activities within the retail company. Purchasing and product management are conducted centrally within the organization, whereas ordering is carried out, as much as possible, decentrally (by the distribution centres or the outlets). Decentralized ordering has become possible thanks to sophisticated, computerized ordering and inventory control systems. Where automatic replenishment has been implemented, planning tasks are shifted to the supplier who is kept fully responsible for the timely delivery of products in the exact quantity needed.

Retail buying: organizational structure

In view of the previous discussions it makes sense that the purchasing function is embedded high in the organization. As a rule, buyers report directly to general management. With regard to the organization of purchasing it is possible to differentiate between a **functional purchasing structure** and a **cross-functional structure**.

In a functional purchasing structure the purchasing department predominantly acts as a separate organizational entity, which operates more or less autonomously from physical distribution and sales and store management. Based on sales forecasts retail buyers prepare their category plans.

In the cross-functional structure the buying function, styling, visual merchandising and physical distribution (apart from store operations) operate in one organizational entity. As has been mentioned before, this often is referred to as 'category management'. Category managers are responsible for assortment policy, product policy, purchasing and supplier management, and distribution policy. Store operations mostly resides outside their area of responsibility.

Developments in trade and retail companies

The purchasing function in trade companies is subject to significant change, and several developments that have important consequences for purchasing policy will now be described.

Changing consumer behaviour

Changes in consumer behaviour have a major impact on the retailer's product-market strategies. It is the retail buyer's job to identify these changes in time and to translate them into new product concepts and design new shelf displays and shop layouts. The following are typical of changes that confront retail organizations in European countries:

- Ageing population, ongoing individualization, more men shopping.
- Increasing income gap between population groups, more one- and two-person households (in large urban areas).
- Growing number of earning couples (two incomes, no children).
- Increased integration of ethnic minorities, exposure to other cultures through tourism, adopting other cultural consumption patterns.
- Increased concern for the environment, manifested in the cry for bio-degradable containers and packaging.
- Increased attention to healthier living, expressed in a strong growth of the number of health food and diet products.

This means that the commodity manager or retail-buyer must constantly tailor his/her product assortment to ever more specific, and often smaller, target groups. This results in a wider variety of products and an increased complexity with regard to managing the incoming and outgoing goods flow.

Concentration

Especially in the chemical, pharmaceutical and so-called high-tech sectors, as well as in the automotive and electronics industries, globalization of competition and concentration through mergers and acquisitions are characteristic developments. This is related to, among other things, the fact that the development costs can no longer be recovered in only one country. (As an illustration, the development and registration of a new drug or medicine often amounts to several hundreds of millions of pounds sterling.)

For manufacturers this concentration means that there will be more mono-production, which makes it possible to achieve better economies of scale. It is expected that there will be fewer and fewer suppliers of food products in the near future and, as a result, retail companies will be dealing primarily with a few very large manufacturers. The trend towards globalization of business and economies of scale will also affect the scale of retail businesses. As a result many large retailers have become very active in mergers and acquisitions over the past decade.

International co-operation

Due to the concentration of power on the suppliers' side, many trade companies are diligently searching for possibilities with which to counterbalance this development. Internationalization is an option seen by many.

It can be difficult to realize internationalization of retail organizations – in Europe, for example, the market often turns out to be culturally determined or dependent on the country. There is only a limited number of products that can be sold internationally with the same marketing formula. Packaging is also culture related; e.g. the French won't eat soup from a can. Furthermore, labels should always contain the language of the country in question. These realities limit the possibilities of achieving further economies of scale.

International purchasing combinations have great difficulty getting off the ground. The Dutch Ahold group of companies has entered into collaboration with six other large retailers in Sweden, France, Great Britain, Finland and Denmark. By buying products jointly, price advantages are being realized. This does not function optimally, however, because there are few 'europroducts' and because (large) suppliers like Unilever, Coca-Cola and Nestlé prefer, for obvious reasons, to sell their products to each country separately.

Private labels

More and more retail companies use private labels or company brands. Private labels support retailer identity and the (quality) image. By purchasing products, giving them a company label and taking over the promotion, the retailer will have the advantage of a higher margin. In future it is expected that it will become increasingly difficult to find suitable suppliers for private label products, because the number of suppliers will keep on decreasing.

Carrying their own private label implies that product liability lies with the retailer. As the product carries the trade company's brand, this company presents itself as the producer of the product. The buyer must be aware of this and should include it in the contract with the supplier. In case of any problems about the quality of the product or customer complaints the retailer then may be able to recover the costs from the producer.

Environmental issues

Ecological considerations are increasingly becoming a dominant issue in purchasing policy. This started initially with the replacement of artificial flavourings and odours by natural products. At present the emphasis is on biodegradable packing materials, PVC-less packaging and a minimum of blister packs. There are some problems, such as the soft drink bottle, that should be solved by the industry in question so that standardization can be achieved (see Memo 16.1). International suppliers bring extra problems, for instance manufacturers of toothpaste have been obliged to eliminate their carton boxes, which they used as a packaging for their end products, due to environmental legislation.

Information

Information technology is an important tool for the retail buyer. Some developments in information technology have an immediate impact on the consumer. They are manifest in, for instance, electronic banking, barcoding and teleshopping.

There are also developments that are far less visible to the consumer. These developments generally relate to the retail trade, wholesale trade and manufacturing companies, the most interesting of which are described below.

- *Videotext systems and E-Commerce.* These technologies enable electronic transactions between retailers, wholesalers and their suppliers. The retailer or wholesaler can see on a screen which products the supplier has in stock, whether there are any special offers, etc. Orders are placed electronically, then traced and tracked through advanced computer systems and, after delivery, paid electronically

- *Electronic data interchange (EDI).* EDI relates to the electronic exchange of data between the retailer or wholesaler and the manufacturer. The objective is to reduce or simplify the transaction communication between the parties involved.

- *Space management.* Since shelf-space is limited, the extensive product lines offered by manufacturers force the retail-buyer to make a selection. In this context computerized space-management systems may support him. They enable the simulation of several display layouts (based on a different number of facings) based on detailed cost information, to decide on the most profitable layout. Important concepts, underlying space management systems, are direct product cost (DPC) and direct product profitability (DPP). DPC concerns all costs that can be allocated directly to the product (including the costs of materials handling, taking in return packaging, pricing, etc.). The retail buyer tries to trace these costs in detail: he compares these to the sales price, and is then able to determine the profit margin per product (DPP).

- *Efficient Consumer Response (ECR).* This concept has received large interest from many retailers and food manufacturers over the past few years. Here it could be defined as 'the competence to react efficiently on individual consumer demand through integrated product management, assortment management and business logistics in order to provide highest possible value to the final customer'. The idea behind it is that retailers and manufacturers all need to work together more closely in order to meet this objective. The idea is 'to work together to fulfil customer wishes better, faster and at less cost' (ECR Europe, quoted in van Goor, 1998, p. 34). ECR implies that retailers develop a concise commercial policy per product category tailored to specific consumer segments and that they communicate this policy with their partners in the supply chain. This should result in optimized logistics and materials flows, much better communication and better sales results from jointly developed promotional and advertising campaigns. Hence, ECR should be considered as an integrated business concept which focuses on improving both commercial and logistics activities of all partners in a specific supply chain. In doing so, companies involved should work on several improvement areas (see Figure 16.3)

Such developments are clearly having a major impact on purchasing in (retail) trade companies. Electronic payment systems and customer loyalty cards provide insight into purchasing frequency, composition of the consumer's daily shopping basket, and the customer's address. Scanning gives the retail buyers an immediate insight into the actual sales in their stores and the stock situation in the distribution centres. Space management enables them to simulate display layouts, based on detailed cost information, so that the optimal return can be realized. Hence, the buyer's role in progressive retail companies evolves from just a buyer to a product group or category manager. This will lead to a different task profile (see Figure 16.4).

Summary

It has been seen that the purchasing function plays a very important role in trade companies. In this chapter wholesale and retail have been distinguished. The

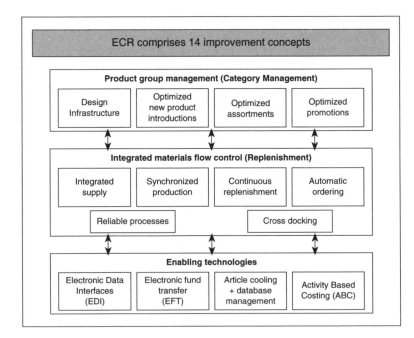

Figure 16.3   ECR includes 14 improvement concepts (Van Goor (p. 55)).

Traditional retail buyer	Modern category manager
● knowledge limited to product and commercial aspects	● knowledge base is much broader (includes marketing, physical distribution, store management, information systems, business economics)
● focus on gross margin (difference between selling price and purchasing price)	
● decides based on gross margin and intuition	● focus on net contribution (difference between selling price and direct product costs)
● acts individually ('buying fiefdom')	● has a co-operative attitude ('supplier is integrated part of retail formula')
● acts for supplier as an intermediary in 'product push' process	● represents to supplier a professional discussion partner, enforcing a tailor-made approach

Figure 16.4   Profile of the category manager (translated from Van der Ster (1993), p. 389).

basic difference between these two types of trade is in the type of customer: the wholesaler sells to other companies and institutions, whereas the retailer sells to the final consumer. Trade companies fulfil the role of intermediary between manufacturer and end user. The buyer's basic task is to translate the customers' demands into a suitable offer of products and services.

Several differences exist in the area of purchasing when comparing retail companies to industrial companies. In retail companies purchasing policy is much more integrated with sales and marketing policy, and company policy is primarily focused on improving turnover and margin. As a result of the fierce competition, most retailers and wholesalers over the years have adopted a strong bottom line orientation. Thanks to modern information technology important progress has been made in terms of integrated logistics, distribution, transportation and store operations.

The buying–selling cycle usually begins with an estimate of the demand for a particular item. Based on this estimate the assortment policy and the distribution strategy will be determined. Then the investigation of new suppliers can be started. At the same time preparations can be made for renegotiating contracts with existing suppliers. In most retail companies the initial purchasing activities are co-ordinated centrally. Ordering, expediting and evaluation often take place decentrally in the distribution centres and/or the retail outlets. Thanks to computerized order entry systems, the number of administrative actions can be kept to a minimum here.

The developments going on in retail buying have not yet come to an end. This is because of the changes that take place in consumer behaviour, which in turn lead to new products and retail formulas. Furthermore, the international competitive environment is subject to change. Subjects addressed were the ongoing concentration on the supply market, the continued growth of 'private labels', and the effects of environmental legislation on purchasing policy. It is clear that these developments considerably alter the role, position and character of the purchasing task in retail companies. The retail buyer should be able to work with modern computer-aided retail concepts such as ECR, DPC, DPP and space-management systems.

Assignments

16.1 An important trend in the food product sector is the development of private labels. The manufacturer's brand name is replaced more and more by the retailer's private label. What are the consequences of this development for the purchasing policy of these retailers?

16.2 Following the previous question, how should manufacturers respond to this development in terms of their marketing and sales policies?

16.3 What actions can retail organizations pursue in order to improve the efficiency of their operations? Differentiate between those activities aimed at improving the sales turnover ratio and those activities aimed at improving the sales margin (see also Chapter 1 for the discussion on the Du Pont analysis).

16.4 Discuss the pros and cons of the functional and integrated purchasing organization structures that can be found in retail organizations. What organizational structures are required in what kind of situation?

16.5 A subject that still receives a lot of attention is the 'battle of the brands': manufacturers' brands are constantly threatened by retailers' private labels. Who do you think will win the battle? Explain your answer.

BUYING IN A FACILITIES ENVIRONMENT

17

Learning objectives

After studying this chapter you should understand the following:

- Trends and developments in the service industry.
- Differences with regard to the role and position of purchasing within industrial versus service companies.
- Key success variables for purchasing in a facilities environment.
- Measures aimed at improving the effectiveness of purchasing in a facilities environment.
- How to improve professionalism of purchasing within a facilities environment.

CASE STUDY:
Purchasing policy in a large insurance company

Four years ago the management of a large insurance company decided to drastically change its purchasing operations. As these activities were scattered throughout the company, internal control on purchasing spend was suffering. Since managers did not give much attention to purchasing decisions, most employees had a large degree of freedom in dealing with suppliers. In some cases, it appeared that this freedom was used for personal advantage. Apart from fringe benefits (such as fairly large gifts at Christmas and luxury study trips paid for by suppliers) some employees appeared to have received large amounts of money in their personal bank accounts as a reward for the business that they awarded to some suppliers. Since the credibility of the company was at stake and company morale was affected, management had to take immediate action. The staff concerned were fired and management started to consider how best to prevent these problems in the future. The ensuing discussion resulted in the decision to centralize all purchasing activities in a single department. A purchasing manager was appointed from outside the company and was given a free hand to form this department. The assignment was simple: see to it that all purchases were made through the department. All departmental managers within the organization were informed about this decision by sending them copies of the new purchasing

Continued on page 322

charter, signed by the president of the company. The purchasing manager and his colleagues set to work.

Three years later the purchasing manager assessed his position. After careful analysis it appeared that only 25% of the total purchasing spend of the company went through purchasing! This was a disappointment – according to the purchasing manager it should have been much higher! However, during the past three years he had found achieving credibility for his department was an extremely difficult matter. Most budget holders and other managers responsible for purchasing decisions seemed not to be very cost conscious; neither were they disciplined in the way they arrived at their decisions. Most had pursued their existing relationships with suppliers, without involving or even consulting purchasing! At best the purchasing department was asked to deal with administrative matters, after supplier selection had been made.

This situation was very unsatisfactory to the purchasing manager because the overall environment prevented him from doing a professional job. He decided that top management should now be informed of the problem – departmental managers should adhere to company policies and procedures and top management should see to it that they actually did! He planned to write a detailed memorandum on this in order to point out the responsibilities of top-management on this matter . . .

Introduction

Earlier chapters have demonstrated that purchasing, as a management discipline in industrial companies, has developed strongly over the last few years. Due to increased international competition, industrial companies have given first priority to issues such as cost reduction, quality improvement and cycle time reduction. At the same time many top managers have focused their efforts on reinforcing their company's core activities. Non-core activities have increasingly been put to the bloc with decisions to outsource these at specialized suppliers. The purchasing department has played an important role in initiating and implementing these management policies.

Companies in the service sector have lagged behind in this development. Here, purchasing activities traditionally have an operational character and are limited to placing orders, expediting and invoice checking. The situation in most companies is reflected by the case study above: purchasing operations are scattered throughout the organization through absence of a professional purchasing department.

However, this picture is gradually changing. Trends towards facilities management, quality improvement, and improving customer orientation have affected the role and position of purchasing in these companies. As in the case study, many (often larger) service companies face the problem of how to improve purchasing professionalism. Managers often try to translate successful purchasing practices, as applied in the industrial sector, to their own organization – this is not without problems. This chapter discusses some of these problems which, for the most part, stem from the fundamental differences between the purchasing function in the industrial sector and in the service sector. First, however, it is necessary to be aware of the most important trends and developments within the service sector in Western economies. Also of importance is the development towards facilities management, which is becoming apparent in many larger service companies nowadays, and how this development affects or will affect purchasing operations. Next the key success factors underlying successful purchasing in service companies will be discussed. Finally, some important measures which may lead to more effective purchasing operations in service companies are described.

Trends and developments in the service sector

In many European countries the service sector is a dominant economic activity. In some countries (for example the Benelux countries) it may account for more than half the total employment. And this share is increasing as more European economies are entering the post-industrial era. A general description (used by the Central Bureau of Statistics) of the service sector is that it encompasses companies operating in:

- transportation and distribution (travel and freight by air, rail, road, water);
- communications (post, telecommunications);
- banking and other financial services (insurance, leasing, factoring);
- professional services (legal, fiscal, accounting, management consulting).

This list is not exhaustive, but it does show the large variety of organizations which are active in the service sector. Depending on the definition used, the public utilities (energy production and distribution, water, gas supply) may also be included and much of what is discussed in this chapter will be relevant to these organizations as well. However, given the high degree of regulation of this sector in most countries, the utility sector is often seen as part of the public sector.

Kotler and Bloom (1984, p. 147) describe service as 'any activity or benefit that one party can offer to another that is essentially intangible and does not result in the ownership of anything. Its production may or may not be tied to a physical product.' Major characteristics of services are:

- *Intangibility*. They cannot be seen, tasted, felt, heard or smelled; essentially, the buyer has to have faith in the service provider.
- *Inseparability*. A service cannot exist separately from its providers; it requires the presence of the one who provides the service.
- *Variability*. The quality of services may vary depending on the person and the moment at which they are provided.
- *Perishability*. Services cannot be stored. This requires a good balance between supply and demand. Often problems arise when service companies are confronted with fluctuating demand, leading to complex staffing problems.

The most important characteristic of service companies is the absence of a physical transformation, i.e. a manufacturing process. Also, a clear and well-defined relationship between input, throughput and output is frequently absent.

Looking at the cost structure of service companies it is clear that the larger part of costs is related to labour. In general these companies represent a large value added. As a result, contrary to industrial and retail organizations, the purchasing-to-sales turnover ratio is rather low. This may run from less than 10% for an accounting firm, to 20–25% for a large banking organization, or even 50% for an international airline company. In general, however, the relative purchasing spend is rather low. This implies that purchasing savings, although impressive amounts of money may be at stake here, only have a limited effect on the return on assets (RONA) of service companies. When discussing competitive strategy, top management in service organizations will understandably spend most of their time on people-related issues and activities. In general they will spend little time and effort on the support activities, among which is purchasing. The next section elaborates on this issue.

Although not true for all organizations operating in the service sector, some companies nowadays face severe international competition. This is true for transport (airlines) and telecommunications. As a result, these companies strive to improve their services to reduce operational costs. In some cases companies have tried to establish international networks through mergers and acquisitions and joint ventures with overseas companies (e.g. KLM and British Airways). Some examples are:

- the introduction of frequent-flyer programmes in order to increase loyalty of business travellers;
- cost-reduction programmes, sometimes resulting in outsourcing activities (such as technical maintenance, cleaning services) and management buy-outs (such as catering services);
- active searches for partners in order to share costs related to information technology and to increase purchasing and negotiating power relative to large suppliers (Boeing) and public authorities (for landing rights).

Similar activities can be found in accounting, banking, telecommunications and transportation, etc. In general, a trend towards a higher degree of concentration in the service sectors can be perceived (as the recent mergers between some large banks and accounting organizations in Europe and world-wide demonstrate).

These developments have affected purchasing operations in several ways.

- *Increased outsourcing of support activities.* Focus on core activities often leads to the decision to put non-core activities to the market test. Those activities that cannot be performed at a competitive level in terms of cost and quality are contracted out to specialized suppliers. This was the prime reason for contracting out transportation and distribution by a major international bank. As a result the bank personnel involved were hired by the transportation company on a five-year fixed contract. Other activities which are often outsourced as a result of this exercise are:

  - security;
  - catering;
  - cleaning services;
  - mail-room activities;
  - maintenance activities;
  - print and photocopying;
  - garden and greenkeeping services.

- *Integration of support activities in a facility management organization.* In order to reduce costs and to improve the quality level of support activities, more companies have adopted a facilities management concept (see Memo 17.1) in which these activities are brought under one managerial responsibility. This development is not without relevance for purchasing: first, it often implies that the purchasing manager is to report to the facilities manager; second, it often leads to more purchases going through purchasing, because this organizational concept facilitates the co-operation between purchasing and the other support areas.

- *Increased scale of operations.* As a result of the growth which some service companies have experienced, opportunities to form a specialized purchasing department have increased. This is especially true for companies which have merged with other organizations. These mergers often result in an impressive purchasing spend which, because of the amount of money involved, warrant treatment by professional buyers. This has encouraged companies to set up a professional purchasing department.

It may be concluded that some service companies nowadays are actively pursuing opportunities to improve their competitive edge. As a result they are looking to reduce labour and operational costs, while improving the quality of their services to the customer. These efforts have not gone unnoticed in purchasing. The trend towards outsourcing means that service companies have a lot to gain from a professional purchasing organization, which can take care of defining purchasing requirements, supplier selection, contract negotiation and control. By adopting a facilities management concept support activities are much

---

MEMO 17.1: Facilities management

Facilities relate to all the physical conditions that enable an organization to conduct its primary activities. This includes the buildings, general installations, equipment, and their related services, and excludes human resources and all manufacturing equipment. Facilities management can therefore be described as 'the management (planning, execution and control) and the realization of housing and accommodation, the services related to these, and other means in order to enable the organization to realize its mission'. It includes activities such as building and technical maintenance, security, catering, travel, reception, transportation and distribution, warehousing and inventory. Traditionally one would find these activities scattered throughout the organization. Within a facilities management concept these activities are brought under one organizational responsibility. Adoption of the concept often leads to a more professional view on each of these activities. Most large companies are aware of the amount of money related to these activities. Moreover, the management of these activities consumes a lot of management's time and energy. The task of facilities managers is to provide their services at a competitive cost and quality level. When these conditions cannot be met, a decision to contract out this activity to outside suppliers is likely. The trend towards facilities management explains, among other things, the rapid growth of some of these industries (catering, transportation, courier services, security, etc.).

better integrated and managed, providing purchasing departments with the chance to work more closely with 'big spenders' within the service organization. Finally, since the scale of operations of many service organizations has increased through mergers and acquisitions, opportunities for a more professional approach to purchasing have increased considerably. The next section will show how purchasing may benefit from these interesting developments.

Purchasing in a service company

The purchasing-to-sales ratio in service companies is, compared with industrial companies, rather low. The products and services that represent the major items of expenditure are illustrated in Figure 17.1.

Buildings, installation and infrastructure	Housekeeping	Temporary labour
• real estate	• energy	• hiring of temporary personnel
• restructuring and renewal	• catering	• interim managers
• maintenance	• cleaning services and sanitary	• consultants
• technical installations	• greenkeeping	• IT programmers, analysts and project managers
• security systems	• removal services	
• office furniture	• security	
• system walls	• garbage removal	
• kitchens and canteens	• clothing	
• temporary buildings	• technical support materials	
Services	**IT and telematics**	**Office supplies and printing**
• transport services	• mainframes, hard- and software	• copying
• cars and transport vehicles	• midrange systems	• office equipment
• travel	• PCs	• office supplies
• accommodation	• peripherals	• paper
• training and education	• data communication networks	• packaging materials
• search and recruitment services	• telephone switching equipment	• printing
• market research	• infrastructure	• representation
• marketing and promotion	• IT projects	• books and subscriptions
• media	• outsourcing	
• events	• information services	
• factoring		
• professional services		

Figure 17.1   Major categories of expenditure (adapted from Rietveld (1995, pp. 138–140)).

In addition to these items some service companies spend impressive amounts of money on investment goods such as specialized equipment (for example airlines on aircraft and kerosine, railways on rolling stock and energy). Using Porter's value chain concept it is clear that almost all purchasing activities are aimed at the other support activities (see Chapter 1). Purchasing for the primary process almost does not exist, since service companies by definition do not have a production process in which inputs are physically transformed to outputs. This is an important difference from industrial companies, where buying for primary activities represents the bulk of purchasing expenditure. It explains why managers in service companies reveal so little interest in the purchasing operations of their company – they consider it primarily as a support activity. From this analysis additional observations can be made.

- Given the low purchasing-to-sales ratio, cost considerations are not prime to internal customers, i.e. departments. They often feel it is more important for suppliers to deliver on time and in the right quantity, than to pursue the lowest purchasing price. As soon as internal users become satisfied with their present suppliers, they will tend to neglect competitive bidding, giving the supplier ample room for commercial tactics.
- Given the specialized nature of most investment buying (information technology, software, construction) the user plays a dominant role in decision making (developing specifications, supplier selection, negotiation), leaving administrative matters, at best, to the purchasing department. This situation develops when purchasing does not possess sufficient knowledge in the appropriate specialist areas to enable it to act as a valuable partner to the internal customers. As a result, strong relationships can develop between internal users and suppliers, which are very difficult to change.
- The purchasing department therefore concentrates on what is left, the general, routine and low-cost items, which are ordered through fixed order routines from traditional sources of supply.

These considerations suggest that in most service companies an impressive potential for improvement in purchasing probably exists. Indeed, a professional approach to these matters, as experience with several of these companies has shown, can result in savings of between 5 and 20%! At the same time, however, it will be clear that improving purchasing professionalism is not a simple matter. Top management will often (because of the relatively low purchasing spend) fail to provide support to purchasing procedures, and buyers will get recognition only by providing a superior service to their internal departments. Purchasing managers operating in a service company should therefore be service driven rather than cost driven!

Key success factors

It has been shown that some major differences occur between buying for production purposes and buying for support activities. In particular, effective purchasing in a facilities environment requires that buyers are sympathetic to the needs and requirements of their internal customers. In practice, however, a considerable gap often exists between how internal customers perceive their needs and requirements, and how these are perceived by the purchasing department. This is illustrated in Figure 17.2.

Most managers of other departments will point to the following success factors for their purchasing department:

- easy access (both by telephone and personally);
- fast reaction to questions and problems;
- prompt delivery of goods ordered;
- short delivery times;
- consistent quality of goods delivered;
- immediate feedback in case of (unforeseen) order changes.

Provided that buyers are able to meet these requirements, users are willing to allow purchasing to take a more pro-active role and to involve them at earlier stages in the purchasing process. The purchasing department will emphasize other aspects in the relationship with the internal customer, such as low price, savings, good contracts, alternative sources of supply and clear specifications, and often consider it their prime task to take care of these issues. It is clear that when the expectations of both the purchasing department and the internal users differ widely with regard to the role of the purchasing department, this will lead to significant boundary problems and friction between the parties involved. Many internal departments prefer to deal with purchasing tasks themselves, simply to avoid these problems when they can.

When improving purchasing professionalism, a prime concern, therefore, is how best to improve the customer orientation of the purchasing department. This issue is discussed in the next section.

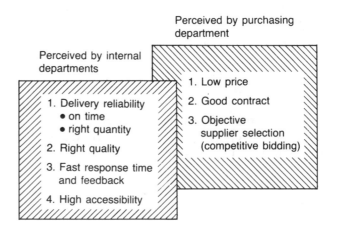

Figure 17.2 Expectation levels with regard to purchasing are not always identical.

Towards more effective purchasing in a facilities environment

In order to improve purchasing effectiveness within a facilities environment the following approach is useful.

1 *Analyse and document internal product/customer combinations step-by-step.* Here the idea is first to find out the total purchasing expenditure per department (often to be gathered from budget and accounting information) and per product group. This sounds simple but is often a time-consuming matter, since many organizations do not keep account of these data in a systematic way. Next, assess what part of the expenditure is contracted through the purchasing department. In this way the internal market share of the purchasing department, both for specific departments and product groups, can be established (see Table 17.1).

Table 17.1   Customer product group matrix (example)

Internal department → ↓ Product group	Computer department	Technical maintenance	Distribution department	Etc.	Total volume
Computer hardware/ software	A _____ B _____ C _____ D _____	Etc.			
Computer supplies	Etc.				
Office equipment					
Office furniture					
Office supplies					
Temporary labour					
Services					
Etc.					
Total volume					

A = Total purchasing volume
B = Purchasing expenditure through purchasing department
C = Market share purchasing department
D = Expected future total purchasing volume ($\nearrow$, $\rightarrow$, $\searrow$)

2 *Assess internal customer satisfaction.* Visit each relevant department to find out how they experience the service rendered by the purchasing department. The attitude here is: 'You are OK, but how are we?' This is easier said than done, since when this investigation is conducted by employees of the purchasing department they will immediately explain or defend themselves against every criticism they encounter. At least one additional objective researcher is therefore essential in this kind of investigation, the purpose of which is to find out what bottlenecks exist in the relationship between other departments and purchasing. These need to be documented and thoroughly analysed.

3 *Target setting.* Based on the information gathered in step 2, targets now can be set with regard to increasing the market share of the purchasing department in each of the cells. It often appears that although tremendous potential for improvement does exist in some cells (for example PCs for the internal computer department) a target cannot be set because of a lack of experience and specialist knowledge within the purchasing department in this area. It should then be decided whether to build up expertise first, in order to increase market share in this area.

   This step should result in a detailed action plan for the purchasing department, indicating:

   - in what customer/product combinations the purchasing department will maintain or reinforce position, i.e. market share;
   - the actions which will be necessary to make this happen;
   - the results which can be expected from these actions (in terms of savings, lead time reduction, less suppliers, etc).

4 *Cross functional buying teams and organizational structure.* The analysis so far often provides sufficient information on what competences are required in order to handle the different commodities. As has been argued earlier, a cross-functional team approach will be crucial for success. Specialists from user departments who work with suppliers and buyers should be put together in cross-functional buying teams in order to develop sourcing and commodity plans. These teams could be supervised by the purchasing manager; they should, however, report to the line management or management team. Apart from a team structure, an appropriate organization structure should be decided upon for the purchasing department. This subject will be covered in the next section.

5 *Develop supply-market strategies.* Each buying team should develop its supply strategies and commodity plans. A valuable aid here is the purchasing portfolio matrix (see Chapter 7). By depicting each product/supplier combination graphically, each buying group can decide on the preferred supply strategy. Each buying group probably will come up with different strategies, depending on the position of a certain commodity in the portfolio. This step should result in a detailed action plan for each buying group, which is presented to purchasing and senior management for approval.

6 *Implementation.* At this stage the plans which have been developed need to be executed. This requires close and careful monitoring by purchasing and general management. Results are to be measured in terms of

- market share per customer/product combination as a measure of how satisfactorily the purchasing department performs in the eyes of internal customers;
- operational measures such as:

  - savings generated as a result of the actions conducted towards suppliers;
  - purchasing customer satisfaction expressed by some form of index based upon a standardized survey, to be conducted periodically;
  - purchasing administrative lead time expressing the responsiveness of purchasing to internal customer needs;

- progress against other targets, as described in the purchasing action plan.

Figure 17.3 provides some practical suggestions with regard to actions which can be taken in order to improve overall purchasing effectiveness and efficiency.

This approach cannot be applied to service companies only. The area of facilities buying is increasingly being acknowledged as an area where large savings can be captured. For this reason, many large companies have initiated large corporate programmes in this area. Among these is Philips Electronics, who started an initiative in 1996 with the aim to reduce 12% on purchasing expenditure in this area (see Memo 17.2).

MEMO 17.2

In 1995 the Board of Management of Philips Electronics ordered a world-wide purchasing benchmark survey to be carried out by an international consulting firm. This firm concluded that, through aggressive programme driven action, the total annual savings in non product-related (NPR) purchasing for Philips could be in excess of 1.2 billion dollars! For this reason a focused cost saving programme was launched under the name OCOO (Other Cost of Organisation) (see Figure 17.4). OCOO is a Philips' global NPR programme focused on a short-term substantial and sustainable reduction of NPR costs. The idea behind it is that every dollar not spent in NPR purchasing will add to Philips' bottom line for the full 100%.

OCOO is a business owned and funded programme that rests on a self-reinforcing approach. A business targeting process aimed at reducing costs in the following areas:

- accommodation;
- personnel-related costs;
- sales-related costs;
- distribution;
- automation and communication;
- office-related costs;
- professional services;
- production- and development-related costs.

(Based upon internal company brochures and press information.)

Improvement measures with regard to the purchasing-customer interface

- Joint efforts aimed at reducing the number of products through standardization
- Joint efforts aimed at supplier reduction ('doing more with less') through:
  - establishing well-defined procedures for supplier selection
  - introducing 'prime vendorship'
  - introducing tender boards, buying committees, or cross functional benefits teams for important purchasing decisions (large investments and service contracts)
- Improve on accessibility and customer orientation through:
  - improving telephone facilities
  - effective help desk
  - improving social skills through training
  - brochures on how purchasing operates
  - improving purchasing systems and procedures

Internal measures to improve the purchasing operations

- Improving product and market knowledge
- Improving purchasing techniques and skills
- Differentiating between routine and non-routine activities; in the case of routine buying delegate order handling (if possible and useful) to internal customer
- Simplifying orders systems by using:
  - blanket order agreements
  - systems contracting
  - electronic purchasing and electronic commerce
  - simplifying authorization procedures
  - simplifying invoice checking and approval procedures

Figure 17.3 Some suggestions for improving purchasing effectiveness and efficiency.

Organizing for purchasing in a facilities environment

In discussing the optimal structure for a purchasing department within a service company the question is posed as to what principle to use. Several options in general exist.

- *Customer characteristics.* The purchasing department reflects the different departments it works for (one group for department A, one group for department B, etc.)
- *Product characteristics.* Buying groups are formed around products with common characteristics.

Figure 17.4   Brochure OCOO Programme Philips Electronics (© Philips Electronics).

- *Service characteristics*. Buying groups are formed around services provided by the purchasing department (for instance a contracting group, an ordering group, a project-buying group).
- *Supply market characteristics*. Buying groups are formed around groups of suppliers.

The basic dilemma is how to secure an effective customer orientation in combination with knowledge of products and supply markets. Although all four options may be considered, the structure most often encountered is that based on product characteristics. Interface problems with internal customers are solved by assigning one of the buying group leaders as the account manager for a specific department. On a daily basis the employees of a customer department can deal with any of the buying personnel. However, policy matters and specific problems are discussed with the account manager. He/she acts as an intermediary between the customer and the purchasing department. The interface with the supply market is often much more easy to manage, given the high correlation between product characteristics and suppliers. Most suppliers sell products within a limited number of product groups and hence often deal with only one buying group. Figure 17.5 provides an illustration of a purchasing department of a large international bank. Here the buying groups are formed around commodities, i.e. product groups. However, routine operations are separated from these groups by means of a special help desk and order group. This group focuses on answering routine questions from internal customers and placing small orders directly. Large orders are transmitted to the appropriate buying groups. Office and computer supplies have been covered by annual agreements with a limited number of suppliers; internal users directly place call-off orders with these suppliers for the materials they need. All products, and the terms and conditions,

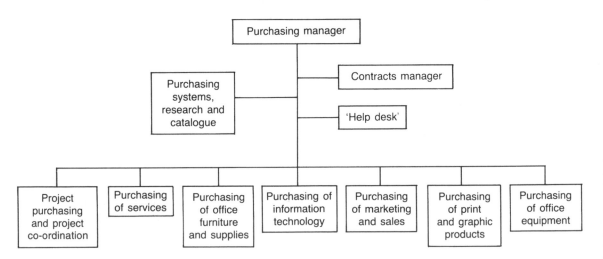

Figure 17.5 Purchasing structure for a large international bank (example).

are available through an attractive catalogue, which is developed and kept up to date by the 'systems, research and catalogue-group'. In this way the organization is able to free up considerable time, traditionally spent on administrative matters by the professional buyers, while at the same time reducing order cycle time for the internal users.

Summary

In this chapter the most important trends and developments within the service sector have been discussed. Service companies represent a growing share of economic activity in most European countries. Purchasing represents, in general, a low share of the service company's overall cost. Purchasing savings therefore have only a limited effect on the company's return on net assets. Moreover, purchasing expenditure is related to a large variety of activities, which are usually scattered throughout the organization. One result is that the purchasing function is far less visible to management than in industrial companies, which is why the development of purchasing management in service companies has lagged behind that in industrial enterprises. This picture is gradually changing, for three reasons: the tendency nowadays to outsource support activities; the trend towards facilities management that can be observed; and the increased scale of operations of many service organizations. These developments have in general increased the need for a professional purchasing approach. As a result many service companies have built up separate purchasing departments within their organization.

Developing a professional purchasing approach in service organizations is a far from simple matter. An important reason for this is that top management frequently fails to support and control purchasing procedures. This explains the freedom exercised by departmental managers in purchasing matters. Also, professional handling of some purchasing decisions requires considerable specialist knowledge, which often is not available from within the purchasing department. In those cases the purchasing department has little value to add to its internal customers. From this it was concluded that buyers, in order to be effective, should be primarily service driven, rather than cost driven. A strong customer orientation and cross functional teamwork are prerequisites for the success of the purchasing department in this kind of organization! In concluding the chapter a six-step approach to improve purchasing effectiveness was presented: (1) analyse and document internal product/customer combinations in order to assess present and future market share; (2) assess internal customer satisfaction in order to discover bottlenecks and problems in the relationship with internal departments; (3) set targets for improving internal service levels; (4) decide on what organizational structure will be most appropriate; (5) develop supply-market strategies for each of the buying groups; (6) implement and monitor progress! The discussion on how to structure the purchasing organization made it clear that professional buyers in service companies have much to learn from marketing theory and practitioners!

Assignments

17.1 Place yourself in the position of the purchasing manager of the introductory case study. What would you do in order to improve the effectiveness of your department? How would you try to gain a better recognition for your department both from other departmental managers and top management?

17.2 How would you assess the degree of customer friendliness of a purchasing department in a service company? What elements would you consider? How would you proceed in order to obtain the necessary information?

17.3 One of the improvement measures suggested was to introduce tender boards or buying committees in order to manage decision making on strategic purchases. How would you construct a tender board, when would you apply one and what do you consider to be the most important advantages of using them?

17.4 Purchasing departments in many service companies deal with many small orders related to standard materials (MRO materials). Much time and effort can be spent on small orders, which prevents buyers from spending sufficient time on the large items. What suggestions would you make in order to reduce the number of small orders?

17.5 Since a high service level and a strong customer orientation are a prerequisite for an effective purchasing department in a service company, purchasing managers should be constantly working on reducing purchasing administrative lead time. How would you define purchasing administrative lead time and what measures can you suggest in order to reduce this effectively?

PUBLIC PROCUREMENT AND EC DIRECTIVES

18

Learning objectives

After reading this chapter you should be able to:

- Identify the most important differences in purchasing between private enterprises and governmental institutions.
- Understand the relationship between public procurement and the EC Directives on public procurement.
- Have an understanding of the basic principles which underlie the EC Directives on public procurement.
- Know the workings and contents of the most important EC Directives and purchasing procedures.
- Understand the limitations and shortcomings of these Directives.

CASE STUDY
Tender procedure for the Storebaelt Bridge

Purchasing and tendering are for governmental institutions no simple matters. This can be illustrated by the problems which have arisen around the public tendering of the construction of a major bridge in Denmark some years ago.

The case concerns the tendering process of a bridge with a length over 6 km which was part of an infrastructural project to connect Funen and Seeland spanning the Great Belt in Denmark. The total distance of the project was 17 km. Tendering for this part of this large investment project had to be done according to the EC Directives for Public Procurement. The Danish government had opted for the negotiation-procedure with prior publication in the EC Tender Bulletin. Out of the construction firms that applied, five combinations of companies (so-called consortia) initially were selected. Finally, the tender was awarded to the European Storebaelt Group. This consortium of companies was controlled by the Danish Government.

However, before the tender was awarded, one of the other consortia submitted a complaint to the European Commission since the tender process obviously had violated the EC Directives.

Continued on page 338

The scope of work, which was submitted to all consortia, stipulated that all parties would use Danish suppliers for all materials and services. Moreover, Danish employees needed to be contracted for the execution of the assignment. Such arrangements were, according to the plea, in conflict with the principle of non-discrimination as laid down in the EC Treaty and its Directives on Public Procurement.

Another complaint concerned the fact that when conducting the negotiations, the bid by European Storebaelt Group had been used as a reference. This, as was argued, would have been at the detriment of all other consortia which applied. A final complaint was that the bid as submitted by ESG did not meet specifications and evaluation criteria as announced in both the EC Tender Bulletin and the scope of work.

Even before the contract was awarded, the European Commission acknowledged these complaints and informed the Danish government on all matters. Next, a formal complaint procedure was initiated, in which it was demanded that the tender process was put to a stop. After refusal by the Danish government, the case was submitted to the European Court. At the same time the Commission requested the Court to demand that all activities were postponed by the Danish government until the Court would have come to a decision.

When the case was discussed before Court, the Danish government had to admit that the non-discrimination principle had been violated. Only after the Danish government declared was that it willing to pay a penalty to the consortium whose interests were damaged, was the procedure withdrawn. According to several publications in the press the Danish government had to settle for a penalty of over seven million Euro.

Introduction

For many suppliers and construction firms the government represents an interesting party. It is estimated that in Europe the volume of public procurement amounts to 900 billion Euro or 12% of Community Gross Domestic Product for the 15 member States (figures relate to 1995: EC, 1999a). This huge amount of money obviously is being spent by a huge number of governmental institutions on a large variety of goods, services and projects. It varies from specialized medical equipment by hospitals, to fuel for government-owned cars and trucks, to the construction of large infrastructural works such as roads, railways and bridges.

Hence, it cannot come as a surprise that the EC has initiated some Directives which stipulate that the market for government contracts should be open to all potential suppliers and firms, regardless of their nationality. This, because a compartmentalized government procurement market would not fit in a 'Europe without frontiers'.

After a short 'tour d'horizon' of the general characteristics of public procurement, this chapter discusses the most important public procurement Directives and procedures. Apart from their content, the consequences for the public procurement policy and organization will be discussed.

When this chapter refers to 'government' it implicitly includes institutions of the central government (ministries and related bodies), the provincial institutions and municipalities, some public bodies such as water supply and energy as well as institutions which are financed or administered by the government. It will become clear that also public utilities (such as energy sector, railways, other public transport and telecommunication companies) are subjected to the EC Directives.

Purchasing policy of governmental institutions

In general, decision making within governmental bodies is far from transparent. This is due to the many stakeholders that are involved, the often conflicting interests among these and the many political aspects that need to be considered. This is not only true for large societal issues, such as health care, employment, national security and environmental protection, but it certainly also is true for large governmental procurement projects. It explains why decision making concerning, for instance, buying defence equipment often is troublesome and difficult to manage. Other examples are large infrastructural projects such as the high speed train from France to The Netherlands or the 'Chunnel' project between France and the UK. As a result of the complexity and duration of the decision-making process these projects usually are executed at higher costs than anticipated and against a much longer lead time.

Political objectives

Governmental purchasing often serves political objectives. At the same time the government needs to spend their financial resources as efficiently as possible. Both objectives do not need to be necessarily complementary. An example will illustrate this. For a municipality, which wants to tender for a new city hall, it may be wise to tender among a large number of construction firms to get the best value for money. However, this may be against their political intent to involve primarily local firms in order to stimulate employment in their region. Social and political objectives often are in conflict with a rational spending of budgets. It means that many purchasing decisions in governmental institutions cannot be made solely on economic grounds. Purchasing management in such organizations, in order to be effective, therefore requires a thorough understanding of their political context.

Budget policy

There are striking differences between governmental institutions and private enterprises in the way they deal with purchasing budgets. Every governmental institution is constrained by the central government's budget policies. These in general point out that the money which is allocated to them in a certain year should also be spent in that year. In many cases it is difficult to build up financial reserves and to shift these to the next year. Postponing procurement projects may lead to a new round of budget decisions for the next year, a situation which many governmental managers want to avoid. Purchasing savings may lead to a similar effect: when a certain department, through smart purchasing, is able to save money, it will be required to return this amount at the end of the year to the local authorities. This explains why many managers in the government consider a purchasing budget as a 'licence to spend'. In general, it is wise to spend somewhat more than your budget in order to get more budget for the next year. Another complicating factor is that in many countries investments and exploitation are financed from different budgets. Hence investment decisions are often made without a careful balancing of costs during the exploitation stage. This prevents the adoption of a purchasing approach based upon total cost of ownership (TCO).

Due to the rigid budgeting systems a clear incentive to save money through professional purchasing within the government is missing. This explains the 'spending-fever', which can be observed in many governmental bodies at the end of the year! Memo 18.1 illustrates this.

Public accountability

Another important difference with private companies is that governmental institutions are publicly responsible for how they spend their money. Reports on this are in general open to the public community. Which is why most institutions are very careful in making decisions. Usually, purchasing procedures are embedded in lots of bureaucracy and require that every superior puts his signature under the intended order. The extensive authorization procedures make purchasing ordering a tedious, laborious and slow process. It explains why most purchasing organizations within the government are procedure rather than result oriented!

Contract management

In the case of large investment projects it is not uncommon that the contract is awarded to the contractor at a reasonable sum, while all parties involved already

---

MEMO 18.1: How to deal with purchasing savings in the government

A couple of years ago one of the EU countries set up a support programme for Bangladesh. Within the context of this programme a large quantity of supplies, facilities and equipment was purchased. Among the supplies was an order for a certain tonnage of fertilizer. European suppliers were invited and it proved possible to buy the intended volume from one of these suppliers. Then, just before the order was awarded, a supplier from Turkey made a bid, which was considerably lower in price. The buyer who was involved decided to place the order at the Turkish supplier. However, at the end of the year he was reprimanded by his superior, since the budget was clearly underspent. Now, his superior was to face some problems since, without doubt, his budget for next year would be cut!

know that the actual costs will exceed the intended budget. Suppliers, of course, in general do not object to such a way of working. In some countries the Minister of Finance has frequently reported about the failing contract management and the lack of consistent purchasing procedures. Most countries still seem to struggle on how to control and monitor governmental purchasing expenditure effectively.

Nationalist approach

Although the Treaty of Rome, which formed the basis for the current EC, was signed in 1957, and most European countries nowadays should get used to the idea of being part of a truly international economic community, national and often regional interests are favoured above EC interests. Many governmental institutions, for a number of reasons, express a clear preference to place contracts at local suppliers. As an example may serve the rumour that occurred when the Ministry of Defence in one of the member countries, acting in line with the Directive 93/36/EEC on the award of public supply contracts, decided to place a large order for uniforms at a supplier located in another member country.

Experiences with governmental procurement projects have learned that a lack of purchasing procedures and a professional approach to purchasing may lead to significant cost overruns and overruns of time schedules. The European Commission estimates that its member countries annually would save at least 4% on their purchasing budgets, provided that they would apply consistent and objective competitive tender procedures in their dealings with suppliers.

EC Directives on Public Procurement

The Directives on Public Procurement, which have been issued by the European Community, have been designed to structure tender procedures for governmental institutions. In fact these are an essential element of the Treaty of Rome, which was founded with the sole purpose of enabling free trade among its member states. As a consequence the Treaty of Rome embodies initial procurement rules which prohibit any discrimination on grounds of nationality and restriction in the choice of supplies or services. However, these arrangements appeared not sufficient to establish a single market in the area of public procurement. Differences between national rules in combination with the lack of obligation to open up contracts to Community-wide competition still enabled local contracting bodies to place their orders at local suppliers. Further legislation was therefore needed to secure that the basic principles as laid down in the Treaty of Rome were being met.

A first attempt was made in 1976 when the European Council adopted a specific Directive on co-ordinating procedures for the award of supply contracts (see Council Directive 77/62/EEC of 21 December 1976). This directive stipulated that government contracts should be advertised to all suppliers in all member states, it banned the use of discriminatory technical specifications and it stipulated that objective criteria would be used for the selection of tenderers. However, this directive did not lead to the anticipated result. Member states still continued their protectionistic and nationalist approach in awarding contracts to suppliers.

Next, in 1988 a new directive was issued to make up for these deficiencies (see Council Directive 88/295/EEC of 22 March 1988). This Directive provided more details on transparency of procedures, the definition of technical specifications and information and tendering conditions but did not bring the results that were expected.

Then more detailed guidelines and Directives were considered to be required. These were decided in 1993, when the Directive on Public Supply Contracts was approved. This Directive brought together in a single text all the rules that were previously dispersed between a number of different instruments.

The objective of all these actions has been to allow public and semi-public bodies to buy goods and services of a better quality and at a better price in order to contribute concretely to economic growth by stimulating competition (EC Brochure, p. 4). At present, the following Directives have been adopted:

- Directive 93/36/EEC co-ordinating procedures for the award of public supply contracts ('Supplies Directive').
- Directive 93/37/EEC co-ordinating the procedures for the award of public works contracts ('Works Directive').
- Directive 92/50/EEC relating to the co-ordination of procedures for the award of public service contracts ('Services Directive').

As we will discuss later in this chapter a special Directive was created for the utilities sector ('Utilities Directive') – entities operating in the water, energy, transport and telecommunication sector. As a result the organizations which operate in this sector do not have to meet the often stringent requirements on public procurement which need to be followed by public institutions.

The aim of these Directives is to provide some general rules that need to be applied when awarding contracts to suppliers. Most Directives cover the following rules:

- Rules describing which public institutions need to work according to the directives and what type of contracts are considered.
- The types of award procedure or purchasing procedure, that need to be followed in a specific situation.
- Rules on how to deal with technical specifications, whereby preference is given to Community standards. The use of discriminatory specifications is strictly forbidden.
- Advertising rules, describing what public institutions must do to communicate their intended purchases to the international supplier community and what time limits need to be respected in the relationship with suppliers.
- Some common rules on how suppliers need to be selected and the criteria that can be used to award the contract in a specific situation.

EC directives need to be translated into the national laws and Directives of each member State. When national governments are negligent on this matter, however, suppliers may submit claims with direct reference to the EC Directives. Hence, the Directives have direct legislative power.

Of course, it should be clear for whom these Directives are relevant. Do these relate to all governmental institutions or are some of these excluded? The same holds for the type of purchases. Need these Directives to be pursued for all types of purchases under any circumstances or are exceptions in some cases possible? The answers to these questions can be found in the Directives themselves. The Directives are relevant to all contracting authorities which are part of the State, regional or local authorities and bodies governed by public law. In fact, this description covers the entire government. However, the working of the Directives is even broader. They are also relevant for private enterprises, who perform public tasks and/or who conduct activities based upon a concession granted by the government. To give an example: although Shell Oil is a private company, it needs to follow the Directive for the utilities sector for its oil exploration activities, which it only can perform thanks to the concessions granted by local governments. Hence, all (sub)contracting activities by Shell for these projects should meet the (somewhat enlightened) requirements of the Directives on public procurement. Or to give another example: in the health sector it is common, when a new hospital needs to be built, to contract an engineering firm for turn-key delivery. Such an engineering firm in most cases is also a private enterprise. The directives may be relevant in this case in two ways: first, the engineering firm needs to be selected following the Directives on public procurement. Second, when the engineering firm starts its activities, selecting the sub-contractors (for civil engineering, installation, construction) will be subject to these Directives. In case of any questions or uncertainties about whether or not an organizational entity will be subject to the EC Directives on public procurement the EC has listed per member-State the institutions which need to adhere to these.[1]

What type of contracts are covered? In fact the Directives relate to all commercial, public supply contracts. In the terminology of the EC: 'all contracts for pecuniary interest concluded in writing involving the purchase, lease, rental or hire purchase, with or without option to buy, of products and services'. Whether a project would fall under the Directive of Supplies, Works or Services depends on the nature of the activities to be performed. If the estimated contract value relates for the largest part to products, the Directive of Supplies needs to be followed. This is relevant since in most cases projects may represent a combination of contracting for goods and supplies, for construction and services. To give an example: when contracting for a new integrated computer network for a public entity, it is important to know in advance what the value of the computer hardware and software will be, as well as the value of the value added services (systems development and design, application engineering, installation services). Usually, the preparation that this takes in many cases leads to the insight that design and development of these systems can be better separated from the

---

[1] See Annex 1 'List of bodies and categories of bodies governed by public law' of the Guide to the Community rules on public supply contracts' of the European Commission.

delivery of hardware and software. As a result, the assignment may be contracted for in two stages: (a) a tender procedure for the appropriate development and design (following the Services Directive), and (b) a separate tender procedure for delivery of the required equipment and supplier (following the Supplies Directive).

The value of the contract under consideration determines whether it should be tendered following the Directives or not. Contracts which exceed a threshold value of 200,000 Euro should follow the EC procedures for public procurement. For this reason it is important to know how the value of a contract is to be calculated. The Directives provide ample guidelines for this. In general the expenditure for the next 12 months within a given product category needs to be considered. This is true for contracts with a duration of a year or less. Of course, in some cases public bodies may engage in long-term contracts with suppliers, without indicating when the contract will end. In those cases the contract value needs to be calculated based on a 48-month period. Of course, in practice, many attempts have been made to bypass the workings of the Directives. One of the ways to do this is by splitting one large contract into smaller portions, each of which is lower than the indicated threshold. It will not come as a surprise that this is strictly prohibited, and when discovered can lead to severe penalties.

The Directives use different threshold values. This is illustrated in Figure 18.1.

Under normal circumstances the EC Directives for Public Procurement will apply. Of course, small, one-time contracts are excluded from their workings, which is fair. This is because a contracting procedure following these directives needs to be prepared carefully, which takes time and effort. Therefore, this time investment only will pay off in case of larger projects and contracts (which may cover 80% of the public entities purchasing budget). Smaller purchases and contracts (often 80% of the transactions, covering only 20% of the budget volume) do not need this type of scrutiny. For these types of purchases the public organization may act much more flexibly and swiftly.

In some cases, which are described exhaustively, the directives may not apply. Such is the case when contracting for very specific purposes, such as research and development (where very special materials are required), for defence (when it concerns weapon systems and ammunition), or when materials are required very urgently due to unforeseen circumstances (in case of a disaster or war).

	Without indicative notice	With indicative notice
Public Supplies	200,000 Euro	200,000 Euro
Public Works	5,000,000 Euro	5,000,000 Euro
Public Service Contracts	130,000 Euro	200,000 Euro
Utilities Directive		
– Supply/Services	400,000 Euro	
– Works		5,000,000 Euro

Figure 18.1   Standard values under the EC Directives for Public Procurement.

EC purchasing procedures

Depending on the situation, the following purchasing procedures are available for awarding public supply contracts:

- *The open procedure*. In this case the public entity will submit a tender through a contract notice in the Official Journal of the European Community and/or the Tender Electronic Daily (an electronic database), on which all interested suppliers may submit their proposals. This obviously may lead to a situation where the contracting authority may receive hundreds of proposals from suppliers, who they do not know. In order to prevent these problems the next procedure may be followed.
- *The restricted procedure*. This is a procedure, where, of the suppliers who have expressed their interest following publication of the contract notice, only those so invited by the contracting authority may submit tenders. Usually, following this procedure takes a lot of time, which the contracting authority may not have. Therefore, an accelerated form of the restricted procedure has been developed, enabling public organizations to move faster, when required. This may be the case when products are required urgently due to unforeseen circumstances. Under this procedure, as under the open procedure, contracts should be awarded without negotiation based upon previously established contract award criteria. This is not true for the next type of procedure.
- *Negotiated procedure*. This procedure is one where the contracting authority consults the suppliers of its choice and negotiates with them the terms of the contract, e.g. the technical, administrative and financial conditions. Although this procedure has more degrees of freedom for the contracting authority, it still needs to adhere to some basic requirements. These are that more than one supplier is being solicited (usually a minimum of five potential bidders) and that all suppliers are treated equally (fair treatment). The Directives describe exhaustively when this procedure may be applied. This may be the case when too few suppliers have responded to an earlier tender, where one of the previous purchasing procedures was followed. The negotiated procedure may be conducted with or without prior notification in the Official Journal.

All Directives are very specific about the lead times which need to be adhered to when dealing with suppliers. First, in case of contracts exceeding 750,000 Euro contracting authorities are obliged to publish an indicative notice in the Official Journal in order to enable suppliers to anticipate on the order. Second, all tenders need to be published in advance through a contract notice (see Figure 18.2). A minimum of 52 days (depending on the Directive pertaining to the situation) should be granted to potential suppliers from the date of dispatch of the notice for publication in the Official Journal for preparing their bids. Of course, longer lead times may be required when suppliers need to make a visit and have a discussion before being able to submit a bid. Third, contracting authorities are obliged to respond within six days to questions raised by suppliers on the potential contract. Fourth, contracting authorities need to be very explicit beforehand on (a) the criteria to be used for supplier prequalification and (b) the criteria to be used for awarding the contract. With regard to the latter, two possibilities exist: (i) lowest price or (ii) most advantageous offer. In the last case the public entity should indicate what aspects will be considered and should list these criteria (in descending order of importance) in the documentation which is made available to suppliers. Finally, when the contract is awarded, this decision should be made public as well through the Official Journal by indicating the contract price agreed, the winner of the tender and the price range between the lowest and the highest bidder. The contracting authority is obliged to maintain a contract report on every tender project in order to be able to inform the appropriate official bodies.

The scope of the Directives, which have been discussed so far on supplies, works and services, excludes contracts awarded by so-called 'utilities' (organizations operating in the water, energy, transport and telecommunications sector). For this sector a separate Directive has been developed due to political, industrial and legal considerations. In general this sector is subject to an 'enlightened' regime. First, the threshold values are higher than in the previous directives (400,000 Euro in case of supply and services contracts; for the telecommunications sector this value is 600,000 Euro). Second, the contracting entities have a free choice between the open, restricted and negotiated procedures.

Government Procurement Agreement

For buyers working for governmental institutions there is more than the EC Directives on public procurement that may influence their work. Traditionally, one of the other guidelines they have to reckon with has been GATT (General Agreement on Trade and Tariffs). This agreement stipulated that all institutions belonging to the central government should open up their purchasing contracts to all suppliers of all member States. The GATT agreement has been replaced since 1996 by the Governmental Procurement Agreement (GPA), which was agreed among the EC member States, USA, Japan, Canada, Switzerland, Israel and South Korea and which proves to be more ambitious. The GPA also covers in addition to supplies, works and services. Apart from this, it covers contracts awarded by public authorities at regional and local level. Finally, it covers the ports, water, electricity and urban transport sectors (EC Brochure 1999, p. 9). It is expected that this new arrangement will open up government contracts to international bidding worth around 350 billion Euro every year.

The GPA is built upon the general principles of national treatment, non-discrimination and transparency and follows the EC Directives closely. Just like these Directives the GPA provides a system of threshold values in order to trigger competitive tendering among suppliers. Also on other aspects the GPA follows the EC Directives closely. Therefore the GPA is not further elaborated on here.

1. Name, address, telegraphic address and telephone, telex and fax numbers of the contracting authority.

2. (a) Award procedure chosen;

   (b) Form of the contract for which tenders are being requested.

3. (a) Place of delivery;

   (b) Nature and quantity of the goods to be supplied. CPA reference number;

   (c) Indication of whether the supplier can tender for part of the goods required.

4. Time–limit for delivery, if any.

5. (a) Name and address of the service from which the contract documents and additional documents may be requested;

   (b) Final date for making such requests;

   (c) Where applicable, the amount and terms of payment of the sum to be paid to obtain such documents.

6. (a) Final date for receipt of tenders;

   (b) Address to which they must be sent;

   (c) Language or languages in which they must be drawn up.

7. (a) Persons authorized to be present at the opening of tenders;

   (b) Date, time and place of such opening.

8. Where applicable, any deposits and guarantees required.

9. Main terms concerning financing and payment and/or references to the provisions in which these are contained.

10. Where applicable, the legal form to be taken by the grouping of suppliers to whom the contract is awarded.

11. Information concerning the supplier's own position, and information and formalities necessary for an appraisal of the minimum economic and technical standards required of the supplier.

12. Period during which the tenderer is bound to keep open his tender.

13. Criteria for the award of the contract. Criteria other than that of the lowest price must be mentioned if they do not appear in the contract documents.

14. Where applicable, prohibition on variants.

15. Other information.

16. Date of publication of the indicative notice in the Official Journal or reference to its non-publication.

17. Date of dispatch of the notice.

18. Date of receipt of the notice by the Publications Office.

Figure 18.2   Example of contract notice (open procedure).

(Source: Guide to the Community rules on public supply contracts, 1999, p. 34)

Consequences

The previous sections have described how the Directives provide to public organizations in any member State objective guidelines on how to proceed in their contractual relationships with suppliers. The purchasing procedures described are congruent with the purchasing process model which was presented in Chapters 1 and 3:

- First of all, they support the idea of preventing customers being locked into supplier relationships by favouring objective and functional product specifications. Any description of specifications which may lead to a captive supplier relationship should be prevented. Therefore the EC favours and stimulates the use of uniform technical standards.
- Second, a large part of the EC Directives is devoted to describing how to arrive at an objective supplier selection. It favours stimulating competition among suppliers by adopting both a uniform supplier prequalification procedure and contract award procedure.
- Third, the Directives favour that contracts with suppliers are conducted in writing, providing in this way an objective basis for the evaluation of the supplier's performance.
- Fourth, when the decision has been made to award the contract, all parties must officially be informed about its outcome. This certainly contributes to a transparency of supplier markets.

In general, the Directives on public procurement have met large resistance, both from governmental officials inside and outside purchasing. Most complaints relate to the lack of flexibility, the level of detail, the time-frames which need to be adhered to, the fact that partnership relationships are not particularly fostered and stimulated through these Directives and the degree of administration which is involved in order to provide an adequate tracing and tracking of the different stages of the purchasing process.

It is clear that working with the Directives effectively, requires a thorough planning and preparation. First, the contracting authority needs to have a good understanding of its purchasing order specifications, which in general will require ample discussions among the users, budget holders, accounting people and purchasing professionals. Furthermore, based upon the specification the requirements need to be laid down, to be used for supplier selection and award of the contract. Based upon this information, it needs to be decided what purchasing procedure will need to be pursued. It should be realized that, when a purchasing procedure actually has started, no changes whatsoever can be made during the process. In case, at hindsight, changes are deemed necessary in for instance the technical specifications, the procedure should be officially stopped. A new procedure might be started based upon the new specification. The same holds when the contracting entity wants to change the criteria to be used for supplier qualification or award of the contract. The idea behind this is 'fair play' i.e. providing every supplier with the same chance to quote for the contract.

In conclusion the EC Directives on public procurement resemble sound purchasing principles. However, at the same time it should be acknowledged that the political climate and culture of most governmental institutions do not foster purchasing professionalism. In general the reward system within governmental organizations does not support a purchasing approach based upon 'getting the best value for money' or 'lowest total cost of ownership'. Next, a coherent control system to ascertain that the Directives are being followed by the member States is not present. These factors may explain why implementation of these Directives in most countries is so troublesome and adoption so slow.

Summary

Public procurement represents an important area within European economies. On average member States of the EC spend 12% of their gross domestic product on contracts with suppliers. This massive amount of money is spent on a large variety of products, projects and services by an even larger variety of organizations.

Central to the idea of the EC is free competition and a free trade between its member States. This has, as seen earlier, considerable consequences for the initial purchasing processes within the governmental institutions and organizations.

This chapter presented some major differences that exist between purchasing for private enterprise and public procurement. First, purchasing decision making is often intertwined with political objectives and issues. Second, the budget system used by the government does not provide sufficient incentive for budget holders to actively strive for the best value for money. Usually, budgets should be spent in the year they have been assigned. Building up financial reserves and shifting these to the next year is difficult. This explains the spending fever that may be observed at the end of each year. Third, most countries still favour a nationalist and protectionistic approach when it comes to placing orders at suppliers. In most cases local suppliers, for a variety of reasons, are favoured.

The EC Directives try to foster a uniform and consistent approach to purchasing decision making within the EC countries. Basic underlying principles are non-discrimination, fair play, transparency of procedures and open communication to the international supplier community. For most governmental institutions three Directives are most relevant: the Supplies Directive, the Services Directive and the Works Directive. In some cases the Directives may also be relevant for semi-governmental and private enterprise. For organizations which operate in the utilities sector, the Utilities Directive will provide guidance in their dealings with suppliers. The latter are more free in their choice of the three basic purchasing procedures: the open procedure, the restricted procedure and the negotiated procedure.

Apart from these Directives governmental buyers need to adhere to the arrangements made within the Government Procurement Agreement, which ties in with other countries such as the USA, Canada and Japan.

Although the EC regulations on public procurement reflect sound purchasing theory and practices, it will be difficult to implement them. This is due to their contextual complexity. Apart from a lack of control by the EC itself, various factors explain why implementation of these directives in most countries is so troublesome and adoption so slow.

Assignments

18.1 Why would public entities often favour local suppliers? What political objectives could be served by such behaviour? Discuss.

18.2 Mention the basic EC Directives on public procurement. List the key elements of each of them

18.3 A municipality within the EC wants to renew its contract for copiers. In order to prevent the contract from surpassing the threshold value it pursues decentralized purchasing: each department needs to take care of its own needs. What is your opinion about this way of working? Discuss.

18.4 When reviewing its car lease contract the police department of a large city thinks about what purchasing procedure to follow. Discuss each purchasing procedure and decide what procedure would be most appropriate.

BIBLIOGRAPHY

Aljian, G.W. (1984) *Purchasing Handbook*, McGraw Hill, New York.

Anderson, J. and Narus, J. (1998) *Business Market Management, Understanding, Creating and Delivering Value*, Prentice Hall, New Jersey.

Aston, M. (1989) 'Method, Trade-offs and DPP', *Focus*, **8**(8).

Barreyre, P.Y (1976) 'La Fonction Approvisionnement dans la Strategie de l'Entreprise', *Revue Francais de Gestion*, Sep–Oct, pp. 61–67.

Brand, G. (1968) *How British Industry Buys*, Hutchinson, London.

Broersma, H. (1991) *Co-makership: cooperation between producer and supplier*, Groningen, Wolterns Noordhoff. (Dutch text).

Business Week (1991) 'The racy Viper is already a winner for Chrysler', *Business Week*, November 4.

Christopher, M. (1992) *Logistics and Supply Chain Management*, Pitman, London.

Clayton, R.F. (1984) *Effective Negotiations Seminar*, Veldhoven, 1983–1985.

Cooper, M.C. and Ellram, L.M. (1993) 'Characteristics of Supply Chain Management and the implications for purchasing and logistics strategy', *The International Journal of Logistics Management*, **4**, (2) pp. 13–24.

Corey, E.R. (1978) *Procurement Management: Strategy, Organization and Decisionmaking*, CBI Publishing Company, Boston.

Corsten, D. and Zagler, M. (2000) 'Purchasing Consortia and Internet Technology', in A. Erridge (ed.), *Best Practice Procurement: public and private sector perspectives*, Gower, London, Chapter 19, pp. 184–191.

Croom, S.R. (2000) 'The Strategic Contribution of E-Commerce to MRO Procurement', in A. Erridge (ed.), *Best Practice Procurement: public and private sector perspectives*, Gower, London, Chapter 16, pp. 160–168.

Crosby, P.B. (1984) *Quality without tears*, McGraw-Hill, New York.

Dobler, D., Lee, D. and Burt, D. (1990) *Purchasing and Materials Management*, 5th edn., McGraw-Hill, New York.

DTI (1989) *Getting the Best From Your Suppliers*, DTI, London.

DTI (1994) A review of the relationships between vehicle manufacturers and suppliers, report of the DTI/SMMT Automotive Components Supplier Initiative Stage Two, p. 28.

Dyer, J. (1996) 'How Chrysler created an American Keiretsu', *Harvard Business Review*, July–August, pp. 42–91.

Eck, A. van and de Weerd, H. (1981) Introduction to Purchasing Market Research (internal paper), Philips Electronics Cy. (Dutch text).

Eck, A. van, de Weerd H. and van Weele A.J. (1981) 'De beoordeling van de inkoopprijs: een conceptuele benadering', *Bedrijfskunde*, **52** (3) pp. 277–288 (Dutch text).

European Commission, (1999a) The Rules Governing the Procedure in the Award of Public Procurement Contracts, Brussels.

European Commission, (1999b) Guide to the Community Rules on Public Supply Contracts, Brussels.

Faes, W. and de Rijcke, J.G. (1982) 'Management in het inkoopgebeuren: noodzakelijk en mogelijk', *Economisch en Sociaal Tijdschrift*, (4) pp. 419–441 (Dutch text).

Faes, W. and de Weerd, H. (1983) 'Research is a must for purchasing', *Purchasing and Supply Management*, September, pp. 36–40.

Farmer, D.H. (1974) 'Training procurement personnel in negotiating skills', *Journal of Purchasing and Materials Management*, Feb.

Fearon, H. (1976) *Purchasing Research: Concepts and Current Practice*, American Management Association, New York.

Fearon, H.E. and Leenders, M.R. (1995) Purchasing's organisational role and responsibilities, Center for Advanced Purchasing Studies, Phoenix, Arizona.

Fisher, L (1970) *Industrial Marketing: an Analytical Approach to Planning and Execution*, 2nd edn, Business Books, London.

Fisher, M.L. (1997) 'What is the right supply chain for your product?', *Harvard Business Review*, March–April, pp. 105–116.

Floor J.M.G. and Schraders, J.G. (1983) *Account Management en Nieuwe Samenwerkingsvorm tussen Fabrikant en Handel*, Samsom, Alphen a/d Rijn. (Dutch text).

Ford, D. (1980) 'Development of Buyer-Seller Relationships in Industrial Markets', *European Journal of Marketing*, 14, (5/6) pp. 339–353.

Giunipero, L.C. and Monczka, R.M. (1990) 'Organisational approaches to managing international sourcing', *International Journal of Physical Distribution and Logistics Management*, (4), pp. 3–12.

Hakansson, H. (1982) *International Marketing and Purchasing of Industrial Goods*, John Wiley & Sons, New York.

Hakansson, H. and Wootz, B. (1979) 'A Framework of Industrial Buying and Selling', *Industrial Marketing Management*, 8, pp. 28–39.

Hakansson, H., Johansson, J. and Wootz, B. (1977) 'Influence Tactics in Buyer-Seller Processes', *Industrial Marketing Management*, 5, pp. 319–332.

Hakansson, H. and Wootz, B. (1979) 'A Framework of Industrial Buying and Selling'. *Industrial Marketing Management*, (8), pp. 28–39.

Hamel, G. and Prahalad, C.K. (1994) *Competing for the Future*, Harvard Business School Press, Boston.

Hammer, M. and Champy, J. (1993) *Reengineering the Corporation*, Harper Collins, New York.

Hart, H.W.V. van der (1984) *Industrial Buying Behaviour in Purchasing Management*, Samsom Bedrijfsin formatie, Alphen a/d Rijn.

Hendrick, Th. and Ellram, L. (1993) *Strategic Supplier Partnering: an International Study*, Center for Advanced Purchasing Studies, Phoenix, Arizona.

Hoekstra, Sj. and J.H.J.M. Romme (eds.) (1985) *Op weg naar integrale logistieke strucuren*, Kluwer, Deventer. (Dutch text).

IBM and Crosby, P.B. (1980) *First Time Right*, IBM.

Kalakota, R. and Robinson, M. (1999) *E-Business, Roadmap for Success*, Addison Wesley, Reading, MA.

Kaplan, S. and Sawhney, M. (2000) 'E-Hubs: the new b2b-marketplaces', *Harvard Business Review*, May–June, pp. 97–103.

Karass, C.L. (1970) *The Negotiating game, How to get what you want*, Thomas Y. Crowell Company, New York.

Karass, C.L. (1977) *Give and take, The complete guide to negotiating strategies and tactics*, Thomas Y. Crowell Company.

Karass, C.L. (1979) *How to fight a price increase*, Karass International.

Keough, M. (1993) 'Buying your way to the top', *McKinsey Quarterly*, 3, pp. 41–62.

Kluge, J.N. (1996) *Simply Superior Sourcing*, 5th Annual IPSERA Conference, Eindhoven, The Netherlands, April.

Kotler, P. (1997) *Marketing management: analysis, planning, implementation and control*, 9th ed., Prentice-Hall, Upper Saddle River.

Kotler, P. and Bloom, P.N. (1984) *Marketing Professional Services*, Prentice Hall, Englewood Cliffs, New Jersey.

Kowalski, Th. (1993) *Purchasing portfolio management*, keynote presentation at 25th International Purchasing and Supply Management Conference, Management Centre Europe, London.

Kraljic, P. (1983) 'Purchasing must become Supply Management', *Harvard Business Review*, September/October, pp. 109–117.

Kudrna, D.A. (1975) *Purchasing Manager's Decision Making Handbook*, Cahners Books, Boston.

Lamming, R, (1993) *Beyond partnership, strategies for innovation and lean supply*, Prentice Hall, Hampstead.

Laseter, T.M. (1998) *Balanced sourcing: cooperation and competition in supplier relationships*, Jossey-Bass Publishers, San Francisco.

Leenders, M.R., Fearon, H.E. and England, W.B. (1989) *Purchasing and Materials Management*, Dow Jones Irwin, Homewood, Illinois.

Lehmann, D.R. and O'Shaughnessy J. (1974) 'Different Industrial Products', *Journal of Marketing*, April, pp. 36–42.

Lehmann, D.R. and O'Shaughnessy, J. (1984) 'Difference in Attitude Importance for Different Industrial Products', *Journal of Marketing*, April.

Lysons, K, (1996) *Purchasing*, Pitman Publishing, London.

Marx, William B. (1996) 'Purchasing's New Muscle', in Strategic Purchasing: Sourcing for the Bottom Line, The Conference Board, pp. 9–10.

Matthijssens, P. and de Rijcke, J. (1982) 'Unieke Dimensies van Industriële Marketing', *Tijdschrift voor Marketing*, July/August, pp. 3–10.

Miller, J.G. and Gilmour, P. (1979) 'Materials Managers: Who Needs Them?' *Harvard Business Review*, July-August, pp. 143–153.

Moffat, P.K., Bettinger, D.E., Howarth, M.A. and Casavant, A. (1993) 'Quality Assurance', in Fearon, H.E., Dobler, D.W. and Killen, K.H., *The Purchasing Handbook*, McGraw Hill, Chapter 13, pp. 403–436.

Monczka, R,M. (1999) 'What is so exciting about purchasing?' *Quality Matters*, Philips Electronics, January, 94, pp. 16–17.

Monczka, R.M. and Trent, R.J. (1991) 'Global sourcing: a development approach', *International Journal of Purchasing and Materials Management*, 27, (2), pp. 2–8.

Monczka, R.M. and Trent, R.J. (1992) 'Worldwide sourcing: assessment and execution', *International Journal of Purchasing and Materials Management*, 28, (4) pp. 9–19.

Murphy , E.E. (1998) 'At Hershey Foods purchasing restructures to tap full supply value', *Purchasing*, June 5.

Ohmae, K. (1994) Competitive advantage in the information age, Northern Telecom, Annual Report.

Peters, T. (1992) *Liberation Management*.

Philips Electronics (1999) 'Purchasing becoming Supply Chain Management', *Quality Matters*, January, Issue 94.

Porter, M.A. (1980) *Competitive Strategy, Techniques for Analyzing Industries and Competitors*, The Free Press, New York.

Porter, M.E. (1985) *Competitive Advantage*, The Free Press, New York.

Quinn, J.B. (1992) *Intelligent Enterprise*, The Free Press, New York.

Rietveld, G. (1995) *Facilitair Inkoop Management*, Academic Service, Schoonhoven (Dutch text).

Robinson, P.J., Faris, Ch. W. and Wind, Y. (1967) *Industrial Buying and Creative Marketing*, Allyn & Bacon, Boston.

Schmidt, R.C. (1986) 'Logistiek Management als instrument voor klantgerich opereren', *Tijdschrift financieel management*, (4), pp. 59–66. (Dutch text).

Sheth, J.N. (1973) 'A Model of Industrial Buyer Behaviour', *Journal of Marketing*, October.

Stekelenborg, R. van, (1997) *Purchasing Information Systems*, Eindhoven University of Technology (PhD dissertation).

Stevens, G.C. (1989) 'Integrating the supply chain', *International Journal of Physical Distribution and Materials Management*, 19, (8), pp. 3–8.

The Conference Board (1996) *Strategic purchasing: sourcing for the bottom-line*, New York.

Treacy, M. and Wiersema, F. (1995) *The Discipline of Market Leaders*, Addisson Wesley, Reading, Massachusetts.

Van der Ster, W. (1993) *Marketing and Retail*, 5th edition, Wolters Noordhoff, Groningen (Dutch text).

Van Goor, A. (1998) *Partnership through Supply Chain Logistics*, Samsom, Alphen a/d Rijn (Dutch text).

Vanhorick, J.F. (1986) Commodity Markets as a Tool for Buying Raw Materials, *Purchasing Handbook*, Samsom, Alphen a/d Rijn. (Dutch text).

Venkatesan, R. (1992) 'Strategic Sourcing: to Make or Not to Make', *Harvard Business Review*, November-December, pp.98–107.

Vigoros, M. (1998) 'Sourcing info and supplier ratings combined on 'Net', *Purchasing*, 5 November.

Vigoros, M. (1999) 'Electronic marketplaces save buyers time and money', *Purchasing*, 14 January.

Vollman, Th.E., Berry, W.E. and Whybark, D.C. (1984), *Manufacturing Planning and Control Systems*, Dow Jones Irwin, Homewood, Illinois.

Von Hippel, E.R. (1978) 'Successful Industrial Products from Customer Ideas', *Journal of Marketing*, January, pp. 39–49.

Webster, F.E. and Wind, Y. (1972) *Organizational Buying Behaviour*, Prentice Hall, Englewood Cliffs, NJ.

Weele, A.J. van (1984a) 'Purchasing Performance Measurement and Evaluation', *Journal of Purchasing and Materials Management*, Fall, pp. 16–22.

Weele, A.J. van (1984b) *Purchasing Control, Performance Measurement and Evaluation of the Industrial Purchasing Function*, Wolters-Noordhoff, Groningen.

Weele, A.J. van (1987) Perspective on Purchasing, *International Management Development Review 1987*, Management Centre Europe, Belgium, Brussels 1987, pp. 383–388.

Weele, A.J. van (1990) *Buying Projects*, Dutch Association of Purchasing Management, The Hague. (Dutch text).

Weele, A.J. van (1990) *Volvo Car BV, towards 'zero-defects' with Suppliers*, (working paper) Eindhoven University of Technology. (Dutch text).

Weele, A.J. van (1991) Purchasing as a Service Center: the Purchasing Audit as a Management Tool, in W.F.G. Mastenbroek (ed.), *Managing Quality in the Service Sector*, Basil Blackwell, Oxford.

Weele, A.J. van. (1994) Inkoop in Strategisch Perspectief: Analyse, Planning en Praktijk, Samsom Bedrijfsinformatie, Alpehn a/d Rijn.

Weele, A.J. van, Faes, W. and de Rijcke, J.G. (1984) *Developments in Purchasing in the Eighties*, Dutch Association of Purchasing Management, The Hague.

Weele, A.J. van and Gelderman, C. (1998) *Purchasing Management*, Heerlen Open University. (Dutch text).

Weele, A.J. van and Rozemeijer, F.A. (1999) 'Getting Organised for Purchasing and Supply Management in the Information Age: towards the virtual purchasing organisation, in D. Hahn and L. Kaufmann, *Handbuch Industrielles Beschaffungsmanagement*, Gabler, Wiesbaden.

Weele, A.J. van and Rozemeijer, F.A (2000) 'The Role of Power in Partnership Relationships: an empirical investigation in the current body of knowledge', in A. Erridge (ed.), *Best Practice Procurement: public and private sector perspectives*, Gower, London, Chapter 10, pp. 90–99.

Weele, A.J. van and Rozemeijer (1998) Mirror, mirror on the wall . . . Let suppliers guide you towards improvement, in Capaldo, G. (ed), *Supply Management*, Chapter 16, pp. 337–355, Edizione Scientifiche Italiane, Napoli.

Weele, A.J. van and Rozemeijer, F.A. (1996) *Revolution in Purchasing*, Philips Electronics/Eindhoven University of Technology, 142 pp.

Weele, A.J. van and Rozemeijer, F.A. (1996) 'Revolution in purchasing: building competitive power through pro-active purchasing', *European Journal of Purchasing and Supply Management*, **2**, (4) pp. 153–160.

Weele, A.J. van and Rozemeijer, F.A. (1996) *Revolution in Purchasing: Building Competitive Power Through Pro-Active Purchasing*, Philips Electronics/Eindhoven University of Technology (limited edition).

Weele, A.J. van, and Rozemeijer, F.A. (1998a) *Getting organised for purchasing and supply management in the information age: towards the virtual purchasing organisation?* Proceedings of the Second Worldwide Research Symposium on Purchasing and Supply Management, London, 1–3 April 1998, pp. 421–431.

Weele, A.J., van Rozemeijer, F.A. and Rietveld, G. (1998) *Professionalising purchasing: towards a purchasing development model*, IPSERA Conference Proceedings 1998, London, pp. 515–523.

Weele, A.J. van and van Hespen, J. (1986) *Professioneel Inkopend Nederland, Deelrapport 1: Inkoopfunktie in Industrieɔle Ondernemingen*, Kluwer, Deventer. (Dutch text).

Weele, A.J. van and van Hespen, J. (1987) Professioneel inkopend Nederland, Deelrapport 1: De Inkoopfunctie in Industriële Ondernemingen, Kluwer, Deventer (Dutch text).

Weele, A.J. van and Van der Horst, H.J. (1992) *Public Procurement in European Perspective*, Kluwer Bedrijfswetenschappen, Deventer (Dutch text).

Weele, A.J. van and Van der Vossen, G.J. (1998) *Purchasing DuPont analysis of some major Dutch companies*, Holland Consulting Group, Research report.

Weele, A.J. van and Veth, A.F.L. (2001) 'Concurreren in het e-Tijdperk: nu of nooit', *Holland Management Review*, March–April, pp. 64–71. (Dutch text).

Wijnstra, F.Y.W. (1999) *Purchasing involvement in new product development*, Eindhoven University of Technology, The Netherlands (doctorate thesis).

Wijnstra, F.Y.W. and Ten Pierick, E. (1999) *A portfolio-approach for supplier involvement in product development: differentiating lean and rich interfaces*, Proceedings of the 8th IPSERA Conference, 28–31 March 1999, Belfast-Dublin, pp. 815–826.

Wijnstra, J.Y.F. (1998), *The role of purchasing in product innovation*, PhD-thesis, Eindhoven University of Technology, 285 pp.

Womack, J.P., Jones, D.T. and Roos, D. (1990) *The machine that changed the world*, MacMillan, New York.

INDEX

Bold numbers denote figures and italic numbers denote tables.